The Real Rainbow Row
Explorations in Charleston's LGBTQ History

Harlan Greene

The Real Rainbow Row

© 2022 Harlan Greene

All rights reserved. No part of this book may be reproduced or transmitted in any form or by any means, electronic or mechanical, including photocopying, recording, or by any information storage and retrieval system, without permission in writing from the copyright owner.

Greene, Harlan. *The Real Rainbow Row: Explorations in Charleston's LGBTQ History*
Published by Evening Post Books, Charleston, South Carolina.

ISBN-13: 978-1-929647-76-7

Cover design by Gil Shuler

Interior design by Michael J. Nolan

Dedication

To all who came before and will come after

And to all who made this possible

Introduction

Much has been written about the city of Charleston, South Carolina in the past 350 years. And, in the future, no doubt, even more will be.

Before English settlers established a permanent presence in April 1670, Spanish and French explorers had crisscrossed the area, later called the Lowcountry due to its flat nature, and sent descriptions back. The English would soon follow. Lush verbiage of over-the-top descriptions of the Edenic atmosphere where it would be easy to make a living lured many from the Old World to the New. Hyperbolic tourist brochures encouraging all comers are nothing new in the Lowcountry.

By the early 1700s, printed descriptions of Carolina were proliferating. Charlestonians were now in on the act of interpreting and documenting themselves. By the time a printing press and newspapers appeared about 1732, a flood of books, manuscripts, documents, and memoirs commenced and would last for nearly three centuries. The focus of their contents has often remained the same, reflecting the views of mostly elite, White men who controlled almost everything. So sure of their assumptions, they recorded them as fact, along with their expectations, accomplishments, and worldviews, using a mirror—more than lens—to document their views. Controlling the laws, the lives of women and enslaved Africans, as well as the politics, the press, and the terrain, these men assumed they had the God-given right to control the narrative, too. And in this way, the supposedly "objective" history of the place was born.

It was reflective of them, their heroics, their ideas, and the way they believed the world ought to be. Every now and then (being the gentlemen they imagined themselves), they made exceptions, and gave room for, and mention of, a Native American, a Jew, a loyal enslaved person, and a woman or two; but history tended to resemble a snobby, White man's club with restricted entry rules.

They founded libraries and archives on the same pattern. Not only did those in charge stock the shelves with books that bolstered their perspective, but they were powerful enough to survive beyond the grave: through the donation of their personal papers, and those of their clubs and organizations, they helped determine what information would survive and transfer down through time to be studied as the basis for Charleston's standard histories. And so, it was a fait accompli, a prophecy. Entering an archive, seeing that only a single sort of narrative was available, one would assume that since the professionals in these temples of knowledge knew what they were doing, this then was the sole source worthy of preserving.

This is how we inherited our official history; the years accumulated and more of the same stories did too. While Charleston has the reputation for holding onto the past longer than most other places, still, it could not avoid the convulsions of change happening elsewhere: we are a peninsula and not an island, after all; and so there is a link, tenuous as it might be, with the mainland and the main currents of change in American history. The shock of change, of civil rights, of the women's movement, etc. eventually were felt locally – if, a tad after the fact, and a bit more subtly.

But society did eventually alter, and in the process, histories did, too. Scholars began to discover and document what had not been valued before: the incredibly rich African American, womens, ethnic and religious elements of the Charleston story. And as different groups proved they had been here all along, and took pride in the past and their accomplishments, they knocked at the gates for admittance.

And the members of the WASPY White man's club that had hoarded all the past and the power, seeing their claims of belonging, had to let them in.

This process took time and, in fact, is still ongoing—unequally. One of the groups long left out of the club, out in the cold, and denied entry has been Charleston's lesbian, gay, bisexual, transgender, questioning and other sexual minorities community. (While the terminology has been in flux and will continue to be, "LGBTQ" is the umbrella term used in these pages for this diverse group of people.) It's not that they haven't been here all along, making history and contributing greatly to the creation of one of America's most distinctive cities, but, even now, with so many people out and acknowledged, marching in the streets, being elected to public office, and marrying in America's second most popular destination wedding city (after Las Vegas), there are still discrepancies. There are no statues memorializing LGBTQ people (while some discriminatory statutes linger), and very few official mentions anywhere. While other pasts blaze brightly, there is just a flickering of knowledge about local LGBTQ history.

So, the question has to be asked: If our history is so long-standing, why hasn't anyone written it down before? Why aren't there volumes of LGBTQ stories rolling off the presses as there are of Blacks, women, Jews, Catholics, and nearly every other group and minority?

The answer is easy: for nearly their entire time here, it was not just an advantage (like protective coloration) to blend in, but a necessity and even a benefit to disappear; for if discovered, those men and women not fitting the dominant culture's stereotyped definition of binary correctness, could have paid (and often did pay) dearly for being identified, for being different, for breaking the unjust laws, for looking queer. Laws on the books could lead to the loss not only of respect, but also of professions, houses, families, position in society, and even life and liberty.

While the mistreatment and abuse of African Americans is the area's ancestral sin, Black people still often managed to create families, communities, sheltering homes, organizations and churches for escape and consolation from the prejudice and injustice of the White minority.

Until fairly recently, the LGBTQ community had none of these. (To be clear, no claims of equivalency are being made of LGBTQ and African American discrimination, abuse, and suffering.) But from 1712 to 1869, those engaging in same-sex acts could be put to death in South Carolina, longer than anywhere else in this country. This state fought hard and long to keep LGBTQ people second-class citizens. Families disowned relatives, made their lives living hells, and then churches and synagogues consigned them there for eternity. While legislators eventually had to bow to political pressure and pay lip service (at least) to Black equality, they still attacked the LGBTQ minority even into the 21st century.

In the 1950s, a man who murdered a gay man got off free; Hate crimes (in a state where there is no hate crime statute, although there is one in the city of Charleston) are proliferating. Local legislators directed hateful speech at us into the 21st century. And while this book was being written, South Carolina law stated that nothing (nothing positive, that is) could be said about LGBTQ topics in schools, unless it was mentioned in conjunction with a sexually transmitted disease.

Despised and dejected, like Blacks in the great migration, gay people turned their backs on Charleston and left for larger more anonymous places like Atlanta or New York City where you could be anonymous (or whom you wanted to be — or both.) And so, if the history of our city is a house or mansion with many rooms, the closet has been the space allotted for the LGBTQ community.Even if someone managed to find happiness with a life partner, family did not gather for a ceremony; there were no announcements or published images in the press, or photos passed down to the next generation. Survivors had to hide their grief; only blood relatives (or those by marriage, denied so long to LGBTQ people) were allowed in obituaries and automatically inherited property. Bosses could dismiss one at will (and can still in some cases); housing and children could be removed legally.

Of course, many people did lead full lives, but most destroyed any evidence of it before dying, so as to not to be outed posthumously, thus concealing from future historians the needed materials to craft narratives and prove LGBTQ presence. If any scrap of paper, suggestive photo, or love letter survived, families often cleansed them and did not donate them to archives; and the gatekeepers there, not seeing such lives as legitimate, often refused to accept such materials if they were offered—unless they came in accidentally. Family members airbrushed or threw away the uncomfortable details to allow a LGBTQ relative to stay on family trees. Stories were rewritten, lies told, details distorted, and slates wiped clean.

Because being LGBTQ was illegal for so long, this history was never collected or treasured. It was devalued and is full of holes, making it hard to look back and identify people in the past who were queer, gay, lesbian, trans, or had other "outlaw" identities. The maxim from the 1980s and 1990s AIDS activists holds true for history: "Silence equals death." Because so many were silenced, there is a dearth of materials to tell their stories.

And yet...

Still...

Nevertheless...

The Real Rainbow Row

There are some glimmers; there are some surviving documents; some stories managed to slip between the cracks. But interpreting the pieces is not often easy. What confronts a historian in this field is comparable to an archeologist's attempts at guessing or reconstructing the shape of a large vessel from tiny bits. But LGBTQ historians are also in the curious position of having to decide if the pieces actually belong to the vessel in question. Behavior patterns have changed as to what is considered acceptable. Customs have too. Even language itself was used differently in eras when words like "homosexuality," "lesbian," or "gay" did not exist. Should 18th-century men who wrote effusive letters declaring love for each other, more than for any other person, including wives and children, be taken at their word? Or was it just that the words they used were, like their wardrobes, so frilly and flowery?

Similarly, what of women who lived together as dedicated couples for decades? Were they lesbians? Or just spinsters who never found the right husband, as their families wanted everyone to believe?

Questions like these leave historians in a quandary; since we cannot know for sure, in some cases, what appears to be plain and logical to modern eyes, often it has to be qualified with phrases like "it seems" or "may be."

What follows is the best this writer could do to piece together the scattered pieces found in books, archives, police records, newspapers, and oral histories. It is not a complete history by any means, but an exploration, a start, a beginning. The chapters follow a rough chronology, each one presenting what is known about particular LGBTQ people found in that era of the city's history — for good or for ill, presented as fact, or as "may be." And sadly, it must be noted at the outset that, even with all LGBTQ history being disinherited and disowned, it nevertheless eerily resembles the parallel "straight" history.

This book, the first one on Charleston LGBTQ history, features a preponderance of White male stories, versus those of women and people of color. It is not by choice, but by necessity.

This has been a weakness of the entire field of LGBTQ studies. One reason is that being male and White has always brought that demographic undeniable powers and privileges, still not shared with women, people of color, or other communities. Just as it has always been easier to be White and male and heterosexual in America, so perhaps it has been easier to be White and male in LGBTQ (and larger) society.

If historians can't turn back time, we can, at least, revisit and revise its leavings; we can do our best to reveal what was hidden, and forbidden, and try to rename and reclaim people, pasts, and places. Too many have been lost or written out of the story and justice demands the righting of those wrongs and the creation of new, more inclusive histories. In local Gullah parlance (and parallels between LGBTQ and African American history do exist), LGBTQ people are not "come heres" but "been heres," longer than just about anybody else, in fact.

A word about the title: Rainbow Row is one of the iconic sites in Charleston, a row of houses on East Bay Street between Tradd Street and Stoll's Alley, some reflecting different pasts, histories, and stories; they have been in place for centuries, once new, then run down, in ruins, and once almost even torn down, deserted, gutted, wearing false fronts periodically. Now most have been restored with integrity and dignity, reclaimed with great pride, and painted with bright rainbow hues, serving as a valid and vivid metaphor for our city's LGBTQ history. (And yes, gay people, like Harry Hervey, did live here in some of these very buildings.)

Finally, as stated, this book is not definitive, but a start, hopefully the first of many. It makes no claim to be

The Real Rainbow Row

Figure 1. Rainbow Row, Charleston, South Carolina

complete (but great attempts have been made to ensure accuracy), and thus the subtitle "Explorations in Charleston's LGBTQ History." It has to be said and repeated vehemently that it is not a blot on someone's name, no matter what descendants or history worshippers and lovers of the status quo might believe, to say that someone was gay, lesbian, trans, queer, or LGBTQ. No one is named unless there is an archival record to prove it or a need to show how those individuals lived and contributed (for good or ill) to the city's larger story. Well-known episodes such as the "candlestick murder" and personalities such as Dawn Langley Hall Simmons may not be documented as thoroughly or discussed at the length that other lesser known events or individuals or institutions are, simply because information on the former can be found elsewhere. That's why previously un- or under-documented episodes and personalities are covered in more depth. "What ifs" and "maybes" may predominate in the earlier sections of the book, but as soon as direct quotations from subjects survive, they are used as much as possible to make up for the enforced silences of the past. This allows members of the LGBTQ community to speak in their own voices and to take charge of their own narrative — at last.

Chapter One

Indigenous Spirits and the First Europeans

Long before Europeans settled the part of the world that would come to be known as Charleston and the Lowcountry, Indigenous peoples, some of whom might be called LGBTQ today, lived in the area as respected members of their community.

It is ironic, then, that one of the last groups to finally get its own history is one of the only few to be native, present before Europeans and Africans came to start what became the "official" story.

In their travels through the South in the 1500s, members of Spanish and French expeditions encountered Native American men and women whose behaviors were so beyond their ken they had no words for them. "Hermaphrodite" was what Huguenot explorer René Goulaine de Laudonnière called a tall Amazon of a woman he encountered in the 1560s in the vague area called "Florida." She was so different from what he expected; her strength and gentleness, he admitted, saved him much suffering. There was an artist on that expedition who painted images of some of these people and the engravings by Theodor de Bry, published in Europe in the 1590s, were eagerly inspected. The strong men with a feminine look who were prized in battle as well as for nurturing the sick evoked astonishment, fear, and wonder. More puzzling still for Europeans was the fact that these unfamiliar people who mixed the traits of both men and women were not just tolerated, but were respected in their society.[1]

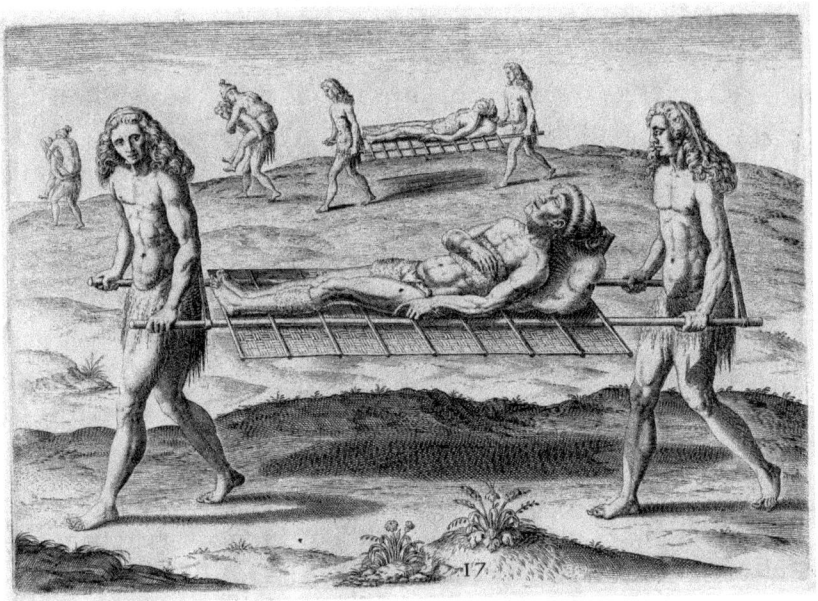

Figure 2. Early image of Native American "hermaphrodites"

In 1588, upon returning from his travels south of Carolina, Alvar Núñez Cabeza de Vaca recalled, "During the time that I was thus among the people I saw a devilish thing, and it is that I saw one man married to another and these are impotent, effeminate men and they go about dressed as women and do women's tasks." Europeans gasped. Proud of their supposedly superior civilization and their hierarchies of beliefs, they could not grasp the idea of gender fluidity that the Indigenous peoples found natural. Not understanding, Europeans condemned these behaviors, and so recorded history, contemptuous of LGBTQ people, began. "Hermaphrodite" was the only way these wide-eyed and gape-mouthed Europeans could describe the sexual diversity and gender role reversals they were seeing among the Cherokee, Creek, and inhabitants of Carolina.[2]

Reactions grew from disapproval to disgust and beyond. "I inferred they must be hermaphrodites, but from what I learned later I understood that they were sodomites," a much later missionary in the American West declared, invoking the disdain of Old World values in Old Testament vocabularies. (It was a long-standing misinterpretation of the sins of the cities of the plain, Sodom and Gomorrah, which had led to the coining of the word *sodomy*.) With condescension came condemnation, and then violence.

The Spanish explorer Vasco Núñez de Balboa bragged about throwing 42 "twin spirited" people (a phrase not necessarily used in the Lowcountry) to be ripped apart by dogs. Along with the European viruses and diseases were the equally virulent ideas and prejudices that infected and destroyed countless lives and cultures in the coming years.[3]

But soon it was not just Indigenous behaviors that upset Europeans. In April 1670, a man aboard the very first ship to land in Carolina was possibly LGBTQ. (And as for the difference between the LGBTQ prejudice of Indigenous peoples and Europeans, consider this: in 2019 a young queer member of the South Carolina Catawba nation said, "I've seen more anti-Native sentiment in LGBT spaces than I have seen explicit anti-LGBT sentiment in my Catawba community.")[4]

With so much of the historical record gone, historians can only wonder if accusations are true about Florence O'Sullivan.

Something of a soldier of fortune, O'Sullivan, a native of Ireland, was in the Caribbean in the 1660s, where he raised troops on Barbados to help attack the French on the island of St. Christopher. Captured, he was imprisoned in France; after a year, the English government paid a fine for his release. O'Sullivan returned to Ireland to work with Joseph West, a man the Lords Proprietors (the principal powers in control of the Carolina colony) had picked as governor. O'Sullivan procured servants for West in the new land, getting along well with the Proprietors, serving as deputy to one, and appointed surveyor general by them. Historian Patrick Melvin notes how the Lords Proprietors perceived him as "trusty and well beloved," praising his "wisdom, prudence, and integrity." O'Sullivan was one of the 93 passengers on board the *Carolina*. No wife is mentioned, though one researcher attributes a daughter to him.

Leaving in September 1669, three ships reached Barbados in October; the *Albemarle* and *Port Royal* wrecked and had to be replaced. The sole surviving original ship, the *Carolina*, reached its namesake colony with O'Sullivan on board. As surveyor general, he was in charge of laying out acreage, a task for which he did not feel he was adequately compensated. He complained to the Proprietors, while others in the colony soon were complaining about O'Sullivan and his surveying skills. The messages back to England claimed he was "of another nature[,] ashamed of nothing... troublesome [and] ill acting." He, according to Melvin, may have come into the crosshairs of factional infighting that beset the colony. (Calling him "of another nature" was close to calling him "unnatural," a euphemism and accusation used to condemn sexual behavior as a "crime against nature.") Not only was O'Sullivan called "no able surveyor" and "knavish" and "disliked," the coup de grace was calling him "an [i]ll natured buggerer of small children."[5]

"Buggery" was the name for "unnatural sex acts," which included any non-procreative sex between men and women, men and men, women and women, and bestiality, outlawed in 1533. (The term itself comes from a medieval Bulgarian sect accused of heresies and loathsome behaviors.) The penalty was death and the loss of all one's property.

Despite being tarred with that slur, O'Sullivan survived. He was relieved of his surveying duties, but he continued to be a presence in the early colony, granted thousands of acres of land, and put in charge of cannons on the island across the harbor from the peninsula, an island that bears his name,

Sullivan's. The fact that he survived the charges might mean they were false, or it could mean that he was too valuable to the Lords Proprietors to lose. But the word "buggery" was uttered, the charge made part of the record, and part of the city's and state's early history.

In 2006, South Carolina state legislators objected to the idea that LGBTQ people might live in the state, or worse, might be welcomed as visitors. As part of an advertising blitz, "South Carolina is so Gay" banners and posters had appeared in London, along with similar declarations about major American cities. Horrified, the lawmakers denied South Carolina's LGBTQ history; they were upset that some state funds had gone into luring tourists to support the multibillion dollar industry. They fired the person responsible and proved they had no idea that LGBTQ people had been here long before any of their ancestors may have reached these shores.[6] They were, in fact, carrying on a prejudice of generations of lawmakers before them, all the way back to 1712.

By that year, mansions and fortunes were rising from the enforced labor of enslaved Africans, and residents of the city were patterning their lives on parents or grandparents back in England. In the city they walled, they began to construct the same social bulwarks enforced across the sea. Lawmakers, seeing themselves working the will of the Deity, passed statutes on what could and could not be done on the Lord's day. They also passed laws to keep Africans enslaved and subservient, and as people imported more Africans, giving them the means to import English goods, they imported attitudes and laws of the motherland, too.

Was there an epidemic of LGBTQ behavior at the time? Texts do survive complaining of "divers evil disposed persons ... bold [enough] to commit the said most horrible and detestable vice of Buggery." Or were the settlers just being as Old World and English as they could be?

For whatever reason, in 1712, the early Carolinians made homosexuality illegal as it was in England; they put it on the same level as mating with beasts, with penalties some of the most severe in the colonies. This is the language they used:

> "FORASMUCH as there is not yet sufficient and condign punishment appointed and limited by the due course of the laws of the realm, for the detestable and abominable vice of buggery committed with mankind or beast: [2] It may therefore be enacted, that the same offence be from henceforth adjudged felony, and such order and form of process therein to be used against the offenders as in cases of felony of the common law; [3] and that the offenders being hereof convict by verdict, confession, or outlawry, shall suffer such pains of death and losses and penalties of their goods, chattles, [sic] debts, lands, tenements, and hereditaments, as felons be accustomed to do, according to the common laws of this realm; [4] and that no person offending in any such offence, shall be admitted to his clergy; [5] and that Justices of Peace shall have power and authority, within the limits of their commission and jurisdictions, to hear and determine the said offence, as they do use to do in case of other felonies."[7]

While the colony's fate was still uncertain, vulnerable to attacks from the Spanish and the Native Americans, lawmakers nevertheless perceived the need to police the city against interior enemies, who somehow were undermining domestic order through their private behaviors. Death was mandated for the "crime" until 1869 (but there is no evidence that sentence was ever handed down).[8]

After outlawing buggery in 1712, lawmakers recycled much of the same language in the next act they passed, now punishing pirates with the same death sentence, forfeiture of goods, lands and chattels, and denying the convicted the benefit of clergy.[9]

While antithetical stereotypes of marauding pirates and mincing pederasts have been reinforced repeatedly in popular culture, historically this was not so. In the early years of Charleston's existence, pirates were feared not just for flouting not only the laws of the high seas, but also the norms of decency. Pirate ships were notoriously democratic, considered a menace in the hierarchical British Navy, which had rigid punishments for same-sex acts. (Interestingly, the United States would not be as strict as the British on this issue, taking a much more lenient stance on sex among sailors than the mother country.) In this male-only world at sea, special onboard relationships developed. "Matelotage," a word derived from the French, was the name given to the civil relationship between male pirates, which, entered voluntarily, involved the exchange of rings, inheritance of material possessions, and in some cases, sexual intimacy. Matelotage, a marriage of sorts between men, eventually gave rise to the term "mate" or "matey" invoked by many today when mimicking piracy.[10]

And just as many LGBTQ people could pass, so too could many pirates, along with those who helped them. Walter J. Fraser, in his history of Charleston, notes how "poor Pyrates" often were hanged while "rich ones appear'd publicly and were not molested in the least."

Those in power and in favor, like O'Sullivan, could escape detection or punishment. It was the outrageously "out" pirate that the city was determined to punish. When a pirate crew attacked ships off the city, and those onboard were stripped of their finery and sent to shore nearly naked, the city was incensed.

In 1718, William Rhett, a leading merchant, colonel in the local militia, and comptroller of customs, and other White men leapt into action. Among the culprits caught was the "gentleman pirate," the effete Stede Bonnet, brought back to Charles Towne; others possibly in league or sympathy with him enabled his escape. One time he achieved this disguised in women's clothing.

He was recaptured and condemned; he went to the gallows not swaggering and cursing, but carrying a delicate nosegay of flowers in his hand. Bonnet had married and sired children in Barbados, but even at the time, it was known he had become a pirate to escape the "[d]iscomforts he found in the married state."[11]

Putting Bonnet and others of his ilk to death was putting an end to anarchy at sea, and an end to social and sexual anarchy, too, in which a single-sex band of men followed their own unsanctioned inclination and rules. That some of the pirates were involved emotionally and sexually with other men is beyond debate.

In 1719, nearly 50 pirates were hanged in the marshes off the southern end of town, which became a public park and cruising ground for gay men in the 20th century. (In the 1980s, Police Chief Reuben Greenberg would express disgust with a gay man who covered up the fact that, upon meeting a man at the Battery, he was later tied up, and, like a pirate, the man had stripped him of his valuables and finery. Greenberg advised gay men to avoid the side of the park containing the pirate memorial, and cruise instead on the waterside.)[12] Nowadays, pirates have been tamed; they are the subject of ghost tours; some guides wear colorful clothes, sport eye patches and parrots, and call the patrons' children, "Matey," unaware of the LGBTQ echoes and nuanced history.

But pirates weren't the only ones at sea who indulged in same-sex relations. Among the anonymous thousands aboard ships that helped make Charleston a flourishing seaport were men who forsook women for a life with others like them. If much local wealth came from rice and crops raised on land, another major part came from the sea, for Charleston's port always was, and continues to be, a major source of its economy. Just as the enslaved helped build the city, Black (some enslaved and some free) and White sailors did too.

Chapter Two

Sex and the Sea-Drinking City: Charleston and Its Seamen through the Centuries

Author William Benemann, in *Unruly Desires: American Sailors and Homosexualities in the Age of Sail*, makes a strong case for the persistent presence of men loving men in the American Navy and merchant marine in colonial days. Benemann argues persuasively that this homosocial and sexual world of men was the reason why many deserted the comforts of friends and family on land for an uncertain and often cruel, unforgiving, and unremunerative life at sea. Through skillful use of diaries, and analysis of ships' logs and contemporary writings, Benemann depicts a world where men could

Figure 3. Sailors from the USS *Charleston*

find other men for sex and society, where homosexuality was tolerated more than it was on land, and even overlooked as long as fraternizing did not cross ranks. (Herman Melville, in *White Jacket*, sharing his experiences in the 1840s, called ships "wooden-walled Gomorrahs of the deep.") Instead of matelotage of pirates, there was "chickenship." In these voluntary associations, an older sailor entered into a relationship with a younger man that often, but certainly not always, involved sexual and emotional intimacies.

Extant diaries and memoirs show that on some ships, homosexuality was rampant, and on others, not. Every man was needed to pull his own weight, so as long as there was no violence or rape, an early Don't Ask, Don't Tell policy prevailed, and men had sex because they wanted to, and at sea found a congenial fraternity. Abiel Abbott, a minister who wrote glowingly of the genteel people he met in Charleston in the early 19th century, took a much dimmer view of sailors. "Too many of you have fatally yielded to the fascination of sinful pleasure, and are willing to become seducers of the rest," he preached to them. If there was any doubt as to which vices he was alluding to, he listed them all, noting, "Fleshly lusts have a thousand forms, in which they creep forth from the heart into act; and there are many forms of sin, which are *not once to be named among Christians.*" The italics were his, and the coded message came through: sex between men, already seen as a sin too horrid to name, was only practiced in foreign lands by infidels like the Turks, but certainly not by God-fearing Christians. America in this era, incidentally, was fascinated by lurid stories of ships captured by the Barbary pirates with the handsome sailors on board taken as sex slaves of men who worshipped in mosques instead of churches.[1]

While ministers admonished mariners, most respectable citizens avoided them, judging them pariahs, a breed apart, not of civil society. As if to prove their unfitness, their uniforms fit too well and drew unusual attention to their anatomy. Recruiters knew this and often installed their handsomest men in front of recruiting stations. As men grew more modest in their dress in Victorian times, the sailors stood out with their hip-huggers and drawstrings in "a conspicuous display of the body to a degree that was shunned by most American males of the period." (In a polite era when piano legs were called "limbs," the obvious maleness of these swaggering sailors, reputed to be more sexually vigorous than other men, must have prompted embarrassment for many — or delight in some.)

When politician and champion of the South and slavery John C. Calhoun realized that fellow South Carolinian Wentworth Boisseau had indulged in same-sex relations, the only excuse he could make for his friend was that he must have "contracted the odious habit … while a sailor to the West Indies," blaming sea-born life and foreigners for perverting him. Calhoun, "shocked beyond measure," saw that Boisseau, due to his homosexuality, had "to give up all ideas of happiness in this life" and that he was "blasted forever in this country. A whole life of virtue could not restore his character." He gave Boisseau money to flee the state, setting the pattern of LGBTQ citizens leaving for more hospitable climes.

Calhoun believed that only by "a life of contrition" could Boisseau "make peace with heaven." But such men with their flagrantly male bodies had souls in them, and so, they might still be deserving of saving. Charleston, like many port cities, began to minister to sailors. In the 19th century, numerous organizations rose to meet this need: the Marine Bible Society, founded in 1818; the Charleston Port Society for the Promotion of the Gospel Among Seamen in 1823; a Temperance Boarding House in 1829; and a sailors home sometime later in the Market (eventually the Harriott Pinckney Home for Seamen opened on East Bay and Market in 1916). A marine hospital was operated by the city in 1834 on Franklin Street, and the Marine Washingtonian Total Abstinence Society followed in 1842.[2]

Active (and segregated) preaching to seamen began in 1819, and a Mariner's Church opened on Church Street soon after 1820. Then came a mariner's cemetery—all signs of philanthropy, yes, but of a certain kind—for all these spaces, even in death, were staunchly removed from polite White society, enforcing a parallel with the enforced segregation aimed at those of African descent. (The marine hospital, quite tellingly, became a school for freed African Americans after the Civil War, and the home for the Jenkins Orphanage, famous for spawning jazz musicians.) With laws prohibiting Blacks from worshipping in their own churches, they had to listen to the gospel from White ministers, with Whites in the best seats and Blacks in the back or in balconies. For mariners, it was worse. Respectable Christians would not defile themselves by having a Navy man or sailor in a pew next to them. In the second annual report of the Charleston Port Society, the duty (and division) said to be due to sailors was "to provide them with Churches and Ministers, devoted to their peculiar use, with a due regard to their peculiar habits and feelings." All believed "[t]he Sailor must have his own house of worship and his own Clergyman." Sailors realized the contempt, one mariner reporting, "if they invite us to church, they shove us up in the n-gg-r's pew by the threshold saying, 'That will do for you.'" So, sailors were kept away from civilians, looked down upon, and treated like sub-humans, just like local society treated the enslaved. The thought seems to have been that Blacks could not help being black, but sailors, White ones in particular, for some unfathomable reason, had chosen a foul lifestyle, a precursor of sorts to the 20th-century arguments of LGBTQ people "choosing" to be queer. Over the years, the Charleston Port Society gave away countless Bibles and tracts, and even sent "floating libraries" out to sea, determined to save the seamen from their sins.[3]

They may not have said it out loud (especially in front of the ladies), but many citizens condemned sailors for their assumed irregular and unmonitored sexual habits, including a penchant for homosexuality. Just as the White minority in Charleston projected images of savage sexuality on Black men and women, they did the same on sailors, believing them to be base and vile in their sexual proclivities. Generations later, in the mid-20th century, Charleston's Merchant Seaman's Club would be winked at as a pickup spot for men, still carrying on a tradition of beliefs from colonial times. While Americans today may have embraced the stereotype of sailors being he-men with a woman in every port, this was not necessarily a past belief.

So, Charleston as a "sea-drinking city" (from the title of a book by 20th-century Charleston poet Josephine Pinckney) was nurtured and created by many homosexual sailors, whose numbers and names have been lost to history, a fate similar to countless enslaved African Americans who built the city. The fact that LGBTQ people among them cannot be named does not mean they were not here.[4]

A Gay Charleston Sailor in the War of 1812?

While rescuing the names of LGBTQ mariners is difficult, historical records present at least one possibility: Joseph Mazyck (or Masick as it was misspelled) of Charleston. Mazyck was imprisoned with many American sailors, captured by the British at sea in the War of 1812, and confined in Dartmoor Prison on the desolate English moors. There, one subgroup of prisoners was so despised by their peers that they were kept in a separate walled area and barracks (known as number four) for their own safety. Racial prejudice was definitely a part of it, as one man jailed at Dartmoor wrote, explaining that building number four was "occupied exclusively by the blacks, except a few whites who have been driven from the other prisons by their bad conduct, and are compelled to take up such accommodations here, as they can find, or the blacks will allot them. They [the hated White men] … are a community by themselves — can mess with none others but their kin in theft, riot and wickedness." Another sailor called them "a perfect set of outlaws and desperadoes, having, no doubt, been selected from the most miserable haunts of vice in all the seaports within the United States."

These loathed White sailors got the name of "rough alleys," a corruption of "raffalés" a term previously applied to French soldiers and sailors imprisoned by the British. The rough alleys were homosexuals who not only did not hide their status, but "seemed to embrace their degradation with an almost gleeful pride, reveling in their own shameful debasement." As if to prove this view, two of the leaders in prison number four, a prideful couple, took the names of Sodom and Gomorrah. As reviled as many rough alleys were, they were nevertheless remembered by others as leaders of culture and entertainment in the compound. They put on plays, created a band, and gave concerts.

These men, along with others, grew restless as they remained in prison after hostilities ended, and the peace Treaty of Ghent was signed in 1815. One small event grew into a prison riot, and although no longer at war, the British nevertheless shot randomly into the crowd, sparking an international incident and a resultant political cover-up. It is through records kept of the injured that the names of some rough alleys have survived. Joseph Mazyck, not denying his sexuality, was segregated, mistreated, and punished for living his life proudly.[5]

Chapter Three
First in the Hearts of Their Countrymen: Revolutionary Histories

While information is often lacking on common soldiers, sailors, and seafarers, it's a different story for those of higher rank. Their names have survived, and monuments recall their deeds. For some of these, however, questions remain, such as in the examples of Francis Salvador and John Laurens.

A monument to the former stands in Charleston's City Hall Park. He is lauded as the first Jewish identified man elected to public office in the colonies, and as the first Jew to die fighting for American independence. While true, he cannot be reduced to just a few facts. A new breed of scholars including Dr. Rebecca Stoil of Clemson University, trying to find the man in the myth, are now positing more nuanced views.

Born in London in 1747 into a wealthy, well-connected, Sephardic family, Salvador married his first cousin and fathered four children before leaving England in 1774. The ostensible reason was to check on some land that belonged to his uncle (and father-in-law) Joseph Salvador in an area near what is now Greenwood, South Carolina. He did not stay in Charleston (as his uncle would when he came over later), striking out instead for the wilds, becoming something of an anomaly: a very civilized Londoner living primitively on the frontier. Standing out for his religion and upbringing, he was elected to South Carolina's First and Second Provincial Congresses. The story goes that Salvador was caught up in the brewing war in which each side tried to involve the Native Americans. Riding like a "Jewish Paul Revere" to spread word of a looming attack, he was scalped and died on August 1, 1776.

But there is more to Salvador: when he left England in 1774, he apparently never again communicated with his wife or children, odd behavior for a supposedly devoted family man. Heterosexual historians, with no basis in fact, describe him as a loving parent and husband, and excuse his apparent neglect of his wife and children due to the political turmoil in the colonies. (But no letters for two years, when business correspondence went back and forth easily? And for all of his praise for being Jewish, it should be noted that one of his sons converted to Catholicism.) Similarly, Salvador also had little to do with his fellow orthodox Jews in Carolina, abandoning his religious peers to be a pioneer. His land was upstate, but like many other planters, he could have stayed in Charleston and managed the land through visits or employees.[1]

At the margins of settlement, Salvador, "not wishing to live alone," as an 1821 published source informs, "resided with his most intimate friend." That was Richard A. Rapley, who was not just a business agent for the Salvadors, but someone trusted enough for Joseph Salvador to have granted him power of attorney. Rapley had left London before Salvador, suggesting that the latter could have followed him deliberately. Rapley was, in many ways, Salvador's equal. Not only did they serve together, but they lived together, as well. (Since colonial times there had been a tradition of single men coming together to make a "joynt crop" being recognized as a social entity, at least in Virginia in the early 1600s. "It was so common," historian William Benemann points out, "that the relationship was given a name: each was the other's 'mate' [echoing the parlance of pirates in these same years]. The relationship between mates was so strongly regarded that it could endure even after one of the men took a wife. Only when both men married did a type of social mitosis occur, two new households being created where previously there was only one."[2]

In the case of Salvador and Rapley, the break never came, for after Salvador's early death, Rapley stayed on in the area and continued to puzzle his contemporaries. He never married. His 1823 obituary mentions his "choicest collection of English and French literature on the coarsest clumpiest [sic] shelves" in his log cabin graced with furniture of walnut and mahogany. The pictures on his walls, and his two unlikely silk umbrellas, one scholar attests, must have raised his neighbor's curiosity, as did other qualities. "He was an ardent admirer of beauty, a very pattern ... of gallantry and ease of manners, yet he lived and died a bachelor."

This was an era when people found that choice of lifestyle abnormal. (But others apparently had figured it out. US Secretary of the Treasury Albert Gallatin, for one, realized that "the Grecian vice [a veiled term for homosexuality] was common among Indians as well as among the back Woodsmen" [a term that could apply to Salvador and Rapley] on the American frontier.) Why else would those who possessed manners, money, land, and wealth turn away from the sophisticated pleasures of cities and live together miles from anyone? And after the untimely death of one, why would his "intimate friend" never marry?[3]

Bachelors like Rapley were considered curiosities, and sometimes even chastised for not procreating. The St. Andrew's Society, Charleston's oldest benevolent society, founded in 1729, open only to White men, penalized their bachelor members with extra fines. True, it was done in a spirit of fun, often encouraged by the conspicuous consumption of other spirits, and the Society also fined members who were married, those who had children and those who did not. Yet, as their historian attests, "In 1769, three [members] who had 'got Bairns' were fined £3 each; and eight bachelors were 'admonished to prevent further enquiries.'"[4] Buried in the wit and male camaraderie lies a veiled threat: bachelorhood might lead to inquiring to the reason for this continued "perversity." Seen as "unnatural," could it lead to "unnatural acts"?

Other unanswered questions about men from Charleston who served in the American Revolution have raised scholars' attention. In 1779, for instance, Sergeant Joseph Grimes, in the Charleston Light Infantry, was "charged with dressing himself like a girl and being out of camp." Grimes wasn't charged for desertion, but just for being out of camp in the clothes not befitting his gender. Dressing up in women's clothes was not taken lightly in these years, since it could cast suspicions on one's masculinity. In 1776, Francis Marion, the Swamp Fox of Revolutionary War fame, dressed four of his followers in lace caps and petticoats to humiliate them as part of their punishment for cowardice and being "unmanly." As for Grimes's motivation and punishment, the record is silent.[5]

John Laurens, another local soldier who has aroused the speculation of historians, had an intense "romantic friendship" with Alexander Hamilton. Their correspondence, sometimes dubbed "love letters," has attracted the attention of such

Figure 4. John Laurens

eminent historians as Jonathan Ned Katz, author of *Gay American History*, and Ron Chernow, the author of a biography of Alexander Hamilton. The affection Hamilton and Laurens had for each other has kept many scholars speculating, and some descendants censuring.

They had met in the strict disciplinary world of the all-male military, each about the same age (Laurens born in 1754, and Hamilton between 1755 and 57). Both served under General George Washington and were aides to the gay "Baron" von Steuben, who left Prussia after being accused of molesting young men. Laurens was the son of wealthy planter and slave trader Henry Laurens, who became President of the Second Continental Congress. The young John, educated abroad, had the very radical idea of treating Black people as equals, or at least allowing them to bear arms—the Black population being greater than Whites in the Lowcountry—to boost defense against the British. When he returned to South Carolina to put forth that idea to the state leaders (who soundly rejected it), a lonely Hamilton wrote to Laurens:

"Cold in my professions, warm in friendships, I wish, my Dear Laurens, it m[ight] be in my power, by action rather than words, [to] convince you that I love you. ... You know the opinion I entertain of mankind, and how much it is my desire to preserve myself free from particular attachments, and to keep my happiness independent on the caprice of others. You sh[ould] not have taken advantage of my sensibility to ste[a]l into my affections without my consent."[6]

Hamilton, biographer Chernow notes, would have known of "sodomites" transported from England for their crimes to the Caribbean where Hamilton grew up. Similarly, Laurens would have had access to knowledge of gay men from his milieu, for among the books in the Charlestown Library Society was Tobias Smollett's *Adventures of Roderick Random*, one of the most popular novels in London and the colonies. An array of male characters with names like Wiffle, Vergette, Simper, and Strutwell parade through the text. They defend the rise of homosexuality (which "in all probability will become in short time a more fashionable vice than mere fornication") and mention the benefit that "the practice of this passion is unattended with the curse and burthen upon society, which proceeds from a race of miserable deserted bastards." As historian William Benemann notes, none of the story's gay men are "punished for their sexual transgressions. Captain Wiffle and his entourage merely sail off toward the horizon, while Earl Strutwell retires behind his gates and burly footmen." We know John's father was a member of the Library Society; and the book was available to readers in this little London of the colonies since 1750, four years before John Laurens was born. This "alternate lifestyle" could possibly have been known to him and his peers.[7]

In another letter, an aggrieved Hamilton noted that Laurens had only sent one missive to the five or six he had sent Laurens. Receiving one back was an occasion for rejoicing. "But like a jealous lover when I thought you slighted my caresses, my affection was alarmed and my vanity piqued."

Another biographer of Hamilton notes the necessity of acknowledging the homoerotic nature of Hamilton's feelings for Laurens, which Chernow likens to a "crush." Hamilton's descendants were wary of it as well, deliberately not including information which styled the relationship with Laurens, "a deep fondness of friendship, which approached the tenderness of feminine attachment." "I must not publish the whole of this," the descendant wrote in the margin of a letter after obliterating words that probably spoke more of their intimacies.

Chernow further explicates that Hamilton was often called "feminine."[8] Laurens was married, but it was not a happy relationship. He had spent most of his time abroad with a circle of male friends and "saved an English's girl's honor" and reputation when he got her pregnant and she gave birth to a daughter. He left them in England and (like Francis Salvador) never saw them again. He nevertheless encouraged Hamilton to find a bride. In response to that advice, Hamilton wrote back, "I empower and command you to get me one in Carolina." Tongue in cheek, Hamilton asked Laurens to advertise his physical attributes to show his worthiness; "it will be necessary for you to give an account of the lover, his size, make, quality of mind and body, achievements, expectations, fortune, &c. In drawing my picture, you will no doubt be civil to your friend, mind you do justice to the length of my nose and don't forget that…"

Historians explain that it was not the size of his nose to which Hamilton was referring, but that of his penis, and the words Hamilton wrote next were cut out of the manuscript by later prudes, dramatizing again how hard it is to document LGBTQ history.

Hamilton did propose to a young lady, and he wrote to Laurens, telling him "your impatience to have me married is misplaced; a strange cure by the way, as if after matrimony I was to be less devoted [to you] than I am now."

His final letter to Laurens, just after the conclusive battle of Yorktown ending Revolutionary War hostilities, urged him to come back from South Carolina and join him in creating a new government. It was probably never read by his friend, who died in a minor skirmish in August 1782; "we have fought side by side to make America free," Hamilton had written, "let us now hand in hand struggle to make her happy."

"Because the style of eighteenth-century letters could be quite florid, even between men, one must tread lightly in approaching this matter," Chernow wrote cautiously in the

2004 book that became the basis for the Broadway musical *Hamilton*. In the less honest, more homophobic decade of the 1950s, another panicky biographer expended energy arguing that the words should not be taken at face value, for if they were, their homosexual content was "certain to provoke a riot in even the best-regulated present-day barracks or mess hall," showing not just prejudice against LGBTQ people, but ignorance of gay presence in the military.[9]

Jonathan Ned Katz explicates it best, saying that whatever the relation between Hamilton and Laurens might have been, they "inhabited a world that was not divided between 'heterosexual' and 'homosexual,' a world in which same-sex love, intimacy, and a touch of the erotic did not make one a 'pervert' or 'deviant.'" In this era where there were no words for such things, one could live more innocently with men friends and express affection, physical or not, more openly.

And in this world, Hamilton and Laurens were not alone. These elite White men of economic means, able to travel and follow literary, artistic, and companionable pursuits, succeeded in finding other sympathetic young men like them. In investigating their networks of friends, scholars have found an exact contemporary of Laurens in Francis Kinloch, who also hailed from South Carolina. They lived away from their parents, pursuing educations in Europe, far more tolerant on sexual issues. While Kinloch did marry and sire a family, he had a coterie of intimate men friends that included not just Laurens, but Swiss historian Johannes von Muller, whose homosexuality was well known. As with Hamilton, Laurens's correspondence with these two suggests deep emotions and like minds meeting.[10]

In the next generation, Francis Kinloch's nephew, bearing his uncle's name, likewise stayed abroad for long periods, and befriended other young men. He never married or returned to the Lowcountry, instead spending his life in

Rome, where he was free to be "artistic" and live beyond the constraints and expectations of his family. He died the patron of two young male artists who lovingly cared for him.

Similarly, Henry M. Rutledge of Charleston found himself the subject of romantic feelings and florid effusions from the very eccentric and effeminate Virginian John Randolph, who wrote to him of "his pure affection between man and man." While Randolph openly courted other men's affection, one is at a loss to explain his eccentric claim that John C. Calhoun "has actually made love to me."[11]

If these personal letters raise questions, how then is one to interpret other documents, even less explicit, some in fact just legalese in wills and deeds, in a search for LGBTQ history? While not as flowery or romantic, dry documents can conjure up an intimate relationship between two confirmed Charleston "bachelors" who, unlike Hamilton and Laurens, lived together as a couple in the early 19th century. Decades ago, another historian, not looking for any hint of homosexuality, concluded that these two men were special companions.

Chapter Four

Schools for Scandal: Men and Boys in the Early 19th Century

In the 1940s, E. Milby Burton, director of the Charleston Museum, was tracing the history of "Charleston's outstanding example of a suburban Regency Villa," when he came upon the intertwined lives of two Englishmen. Even in that pre-Stonewall era when homosexuality was illegal and not fit for polite discussion, Burton used language to suggest he saw something special between them. For in referring to Patrick Duncan and James Nicholson, he used the term "intimate friend[s]," the exact words a historian over a hundred years earlier had invoked to describe the bond between Richard A. Rapley and Francis Salvador.

Duncan, a Scotsman, had arrived in Charleston soon after the Revolution, possibly by 1783, and worked as a tallow chandler (or candlemaker), in the neighborhood then known as Cannonsboro, beyond suburbs spreading north of the city. It was an odiferous process, involving animal fats and such, so being away from the crowded downtown made sense. Duncan succeeded well enough to be named a director of the Planters and Mechanics Bank by 1818. City directories list him residing in this area, and the house he had built, possibly designed by the English architect William Jay, is thought to have been finished by 1816. Soon his profession shifted from messy manufacturing to acting as a factor, someone doing business for planters and others.

Records show another man associated with him, sharing the same house, the same profession, the same hobbies, and more: certainly, an emotional and possibly a deeper intimacy. James Nicholson, born in 1758, shows up in Charleston by 1786, a few years after Duncan. Nicholson shared Duncan's interests in manufacturing and mining, noting in advertisements that he was seeking mineralists and artisans who could make porcelain out of "real china clay." City directories were soon referring to him as a tallow chandler, too, and put him living and working in the exact same neighborhood as Duncan.

They were not neighbors, but housemates. The census for 1830 (which only names the head of a household and gives demographics of others in the home) shows Nicholson living with another man, his own age (both in their 70s), with no women, most probably in the house built by Duncan. (Odd that the census takers would list the newer arrival to the premises, and not the owner, as the household's head.)

They did not just spend time together under the same roof, but also on the grounds, as both loved to garden. In 1836, Nicholson was awarded a silver medal for his tulips by the Horticultural Society; and in 1819, a visitor to town was taken to "the seat of Patrick Duncan, Esq, ... the head of a bank in this city. He is a rich, knowing old gentleman, living in the garden of the choicest flowers and fruits, breaking down the trees with their weight." It's a lovely image: two senior men, together during the day at the same sort of work, together later in their garden, raising flowers, living in one of the most elegant of the city's mansions, sequestered on their estate from prying eyes. (So discrete was their residence that some accused of plotting in the purported Denmark Vesey slave insurrection felt safe enough to do their talking under the garden's trees.)

While we lack correspondence between Duncan and Nicholson, there is other evidence to suggest what they meant to each other. When Nicholson died in 1836, he left everything to his "good friend" for his natural life, just as historian Nic Butler suggests, one would grant "a life-estate extended to a spouse." At Duncan's death, everything he inherited reverted to Nicholson's siblings, his blood relatives, showing that Nicholson held his chosen family, Duncan, closer to him than his blood kin. Two years later, Duncan died in England, having never married.

Exactly when Duncan left Charleston for England is not known. But something of their memory lingered in the house, something that suggested a bond. Milby Burton noted that the house that Duncan built was long known as the "Nicholson House after Duncan's friend... who lived with him for many years and remained in the house after Duncan moved to England." (Nicholson and Duncan, coincidentally were involved in a legal case regarding the lands once owned by the Salvadors.) These men who by profession in candlemaking served to light the city, might be illuminating a dark corner of LGBTQ history.[1]

The house eventually became the property of George A. Trenholm, who served as Secretary of the Treasury for the Confederacy; and then it was home to Charles Otto Witte, whose six daughters, legendary for their beauty, wit, and charm, married into the highest social circles and became cultural leaders of the city. When the property was sold to Miss Mary Vardrine McBee in 1909, she started a school on the premises. The mansion that became the famous Ashley Hall single-sex school for girls had begun as the home of a single- sex couple of men.

At the same time these older men were living together, two young South Carolina College boys were finding carnal enjoyment with each other. While the story is more of Columbia's LGBTQ history than Charleston's, its coming to light demonstrates the difficulties of documenting this topic and reveals to what lengths even professionals charged with saving the past will go to obscure LGBTQ history.

Recalling their time in college together, in 1826, Thomas Jefferson Withers wrote to his friend James Henry Hammond:

> "I feel some inclination to learn whether you yet sleep in your Shirt-tail, and whether you yet have the extravagant delight of poking and punching a writhing Bedfellow with your long fleshen pole — the exquisite touches of which I have often had the honor of feeling? Let me say unto thee that unless thou changest former habits in this particular, thou wilt be represented by every future Chum as a nuisance. And, I pronounce it, with good reason too. Sir, you roughen the downy Slumbers of your Bedfellow — by such hostile, furious lunges as you are in the habit of making at him — when he is least prepared for defence [sic] against the crushing force of a Battering Ram. Without reformation my imagination depicts some awful results for which you will be held accountable — and therefore it is, that I earnestly recommend it. Indeed it is encouraging an assault and battery propensity, which needs correction — & uncorrected threatens devastation, horror & bloodshed, etc....
>
> With great respect I am the old
>
> Stud,
>
> Jeff"

There is much to parse (and very little to decode) here, especially the sheer unashamed frankness and fun of Hammond's sexual exploits with his male friends. These elite White men were powerful and wealthy enough not to feel guilty about anything. Withers went on to attend the South Carolina Secession Convention, taking the first step to disunion and Civil War, and Hammond served as governor and United States Senator. He fell into disgrace due to his unleashed libido, taking liberties with enslaved women on his plantation, as well as with the nieces of Wade Hampton, later a Confederate general and Reconstruction governor.

Hammond's papers, with the few racy letters buried in them, were well known among historians; Hammond family descendants had given the materials to an archive to preserve and make them accessible. While they were made available to scholars, in 1981, permission was withheld from gay scholar Martin Duberman who wanted to show that two South Carolinians of distinguished rank had been bedfellows in their youth. Fearing that would taint them and their descendants, the archivist refused to answer Duberman, who, after repeated rebuffs published the letters to cast light on the topic of early 19th-century male-to-male sexuality.[2]

The lack of guilt felt by Withers and Hammond was not shared by all men and boys at school in these years. Letters in another archive dramatize a lesser-known story that took place more than a generation later, involving a young Lowcountry boy. He was of high rank, too: his father was R.F.W. Allston, a governor of the state. The family plantation, Chicora Wood, outside Georgetown was their traditional home, but they also owned one of the most elegant mansions in Charleston, the Nathaniel Russell House, now a museum.

Aged 13, Charles Allston was away from home, attending Octavius R. Porcher's Willington Academy in McCormick, South Carolina. Benjamin, his older brother, was worried about what might happen in this all-male environment, and wrote Charles in March 1861, responding to the information that Charles was sharing a bed with another student.

"Where is your own bed?" the older Benjamin inquired; "have you not one? I would ask Mr. Porcher to allow you to use your own mattress, even if you have to put it upon the floor."

"If you cannot affect this," Ben advised, "well you must submit, but be very careful Charley, boys in sleeping together sometimes teach each other very bad habits which in long after years will give you much trouble and pain, if they do not even worse than this, sometimes men become insane, and are obliged to be sent to a madhouse, from the practice of habits learnt in boyhood."[3]

He was warning him against masturbation, believed by many to drive one crazy; and perhaps he was warning him of things he himself had seen. Ben Allston, 15 years older than Charley, had gone to an all-boys school, too, one run by a Mr. Coates on Wentworth Street in Charleston. While there, his mother pleaded with him to behave; later in West Point, Ben complained of a most eccentric roommate that made him want to leave.

It seems likely that in Charleston, in an academy run by a man from England, where all-male schools were rife with opportunistic same-sex activities, or at West Point, another all-male environment, Benjamin had witnessed behavior between men, mutual masturbation or something beyond that, and he felt he had to warn Charley.

He had to speak clearly: "I refer to the handling of your private member. Let nothing tempt you to do so, yourself, or allow others to do so for you. If there is anything which you do not understand write me frankly about it and I will explain. Life is one long struggle Charley against what is bad and for what is good."[4]

Charley's replies to Benjamin have not been found, but letters to his mother survive. After the exchange with his brother, he wrote her, "I am in a room with five boys besides myself and they make a constant noise I can hardly read my Bible or say my prayers ... the only way to remedy it is to try and get into a room with one boy next year."

He did not know what to do. "I feel entirely lost without someone who I can talk to freely and be under no restraint for there is no one up here that I care to bother with my little problems or to whom I can go to with any hesitation for advice when I am in difficulty."[5]

Charles survived his childhood quandaries, married, and became a clergyman, the father of many children.

Charles' sisters and other elite, White women attended their own schools in these years. Although right before the outbreak of the Civil War a pre-eminent institution would hire a very progressive lesbian, (more on Anna Brackett to follow), the historical record so far has not yielded any suggestion of same-sex desire between girls or women in the city in these years. They were held to higher standards, assumed "pure" and above reproach. Women of color and others seen as lower on the social economic scale, however, were judged, and written about differently.

Chapter Five
Misbehaving Women

From the early 18th century on, organizations focusing on misbehaving and promiscuous women also sought to curb the actions of transgressive men who acted like women. It is no wonder that in the 20th century, feminism and the fight for LGBTQ rights would always be linked. Women transcending their traditional roles have a long history in the Lowcountry.[1]

One of the strongest Indigenous rulers the Spanish encountered in their 1540s explorations of South Carolina was female. The Lady of Cofitachequi ruled from the Pee Dee region of the state to the Piedmont, maybe to the mountains, and possibly as far south as the sea. Although the Spanish captured her, she escaped, and probably returned to rule her people before she disappeared. Her empire soon crumbled after the arrival of the English in 1670. That was the year young Affra Harleston endured the same rough voyage on the same ship that brought Francis O'Sullivan; just as he is remembered by Sullivan's Island, the downtown neighborhood of Harleston Village, land she was granted, continues her memory.

In the 18th century, Sophia Hume, born in Charleston in 1702, defied convention by publishing and preaching. Though understudied, Hume is considered the mother of American feminism among Quaker leaders. Henrietta Johnston, arriving here in the early 1700s, may have created lady-like pastels of early Charlestonians including William Rhett, who went to capture pirates, but she, as her husband confessed, was the breadwinner in the family. Enslaved Black women in the market were chastised for being "loose, idle and disorderly," their behavior deemed unruly in demanding certain people purchase goods from them. While White men controlled most everything, White women could petition the courts to become femme soles who could thus engage in business in their own names and avoid their husband's debts while holding onto their own property. Many Charleston women fought for their individual—and all women's—rights in the 19th-century. The Pollitzer sisters, two of whom did not marry, became leaders for women's rights in the 20th.

It's only been a recent development, in a monument unveiled in 2015, that the Lowcountry has publicly embraced the 19th-century Grimké sisters, Sarah and Angelina, who spoke out against slavery and for the rights of women, and so were considered disgraces to their sex and family. The images of them that have come down to us show dour, stern, grim visages. One scholar suggests that these "portraits" were actually drawn by the opposition to deliberately depict them as unfeminine and masculine to show how they had "unsexed themselves" and betrayed their supposed God-given roles. Their great niece Angelina Weld Grimké, granddaughter of their brother Henry and free woman of color, Nancy Weston, became a celebrated Black lesbian writer of the Harlem Renaissance in the early 20th century. But she'd feel prejudice's double sting. Although lauded as one of the first Black women in this country to write a play to be produced, be staged, and praised by the NAACP, she'd find her poetry on women's sexual love for other women reviled and unwelcome.

The double standard was long in vogue. James Louis Petigru's daughter, Susan King, was ostracized for her lack of femininity. While her father was respected for taking up legal cases of Black people and White women, and for being a staunch supporter of the Union during the Civil War, she was disdained for writing books that complained of the status consigned to women, for being "fast," and speaking her mind to such literary lions as William Makepeace Thackery when he visited the United States in the 1850s. Worse yet, after the Civil War, she married a Yankee.

Another woman who embraced her sex and sexuality and may have had lesbian affairs has been written out of the city's history entirely, due to her antics, and her ties to one of the most visible gay men of the 19th century.[2] She was born Ada Agnes Jane McElhenney in Charleston in 1834. Like the Grimkés, she was not content with the lot assigned her as the "lesser" sex. A tomboy when young, she preferred rough-and-tumble sports but had to assume behavior expected of her as a girl. She attended the Miss Bates all-girl school, pursuing math and other unladylike subjects. She wanted to be a writer, and though she was related to Charleston lyric poet Paul Hamilton Hayne, this was an era when only men like him and William Gilmore Simms were encouraged. "Defends slavery, is too wordy, but has good descriptions," was the verdict of Walt Whitman on Simms. But McElhenney published articles in the College of Charleston's magazine—a school she could not attend due to her sex. She hid her identity, using initials only. Chafing under what was expected of her, she broke the law to free herself, committing a crime her family tried to keep secret for years.

Searching for funds to leave Charleston, she stole money that the Ladies Calhoun Memorial Association had raised to build a statue to the Southern states' rights champion John C. Calhoun, delaying its eventual erection from the 1850s until the 1880s. That she was related to Calhoun by marriage and had once stayed with him and his family might have angered and upset her relatives even more.

In a single act, she kept Calhoun off a pedestal and removed herself from the one she, as a woman, would have been forced to occupy, metaphorically at least. In New York, she took the name Ada Clare from one of Charles Dickens's heroines; she became a journalist, refusing to simper and say sweet things; she cut her hair, and was not reluctant to use her witty, tart, and acid tongue. She became an actress, and a novelist. The characters she created were "women who ought to have been men, and men who ought to have been women," according to one critic. But what scandalized folks most, especially her Charleston family, was her overt sexuality, and her bearing a child out of wedlock. She claimed Louis Gottschalk, the most famous musician of his day, as the father. "Miss Clare and son" was how she proudly signed hotel registers when traveling. She was called "the Queen of Bohemia" by the artists, poets and other social outcasts who gathered together in Pfaff's Cellar in New York City, ground zero for many of the new art forms and social movements then brewing.

One of her most ardent admirers was the good gray (and gay) poet Walt Whitman, an icon in American literary and LGBTQ history. Another of her best friends was the very effete gay poet Charles Warren Stoddard, with whom she traveled in California and Hawaii. A sexual rebel herself, she was very comfortable with the sexual outlaws of her gay male friends. Clare herself may also have been bisexual or lesbian. She was very intimate with the equally scandalous actress and cross-dressing celebrity Adah Isaacs Menken, who, when not having affairs with women, played men on stage, and often appeared in roles seemingly nude on horseback. Menken's and Clare's romantic behavior together outraged men witnessing it (once driving Samuel L. Clemens — "Mark Twain" — from the room) and "generated many questions about their sexual desires." No doubt those aghast at her behavior felt vindicated when Clare died in 1874, at the age of 40, victim of a bite from a lapdog with rabies.[3]

Women like Ada were watched and chastised for infractions of femininity, while men were allowed great liberties and allowed to be sexual libertines. Whitman brazenly celebrated love between men in his poetry, and Stoddard wrote of his love affairs with the beautiful native men of Hawaii, but woe to any woman "outed" for flouting assumed gender roles. Stoddard and Whitman wrote in code and at first escaped censure, until readers and critics began to understand their homosexual themes. Women were condemned for even minor infractions of the code imposed on them by society, which cast them in the role of goddesses of delicate femininity.

Jezebels of the City

Women in Charleston who worked as prostitutes were condemned as sexual outlaws. When caught, they were punished with fines and imprisonment, but the penalties were not as severe as those for buggery. While their names and stories might have been saved in police reports, most of those records from before the Civil War don't survive. Following the rules of Victorian decorum, the local paper, *The Courier*, and others, refused to name them. So, like the early stories of LGBTQ people and other sexual outlaws, mentions of women who broke the rules are few. But we can get a glimpse of the antebellum demimonde of the city thanks to a Charlestonian who styled himself "Buzzard." Like his namesake, he lived off the dead reputation of others. He was obsessed with those who broke the rules, and in doing his "moral duty," he sent information the local papers would not print to one that would: New York's *National Police Gazette*, a tabloid scandal sheet which was sold on Charleston streets. While prostitution was the main focus of the paper's exposé on social evils in Charleston, the paper would report on men who broke gender norms too, further evidence of the link between homophobia and misogyny.

In the November 28, 1859 issue of the *Gazette*, under the heading "Charleston Correspondence," Buzzard said he had to "call attention to the mayor of the neighborhood of Archdale Street, between Magazine and Beaufain … Last night, while passing through the neighborhood, I saw the inmates of the brothels there walking up and down the pave[ment] to see whom they might entrap, and making night hideous with their noise and indecent exposure." One pictures the poor men being lured into clutches of these terrible women, like insects into Venus Flytraps.

On July 2, 1859, Buzzard wrote of other brothels and their inhabitants. As for the "the Elliott street crib," the bordello's owner, "one of the heroes of nullification ... is the son of old Mother Smoke, of Bedens [sic] alley notoriety, who kept a den of the lowest order in what was then known as Mullatto [sic] Alley. ... This hero, her son, was at that time a kind of waiting chambermaid for the lady boarders of his ma's crib." This unnamed man had kept "a house of prostitution and fence for thieves. At this

Figure 5. Charleston prostitutes repenting, 1886 earthquake

time, he kept his den on Elliot Street, opposite Beden's [sic] Alley and Kate Welch, and Margaret McCloud, alias Laughing Jack, two notorious thieves, were his boarders and pals."

Buzzard continued enumerating. "31 Beaufain Street. This crib is inhabited by Martha Downing alias Martha Cox, and Ellen Hennessy. Next is No. 35 Beaufain Street. The occupants of this brothel are Lucy Riners, Gilly Prier (a shoplifter) and little Moll Collins. ... The next and most vicious, the most patronized—in fact, the worst sink of a crib in the city is kept by one Miss Ashley, in Beresford street [sic]; I say the worst, because more rum is sold there than at all the rest — because more young men have been there. Among the actors in this crib are Emma Demarest, Fanny Livingston (an old thief), Ida Clifton (an old decoy), the very graceful Florence Washington, and Clara Fisher (both Philadelphia thieves), and three others whose history I have not yet obtained."

When Buzzard fell down on the job, or didn't follow through, a writer named Pink took over the "Charleston Correspondence." On April 20, 1861, just over a week after the start of the Civil War, Pink wrote of goings-on in one whorehouse Buzzard had mentioned: "Old Alice Ashley has turned old scabby Hettie Ware out of her ranch, and says she don't want anybody in her house who will be the cause of getting 'Pink' to write against her ... I will drop into Alice's tonight to see if I can get anything worth mentioning."

Pink accused the police of corruption, noting that more than anything else, they were the ones who wanted to ferret out his identity. "It is no wonder they are not able to pay their boarding-house or clothing store bills. How can they, when it takes every dollar they can make to keep these prostitutes? Any one can see this grade of guardians two days after getting their salaries, hanging around bar-rooms, trying to sponge a drink, when their mulatto and white mistresses are in King street, buying silk dresses. ... Let any one [go] to a negro [sic] fandango, and see these very mulattoes dressed in their silks and satins, and ask one of them where she obtained the means to dress in such style, and the answer he would get is, that she is officer So-and-so's woman." Employing a flagrantly sexist double standard, Pink wrote, "I do not wish to put these men's name in public print," — but he, like Buzzard before him, did not hesitate to call out the women.[5] One of the few times Buzzard would ever name a man was when he found one pretending not to be one. (More on that story below.)

If outrageous women who broke the rules, sexual or social, were not enough to upset Charlestonians, they must not have known what to do when their city was suddenly the scene of a national scandal unfolding on gender reversals and dubious sexual identity. Eventually, they did figure out what to do — they ignored it, refusing to cover it in the press. But if Charlestonians looked the other way, others did not. The story was eagerly taken up by the *National Police Gazette*, along with other journals around the country, titillating their readers with a story that had more twists and turns than a corkscrew.

Chapter Six

Intersex in the City? Charlotte Myers and Rufus Griswold

Charlotte Myers was born in Georgetown, South Carolina, in 1802 to Moses and Anna Myers, both from Lowcountry Jewish families. A surviving relic from her childhood is her commonplace book. Once very common indeed, their contemporary analogy would be Facebook: in a nearly empty volume repurposed from her father's business, she spent a considerable amount of time, if not posting, then pasting her "likes"—laying in snippets of news and images from newspapers that caught her fancy. Instead of a glut of selfies, she glued in engravings of women in gorgeous gowns, and beauties in bonnets she hand-colored. In an era when dainty skills were prized, Charlotte proved her feminine dexterity by creating delicate paper cuts that, with a pull of a cord, balloon out into fabulous if fragile geometric shapes, still working two centuries after she made them. She also showed interest in topics then considered masculine: global issues, world leaders, and politics. An omnivorous reader (and clipper), it's quite likely she came across the man who would carry her name into the scandal sheets (which she determinedly did not clip).[1]

Rufus Griswold had been born in Vermont in 1815, 13 years after Charlotte. Wild, restless, and unruly, he eventually clawed his way to the position as a journalist and editor. With little talent of his own, he spent most of his career making and breaking the reputation of others. If not for his relationship with Edgar Allen Poe, he would have not even been a footnote in literary history.[2]

Poe and Griswold had started out friendly enough, until Poe realized Griswold's mediocrity, and the latter was consumed with envy. When Poe died, Griswold claimed that the poet had chosen him as his literary executor. But he acted more like an executioner, originating many of the unsupported claims of Poe as erratic, a drug user, and mad: untruths scholars have combatted for years.

Somewhere along the line, Griswold picked up the title of "reverend," maybe having been licensed to preach, or maybe not. He was a liar and forger; a "defender of copyright," he plagiarized widely. The sex and sexuality of male and female poets and the latters' "transgressions" of their God-given roles (as he perceived them) obsessed the reverend. He castigated women writers who disagreed with him and praised those who favored him. Furthermore, he appears to be the sole contemporary critic who detected the homoeroticism of Ada Clare's friend, Walt Whitman. Griswold called Whitman's verse "filth," full of "the vilest imaginings and shameful license." With no word like homosexuality at his disposal, he called it (in Latin) "the horrible

Figure 6. Charlotte Myers

Figure 7. Rufus Griswold, ca. 1855

sin, among Christians not to be named," linking it to sodomites, bestiality, and buggery.[3]

If he lacked an exact word for Whitman, he certainly had no trouble finding the mot juste for the many female writers whose enmity he earned. Griswold dismissed and insulted them as "hermaphroditish [sic] disturbers of the peace," women who unsexed themselves in trying to invade the male sphere of literature. With Charlotte Myers, those words would come to haunt him.[4]

They met in Philadelphia in 1845 where the 43-year-old Myers was summering with her aunts Sarah and Hesse. By then a widower with two daughters foisted off on his dead wife's kin, Griswold paraded like a peacock and courted Myers, hearing she was rich.

Griswold proposed and Myers accepted. But he immediately got cold feet. (Was it because he would be criticized as a reverend married to a "Jewess"?) Griswold said he tried to retract his offer of marriage, but the aunts insisted he go through with the ceremony. The wedding took place August 20, 1845, in New York City.

And then what did or did not happen on their wedding night eventually provided titillating reading for those who followed the story. He left her side, he said, at 3 a.m., and claimed that, although they saw each other over the next few years in Charleston, Philadelphia, and New York, they never had a true marriage.[5] This is hard to square with the fact that he moved down to Charleston, bringing his daughter, Mary Caroline, known as Caroline, to live with Myers and her aunts in Myers's home on what was Aiken's Row on Wragg Mall. Myers became Caroline's legal guardian.

Myers paid for everything; and Griswold demanded all her financial papers and deeds. Arguments over money ensued; Griswold abandoned his wife and daughter to pursue his literary career while he was wooing other women simultaneously. (When considering proposing to a writer, he abandoned the thought, having "seen and read too much of literary women to believe they were apt to make good housekeepers," so he switched his attention elsewhere.)[6] He needed a divorce, something South Carolina would not legalize until the 1940s.

In her version of what happened, Myers fled the place they arranged to meet, suspecting Griswold might waylay and snatch her adopted Caroline (Griswold's child) for ransom. He did exactly that. He vowed he'd only return Caroline to Myers if Myers signed a statement attesting she had abandoned Griswold so he could have grounds for a divorce.

In 1852, right after Myers signed (and Caroline, who never saw her father again, was returned to her), Griswold swore he presented that document to a Philadelphia court, and on its strength, he was granted his divorce.

Myers immediately challenged the decree, saying her signature had been obtained under duress.

The case went to court in 1856, and the *Police Gazette* and other papers had a field day attacking Griswold for his hypocrisy. Everyone waited with bated breath for the decision of the judge. The saga, one journalist wrote, was more scandalous even than the "inventions of the French novelists."[7]

The judge dismissed Myers's complaint, but in his due diligence, searching the written record, he found no trace of a divorce decree: no filing, or petitioning, or judgment or indexing. There was no proof Griswold had ever presented papers or been divorced in the first place, as he claimed. Evidence suggests he made that up.

As soon as the verdict was announced, with his recently wed wife in Maine refusing to see him (they never met again), and the jilted one in Charleston despising him, Griswold sat down to seek justice from what he saw as a higher source: the court of public opinion. It has been his version of things (still studied in the course of American divorce history) that has come down through time. He had a pamphlet printed and dispersed to the four winds before his death. It is now preserved in over 100 libraries and is downloadable on the Internet for free.

In defense of himself and his attack on Myers and the court, he wrote like Poe, enticing his readers with ominous hints, unmentionable gothic secrets of the wedding night, a conspiracy of aunts, the unnatural rumors around Charleston about Myers. He was not a bigamist, but blameless. In fact, he never had needed a divorce from Myers in the first place. The marriage was never valid, legal, or moral either in the eyes of God or man because, he said, it was tantamount to one "taken place between parties of the same sex, or where the sex of one was doubtful or ambiguous." Myers, he told the world, was not a woman at all! She was either a man, a hermaphrodite, or intersex. Thus, he said, no marriage with such a monstrous creature was valid.[8]

The accusation (true or not) in the Victorian era must have been devastating to Charlotte and her family. Did her neighbors in Charleston know? How did she react? Again, the few clues left to us are from her commonplace book. She kept clipping and pasting as if nothing had happened.

Rufus Griswold might have turned in his grave at some of the stories she pasted in. (He died on August 12, 1857, just a week after what would have been his and Myers's twelfth wedding anniversary; his affairs were such a mess, however, it took six years for him to be buried.) But now the daughter he had abandoned had become a writer herself, turning, like Myers, into one of the manly "hermaphroditish" women he despised.[9]

Myers, her aunts, and her adopted daughter survived the Civil War. The women banded together to teach school, but it did not last. The aunts died, and then Caroline did too—young. Her death record notes consumption, and dated October 6, 1874, it gives her age as 36. But it also states she had lived in Charleston for 35 years, impossible since she was about seven when Myers and Griswold married. It seems Myers might have been trying to pass Caroline off as a daughter she had birthed. Myers lived on, moving to smaller and more squalid places until she died of heart failure on February 17, 1891, at age 88. Did her death record contain inaccuracies, too? On it, she was pronounced "female."[10]

After his death, Griswold's letters were collected and published; they raise a suspicion that he himself may have experienced what he fulminated against in Walt Whitman. At 15, the object of "an affection which knew little restraint," he ran away from his family to live with a 20-year-old man named George Foster. They read romantic poets together in their shared room; their "emotional abandon and freedom must have been exhilarating."

Foster wrote of "the flames of passion" he had for Griswold. "I have never felt towards any human being—man or woman—so strong and absorbing an affection as I bear you." He compared their love to that in a poem they had memorized—Byron's *Don Juan*. "You are to me what the shipwrecked Juan was to Haidée," he wrote. In the poem, the lovers form,

> a group that's quite antique,
> Half naked, loving, natural, and Greek.

Foster ended his letter to Griswold, saying "my love, my devotion (we may both I trust use the word,) is unaltered and unalterable. ... come to me if you love me."[11]

One cannot but wonder at those words, fervent as those between Alexander Hamilton and John Laurens. Griswold was a man who had feckless relationships with women, who was obsessed with hermaphrodites, on the lookout for men who acted like women and women who acted like men, a critic who had recognized Whitman's homosexuality. Had all the agony and angst he caused himself and others stemmed from his inability to deal with his own sexual attractions to men? Did he make up the whole story of Myers being intersex because of his own complicated sexuality? One cannot deny the possibility, making the whole saga a cross between a farce and a Greek tragedy.

As singular as the Griswold/Myers case was, it was not the only one of gender confusion in the press in these years. In 1859, some years after this affair rocked the Lowcountry, another one was in the news, once more in Charleston, and once more playing out in a variety of places.

Nic Butler of the Charleston County Public Library found the story in the local press. Charleston citizens, accustomed to keeping an eye on Black men and Black women, fearful of what the enslaved majority might be up to, grew suspicious of a White woman new to town seen associating with enslaved people on the street. She was brought to the attention of the chief of police, who had her arrested. She claimed to be Caroline Wilson, but while in custody, her secret was revealed. She was, in fact, a man named Charles; he "made a full confession, in which he stated that he had regularly appeared in women's apparel since he was ten years old, but refused to give any reason for such strange and unaccountable conduct." Back then, citizens had no vocabularies to ask if Wilson was a transvestite, a gay man trying to seduce other men (a Black man?), or someone doing all they could to express the gender they believed the proper one. Charlestonians, on the verge of the Civil War, theorized that this subversive act might represent their greatest fear. Charles, dressed as Caroline, might be a spy, consorting with the enslaved, possibly acting in secret as "an Abolition emissary."[12]

Caroline/Charles was encouraged to move on. And if she no longer was covered in the local press, New York papers took up her story. The reporter noted that Charles, now passing himself off as Caroline Walters, presented as "quite a handsome female," and though she had made the rounds from New Orleans to New York, her "debut in Charleston," garnered more attention. "She visited the city during the prevalence of the yellow fever last year [1858], and tendered her services to the Howard Association ... for the purposes of nursing the sick, and was boarded for a time at one of our first class hotels.

"Possessed of a fine exterior, neatly attired in black, with a fair sprinkling of furs and flash jewelry, she made quite an impression on some of our young bloods, and doubtless not a few older ones sent sidelong glances at the fair Desdemona. While here she laid claim to Philadelphia as the place of her nativity." From Charleston, Caroline apparently went to Memphis, convincing the mayor there that she was a damsel in distress, "an innocent female" who "had been seduced in Charleston, the gay Lothario having promised to meet her in Memphis, where he swore by that love, at the alter [sic] of which she had yielded herself and been prematurely immolated, he would straighten up matters in true matrimonial style." But what were people to think, presented with the story of a man dressed as a woman, saying he had had sex with another man, who promised to marry, but then jilted, him?

When the beau did not turn up, "she went raving, crazy, created considerable excitement and sympathy, and probably realized something by the operation," suggesting that the public took pity on her and supported her with money and shelter, until somehow the truth came out. The writer spoke of similar hoaxes in other cities. In Philadelphia, claiming she came from Charleston, Caroline was arrested for stealing a watch from a Black man she knew. Leaving for other Southern destinations, she carried no baggage, "contriving by some means to be on par, in manner of dress, with the most fashionable of the sex." The New York press said she returned to town a few months before and was kept under watch. "Later accounts affirm that the same individual ... arrested in Savannah, and upon examination, having proved to be a veritable man, he was furnished with a suit of male attire, placed on board a vessel, and given a free passage to New York." No one seemed to know what to do with this self-dramatizing man who dressed as a woman, who always managed to get caught despite a lovely façade. The solution seemed to be to send Caroline/Charles somewhere else.[13]

If gender lines were being crossed willy-nilly, political lines, on the other hand, were not. They were, in fact, hardening. The country was becoming two armed camps, North versus South, slaveholders versus abolitionists. In 1860,

Charleston was the site of the Democratic National Convention, which split over the issue of slavery; after Abraham Lincoln was elected president in November of that year, the lines hardened further, and the die was cast. On December 20, 1860, South Carolina seceded from the Union, demanding a divorce of sorts from the North, that its own private citizens could not achieve. As noted, one of the signers of the Ordinance of Secession was Thomas Jefferson Withers, the bedmate of racist Southern demagogue, James Henry Hammond. With politics making strange bedfellows, there was apparently room enough for Southern orthodoxy to bed down with sexual hypocrisy.

And just as America was teetering on the cusp of violent change, two extraordinary sexual radicals who would come to challenge gender rules in the coming years were in town biding their time, not tipping their truths to anyone.

Chapter Seven

On the Cusp: Theorists in the City

Both of these progressive advocates of change were from the Boston area; both were involved in education, and both were in Charleston just briefly.

Anna Brackett, born 1836, educated in leading Massachusetts female academies, arrived in 1860 to teach in the recently established Whites-only Girl's High and Normal School, soon re-christened Memminger after Christopher G. Memminger, later Secretary of the Treasury of the Confederacy. Frederick Adolphus Sawyer, a graduate of Harvard, was brought down as principal, and Brackett was vice principal and teacher. She was a strict disciplinarian, dedicated to women's education (a normal school, by definition, produced future teachers) and loved by her pupils. Brackett was visiting a plantation when the attack on Fort Sumter began in April 1861. Most Northerners saw this as a signal to leave, but Brackett stayed, one of the last to get out of Charleston before the port was blockaded by Union ships.[1]

In her subsequent career, she gained fame for her feminism and visibility as a woman who loved women. In 1863, in St. Louis, Brackett became the first woman in American history to become principal of a secondary school. She authored articles and books on the topic, fighting for co-education, knowing women had a role to play beyond the domestic realm. Co-education, she argued, would keep women from becoming vulnerable to men.

Defying convention, she lived with her "domestic partner" Ida Eliot, who founded a school for African Americans in St. Louis, where Brackett hired her. They moved to New York and adopted a daughter, Hope, in 1873 and another daughter, Bertha, in 1875. In a poem for her partner, Brackett wrote, "How did I know she loved me?" The next line was "How did I know I loved her?"

While her time in Charleston had been brief, her impact lasted. Her student Henrietta Aiken Kelly remained single and founded the Charleston Female Seminary before going off to Paris to study botany; others became teachers, and Celia Campbell managed the house of rest for impoverished women, orphans, and children. It's impossible not to wonder what Brackett might have accomplished locally had she stayed.[2]

The same holds true for a very articulate gay man who'd come to defend homosexual lives and love in future years. James Mills Peirce, born in 1834, two years before Anna Brackett, was the son of a Harvard professor and grandson of a Harvard librarian. Following in their footsteps, he graduated from the school in 1853, went to Harvard Law, and then to Divinity School. Starting in 1859, he spent two years in the ministry, in Massachusetts and then in Charleston. An 1860 newspaper story puts Peirce in the pulpit of the Unitarian Church on Archdale Street. His was just a brief stay, for he soon gave up the ministry for a Harvard professorship in mathematics. Back in Boston, he pursued a number of romantic friendships with young men and colleagues.

At the end of the 19th century, closeted British writer John Addington Symonds, who corresponded with Walt Whitman, privately published *A Problem in Greek Ethics*. In it he examined male love through the prism of the pederasty practices of classical Greece. Peirce secured a copy and wrote Symonds of his theories on the topic.

While Symonds had prevaricated, Peirce saw no ethical problem with being gay, asserting instead how natural and healthy it was. "I believe," he wrote, "that the Greek morality on this subject was far higher than ours, and truer to the spiritual nature of man. ... We ought to think of homosexual love, not as 'inverted' or 'abnormal,' as a sort of colour-blindness of the genital sense, as a lamentable mark of inferior development, or as an unhappy fault, a 'masculine body with a feminine soul,' but as being in itself a natural, pure and sound passion, as worthy of the reverence of all fine natures as the honourable devotion of husband and wife, or the ardour of bride and groom."

Historian Jonathan Ned Katz notes how astonishing this was for the time. Peirce demolished accepted beliefs about homosexuality being immoral or a disease. Nor was it a medical malaise, or degeneracy, as Freud was positing. Symonds was shocked at such an unapologetic and even proud defense of gay male sexuality. Havelock Ellis, his co-author, was so bothered by this open acceptance of sexuality that he had Peirce's ideas expunged from editions printed after 1901.

Peirce died in 1906, when America and Charleston were still decades away from accepting this startling idea. Seventy years would pass before another gay minister at the same Unitarian Church in Archdale Street would echo these ideas.[3]

The trailblazing Brackett and Peirce, as far as is known, never spoke of their advanced views while in Charleston. (In the 1890s, Brackett penned an article about her memories of Charleston.)[4] Perhaps the city's staunch conservatism kept them from speaking out, or maybe they had yet to develop their ideas. While they may not have been aware of same-sex desire among the populace, a contemporary of theirs was.

The son of the actor Junius Brutus Booth, Edwin Booth began to attract attention for his acting in the 1850s. He caught the eye of critic Adam Badeau, who fell for the twenty something's handsome good looks, stalking him like an obsessed fan. Badeau insinuated himself into Booth's life, and boosted

Booth's career with lavish critical praise. He bragged of their intimacy and flaunted in print that they had once spent the night together. While Booth was grateful, it's unclear to what length he returned his fan's affection. (Achieving the rank of US general in the Civil War, Badeau would fall for Ulysses S. Grant so obviously that one of Grant's later biographers would "out" Badeau as a gay man.)

When Booth came to Charleston in 1858, he wrote frankly to Badeau about a phenomenon he witnessed. Whether they were loitering at the stage door or making direct advances in letters or in person is not known, but Badeau got the message that Booth knew men in the audience were attracted to him. His letter does not survive, but Badeau's answer does. According to Ada Clare, who saw Booth perform, the actor "possessed that rare and mysterious personal magnetism, which ... woos, enchants, and ravishes an audience." It seems some men in Charleston wanted to be ravished by him.

"So the fellows have gone mad about you in Charleston," Badeau wrote mockingly back to Booth, "not the women; complimentary truly: that's what you get for being so handsome!" And then he added, "Wouldn't you be in demand in Turkey?" Turkey, Badeau knew, had just made homosexuality legal, which is why he suggested Booth would be popular there. Badeau clearly understood what men in Charleston were feeling for the actor, yearning over his physical grace in a darkened theatre where they could gaze on him legitimately and then maybe fantasize privately.

Booth is usually remembered for a "fit" he had in the Planters Hotel where he was staying, attacking his male manager. Earlier biographies suggested Booth could have been epileptic; more recent writers have been more open about Booth's alcoholic bouts. Perhaps some goading about this sexually aroused male fan base of his, or even a move from his manager, precipitated the violence.[5]

Figure 8. Edwin Booth

We may never know, but the real value of the Badeau letter is what it reveals: those we would perceive today as gay or bisexual males were present in Charleston before the Civil War, and were obvious enough to make it known. Brackett and Peirce held their truths in check in church and school, but Booth recorded what he saw.

Lesbian actress Charlotte Cushman (who played female and male parts, sometimes in trousers—she was well known for her Romeo) was seen on the Charleston stage in these same years, but no mention has been found of a similar effect she might have had on women. Hortensia Mordecai, a proper Jewish young lady, mentioned seeing Cushman onboard the ship on which she was traveling; later in Italy, Mordecai visited the studio of lesbian sculptor Harriet Hosmer, a great friend of Cushman's. While she dutifully noted her sighting of celebrities, she inferred no knowledge of Cushman's or Hosmer's sexual identities.

Although both Booth and Cushman were famous, neither achieved the notoriety of Booth's brother, John Wilkes, who made the greater impact on the national stage. (Another Booth brother, Joseph, had been a medical student in Charleston.) The day John Wilkes Booth assassinated Abraham Lincoln at Ford's Theatre in Washington was the same day that the Stars and Stripes was raised again over the vanquished ruin of Fort Sumter, on April 14, 1865.

With the Civil War over, a curtain rung down on the country and one act was over. Charleston lay in ashes, and throughout the South, Confederate leaders were fleeing. One of them, once a Charleston resident, scholars now suggest, escaped both the state and detection as a gay man.

Born to British Jewish parents in St. Croix in 1811, Judah Philip Benjamin accompanied them to the United States, settling in Charleston in 1822. His father became involved with the first Reform Jewish movement in America, at Kahal Kadosh Beth Elohim (in the 21st century becoming extremely LGBTQ friendly, having an out gay male Rabbi). Around this time, Judah, beginning his education, thrown out of Yale a few years later, returned to Charleston, and then went off to New Orleans. There, the rumors of his sexuality began circulating. He married a wealthy young Catholic woman of French descent. Only after ten years did they finally have a daughter, and his wife left him immediately to live in Paris, where he visited mother and child periodically. As the scandal grew, it became clear to others that Benjamin, who destroyed every letter sent to him and bragged about leaving no trace for biographies, never sought consolation with other women, White or Black, as New Orleans gentlemen did frequently. Elected to the US Senate, he was called a "eunuch" and praised for his smooth face, lovely voice, and feminine grace. Once the Civil War began, Benjamin became known as "the brains of the Confederacy," serving as its attorney general, secretary of war, and secretary

Figure 9. Judah Benjamin

of state. His portrait graced the Confederate two-dollar bill, and while most office holders were captured by federal troops, Benjamin escaped to England, where he became a distinguished barrister and wrote a treatise still considered one of the basics of English civil law. While he never renounced his Judaism, he did not practice it; he never addressed his sexuality. Nor did he ever return to Charleston, a city he would not have recognized.

With the fall of the slaveholding Confederacy, freed men and women embarked on a new era of civil rights; a change in gender norms and sexual expression for LGBTQ people was coming, too.[6]

The Imaginary War

In his book *A Queer History of the United States*, (which makes almost no reference to the South), Michael Bronski notes, "many of the most important changes for LGBT people in the past five hundred years have been a result of war."[7] It's easy to understand how in World War II, young men and women, believing they were the only gay men or lesbians in their small hometowns, joyously found others like them in the military. It happened in earlier wars, too. But the idea of it has intrigued others and lit the imagination of fiction writers with various degrees of success. Since no histories of local LGBTQ participation in the civil war have come to light (as of yet), here's how fiction writers have imagined it may have been:

The metaphor of such a war being one of brother against brother has been taken up as lover against lover. There is a two-volume saga depicting young gay soldiers from Charleston and Portland, Maine, falling in love but fighting on opposing sides of the war. One audacious X-rated short story dramatizes the love affair between the two male heroes of *Gone with the Wind*, Ashley Wilkes and Rhett Butler, who only flirt with Scarlett O'Hara to catch the eye of the other. In this version, Ashley and Rhett finally consummate their love in Civil War–torn Charleston.[8]

But another much more serious work of art set in Charleston is actually part of LGBTQ media history. Born in Paris to parents from Savannah, Julien Green (1900–1998) grew up on stories of the Civil War. A devout Catholic, in his youth he was tortured by his attraction to men. He depicted homoeroticism in many of his novels and diaries in a long, distinguished literary career. He took it to a whole new level in his play Sud (South), portraying the decisive moment in the life of a Polish exile in love with a handsome Southern gentleman on a plantation outside Charleston. The time is April 1861, just as guns fire and the Civil War begins.[9]

Sud is a tale of civil strife within the heart of the Polish officer, Jan, torn in his divided loyalties between his fiancée Regina and his fatal attraction to Erik, the dashing young army officer. Written in the mid-1950s, the play defied convention when it was staged in England, first on radio, and then in 1955 before a live audience — despite the fact that the Lord Chamberlain refused to grant it a license, declaring its homosexual theme obscene. The producer countered that the play was about "extremes: North versus South, white man against colored man, the old world of Europe in contrast to the new world of America, the difficulty that the sexually normal have in understanding the sexually abnormal." When it was staged for British television, one critic noted he was not interested in the "agonies and ecstasies of a pervert. ... There are some indecencies that are left to be covered up." But the fact that it was not covered up, and that the play was shown on television at all is now considered "a milestone in gay cultural history." Its broadcast on November 24, 1959, makes it one of the earliest, if not the earliest, surviving gay TV drama ever shown in the United Kingdom. Graydon Gould, who played the straight love interest, a heartthrob for many women, (and one of the inspirations for Mike Myers's Austin Powers character decades later), was actually a closeted gay man in a long-term relationship with Alan Bates. "It's better not to know what men are thinking, it's always almost sad or shameful," the gay character Jan says. "I'm not ashamed, but I am alone. Hopelessly alone."[10]

That must have been what it felt like to be gay in Charleston in 1861, or even in the 1950s when the play premiered, but still it gave many gay men one of the first positive views of homosexuality despite the tragic ending.

One would have hoped it could have served the same purpose when the play, which became the basis of an opera, was finally staged in Charleston. Due to segregation, it had taken 35 years for *Porgy and Bess*, an older opera with a Charleston setting, to premier in its native city. *Sud*, on the other hand, took even longer; the play was not performed in Charleston until 2004. A reviewer noted, however, that the gay element was so downplayed and hidden by the production that it was downright "murky." Sadly, the director in England in the homophobic 1950s had been braver than the local Charleston director half a century later.[11]

Chapter Eight

Civil Rights and Wrongs and Addressing Cross-Dressing

After 1865, the city that had been known as "the Queen City of the South" was changed utterly. Fire and bombardment had left their marks but more monumental was the overthrow of slavery. Whites mourned a lost world, but African Americans welcomed a new one, with Black men enfranchised. White women, still disenfranchised, nevertheless had gained some authority, working in the absence of men who were on the battlefield. Many gladly surrendered that role and retook their spot on the pedestal of pure womanhood, but others used their new power to work for social causes, coming together in associations, clubs, and charities, some memorializing the fantasized glories of the Confederacy.

For African Americans, Reconstruction meant freedom and autonomy, the ability to go to schools, and, while federal troops occupied the city, a chance for justice and economic parity. But LGBTQ people, Black and White, men and women, still had to hide. In 1868, White and Black men drafting a new constitution for South Carolina (a prerequisite to be let back in the Union), did not list buggery as a crime meriting the death penalty. But it was an oversight, suggesting how few people even considered it. Realizing the omission, they included it in 1869, reducing the penalty from death to a fine of up to $500 (at a time when farm laborers made less than a dollar a day) and up to five years in prison.[1]

New times required new laws, and Charleston joined the movement of many cities across the country banning cross-dressing. While that law itself was new, the city nevertheless had been obsessed with the topic, for Black communities especially, for nearly two centuries.

Before the war, the newspaper correspondent "Buzzard" had written disgustedly of having to encounter Black and mulatto women in silks and satins. He was not alone, for from the 18th century on, the statute books were filled with laws restricting what enslaved people could or could not wear. Black men were not allowed to carry canes. Black women were restricted to certain fabrics, so as not to rise above their station.[2]

The lawmakers were onto something, in the realization that one's appearance was often one's destiny. Jehu Jones (1769–1833), a free man of color who ran one of the best antebellum hotels in Charleston, ran afoul of a law stipulating that if a free person of color left South Carolina, he or she could not legally return. It's said that Jones, who had gone to New York to visit family, only got back into the state dressed as a woman.[3]

Ellen Craft (1826–1891) was even more outrageous in her cross-dressing. A light-skinned, enslaved woman in Georgia, she hatched a daring escape plan. She dressed as a man, donned dark glasses, and pretended to be an invalid, putting her arm in a sling to disguise the fact that she could not write, necessary to sign hotel registers. She passed off her husband William Craft (1824–1900) as her enslaved manservant. In this masquerade, she entered the city of Charleston, where master and servant stayed in a hotel before boarding a ship to take them to Boston. Once their escape was known, they became international celebrities with the publication of their book, *Running a Thousand Miles for Freedom*. White Southerners were incensed by the Crafts' audacity in cross-dressing and role-playing. Laws banning people of color wearing disguises were already on the books and no doubt now doubly enforced.

But White women were punished for the crime, too. Charleston Civil War–era police records show that at least three who first came to attention for being inebriated were also fined or imprisoned for cross-dressing. On January 29, 1862, Mary Ann Zanuga (or Vanuga), with over $15 on her person and wearing a watch with a gold chain, was fined $10 for disorderly conduct and "being dressed in male attire." Sarah Alchiso, dressed in men's clothing, was sentenced to 10 days in the House of Correction and fined $10 for that and for being drunk and disorderly. Mary Martin received the same sentence when she was arrested on November 25, 1862, for being in the clothes of the opposite sex.[4]

After the Civil War, each law about slavery was voided. Soon new ones were passed, some still focusing on dress. It's not known what prompted the city of Charleston to decree what was appropriate dress, but many cities across the country were passing similar statutes. Metropolitan centers grew, offering refuge to people who could leave communities where they were known. Light-skinned Black people could cross the color line; people could create new pasts to make new futures. One could dress above one's station, or even claim a different gender. With the enforcement of these new wardrobe laws, some early vignettes of what may be Charleston African American LGBTQ history come to light.

Passed in April 1868, an ordinance forbade anyone to "appear in a public place in a state of nudity, or in a dress not becoming his or her sex." It was also against the law to create or sell lewd books—with a minimum fine of $20, a maximum of $100, and up to a month in jail.

Charleston at the time was run by a brevet colonel with the Union Army still occupying the city, making one wonder if that prompted the change, as military men often attracted sexual camp followers. While there is a vague reference to two Black youths "making unlawful love to sundry pieces of under male attire" in 1868, a definite case of cross-dressing occurred near a military installation. In 1871, "George Robinson, a colored youth of about 18 summers, was arrested on Monday night in Meeting street [sic], near Calhoun," which would put Robinson at or very near Marion Square, the parade ground of the South Carolina Military Academy before the war, and now where Union troops were garrisoned. Robinson, it was noted, "was arrayed in all the habiliments of a colored belle." For his plea in mayor's court, Robinson claimed "that his mother had made him assume the garb to keep him at home," a ploy the court obviously did not believe, since Robinson was sent to the house of corrections for 30 days.

Jehu Jones kept his freedom by cross-dressing, and Ellen Craft had earned hers the same way. It may be that George Robinson was claiming his freedom, too, a freedom to assume a truer identity.

Other arrests followed. In 1873, a young African American fellow, employed as "a waiting man," was discovered in women's clothes. His full name was not given in court records, but they do show his assumed name. "Sarah Jane" was sent to the house of corrections.

Police records from 1901 give us what might be an early documented instance of lesbians of color in the city. All that is known is noted in a published police report. The headline was attention-grabbing: "WOMEN DRESSED AS MEN: Two Colored Damsels Fined for Wearing Male Attire.

"Clad in male attire, Florence Tension and Ida Richardson, colored, appeared before the Police Court this morning on the charge of disorderly conduct, masquerading in male clothes."

They created something of a stir as they proceeded from the prisoners' room to the recorder's desk. "Acting Recorder

The Real Rainbow Row

Figure 10. Federal troops on parade, Marion Square, at The Citadel, 1877

Memminger looked surprised as the women sauntered forth dressed in trousers, shirt, vest, coat and hat. Their make-up was complete and the negro [sic] spectators sniggled out loud at the show and the orderly sergeant was forced to cry out 'Order in the Court' to suppress the laughter."

It's sad that their peers, other African Americans entangled in an often unfair legal system, felt no camaraderie with the women, but ridiculed them. The White presiding officer took no pity either. As the paper noted, "Ida and Florence were found in Rodgers Alley yesterday afternoon and were arrested and sent to the police station, charged with appearing in public in dress unbecoming their sex. They told the Recorder that they were funning and promised not to do so again if he would dismiss then. Their appeals were to no avail, each being sentenced to a fine of $5 or twenty days in jail."[5]

At the time of the Rodgers Alley incident, a certain teen-aged White boy longing to be a writer, now a dropout from school, was working to support himself and his family. In his various jobs, he was fascinated with the teeming African American life he saw. Born in 1885, DuBose Heyward was intrigued with life "beyond the color wall," as he called it. His story based on a handicapped Black man he met on the streets would gain him fame. Sammy Smalls could not walk, and so propelled himself through town begging in his goat cart. Heyward, though White and elite, felt a kinship with this poor Black man, both of whom likely had been affected by polio. Smalls was Heyward's inspiration for his eponymous 1925 novel *Porgy*; in theatrical and operatic form of *Porgy and Bess*, the beggar would act as a cultural ambassador, taking a tale of Charleston to all inhabited continents of the world. Heyward always affirmed that, yes, Porgy was based on the real-life Sammy Smalls.[6]

Heyward often put real-world people into his books. In his novel *Lost Morning*, he'd adapt the story of the death of a woman he had known. And in his third novel called *Mamba's Daughters*, there is a major character bearing strong similarities to local African American women like Florence Tension and Ida Richardson. Heyward's very masculine female character Hagar dominates the story of three generations of African American women in counterpoint with a White family based on Heyward's. Critics agree that this book is the most autobiographical of all of Heyward's books, so this argues for trying to determine what facts Heyward might have appropriated from real life, and which African American characters he knew or had seen.

In his book, Hagar is always presented in men's clothes, ("trousers, shirt, vest and hat"), doing a man's work in the phosphate mines, stronger and a better fighter than the males around her. She's a tough from the alleys of the city, her arms "muscled like a stevedore's" and she has "masculine shoulders." Heyward is quite specific: "Below the chest, the body [not "her" body] was not ungainly, the swell of the hips barely noticeable, and the legs, slender and powerfully thewed, seemed wholly masculine." Hagar, despite displaying an "enormous maternity" has "the muscles of a fighting male." In the play version of the novel, co-written with his wife, Dorothy, Hagar is first seen in court, as Ida and Florence were; Heyward did go to courtrooms to do his research. She is described as "a young woman of large proportions, unusually tall, unusually broad and giving an impression of great strength." Again and again in the novel, as in the play, we are told that above her "superb body is a pleasant, childlike face." And not only does Hagar take on the work of a man, she assumes a male name as well, the much more gender neutral (or "butch") "Baxter."

Just as it's known that Heyward watched people on the street and the courtroom and appropriated them into his fiction, so it's also known that he was in New York in the 1920s, where he frequented the Black jazz clubs of Harlem. What is not known, however, is if he ever heard this song that parallels his description of Hagar/Baxter:

"B.D. women, you sure can't understand. They got a head like a sweet angel and they walk just like a natural man." B.D. means "bulldagger," a slang word for a butch lesbian in the African American community in this time.[7]

Heyward never went on the record, as he had with *Porgy*, from where his model for Hagar/Baxter came; but there is no reason to believe that she did not spring, as Porgy had, from the streets of the city—if not Ida or Florence, then a strong, proud, masculine woman like them.

Never is the word "lesbian" mentioned in the novel. (Heyward was a gentleman and usually squeamish on the issue of sexuality, although he did once critique his wife's dialogue saying her characters spoke like "fairies.")[8] Most readers would not have noticed such things, especially since Hagar has a daughter. But she shows no sexual attraction to any man throughout the book, and instead lives a life like that of her biblical namesake, an outsider, and outcast, apt descriptors in this era for lesbians.

But one Black lesbian who read the novel took it to heart and saw herself (and her mother) in Hagar. To portray Hagar on the stage, she said, was not just her dream, but her destiny.

Ethel Waters achieved her goal; as Hagar, she reached a peak in her life and made theatrical history. Starting as a blues singer, Waters took several husbands, and eventually shocked her friends by becoming not just religious, but also by denying her earlier years as a fairly out lesbian. Like Hagar, Waters got into violent fights with men and women, usually over her female lovers. She appealed to the Heywards to write the part for her, and they did. The play *Mamba's Daughters*, rewritten around the figure of Hagar, opened in 1939, and for the first time in Broadway history, a Black actress in a dramatic (really melodramatic) role got top billing—and rave reviews—from nearly every New York critic. From *Mamba's Daughters* she moved to films and television. It was then, in the public eye and with a reputation to uphold, that she began to recast her past, omitting her lesbian love life from her autobiography. In it, she went out of her way to make gratuitously snide comments about "he-she-and-what-is-it types" in referring to her drag queen friends to whom she lent her clothes. A Black lesbian on Broadway played a Black woman who looked and acted like a lesbian. "I was Hagar," that night, she wrote of the opening. "Seventeen curtain calls ... for me alone."

"Before that, I'd always been cursing outside and crying inside." Now, as Hagar, she could show her true face, despite having to use stage makeup. "Playing in *Mamba's Daughters* enabled me to rid myself of the terrible inward pressure, the flood of tears I'd been storing up ever since childhood." By acting out, she could claim herself, enabled by make-believe and cross-dressing.

Waters never gave up Hagar. She performed a vignette from the play on her television show, the first program hosted by an African American woman. That a bulldagger glimpsed in Charleston could have inspired such success and visibility (even when people did not realize what they were seeing as

Figure 11. Ethel Waters as Hagar

Ethel Waters did) is a real possibility. Hagar and Ethel Waters stand in the place of many such women of color of whom we have little, or no, documentation.[9]

As time passed, Blacks and Whites in Charleston continued to be persecuted for flouting gender roles. In 1895, an unnamed male was charged with "Masquerading in Female Dress." In 1902, two White women were charged with "Appearing on streets improperly attired," possibly cross-dressing, the same charge against African American William Taylor lodged in 1904. In 1912, a White woman on a train from Manning was found out, under a man's hat, to be a blonde woman "fair of face."[10]

With time, the crime of cross-dressing and the crime of sexual deviancy became twined in the public mind; the unnatural attire signaled something amiss; and it was none other than Oscar Wilde, perhaps the most notorious gay man of the 19th century, who gave locals the link. He was to bring the topic out of the closet into the consciousness of the city.

Chapter Nine
Wilde Men and the French Offence

In 1895 Oscar Wilde's trial for having sex with other men was a worldwide phenomenon. But even before his case grabbed the headlines, Wilde raised the suspicions of locals —based on the transgressive clothes he wore.

Wilde visited Charleston in July 1882. Before his appearance at the Academy of Music, reporters laid in wait at the massively pillared Charleston Hotel. All hell broke loose "when they saw the arrival of [his manservant], a dapper little red whiskered man, and finally two hundred pounds of avoirdupois of aesthetic human flesh and bones done up in a mouse-colored velveteen shooting jacket and salt and pepper small clothes. The head was ornamented with long ambrosial locks of very dark hair, and capped with a broad brim, dim colored slouch hat, something out of the style of Buffalo Bill or Texas Jack. 'That's him,' cried Ingliss, the barber, who had come out to see the sight, and there was a rush of the few persons who were loafing about the hotel in the direction of the show, while the storefronts in the immediate vicinity were speedily adorned with idle salesmen and drummers. The door of the ladies' entrance being locked, the 200 pounds of aestheticism posed about on the doorsteps, grim and dusty, and uncomfortable, but looking all the same like a magnified photograph of Geo. Denham in the role of 'Bunthorne'," a reference to a buffoonish character in the Gilbert and Sullivan show *Patience* actually based on Oscar Wilde.

Much was made of the fact that he went to the ladies' entrance and the press helpfully dredged up a disparaging ditty about his manner and ways:

> "Oscar dear, Oscar dear,
> How utterly, flutterly, utter you are;

Oscar dear, Oscar dear,
I think you are awfully wild, ta-ta."

Once Wilde settled in, the reporter immediately focused on how non-conforming Wilde's behavior and apparel were, linking clothes and character. "The great aesthete was 'lolling' upon a sofa, his ambrosial locks parted in the middle resting upon a pillow, and his feet, ornamented with red-striped socks and sharp-pointed shoes, occupying the other end of the sofa.... From his collar there hung the ends of a salmon colored silk neck handkerchief while a pale violet-colored kerchief peeped out from the breast pocket of his coat."

While ridiculing him for the off-nature of his dress, the reporter admitted later that day that Wilde acquitted himself admirably. His lecture at the Academy of Music was well attended. "Perfectly self-possessed, earnest, yet never carried away, he talked rather than spoke, with a clearness of enunciation that enabled him to be heard in all parts of the house without once raising his voice above an ordinary conversational tone. The lecture was ... on decorative art, [usually considered the province of women] its neglect by the people of the present day, our duty to restore its powers in life and how that duty is to be performed. The lecture lacked method, but abounded in beautiful descriptions, happy illustrations and poetic thought, while an occasional scintillation of humor was not wanting. ... He finished and left the stage as quietly as he had entered, in the midst of a round of applause which was followed by subdued murmurs of approving comment as the audience dispersed."[1]

According to Wilde's biographer, if not right then, soon afterwards, Wilde went strolling on the Battery seawall, where tourists inevitably go, and where gay men would cruise in the next century. He commented on Charlestonians after he left, noting how mired in the past they were, preferring a romantic vision of antebellum life over a realistic present. Turning

Figure 12. While in the US, Wilde was the butt of many jokes, here getting burned for disregarding American institutions

the observation into an epigram, he said that when he had remarked on the beauty of the full moon from the seawall on the Battery, Charlestonians disagreed, saying the current moon was inferior; it had been much more beautiful before the Civil War.[2]

Years later, when British headlines trumpeted the story of him being called a sodomite by the father of his lover Lord Alfred Douglas, Charleston papers followed suit, covering his trial for "gross indecency." "Wilde Under Arrest," the press announced. "Oscar Wilde On Trial" came next; "The Case Against Wilde" was then presented; and finally, "Two Years for Wilde."[3]

The nicknames used for Wilde were various. "The Fallen Dude" was one; "The Poet Culprit" who dressed faultlessly and wore rings on his fingers was another. But when it came to naming his actual crime there was silence. The closest the papers came to explaining his "gross indecency" was a quote from the sonnet Wilde had dedicated to Douglas, referring to a love "that dare not speak its name."

When asked to explain, Wilde replied, "It is love not understood in this country. It is the love of David for Jonathan; a deep spiritual affection, as pure as it is perfect. It is something this age does not understand. It mocks at it and sometimes puts one in a pillory." But the public in Charleston thought the pillory apt, despite the fact that "misdemeanors" was the only other noun the press used to describe the charges. Stories noted that Douglas was to be charged, too, though for exactly what was not stated. By not daring to name it, people were condemning it as one of the worst crimes imaginable; apparently vocabularies rife with words like rape, murder, torture, and incest would not do. What made it worse to many was the news that Wilde had not only consorted with gentlemen of his class, but with commoners, waiters, and errand boys who were given gifts for sharing their favors with him.

"English Justice is Again Vindicated," was the *Evening Post*'s endorsement when Wilde was convicted.[4] Unwilling to let go of a salacious story, a reporter went to the Charleston Library Society "to see what effect the Oscar Wilde scandal had had on the calls for his works." The librarian, Mrs. Dawson, "said that she doubted whether there was one copy of the writer's novels in the library, as she could not remember ever having received a call for one." (Indeed, Wilde only wrote one, his published work up to this time consisting of poetry, essays, and plays). Smugly, Mrs. Dawson reported, "No requests have been made for his works since the scandal."

Booksellers were also quizzed. Mr. L. Hammond, with his popular shop on Broad Street, "said the demand for Wilde's books has always been very light." Another merchant "stated that he would refuse to be interviewed on the subject and would not permit his name to be used as having been called upon, so thoroughly disgusted has he become with the man since he read of his disgraceful conduct." A third bookseller, C.L. Legerton, assured the reporter, "There has never been any demand as far as I have ever been able to learn for his books. In fact, the reading public have apparently never cared for his style or subject matter." Legerton even denied that the public wanted the newspapers dealing with it. The editors did condemn the burning of Wilde's books by a library in New Jersey, while showing Charleston's moral superiority: "Was Never Popular" was the headline of a story about locals never having expressed interest in Wilde, somehow suggesting the city's uncontaminated moral superiority.[5]

Wilde had taken homosexuality from whispers to headlines that condemned the sinner without mentioning the sin. He became a joke, even to the prostitutes and madams of the city, who perhaps felt they alone understood the correct nature of male sexuality. In 1901 enterprising business folks published a booklet advertising the addresses of brothels where men coming to town for the South Carolina Inter-State and West Indian Exposition could find women willing to gratify them for a fee. Other than names, addresses, and delicate turns of phrase, the booklet included a mild joke and a poem:

> The boy stood on the burning deck
> With his back against the mast
> "I will not stir one step," he said
> "Till Oscar Wilde has passed"[6]

This ditty confirms that sex between men was known and assumed to be behavior practiced aboard ship by sailors or pirates. Such acts were to be scorned, not indulged in by

Charleston's solid and moral citizenry, who often nevertheless frequented brothels and exchanged heterosexual sex for cash.

These solid citizens must have been startled when a scandal like Wilde's broke, not in London, but locally, just a few years later. This time, the city gave it a completely different spin.

On a Sunday night in May 1899, "a well-known gentleman of this city" discovered that his grandson was missing. When the gentleman, obviously White, somehow discovered the site of his grandson's whereabouts, he called the police. A Lieutenant Dunn "sent out a squad of men and had the house pulled."

Under the heading "A VILE RESORT," a story was filed the following morning:

> A notorious negro dive on Wentworth street, between King and Meeting, inhabited by negro male degenerates, was pulled last night by a special squad of policemen and five inmates were arrested and sent to the station house. The dive is of the worst type known to the police and has done more to wreck the morals of young boys than any other resort in the city.

Apparently, the police knew of its existence since the paper could report, that it "had been in operation by Ed Drayton, a coal black negro" for some time.

Never elaborating on why this place was so "vile," or on its impact on the morals of the (assumed) White youth, the article centered on the latter, noting, "Three young [obviously White] boys [including, no doubt the missing grandson] who were there last night appeared in court this morning and testified against the negroes. All of them testified that the place was a house of ill fame."

In other words, it was a place of prostitution, a brothel.

Apparently saved by their white skins, and possibly by their prominence, the boys were not named. Although they were likely participants in the activities, they appeared in court not to defend themselves but to act as witnesses against the Black men.

Discretion shielded their names, but not so for the hapless African Americans: "Gus Green, Ed Drayton, Henry Mitchell, Henry Green and Ed Anderson." All but Henry Green were fined $100 or given 30 days on the chain gang. No women were named, so what sort of "house of ill fame" was it? A brothel for Black (and White) men?

Unlike the conspiracy of silence with the Wilde case, this time the offense was named — in a way. "After serving out their sentence they will be taken before Magistrate Rouse to answer the charge of committing an unnatural offense," a code word for "crimes against nature," i.e., homosexuality, or the old bugaboo of buggery.[7]

The story emerges that some White youths of good family were found in a male brothel, run and visited by Black men, where "unnatural" acts were committed. "Unnatural" male-on-male sex was one thing, but indulging in it across the color line must have been especially horrifying in the Jim Crow era. While it was common practice for White men to have Black mistresses, as the screeds of Buzzard attested back in the 1850s, this was a first for White and Black men having sex with each other. And with all the contemporary accounts of cross-dressing, one has to wonder if they were all really Black women being kept by White Charleston men, or possibly men dressed as "colored belles" in those silks and satins as antebellum papers had it.

In England, the elite Oscar Wilde had been charged, named, and punished, but many of the boys he consorted with were not. In Charleston it was the reverse: upper-class Whites escaped, while working-class African Americans did not.

A few days later, a small article appeared with more details and a possible explanation. Specific charges were leveled at Gus

Green for being the worst of the worst. But oddly enough, this horrifyingly evil Black man was now represented by one of the most prominent White attorneys in town, Drayton F. Hastie, of the planter class, historically tied to Magnolia Plantation. Hastie "made a motion for a new trial against Gus Green, one of the negroes who was arrested last Sunday night and sentenced to thirty days in jail."

"Green was arrested in a most notorious dive on Wentworth street for engaging in a most horrible practice, together with several other negroes," the reporter explained. To remove the blame from his client, Hastie blamed it on foreigners. "The crime for which he was arrested is of the worst form of degeneracy, and seldom known in this country, being confined exclusively to Paris, although of late years has spread in the larger cities of the United States."

It was not uncommon at the time to blame other cultures for tolerating homosexuals and infecting morals of other countries. Homosexuality had been decriminalized in France in 1791, and so, in the 1850s the antics of Rufus Griswold, in his irregular sex habits, had been compared to the plots of French novels. Similarly, seeking peace after imprisonment, Wilde moved to France to live out his last years.

But now the French vice had infected Charleston, and people had to admit it. It was one thing to read about titled elites in newspapers from across the sea, but this involved neighbors and peers. This 1899 episode was something else entirely: a wholly male house of ill repute, involving Black men and sons of prominent White families. "Recorder [Theodore] Jervey refused to grant a new trial, whereupon Mr. Hastie gave notice that he would appeal the case."[8]

The next day, "Mr. Hastie again appeared in court to secure the release of Henry [sic?] Green," the papers reported, not Gus, as previously printed, possibly a reporter's error. He could do this because "[o]ne of the most prominent gentlemen in the city went on Green's bond." Again, the prominent gentleman's name was not given, he possibly being the same "well-known gentleman" whose grandson was found in the vile dive. Was he trying to save his grandson's unreported good name by posting bond for the man who could testify against him?

Hastie claimed he would not have been involved in the "very unsavory" affair if he did not believe in the innocence of his client, and he had not been approached by Green's mother, "who is one of the most respectable women of her color in this city and a family servant." One wonders if she did not serve in the household from which the White youth disappeared that Sunday. Green, Hastie averred, was "innocent of the horrible charge" and had he been given counsel, he would have not been charged. Hastie never explained what his client was doing in that house of ill fame. He did say he had "two unsolicited testimonials to his excellent character and steadiness from a gentleman and a lady of the highest social standing."[9] Obviously, if you were of high moral character you could not be sexually attracted to members of your sex. (Elite Whites standing up for accused Blacks often resulted in the latter being treated more leniently, as portrayed in Heyward's *Mamba's Daughters*.)

While the case disappeared from the papers, other surviving records of the recorder's court suggest that in July 1899, Hastie's appeal to have charges against Green dropped was denied. In court records now lost, another twist developed. Apparently, the charge Green faced was soliciting sex with another man, and although the outcome of the case is not known, the tactic is intriguing. For now, the charge of homosexuality was not denied by Green's attorney (suggesting that Gus Green really might have been having sex with Black or White men or both). The attorney argued instead that Green should go free on a technicality (possibly in return for his silence) because a man could not be charged with soliciting for sex from another man because there was no law forbidding it![10]

This was a clever legalistic tactic that would not necessarily have saved Green's reputation but would have saved him from a fine or time in prison. Women could be convicted of soliciting sex with men, and men for consorting with prostitutes, but lawmakers had not planned for men being caught in that eventuality; the attorney's argument was that a crime existed only when men had homosexual sex, but there was no law on the books for soliciting it.

The exact outcome of this intriguing bit of history is not known. But the episode nevertheless offers several interesting and undeniable facts about 1899 Charleston. There was a place where Black and White men congregated for sex, a brothel in the police's estimation. While White men visiting Black female prostitutes certainly reeks of exploitation and bigotry on numerous levels, no one knows what the relationship was between the men of different colors. Apparently the youths testified in court to save themselves. But what if they had not been caught? Would being homosexuals together have trumped racism and created camaraderie among them?

As for those who were arrested, they are hard to trace due to the lack of records, specifically about impoverished African Americans. A Frank Drayton, listed a year before in the city directory, worked in a basket factory. Of the others, none can be traced definitively. As for the exact location of the place, other than between Meeting and King on Wentworth Street, directories and plats offer few clues, listing only businesses, homes of prominent citizens, and paramilitary organizations.

Rooting out the identities of the White boys involved is even harder, given the scrim of secrecy and the press's silence. No one would have owned up to having been found performing "unnatural" acts with a Black man. Yet one young, gay White male from a "most distinguished family," the approximate age of the "muscular" Gus Green, offers a possibility. While some links aren't exact (the man's paternal grandfather was not living at the time and the status of his maternal grandmother is not known), in later life, he encouraged youths to revel in sex. Furthermore, he is thought to have been attracted to Black men. This does not necessarily link Huger Wilkinson Jervey to the bordello event, but a closer look suggests what the life of an elite White gay male from Charleston was like at the beginning of the 20th century.

Find Jervey in any biographical directory and you'll encounter no mention of his sexuality. Born in Charleston September 26, 1878, "of English and Huguenot [that fated French!] origin, and a direct descendant of Arthur Middleton, a signer of the Declaration of Independence," he was about 20 years younger than his relative Theodore Jervey, the court functionary who refused to dismiss charges against Gus Green. Huger attended the High School of Charleston, and in 1897 entered Sewanee: the University of the South, studying Greek and literature. Following further study at Johns Hopkins, he returned to Sewanee as a professor of Greek.[12]

Many educated gay men of this time turned to the classic Greek texts (and art) that celebrated male-to-male sexuality and the glorification of the male body. This invocation of ancient cultures could be used to counter the growing middle-class disgust for homosexuality, a term just coming into vogue. Those who were schooled in the classics could cloak themselves in the grandeur that was Greece and say that their love of male beauty rendered them a cultured elite, making them similar to the great men of antiquity. If they could find no peers or mentors in the present, the past would do for them. The South in particular valued Greek and Roman classics more than other areas of the country; the College of Charleston, for instance, did not surrender its mandatory study of both Latin and Greek until 1897, allowing students to study just one. Charlestonians read the great orators of antiquity, had a statue of John C. Calhoun in a toga in City Hall, and likened their city-state of cultivated free men based on slavery to ancient Greece. But the brother of the abolitionist Grimké sisters, Thomas S. Grimké, believed that those scurrilous classics should be banished, and education based entirely on the Bible; it was well known that Greek culture (read male love) was immoral to its core. Ministers in Charleston pulpits would preach on the depravity of Greece into the second decade of the 20th century.[13]

It was at Sewanee, as author Benjamin E. Wise notes, that Huger Jervey found a contemporary circle of gay friends. There he "explicitly linked his own teaching of Greek with his own homosexuality." Jervey's most famous student was William Alexander Percy, who followed his mentor "in interpreting classical history as legitimizing and celebrating homosexual love." Jervey was seven years older than Percy, whose poetry was later published by Charleston's Poetry Society of South Carolina, and who gained fame for his memoir, *Lanterns on the Levee*. (He eventually became the guardian of the novelist Walker Percy, who expressed negative views on homosexuality.) "Percy and Jervey became close in Jervey's Greek classes. ... They remained close throughout their lives, traveling often to Greece and Italy, and purchasing a summer house together in Sewanee."

After service in Europe in World War I, Jervey eventually became a professor and later dean at the Columbia Law School. A perennial "bachelor," he had the integrity not to pretend to be heterosexual and marry. Jervey was "out" for his time, advising young gays and lesbians "to be wild as sin" while they could. Percy came to New York to visit Jervey every February "likely [to attend] the most famous gathering of homosexuals in the 1920s and 30s." Harlem's large drag Masquerade and Civic Ball attracted thousands, an opportunity for Black and White men and women to come together.[14] While Percy's biographer assumes his subject had sexual liaisons with Black men, it's impossible to know if his friend and housemate Jervey did. When he finally returned to Charleston in 1949, it was only to be buried in Magnolia Cemetery.

There is one other detail to add to the story.

In the chief of police's report in the 1899 *City Yearbook*, for the first (and apparently only) time, the annual tabulation of crimes included the entry "inmates house of ill fame," referring not to bordello owners, but the sex workers within. No White men or women were listed, but six "colored men" were, a direct confirmation of the "vile" homosexual affair. In the original case, however, only five men had been charged. Did police go back with no press coverage and arrest another? No matter the answer, it seems that the penalty for the "French" vice was enforced on people of color only. And, in 1912, a more horrifying scenario played out in Blacksburg, Cherokee County, when two Black men were jailed for an "unmentionable" and "most horrible crime" [oral sex], while drinking whiskey in a cemetery with a White man, found drunk and half undressed with them. "Interracial camaraderie that degenerated into homosexual activity" had "explosive" results. Black Frank Whisonant and Joe Brinson were kidnapped from jail and lynched. White Jim Childers was untouched, proclaiming his innocence, a sad commentary on how racial bigotry and homophobia could be linked.[15]

In Charleston, arrests continued. Edward Williams had been arrested and accused of buggery in 1895; in 1898, the charge was levied against Samuel Ellsey (or Ellsly); then at Timothy Madden in 1901. People were arrested for being disorderly, running a disorderly house, exposing their person, and the like, with possible, but unstated, LGBTQ links. Unsanctioned sex was definitely an issue.[16]

Calling for reform, in 1913, following a pattern of other American cities, Charleston citizens formed a Law and Order League. The League was started primarily to stem the flow of illegal liquor in bars and corner grocery stores, spots locals called "blind tigers." But sexual outlaws were a target, too.

Women joined men in the League; the Episcopal bishop dedicated a prayer to the mission as headlines declared the organization aimed to shine a divine searchlight on vice and crime. But after one large advertisement calling for closing the red-light district near Memminger, the girls' school, the League had to abandon the "searchlight" series.

Ten years later, Mayor John P. Grace, in his annual report, stated that it was the aristocrats, the blue bloods in the South of Broad Street neighborhood, who interfered with reforms and resisted cleaning up prostitution (and other sexual irregularities). Mayor Grace's statement infers that they were above the law, and that the red-light district establishments were a tradition of sorts and not worth combatting. The middle classes disagreed; they were the ones joining and leading the Law and Order League.

Mass meetings continued, and the League published a special report in 1913. Targeted crimes included many of the same tallied in the police reports. Protecting children from lewd and indecent publications became a priority, along with proper sex education, coming only from parents and those trained on the topic.

The special report also had a "Perversity" category, but the anonymous author was tight lipped. "Perversion is declared to be prevalent in Chicago," he or she stated, again inferring that homosexuality came from other places and could not be home grown. Yet: "The results of investigations made in Charleston would seem to indicate that there is more of it here than the average citizen has any idea of. These persons could be prosecuted under the law relating to 'infamous crimes.'"[17]

Despite the threat of heightened prosecutions, no increase in statistics is reflected in crimes tallied in the *City Yearbooks*. One White man was arrested for buggery in 1915, three White males and one man of color were charged in 1921, and three White men were charged in 1924, with no more arrests noted in compiled police records until the early 1950s.

The League demanded more prosecutions. One unidentified minister involved with the League preached on the imperative to return Charleston to what he identified as Christian values. In his sermon, he blasted nearly any religion and civilization not his. Babylon and Persia were dismissed; China and India, full of people of color, were singled out for their inferiority, and the minister took aim at antiquity studied by the elites. "The Greatest man of Greece," he wrote in his notes for a sermon, "in the matter of the soul, Socrates, not only countenanced but advised the grossest and most unnatural immorality and the most cursory knowledge of Greek romances show us the bestiality which underlay the beautiful shell of Art and Philosophy." Although that man of the cloth had trouble writing out those words (to which his extensive cross-outs and word changes attest), he nevertheless knew what code words to use — "unnatural" and "bestiality," the vile nature of the homosexuality of Socrates and the whole of Greece.[18]

If someone could refer to "unspeakable" vices from the pulpit, and suggest their presence in Charleston, a shift had come. With more frequent mentions of same-sex desire, more people were now vigilant and on the lookout for it. New ideas were coming in with the new century, and among the change agents challenging old ways were gay men and lesbians.

Chapter Ten

Renaissance Women — and Men

Laura Mary Bragg, born in Massachusetts in 1881, arrived in 1909 to work at the Charleston Museum, then housed in the main building at the College of Charleston.

She was from a progressive family (her minister father having worked in the South) and had an advanced degree, being in the first graduating class in library science of Simmons College in Boston. The single White woman in her late 20s was coming south not to preach morality but to teach science, ideas, and rationality. She needed a place to effect change and channel her energy. She found her niche in Charleston, a city with a heritage of sophistication that was reluctantly adapting to the demands and shifts of 20th century. Bragg encountered a great naiveté on many topics, including sexuality.[1]

"Lots of women were lesbians when I came to Charleston," she said in a 1970s interview, long after she had retired and become a local legend. "It was all very innocent," she prevaricated, as if realizing what she had revealed. "I had at least five friends who were." In fact, "[n]o one knew what it was until Lillian Hellman wrote *The Children's Hour* [a 1934 play about two women friends, teachers, accused of being lesbians]. Of course, I knew all about Greek boys and girls, but I had never put it together." Being coy and confessional simultaneously, she concluded, "There was just a shortage of men and it was as though women were married." She walked back every admission or knowledge of lesbianism to innocence and ignorance of the topic, a sort of doublespeak, a wanting to come clean and be closeted simultaneously. Some of the same attitudes she had faced in 1909 were still present when she was interviewed in the 1970s.[2]

As for it being "as though women were married," she was right. Such relationships, often called Boston marriages, flourished in Charleston. Local women set up housekeeping together, divvied up domestic duties, and supported each other's intellectual and artistic pursuits (which a typical husband in the early 20th century might not have done). While some of these "marriages" were intensely intimate and physical, others were not. And just like any other romantic involvement, some of these arrangements were a source of happiness, others despair. To be fair, there was a shortage of men in Charleston in the era after the Civil War. When Henry James, the great gay Anglo-American writer, visited in 1905 he saw a place inhabited mostly by women. He unwittingly described Charleston as a trans city, "masculine, fierce and mustashioed" before the Civil War, but now "feminized," in the early 20th century.[3]

Miss Bragg (as she demanded to be addressed even by lovers and peers), and her companions lived together, careful to avoid suspicion of anything untoward, which was not difficult as Lillian Faderman attests in her book Surpassing the Love of Men: Romantic Friendships and Love between Women from the Renaissance to the Present; most looked upon women living together as "innocent" until the larger public gained knowledge of Freudian theories after World War I. Louise Anderson

Figure 13. Laura Bragg

Allen, Bragg's biographer, confirms this, stating, "Few of the educated in the city ... had read anything about female sexuality, sexual inversion or lesbianism." Miss Bragg's cohabitation with a woman named Hester Gaillard was thought of "as a friendship between spinsters." Jenn Shapland further explains, "It is by no means easy to track or trace relationships between women, past or present. Women's relationships with other women are often disguised: by well-documented marriages to men, by cultural refusal to see what is in full view or even to believe that such relationships exist. In a world built for men and their pursuits, a woman who loves women does not register—and is not registered, i.e., written down."

At the time, many Charlestonians were wary of Bragg's suffragette beliefs and her Yankee roots. Were any sexual improprieties perceived, she could never have gained the traction she did with the power structure in the city to create the changes she desired. But hidden, she succeeded. "She changed the course of history through her actions and her will," writes Anderson.[4]

She was in high profile, working with children, and soon helping to move the museum a few blocks away from the college campus to Thompson Auditorium, constructed for a meeting of Confederate veterans. Her visibility rose in 1920 when she became the institution's director, the first woman to head a natural history museum in the country. She further broke the mold in this segregated society by opening the institution to Black visitors, and helped found the local public library. In her museum work, she documented the past, saving local material culture, including previously uncollected works by African American artisans, and helped foster the preservation movement. Museums, she believed, could be tools of progress, introducing people to the idea of the march of civilization (the name of a series of dioramas she commissioned from a local gay man named Ned Jennings), and to the concept that culture was constantly evolving. This, in turn, suggested the status quo would give way eventually to newer beliefs. She held advanced views on race, sex, art, and civic and social responsibility. In her nineties, she would tell a young man (the author of this work, then in his early twenties), that she had nothing against homosexuals, except that most she knew were unhappy. She also divulged one night (she was a night owl, her bookplate being an owl with a candle burning) that one's sexual desire never died.

In 1920, she and DuBose Heyward, eight years her junior, and a few others founded the Poetry Society of South Carolina. Its Pulitzer Prize–winning successes prompted the founding and flourishing of other cultural organizations such as the Preservation Society of Charleston. The city became a tourist destination, instigating a boom that transformed the economy. Laura Bragg was a major player in this era known as the Charleston Renaissance; a scientist more than a sentimentalist, she also changed individual lives, helping those she mentored achieve great things. While the city has acknowledged her contributions, mostly hidden and unacknowledged has been her love of women.

After leaving Hester Gaillard, she lived with Belle (Isabel) Heyward (a cousin of DuBose) on Gibbes Street. Their time together was intense, as their loving letters attest, but in 1926 Heyward was found almost lifeless due to gas poisoning. She was revived, but soon after succumbed to a fatal overdose of gas. Around the same time, Bragg befriended the younger Helen McCormack (1903-1974). Bragg's biographer suggests that this might have made Heyward jealous and triggered her despair. Bragg denied that it was a suicide, and claimed murder, removing any suspicion of intimate improprieties.

McCormack was her new love interest. The former wrote "Dear Miss Bragg" in 1928 when she, McCormack, was in North Carolina. "Oh! Darling," she exclaimed, "as nice as it is here... I'd much much rather be there with you... I wanted you so [as she watched the sun go down]. I thought of the pale sunset we had watched on the Hudson, and the bright lovely ones at Snug Harbor [Bragg's weekend retreat outside of town]. I wanted your arms around me. I wanted to hold your hands in mine." "I'm weeping from loneliness for you," she wrote soon after, "but nobody knows," showing how she had to hide their relationship; "remember that I too love you and love you and love you."

"Whether there was a physical side to their relationship or not, Helen was Bragg's emotional partner for the rest of her life, even when Bragg moved on to other women," Louise Anderson writes. (While never "outing" her in her biography, Anderson is much more direct in an article co-authored and published in *The Journal of Homosexuality*.)[5]

McCormack, like her mentor Miss Bragg, also was a change agent. Leaving Charleston, she headed the Valentine Museum in Richmond, Virginia, from 1930 to 1940; and when she returned she served as archivist of the South Carolina Historical Society, before becoming director of the Gibbes Museum of Art. McCormack was one of the authors of a vital landmark architectural inventory and classic guide to the buildings of the city, *This is Charleston*.

Many men and women followed her example in helping preserve the city. They included gay leaders of the Preservation Society of Charleston, the Gibbes Museum of Art, the Historic Charleston Foundation, the Charleston Museum, and the South Carolina Historical Society. Like McCormack, many worked at those institutions in times when their sexual orientation would be unacceptable to their employers.

If Miss Bragg was reticent about herself, she was nevertheless outspoken in her support of others. Her sex was incidental, recalled one of her "boys," the name she gave to the younger men she mentored (this author being the last of them). And she had her "girls," too. "Her gender never defined her actions because she saw herself as person who was dominant and controlling."⁶

Laura Bragg and Helen McCormack lived long enough to see themselves recognized for their gifts; their papers were saved for posterity in museums and archives. But for women of color, it was different. Black accomplishments were seen as threats, ignored, or downplayed by the White community. Dart Hall, the "colored" branch of the public library, did amass some historical documents, but the Avery Research Center for African American History and Culture at the College of Charleston was not founded until 1985 and the college did not focus on LGBTQ materials until about 2018.

The path to success and social acceptance in the African American community demanded rigid conformity to social norms and sexual respectability. In this segregated era people were pressured to stay closeted for the reputation of the race. Yet some African American women refused to pretend otherwise, and like Bragg and McCormack cleaved to each other as they lifted the community.

Figure 14. Laura Bragg's bookplate.

Dr. Huldah Josephine Prioleau's obituary suggests she was born around 1880, though her tombstone says 1866. After education in segregated South Carolina schools, she attended Howard University, and returned to Charleston in 1904, the second Black female physician in the city.

In World War I, Prioleau worked for interracial cooperation as head of the Colored Branch of the Red Cross. Focusing on Black youth and refusing to kowtow to the local White power structure, Prioleau knew how important it was to mentor the next generation and to instill pride in children in a stigmatizing society. She fought for a statewide "colored" industrial school to teach trades to those who would lose their fathers in the war. Her dedication to children's welfare extended to mothers as well, for she worked to educate single mothers especially. It was a lonely uphill battle until she found a companion to share her passion and her household.[7]

According to city directories, Beulah J. Crawford moved in with Prioleau in 1913. Referred to as a trained (or registered) nurse—again unusual for a Black woman in these years—she worked alongside prestigious White doctors doing tuberculosis testing in Black schools. Crawford was also a city employee, charged with physical education of "colored" children at Charleston's segregated playgrounds. She was director of Harmon Field, one of only two playgrounds for Black children in town. Crawford arranged sporting events and was praised for the good she did for her race.[8]

This was another passion Crawford shared with Prioleau, who was respected enough to be addressed as Madame (but not "Dr.") by Whites like attorney Theodore Jervey. (Black men were never "mistered," and both men and women were usually just called by their first names.) Prioleau urged the city to establish playgrounds for "colored" children, once chairing a committee of

African Americans willing to donate land, an old cemetery on the east side of town. She had volunteered as head of Harmon Playground, also on a cemetery on the west side, possibly working with Crawford until the land was taken over by the municipality.[9]

In one newspaper article, they were both thanked, their names linked for their dedication to the needs of African Americans in the Depression. At their home on Rutledge Avenue, known as the "Home of the Better Baby," their names were conjoined on letterhead stationery: "Dr. Huldah J. Prioleau, Physician in Charge" and "Beulah J. Crawford, R.M., [sic] superintendent." "No race can exist that does not care for it's [sic] women and children" appears above Prioleau's name; and "No child comes into this world of its own will and its greatest heritage is good health and honest parents" is above Crawford's.[10]

They worked until Prioleau's death in 1940. She left no will, but a relative appeared. As "real" and "blood" kin, the assumptive heir demanded the inheritance, and Crawford found herself having to buy back the house where she and Prioleau had lived and worked for years.

Crawford continued there, working and giving money to charity, periodically taking in lodgers. She must have been proud to see Prioleau honored in the name of a daycare center for working mothers at Plymouth Church.[11]

But Dr. Prioleau's name soon disappeared.

When leading Black physicians and historians in town began a project at the Avery Research Center for African American History and Culture to document the community, they could only vaguely recall Prioleau's name, and Crawford's not at all. Was it the fact that they were women and not men? Had this household of "spinsters" held itself aloof from the community? (The listing of their names and actions in a White-controlled newspaper that even published whole unedited articles by Prioleau argues strongly for their prominence and visibility.) Would any community, Black or White, have accepted lesbians working with children if they had been known or suspected, as evinced in *The Children's Hour*? In 1950, a woman named Beulah Crawford participated in an anniversary event at Allen University, but by 1958, other people were living in apartments that once had been the home and workplace of Nurse Crawford and Dr. Prioleau, caretakers of their community.[12]

Along with Prioleau and Crawford, other Black men and women defied convention, living fairly openly, disregarding (but having to contend with) the pressure of family, community, church, and peers. Of the funeral home-owning Mickey family siblings, sister Ellen was much more brazen and out than her brother Edward. She, her family knew, "slept on the far side of the bed" — meaning she was lesbian. "She was sort of manly, and she wore her hair pretty short...." In the funeral home's heyday of the 1920s and 30s, she often drove the hearse. Family thought of her as the black sheep. "Heaven knows what Aunt Ellen did to find girlfriends," Edwina Whitlock reminisced, "or what she did with her girlfriends once she found them. [One was a minister's wife apparently.] But she had a temper and was always having confrontations with someone." Indeed, in an argument over a lover, a married woman, and possibly that minister's wife, "Ellen waited for the unsuspecting fellow, her rival, and then just shot him." For once, all the shocked family members rallied; to save her and the family name, they spirited her out of the city and she vanished from the local scene and local memory.

Her brother Edward's life was not as dramatic. Described as a dandy, and known to be gay, he began in the family business before his sister. He led funeral processions when hearses were pulled by horses, calling attention to himself with his tall black hat and cape. Perhaps being one of the family in charge of the firm and needing to cut more of a figurehead, he bowed to convention and married. He surprised many when a newspaper announcement declared his wedding to the daughter of the late Alonzo McClellan, the second African American midshipman to attend the US Naval Academy before founding a hospital for Blacks in Charleston, with which Dr. Huldah Prioleau was affiliated. But the marriage was doomed — though gay men would continue to marry in the city for social acceptance. When his true identity became known, Mickey's wife left him. The funeral parlor failed in the Depression, and Edward Mickey, like his sister, left town. He moved to New York where he founded another funeral home and, to some extent, found himself. When Edwina Whitlock visited her "gentle and elegant" kinsman in the 1970s, he turned over a treasure. Lacking a family of his own, as she noted, with no children or grandchildren, he had become the family archivist, saving documents telling the stories of several distinguished extended Black and White interconnected Charleston families, the Harlestons, the Jenkinses, and the Mickeys. This led to the publication of a book about them.

But he had not just saved history; he helped make it, defying conservative Charleston in yet another way in the early part of the 20th century. In 1917, with his cousin, African American painter Edwin Augustus Harleston (whose career Laura Bragg had tried to advance, and who DuBose Heyward had used as a character in his novel *Mamba's Daughters*), Mickey, with a few other very brave, forward-thinking Black men, founded the state's first chapter of the National Association for the Advancement of Colored People (NAACP). Since then, the Charleston Chapter of the NAACP has stood up for LGBTQ rights consistently. Apparently he found more support in Charleston being Black than being queer.[13]

The Real Rainbow Row

Another branch of the clan, the Jenkinses, also felt sexual and social tensions in their very visible lives. Born into slavery, the Reverend Daniel Jenkins (1862-1937) founded an orphanage for Black children just before the turn of the 20th century, which White locals helped support. To further finance the institution and provide a way of life for some of the children, Jenkins had launched a musical program in the old marine hospital on Franklin Street. Various bands toured the East Coast, played for presidents, and had a following in England; many veterans of the Jenkins Orphanage Band landed jobs with some of the jazz greats of the 20th century. When Edwin Harleston's sister Eloise had an illegitimate daughter named Olive with the married Reverend Jenkins, she was raised out of sight in Wales, the only Black girl in an entirely White community. The United Kingdom provided an escape route for another Jenkins, too.

Edmund Thornton Jenkins, or "Jenks," born in 1894 to Rev. Jenkins and his wife Lena, called effete, precious, aloof, and arrogant, was somewhat of a musical prodigy. He mastered the violin, clarinet, and piano, and was a cypher in his sexuality. Jenks went to England with an orphanage band in 1914, but stayed on in London when others returned home. He enrolled in, and spent years at, the

Figure 15. Edmund T. Jenkins

Royal Academy of Music, winning prizes and certificates for his musical proficiency on various instruments and composing. He became a jazz band leader in London and in Paris, and once thought of proposing to a woman, but pulled back almost immediately. He was just starting his European career as a classical composer, using Black musical themes from the streets of Charleston, when he died unexpectedly in Paris in 1926, listed as a bachelor on his death certificate. His burial in Charleston was supervised by none other than the gay Edward Mickey. Many in the family believed Jenks was gay, and while now celebrated in his native city that once ignored him, he, along with Edward Mickey, Huldah J. Prioleau, and Beulah Crawford have not had their full stories included in the fleeting mentions afforded them.

While Black artists like Edwin Harleston and Edmund Jenkins were mostly ignored in the Renaissance, Whites cashed in. Their paintings and prints, especially etchings, sold in countless editions and, reproduced in books, newspapers, and magazines, did much to broadcast and set the image of Charleston for decades to come, helping to make it a tourist city and bringing infusions of cash into the economy. The introduction of etching to Charleston, vital to the success of the Renaissance, came about through two women who loved each other and the city. Their story, too, has been left out of local histories.

Before they started wintering in the South, both Gabrielle de Veaux Clements (1858–1948) and Ellen Day Hale (1855–1940) had ties to the Lowcountry. Clements's mother, Gabrielle Esther de Veaux, born in South Carolina, was a relative of Revolutionary War hero Francis Marion, the Swamp Fox. Clements, born in Philadelphia, studied printmaking at the Philadelphia School of Design, and painting under Thomas Eakins. She had to go abroad to further her studies at the Académie Julian in Paris, which admitted women. In 1883, she met Hale, who became her life partner. Hale had been born in Boston to an equally distinguished family; her father was author Edward Everett Hale, who served as a Unitarian minister to the US Senate for five years. He had filled in for Reverend Samuel Gilman in Charleston's Unitarian Church (where gay rights defender James Peirce had preached before the Civil War), also providing Hale a link to Charleston. She would eventually donate a portrait etching of her father to the church.[14]

Hale's artistic life mirrored Clements's: training in Philadelphia under Eakins and later in Paris at the Académie Julian. They traveled the world, and after returning to America, set up housekeeping in a home they called "The Thickets" near Gloucester, Massachusetts.

In 1916 or so the women began wintering in Charleston, making friends, pursuing their art, and lecturing. When they knew in the mid-1920s they would not return, they decided to leave a lasting legacy.

They chose women to teach. (In Charleston in these years, the arts were not considered a masculine territory.) Artist Elizabeth O'Neill Verner later reminisced that they gave more than instructions; they "turned over to Alice Ravenel Huger Smith not only their good will, but big bottles of green, well-seasoned mordant, some bits of copper, and cones of smooth bees-wax [all necessary in etching], as well as valuable addresses of Paris suppliers." Hale and Clements, called "close friends whose careers overlapped," in Martha Severens's book on the artistic history of the Renaissance, "planted the seed for an etching club, allowing Charleston to participate in the nationwide fervor for prints."

Severens accords them their due, noting "they helped to shape the art of the Charleston Renaissance." And that in turn helped shape the development of the city. While the nature of their contributions to Charleston has been acknowledged locally, the nature of their relationship has not, another example of lesbian invisibility.[15]

The same attempt to airbrush sexual orientation away is evident in the story of a young man who joined the Etchers Club founded by Hale and Clements. Edward I.R. Jennings (1898–1929) was a sensitive youth made more sensitive by a speech impediment. As a teen, Jennings gained the attention of Miss Bragg, who made him one of her "boys," taking him under her wing. After serving in Europe in World War I, studying in Paris, and in Pittsburgh at Carnegie Mellon, Jennings returned to Charleston. He created stage scenery and costumes for theatrical groups and events, and crafted dioramas dramatizing the march of civilization that fascinated Charleston children for generations. Employed as children's curator at the Charleston Museum, he created fanciful, light-hearted art for them.

But Ned, as he was called, had dark moods and felt the pull of modernism, being the first artist in town to veer towards non-objective, or abstract, art. He influenced the young William Halsey (1915–1999), who became one of Charleston's most lauded abstract artists.[16]

As a devotee of Isadora Duncan and the Denishawn group of modern dancers who had performed in Charleston, Jennings would dress up, or undress, and fling himself into extravagant rhapsodies of movement at social functions. John Bennett, an author who befriended the young man, described these dances as "remarkable" and "strange things." Draped in fabric and Spanish moss, he'd perform on moonlit nights where others gathered to listen to concerts by the Society for the Preservation of Spirituals, a White group of plantation descendants who sang Black spirituals. Jennings designed their backdrops and costumes. As someone who had to disguise his sexuality, masks had a special appeal to him. He made wild, imaginative faces, behind which he could assume different identities.

It was on his masks, these "strangely and pitifully theatrical and macabre" objects, that Jennings "spent so much of his real but unfortunately morbid genius," opined Bennett, who watched him being pulled from their "quiet although sympathetic ring, into the swift and cocktail drinking set." Charleston had lent its name to the dance that epitomized the Roaring Twenties and despite the city's attempt to keep it at bay, bohemian behaviors were not unknown in garrets and basements among some of the young in the city. Jennings met a young man (possibly Robert Sellers), a teenager who lived nearby, with whom he began a seemingly sexual relationship. Bennett called him "a friend, who

Figure 16. Edward Jennings

had for some time made his home with him." One afternoon in May 1929, "There came a stormy scene between him [Ned] and the ephemeral companion ... thoroughly frightening the latter. ... A lad named White was with him [that] night, who says his [Ned's] conduct was irregular and extraordinary, wild, nervous and disturbed," as the behavior of someone who had broken up with a lover might be.

"Next morning, he did not appear about his usual haunts; the friend hurried to the Jennings' house in Tradd Street, and much perturbed, advised them [to] break in Ned's studio." It was there that they found him "twelve hours dead, almost high noon, still sitting in his chair, a Bible opened in his lap, a dry and empty champagne bottle ... upon the table at his side, and a revolver brought from home dropped from his hand; he had shot himself through the head." He sat "surrounded by his masks and faces watching from the wall."[17]

There were many other, less dramatic "red endings" for sad and lonely LGBTQ people in those years, men and women who killed themselves believing the evil things society said of them.

It was Miss Bragg who stepped in to save her "boy's" legacy, collecting his art before others could destroy it. Among Jennings's fantasies and frivolities for children, she found homoerotic works featuring phallic shapes and devouring maws, a cross between nightmares and dreams—taboo subjects for which society condemned him, and for which he condemned himself.

Decades later, family members born after Jennings's death continued the story that his suicide had been prompted by stress sustained in the war, and his loss of a fictitious female lover.[18]

In fact, it was the reverse. A woman a few years older than Jennings fell in love with him only to discover his homosexuality. In him, Elsa Gamel Woolsey (1895–1968) found a partner with whom she could escape reality into a world of dreams, myth, and fantasy, a world she lost when she lost Jennings and left Charleston. But she never forgot him, and her remembrance blended into her romanticized view of the Lowcountry, a lost and lovely civilization beyond recovering. In a poem dedicated to him, she addressed his shade, saying:

> When you died
> That gay world
> We only knew
> Only together,
> Our world-bubble, vanished, too
> (You mirrored in my face
> And I in you.)

She knew he was homosexual, and although the word "gay" was not unknown in that day, it was not much in vogue, yet, poet that she was, she could have chosen it deliberately. She abandoned the name "Elsa," becoming known as Gamel Woolsey, a bohemian in the tradition of Ada Clare. Married to one man, obsessed with another, she spent decades with a third, Gerald Brennan, a scholar and writer in the outer ring of the Bloomsbury set of English artists. (Brennan himself had been in love with artist Dora Carrington, who had killed herself after the death of the gay man she loved, Lytton Strachey.) Gamel Woolsey was influenced by, and never forgot, her beloved friend Ned Jennings.[19]

In 1929, people did not speak judgmentally of Jennings out of respect for his memory and family, but it was altogether different for his friend. Harry Hervey (1900–1951), was not only "out," but also published what can be considered the first gay novel set in Charleston.[20]

Unlike Jennings who had lived most of his life in Charleston, Hervey had appeared as a lone wolf in the mid-1920s, moving to town as a world traveler with several books to his credit, despite being only in his mid-twenties. But he was not a lone wolf, though some would come to consider him one in sheep's clothing. He had arrived with a handsome younger man in tow: Carleton Hildreth who had just traveled halfway around the world with him.

While his books passed muster with the critics, Hervey tipped his hand to gay readers of his travelogues and novels by employing thinly veiled references to, and winks at, gay male experience. For instance, he named one character "Dicky Manlove," and wrote with unabashed admiration of the naked male natives he encountered and obviously bedded in Southeast Asia. Authoring one of the earliest books on Angkor Wat, Hervey said he had solved the riddle of the place, claiming the temples' large cone shaped towers chanted "the creed of the phallus," happily joining in the chorus. He convinced the parents of his underage lover to let Hildreth go abroad with him under the guise of serving as his secretary.

John Bennett, the grand old man of the Charleston Renaissance, and his wife Susan called on the lads in their apartment in "the Pirate House" on Church Street only to find them nearly naked. The excuse offered was that Hildreth and Hervey had just been in a traffic accident, which the Bennetts accepted.

Even when Hervey did his version of drag, he got away with it by cloaking himself in clothes and rituals of other cultures. He entertained, not in women's dresses, but in kimonos from Asia, and sometimes appeared in a revealing sarong. (The British edition of his most autobiographical novel was titled *The Gay Sarong*.) The feminine guise spilled over into

Figure 17. Harry Hervey

his fiction, for in writing of glamorous femme fatales, he used their point of view to express appreciation of, and desire for, men's bodies. In his novel of Charleston, he defied convention, portraying the city as a seedy backwater. His story told of two brothers in a sadomasochistic relationship presided over by a castrating mother. There is a disguised cruising scene of sorts, and the main character, who cannot physically make love to a woman and, unable to be the virile man he thinks he should be, leaps to his death in a red ending, the title of the book. *Red Ending* was released just a few months after Ned Jennings's suicide.

By this time, people realized Hervey and Hildreth were not "innocent" friends, but instead were "guilty" of being deeply in love with and dependent on each other. Bennett, who had not named Jennings's "ephemeral companion" or their type of relationship, tried his best to use code for the link between Hervey and Hildreth, referring to folks from Essex, Sussex, or Middlesex, with Hervey and Carleton, gay men, in the latter, middle-sexed, category.

Hervey had been kind to people in Charleston, but even the young crowd began to shun and avoid his supposedly shocking costume parties fueled with alcohol, the "swift, cocktail drinking set" that had seduced Jennings. Charlestonians dropped Hervey (which fueled his negative view of them in *Red Ending*) for not pretending to be straight and for not conforming.

The local papers slammed his novel, yet Hervey never lost his affection for the city. He and Hildreth had a series of successes: *Congai*, a play they co-wrote about a Vietnamese woman using her sexual wiles to survive, was a hit on Broadway. Hervey's next play, set in a steamy homoerotic all-male prison, was so blatantly gay that producers abandoned it, knowing the New York law forbidding gay or lesbian depictions on the stage would result in arrests and closing the production. Hervey quickly turned it into a novel, upending the traditional tragic story of doomed gay love. In *The Iron Widow*, an oversexed

Figure 18. Hervey's novel *The Gay Sarong*.

woman, preying on handsome men, meets her doom as the two main male characters go off happily together.

After Broadway, Hervey and Hildreth went to Hollywood. Hervey's scenario for the classic Marlene Dietrich film, *Shanghai Express*, was his best work. But he was on the skids soon, drinking too much, and panicking when one of his male pickups resorted to blackmail. Pawning all he could, he and Hildreth fled to Savannah, where Hervey's mother worked. Hervey wrote better and better novels, dying in 1951, utterly forgotten by Charleston.

But he left a legacy. Few realize that his book *Red Ending* influenced the most "Charleston" of all Charleston Renaissance novels, *Three o'Clock Dinner* by Josephine Pinckney. He and Pinckney were friends, and he gave her his typed manuscript; an astute analysis reveals that she re-used its basic plot elements, stripping it of *almost* all its homoerotic underpinnings, while still focusing on a younger brother trying to live up to the virility of an older one. While she fashioned a much different work of warmth, wit, and wisdom as a tribute to her native city, still, this epitome of Charleston fiction has an undeniable underlying gay genealogy—an apt metaphor, perhaps, for much of what stayed hidden in Black and White LGBTQ lives in the Renaissance years.

Chapter Eleven

Passing In, and Passing Through, Charleston

In December 1934, when Edna St. Vincent Millay (1892–1950) was a featured lecturer at the Poetry Society of South Carolina, curious folks turned out to see this flame-haired poet who was famous for her words, "My candle burns at both ends; it will not last the night; but ah, my foes, and oh, my friends—it gives a lovely light!" And by "both," many saw her bisexuality.

She read at the Academy of Music (where Oscar Wilde had lectured), but because locals had been tipped off about Millay's wild ways by a closeted lesbian, no one would host her or her husband, Jan Boissevain. Instead, a winter resident, novelist Owen Johnson, stepped up and opened his house to them. Yet one sophisticated Charleston lady later regaled her bridge partners with stories of how she had been propositioned by both Boissevain and Millay, serially and individually, on the same day. She never did divulge if she took either up on their offers; and Charleston later ignored Millay's male lover, George Dillon (1906–1968) when he lived in town, despite his editorship of *Poetry Magazine* and his winning of the Pulitzer Prize for poetry.[1]

Earlier, another Pulitzer poet, the Boston Brahmin Amy Lowell (1874-1925), had visited Charleston. In 1922 everyone stood when she entered South Carolina Society Hall. She raised no eyebrows while staying with writer Josephine Pinckney in her mansion on King Street. It was just "spinster" Lowell's manly cigar smoking that set people's tongue's wagging, that, and the fact that she did not like the color magenta, the predominant hue of the azaleas at Middleton Gardens.

Besides, Lowell, as well connected in Boston as Pinckney was in Charleston, was strictly closeted. She avoided embarrassment for her prestigious family, not traveling with her partner Ada Dwyer Russell, to whom Lowell addressed some of the best love poems since Sappho, said some. Russell, at Lowell's demand, destroyed all their correspondence at her death, and it was Lowell, in fact, who had warned Charleston of Millay's "Sapphic" tendencies.[2]

After Millay, in February 1935, came Gertrude Stein.

The press categorized her as "half-way between an old maid and a Roman senator," with digs at her appearance and sexuality. "'Hard to get Gertie,' as she is sometimes affectionately known, has been called everything from a super-genius to a floor-flushing publicity seeker," the *News and Courier* warned. Stein, readers were told, was going to be accompanied by her "secretary-companion," referred to in another article as "the ever-present Alice B. Toklas," perhaps another dig at their lesbianism.[3]

On the appointed night, Stein appeared "in a dress of some rough material cut very much like a monk's cassock with the hood. Around her neck she wore a plain yellow scarf, which she removed before she started to lecture. And she wore spats, not petite, sissy, drug-store cowboy spats, but big brown, hairy, masculine spats that made her ankles big and shaggy, like those of a dray horse." As if Nicholas Hobbes, The Citadel cadet writing in the school's literary magazine, had not made his point forcefully enough, he said that, if limited to a single word for Stein, it would be "masculine." Her talk of diagraming sentences and the ineffectiveness of interjections ("Interjections have nothing to do with anything, not even themselves") puzzled everybody, suggested the *News and Courier*, but Hobbes found her "a source of genuine aesthetic delight." DuBose Heyward, who had tried to introduce her, was confused when she declined the honor, until a more cosmopolitan citizen explained that in France, where Stein had been living, the custom was that, at the appointed hour, the lecturer simply appeared and began to speak.[4]

He and his wife Dorothy accompanied Stein and Toklas for a boat trip through the lagoons of Cypress Gardens. There, Stein charmed young reporter Frank Gilbreth with her fierce intelligence, enormous sense of humor, and prodigious belly laughs. Gilbreth showed up later in their room at the guesthouse, the Villa Margherita; "there was a great deal of small talk of how-do-you-like Charleston variety" and an oddness Gilbreth reported on. "Throughout the interview, Miss Alice B. Toklas, Miss Stein's secretary-companion, sat in a corner, typewriting. She was thin and dark and would have looked more natural if she had been knitting." Taking the wrong door upon leaving, he ended up in the closet. When "he turned and walked out the right door, Miss Stein roared." Maybe because of her celebrity, and the fact, as he confessed, that he did not always understand her, Gilbreth gave her a pass, and often in the future told the tale of their meeting in his column "Doing the Charleston." But if he remained reluctant

Figure 19. DuBose Heyward, Gertrude Stein, and Dorothy Heyward

to write of a celebrity's sexuality, he condemned others for it. (In a January 18, 1968, piece, for instance, he listed "perverts," drug addicts, oddballs, and murderers in the same category.)[5]

Stein and Toklas were probably still being talked about when poet Frances Frost closed out the 1935 Poetry Society season in April. No doubt, the audience was relieved when she just read her very lyrical, New England-based poetry. "She wore a simple-low-cut evening dress and her hair was short, black and curly." She was, the paper noted, "as a poet is expected to be, shy and seemingly embarrassed ... [and] took the platform with several quick, nervous movements that bespoke self-consciousness." This was quite odd for a woman who before coming to Charleston was described as "mannish." The first woman to smoke in public in her St. Albans, Vermont, hometown, Frost was tomboyish, husky of voice, and known as a sexual libertine "who detested social rules." She had a history of mocking "conventional behavior" for a "devil-may-care flamboyance" which resulted in pregnancy, a hasty marriage, and dropping out of college. As a child she wanted to be a lady pirate, and when told ladies could not be pirates, she became a lady poet instead, bending convention and making her readers uneasy.[6]

Standing in front of a conservative Charleston audience, however, she corseted herself, keenly aware that the city was judging her. She had recently married Samuel Gaillard Stoney (1891–1968), one of the city's favorite sons.

Theirs had been a whirlwind courtship frowned upon by Pinckney. The latter had invited Stoney to visit her at the MacDowell Colony in Peterborough, New Hampshire. Frost was there too. The divorced mother of two, and the subject of scandal due to her sexual affair with colonist Irving Fineman, she and Stoney met and were instantly married. Josephine Pinckney attended the ceremony, cordially disliking the "vamp." Frost returned the favor, nearly "beaning" Pinckney with the wedding bouquet.

The marriage was doomed. Not only did Frost keep her surname, she refused to give up her career, ceding care of her two children, son Paul Blackburn (a future poet) and daughter Jean (to become a nun), to her parents and the dutiful Stoney. This was the reversal of sex roles expected in Charleston. (One reason Pinckney dodged matrimony altogether was because she knew that she could never have a career if she married.)

It was Pinckney who prevailed on her gay artist friend Prentiss Taylor to design a book jacket for Frost's *A Woman of This Earth*, which Frost dedicated not to her husband but to her lover Irving Fineman, who promptly began an affair with married South Carolina writer Julia Peterkin and other women. (And people shook their heads at supposed LGBTQ promiscuity!)[7] For the most part, Charleston writers and artists were more circumspect and observant of societal rules than those bohemians in New York, New Orleans, or Bloomsbury. Pinckney herself carried on a clandestine affair with the married Thomas Waring, editor of the local paper, for years.

After leaving the confines of her marriage (through a divorce), Frost continued to publish vigorous, lyrical poetry, and some disturbing novels of childhood that suggest how unhappy and maybe sexually traumatic hers had been. *Kate Trimingham* shares much with Lillian Hellman's *The Children's Hour* in a plot that revolves around a female teacher, a child, and whispered rumors of lesbianism.

An alcoholic, Frost took odd jobs to make ends meet, including a stint as a taxi driver. For funds, she began writing stories for children and published a novelization of *Amahl and the Night Visitors*, an opera by composer Gian Carlo Menotti. Her life improved "when a relationship formed that smoothed Frances Frost's middle age and made her more productive and less troubled." The relationship "was with a woman, and the two of them lived together in the hectic privacy of Greenwich

Village." Norene Carr Grace was named in a source as living with Frost there; Frost dedicated her novel *Uncle Snowball* to her, and Grace apparently was Frost's executrix.[8]

Frost never wrote about Charleston, except for brief glancing mentions in her poetry. Everyone took the side of the man who had loved and lost her, Samuel Gaillard Stoney. So, she was not claimed, and despite her prize-winning poems and well-regarded novels, she has slipped from sight, due to her secret life with another woman.

Anne King Gregorie (1887–1960) and Flora Belle Surles (1887–1971) also succeeded in hiding their relationship, ironic due to their championship of women's rights and dedication to the truths of history.

The boyishly slim Surles left her native Alabama in 1917, moving to Washington, D.C. Schooled in business, she took a position with the Women's International League for Peace

Figure 20. Anne King Gregorie

and Freedom, becoming a friend of Jeannette Rankin, the first woman elected to a federal office (US House of Representatives from Montana in 1916). Surles became active in over a dozen women's organizations, participating in national and international feminist gatherings.

Gregorie was the first woman PhD in history from the University of South Carolina, her first publication coming through Laura Bragg. Surles's and Gregorie's paths crossed when the latter began teaching at Alabama College in the early 1930s while Surles was there pursuing an advanced degree. When the school let Gregorie go due to the economic downturn of the Depression, she returned to South Carolina. Surles followed her, each unsure of the outcome. "On the day of Flo's final arrival they sat on the open terrace and gazed over the gleaming marsh. With the full realization of her dream at last beginning, so contented was AKG that she took Flo's hand in her own ... and said quietly, 'It's just as though we'd both died and gone to heaven!'" They vowed then "that, together, life for them would be sustained. When AKG became head of the South Carolina Historical Records Survey [a WPA project to help locate, inventory, and preserve local records], Flo followed her as supervisor [of a related project.] ... Thus at every step she was associated with AKG."

Retiring, "they settled down happily and lived with maximum contentment ... and during their 29 years of companionship, the bounds of their common resources widened and deepened. AKG was the homemaker-hostess and scholar; Flo was her aide-de-camp, filling a lead role only as yardboy-fisherman and dog keeper," with a doghouse she built herself.[9]

While they were obviously as committed and as domestic as Stein and Toklas, Flo and AKG were not out; nevertheless, there are striking parallels in the couples' published biographies. Stein manipulated Toklas's voice to write about herself (*The Autobiography of Alice B. Toklas* being a book

Figure 21. Flora Belle Surles's card

instead about Stein) and in Surles's worshipful 1968 biography of Gregorie, she included herself in the third person, while simultaneously narrating her partner's life. The descriptions by Surles of their shared bliss, quoted above, are not in the main text, but oddly, in the footnotes. Yet Flo was not a footnote at all to AKG's life, but an integral part of it.

Flo wrote of AKG and their life together only after the latter's death, perhaps a defiant feminist overcoming a too discrete historian, worrying about local family. She herself created the terms AKG and Flo; and if there is any doubt about their relationship, consider Surles's valentine to Gregorie: "Roses are red, violets are blue, You love me and I love you, you are big and I am petite, And both of us do love a sweet!"

On her tombstone, Flo might have tipped her hand deliberately with one final confession: Under her name, dates, and parentage, are engraved these words from Psalms 5:61, "But, lo, thou requirest truth in the inward parts."[10]

In her own way, Flo was showing her desire to tell the truth of their lives together and adding their note to local LGBTQ history, something studiously avoided by a contemporary in his autobiography.

Schuyler Livingston Parsons (1892–1967) was born "into the inmost circle of those old New York families who ... kept their position in the social life of the most changing city in the world." (Or so the dust jacket to his memoir states.) His "boyhood was passed in the America of gaslit ballrooms, when ladies rode out each afternoon to make their calls in glistening carriages ... with two smartly liveried men 'on the box.'"

Parsons grew up "with a passion for the stage and its people," a trait trifle suspect in a man. At his home on Islip, Long Island, he welcomed celebrities like Beatrice Lilly, Gertrude Lawrence, George Gershwin, Cole Porter, Tallulah Bankhead, Noel Coward, and Elsa Maxwell, a fair sprinkling of gay men and lesbians among them. But after the 1929 stock market crash and years of riotous living, he was reduced to selling antiques to many of his old friends.

Aiken, South Carolina had long been popular with wealthy Northerners seeking Southern sun, and Parsons went there, moving back and forth between the horsey society set in Aiken and the South of Broad set in Charleston. He entered into business with local designing doyenne, Marguerite Sinkler Valk.[11]

Gay men could not afford to be out if they sought acceptance in society. So, many married, having a wife in the drawing room and a lover elsewhere. (A closeted gay naval officer would still see it the norm decades later in the 1960s.) Parsons had no wife to exhibit in South Carolina, but he could speak of having had one once. In 1920 he had married Betty Pierson (1900–1982). She, too, was from a distinguished New York family, but one with enviable Charleston links. Her grandfather, William Porcher Miles, had been a professor at the College of Charleston before becoming mayor in the 1850s, and

The Real Rainbow Row

later a US Congressman. Miles ultimately was credited with the basic design of the Confederate battle flag.

Granddaughter Betty, a confirmed bohemian, became an artist, claiming she had inherited the talent from her Confederate grandfather. As the owner of the eponymous Betty Parsons Gallery, she became better known for encouraging other artists. Among the first champions of the avant garde, she represented gay South Carolina painter Jasper Johns, famous for his flag paintings, as well as Johns' lover Robert Rauschenberg, who photographed Charleston and used city motifs in his work.[12]

It was to "save" her that she had been married off by her family to Schuyler Parsons. After three years, they divorced amicably in Paris, both knowing theirs had been a "blanc," or white marriage, one of convenience, to hide the fact that she was lesbian and he gay.

While she lived the rest of her life out as Mrs. Parsons, helping to change tastes and the artistic landscape, Parsons never mentioned his ex-wife by name in his autobiography, but he dropped Charleston names galore. He spoke of Josephine Pinckney, of the Society for the Preservation of Spirituals, and how he was a member of the downtown set, entertaining lavishly. But he still kept focused on his goal, membership in the most elite organization in town, the St. Cecilia Society.

He failed to get in, not because he was gay, but because, ironically to prove that he was not, he had once married. Divorce was not tolerated in the society if the ex-spouse was still living. It was that, Parsons claimed, which denied him entry. That he chose to write about it suggests how important it was to fit in, and, no doubt, why he was mum on his homosexuality. The title of his book, *Untold Friendships*, is a sad double entendre, exposing all that was untold in his supposed tell-all autobiography.[13]

A contemporary of Parsons was Charleston native Murray Bennett (1896–1973) who left at an early age for New York City. There in the 1920s and 1930s, he appeared with distinguished casts in numerous Broadway plays, returning for a final performance in the 1950s in Tennessee Williams's *Cat on a Hot Tin Roof,* with its theme of repressed homosexuality, a trait tantalizingly present in Bennett's own poetry. His collection, mostly sonnets, was published in 1961, following his return to the Lowcountry. Living in nearby Mount Pleasant, Bennett directed and appeared in plays, hosted a radio show and lectured to the Poetry Society, on (bisexual) Edna St. Vincent Millay, (gay) Rupert Brooke, and (sexually free) Elinor Wylie, whose work provided Bennett's book an opening epigram. Instead of quoting Oscar Wilde's "The love that dare not speak its name," he invoked Wylie's "The love that speech can never render plain." In his poem "Marion Square," for instance, he wrote cryptically of Southern poet Henry Timrod (dubbed the Poet Laureate of the Confederacy) meeting gay Northern poet Walt Whitman only to have "A guardian intervene … to keep things right —Where are you boys bound? Move on, It's night!" There was a nearby bus stop to the Navy Base, and apparently cruising went on in Marion Square on dark evenings.[14]

Another poem "Island Legend" reads:

> My love's intention is withheld,
> His matchless beauty drained and welled,
> Entombed from me
> I cannot live without my love
> He lies tonight beyond the cove.
> North of Santee

Hidden in code like Poe's "Annabel Lee," a lost love in "her tomb by the sounding sea," is the mention of the "cove," a bar on East Bay Street where gay men drank beer. As for his lover, it is not her but "his matchless beauty" that is celebrated.

The Real Rainbow Row

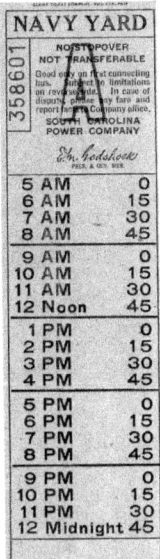

Figure 22.
Bus ticket to the
Navy Yard

"Angel in the Park" suggests a cruising scene with the narrator taking "A second tour upon a fertile lane" to "tranquilize a passionate heart's despair." He sees "A radiant being of appointed Good,/ His hands bestowed the everlasting seed;" Then, "I saw him by the fountain in the park,/ And when I touched his arm to ask the way," he disappeared.

The poem "Return" refers to a man with "the mark of his kind" with:

> … haunted eyes, irresolute and meek,
> A hand that moves too swiftly to my breast,
> That overstays a touch against my cheek.

And in "Funeral," the poet laments:

> I will return an alien to our land,
> I will be patient in my thin disguise,
> No one shall guess the substance of my hand,
> I will be cautious to deceive the wise.

In marking the death of a loved one, he is forced to grieve in disguise to deceive those who might grow wise to—what? The gender of his beloved?

The "disguise" does not totally "deceive" however, for glimmers of a same-sex love come through with more poems addressed to "he" than "she." The local reviewer, who knew Bennett, understood, writing in the *News and Courier*, "Mr. Bennett [is] more concerned with the quality of experience than with any explicit statement of its basis. The reader who wants to know 'what happened' will sometimes be frustrated because the poet has wholly transmuted the event into the emotions it evokes." So instead of invoking a lover, the poet just speaks of his love. The title of his book, *Invisible Pursuit*, rings all too poignantly true, rife, like *Untold Friendships*, with double meaning, hiding truth under the cloak of invisibility.[15]

If Timrod, whom he invoked, is known as the Poet Laureate of the Confederacy, Bennett might be hailed as the Laureate of the Closet in the city.[16]

Chapter Twelve

Passing Strange: Lives Lost and Found

The fear of being rejected for one's sexual identity was real for many Charlestonians in these years. If men with social positions like Schuyler Parsons and Murray Bennett had to hide, what was an impecunious young student coming to the College of Charleston to do?

He could only turn to his diary, a poignant and heartbreaking record that reveals the angst and torture he endured. The writer understood it could be social suicide to admit his homosexuality. The loneliness and fear he experienced led to internalized homophobia and self-loathing; his struggle shows how difficult it was to be different in Charleston in the 1930s.

In 1933, the young man, whose name is withheld at the request of his family, was at a crossroads. Throughout his college career, he worked intensely to master the skills needed in his chosen field. That gave him the reputation of being aloof and interested only in his studies. But then he met a young man named Richard and discovered how easy and relaxed he could be in his company.

On May 3, 1933, he wrote, "My friendship with Richard … is on the rocks. I was again too hasty in drawing conclusions and thinking that he might be that exception who understood and was willing to be my friend wholeheartedly."

In January 1934, he felt close enough to Richard to tell him of his "complex of weakness[es]—mainly physical, but now ethical as well," falling into the trap James Mills Peirce had avoided, not believing same-sex attraction made one morally or ethically weak. On February 24 came a "dreadful day of reckoning! God! I've just found out what has been my feeling toward Richard. I have loved him and didn't know it. Last night I played the fool…." He went with Richard and friends to the Rathskeller, a bar with mixed gay clientele. "Things broke up and we came back here, for a while." Something happened (a small intimacy?) that the young man could not even articulate in his diary. "Oh God," he wrote afterwards. "What fools and all the other expressions of self-reproach. But nevertheless we were both guilty of human weaknesses. Nothing that really mattered. After all it was nothing. Both starved and we minced words. I'm not sorry. I have no regrets. Because now I know just that more of life. … Of course, I can see how a habit could lead to biological or material displeasure, but from a moral standpoint it was nothing.… How comforting to feel, though, someone else near, very near to me. Days of loneliness fled and I was so content and relieved in the realization of nearness. Even the music we play when repeated in the daylight had no disconcerting memories."

Richard spent the night. "I am not a sensualist," the student diarist argued. "It's just that I crave companionship. … And for one moment I would have willingly foresworn a lifetime. To die would have been indeed sweet." Seeing Richard again on February 25 filled his admirer "with the joy of living." The music that they listened to was *Don Juan*, and now the student listened to it repeatedly. "Sane thoughts are lost," he realized on March 25, "and fancy runs riot. Success, career, my love, repression, sex, loneliness, [and] Richard," were on his mind. On April 3, fighting his demons, shifting into denial, he turned to Freudian theory. "As for Richard—I am not in love with him. He is at present just a convenient item for projection. I really don't want him; I quite normally want expression of the sex drive, and the answer is the normal course of action. I have profaned him by thought of perversion."

Figure 23. Rathskeller matchbook

On April 12 he wrote a letter to Richard he did not send, "It's time[s] like this that I need you ... my arms ache and ... About my brain a tightening wire sends ... encircling maddening whirls." Having expressed his feelings, he found release in sleep.

Yet there was no long-lasting peace. He made a decision; on July 13, he was sure there would be no more "[m]ooning over Richard. ... What I felt was not reciprocal in him. Thank God!"

Our young man believed that by consummating a relationship with his idealized Richard, he would somehow besmirch and dirty him, yet one thing he could not omit admitting even to himself was how he "envied Richard ... his fine physique."

"I'm determined to be normal," he wrote Richard on July 30, 1934; whether he sent it or not there is no way of knowing. "No homosexuality for me. God! I've seen enough of it illustrated in others here to see its unhealthiness—[so apparently gay life was obvious in Charleston and maybe at the college] there's no satisfactory climate in it. ... Homos are the result of people who were afraid to follow their natural instincts in expression, namely, were afraid of women, and so took the path of least resistance which was intercourse with men. Habit followed and could not be broken, or rather replaced the natural expression by its substitution."

The fellow seems to have been reading the tripe passing for science and psychology that might have been on the shelves of the college library. He seems to have soaked up every contemporary self-hating stereotype. "And for the most part the loves of homos are not lasting things — they are temporary though they give the illusion of permanance. ... The whole thing of homo is decisively futile for there is no hope of permenence of any sort. Normal love lives on through children for posterity. Homo is the expression of selfish passion." Within a week he was saying he was "disgusted" with himself.

He did not enter therapy; he did not kill himself. He was determined to sublimate his evil desires through hard work. But while playing the piano, a mentor spoke to him, warning him to limit his skill. He was told that "[t]he tendency was for a man who worked continually with the details (art) to become effeminate. And nothing is worse from a social (broadly defined) [point of view] than an effeminate man except a masculine woman."

So, the young man now had even a further cause of concern. "In any phase of art a man has to beware of becoming 'arty' [or] of joining the 'fairy' class. These latter are soft physically and morally; they can talk only on one subject and cannot hold their own in normal society." The solution was "to associate socially only with masculine men, 'he-men' [like Richard] and avoid the artys." He then determined to "walk with big strides, use broad gestures and talk with great variety in pitch and inflection. Above all, be a man!" The pep talk suggests the sad life of Ned Jennings, dead for about five years. This young fellow was going to wear a mask, too, and pretend to be someone he was not.

When visiting New York, a sight horrified him, confessed in an entry dated August 25, 1935: "In the cafeteria a party of fairies shrieking their soprano laughter ... the near sighted bespectacled one, the lapid fish-skinned effeminate one, and the handsome sunburned tallish one." And back in Charleston, he let Richard read his diary—all of it (was it an attempt at honesty or masochistic?). To his joy, he found that Richard was not disgusted, that Richard thought him brave for all the agony and soul searching he was going through, and Richard, in his way, confessed his love for him. It was so heartening, so encouraging, but it was not enough. The diarist wanted more, and on December 15, 1935, he told Richard "what I thought about sex and love; of how I admitted homosexuality when there was love between the two—how that sex was a means of reaching a culmination of a mutual feeling and understanding where intellect and emotion were incorporated, then sex was but an added factor." He thought sex for sex's sake "prostituted" it and made it abominable, but he had suddenly come to the conclusion that James Mills Peirce had: love could consecrate sex. Richard replied that he respected him but could not return that sort of affection. "And oh, how true and right is his opinion," the diarist wrote, immediately deserting his breakthrough to fall back to self-loathing. "His is the healthy view. It is capable of full culmination—of satisfaction—of marriage [and] birth."

He was so upset with himself for being gay that when another gay man named Bruce approached him, he did not know what to do. "I'm afraid he is in love with me. ... I would go to him, but I know I would ruin it all, because I'd probably fall on his neck, and let go all my physical desires, not for him particularly, but for any male. And God! I can't do this; I just can't. I'd just as soon kill myself as be an effeminate male."

The poor young man, trying to be himself, was stymied by the "truths" in which society believed and demanded he uphold. He denied himself, graduated college, became a success in his field, married, and had a family.

Nearly four decades after putting down his diary, he resumed. Again, it was his frustrated sexuality that prompted him to pick up his pen, though he had survived into a more tolerant, but still judgmental, era. A chance glance at another man brought up memories and longings and prompted poetry:

> Across the room
> A smile, a look,
> Enchanting, nay, appealing —
> Oh! that life can hold such beings.
> But not for me.
> Oh! do not respond,
> Yet the urge is there;
> The denial is there.
> These are tempting illusions,
> The stuff of dreams —
> But denial is requisite,
> It must be mutual —
> Yet how does one know?
> A look in the eye?
> Perhaps they too deny
> And so a passing glance
> That knows no fulfillment
> Is all there is,
> When young, such looks promised requital,
> With age it is remembrance
> And acceptance.
> Dream.

Although this man had many peers in his circle who married and carried on secret affairs with men, he refused to do so. He was true to his wedding vows, and of him there was not a whisper. When he died, he was mourned by the city.

Decades after his death, his diaries surfaced. Despite all the agony and angst recorded in their pages, the note he had attached to the very first volume might be the most moving.

"These were the bad times, when I had nowhere else to turn," he wrote recalling his youth; he continued:

> The good times — there were many — never prompted more
> than what they were —
> I distrusted them — hubris!
> Why keep a reminder of miseries? Perhaps to shame
> So you will know you are not alone.
> My regrets are many, for wrongs I committed.
> In fact, I fell, a human, and learned
> Tolerance, a need for compassion.
> My miseries, which I confined to paper
> I hoped to conceal from others, and yet
> I leave them here. Why?
> A hope for compassion, that another soul
> Might not find a literal complaint
> But a cry for understanding.
> I trust God will pardon my intent.

He who denied himself hoped that by sharing his experiences, his sufferings might not have been for naught, and others could be saved from loneliness and grief.[1] Flora Belle Surles had a quote from the Psalms on her tombstone. Murray Bennett had inferred much in his poems. Our young man did not destroy his diary. It's a nobility of spirit evident in him and in the permission granted by his family to reproduce some of these pages here.

Revealing documents such as these on the issues of sexual identity in the first half of the 20th century — in the South — are rare indeed. Other writings on the same or similar traumas were often destroyed by their authors or heirs, leaving no trace of LGBTQ lives other than rumors, whispers, or obliquely worded obituaries.

Yet defying the odds, we have two other stories of suppression and survival, one found in another diary, and the other published in the pages of *Ebony*.

Even as that anonymous student at the College of Charleston was recording his daily ups and downs in his diary, the president of the school was doing something similar.

Born in Louisiana in 1871, the scion of distinguished Southern families, Harrison Randolph had graduated from the University of Virginia, showing success in two diverse fields: music and mathematics. He taught at his alma mater and the University of Arkansas and was offered the dual role of professor of mathematics and president of the College of Charleston in 1897. In the following four decades, he changed, expanded, developed, and modernized the institution. Randolph added sciences to the curriculum, along with the B.S. degree, and began recruiting and admitting students from beyond the Lowcountry. He'd prompt the founding of the first dormitory and students' activity building, and open the college to women (by giving in to their active agitation and work for it) in 1918—all acts increasing the institution's viability and prestige (and the size of the student body by fourfold) by the time of his retirement in the 1940s. A nearly one-man administration, he kept track of his college and personal activities in his multi-volume diaries, which he kept in a tiny, cramped hand, sometimes in full sentences, sometimes in telegraphic bursts. On his wedding day, for instance, marrying Louise Wagener in 1911, he wrote, "Married. Didn't go to office."[2]

Randolph knew nearly all of his students, and they respected and were somewhat in awe of this balding scholar who always appeared literally buttoned up and dressed impeccably, reserved, and austere. He noted in his diary the presence of the student diarist, and in return, the student noted him in his.

In those handwritten pages, Randolph lived up to his reputation of being rather prosaic, recording by rote the days of his regularly scheduled haircut, when he woke, his illnesses, to whom he spoke—generally about College business. In the decade of the 1930s, however, he began to make frequent mentions of a young man hired to head the night school.

"Georgie," or "Dicey," the nickname by which everyone called him, was a local boy who had graduated from Columbia University, and had been a principal of a local public school before joining the college. He was in his early 40s, "delightful" and "too attractive" according to diary entries by Harrison Randolph, who was 20 years older, and starved for an outlet for male affection. He gushed like a schoolgirl, noting how nice Dicey was, wondering what he was thinking, and wasn't he good looking? Every exchange with Dicey was jotted down and mused over, with Randolph growing more excited with each new intimacy. They had splendid talks, whispered to each other during theatrical performances, and, as they spent increasing amounts of time together at work, Randolph could barely restrain himself. "His good humored cleverness brings a belly laugh at once. I tell him his ability to get people in a good humor ought to get him a fortune"—a prophecy that

Figure 24. Harrison Randolph

would ring true, bringing Randolph both angst and ecstasy, and a bright future for Dicey.[3]

Riding home together after watching the movie *It Happened One Night*, it happened for them, too. Randolph's reserve melted to rapture as they began to touch. Cataloguing in his diary exactly what caresses and groping had been exchanged in the automobile, Randolph lapsed (as he would in the future) into another language, eventually including Latin, Italian, and German. It was like morphing into a different man with this younger sexy employee, and in doing something so divorced from what was expected, ordinary English would no longer suffice: it lacked the vocabulary to describe newfound pleasures, forcing him to abandon his reserve and his mother tongue simultaneously. Except for a slip or two when mentioning which anatomical parts had been touched, he coded his entries in foreign tongues. So even in his secret diary, the reserved and austere Randolph, the dry mathematician who loved music, had to hide, disguise, obfuscate and be duplicitous as he masked his December-May love affair.[4]

Students under his charge at the college would have been expelled (and possibly jailed) if discovered indulging in what he and Dicey were doing. Statistics in the paper carried grim news of those charged with "buggery." In 1930, Leon Simmons, a 12-year-old Black lad, was sentenced to serve in an industrial school until age 21 for the crime; a man named Alonzo Scott was arrested for attempting it in 1938; Prince Ckhioati was sentenced to two years for the crime in 1937.[5]

But being of the elite class and married, Randolph may not have worried as he continued his "trysts" and assignations with Dicey. "Tell him I love to be with him," Randolph recorded in his telegraphic style one night before he went to sleep. "I love him," he admitted more bravely. Later, he "awoke in night [to] think constantly of [him]. ... Says he is

Figure 25. George Grice

going to get his stomach in shape so we can have our evenings together."

Afternoons followed, evenings, too. Dicey's presence made meetings with others incandescent and could turn an ordinary day into a "red letter" one he noted in his diary. Who would suspect that these two seemingly heterosexual married men were not just working on college business late into the night, but having assignations in cars and rooms?

These were moments of rhapsody for Randolph, ("Home with Dicey," notes one entry. "Drive around park first; delightful charming talk"; a shift into Italian describes how they touched; when they saw each other later, Randolph wrote, "Ecstatic.")[6]

Dicey, however, apparently well named, was not above turning morose and having mood swings, torturing Randolph into fits of jealousy.

On a college trip, which included Randolph and his wife, as well as other personnel, Dicey was introduced to some women at the same hotel, including a friend's niece. Dicey started flirting with her, even though he was married. Randolph was so upset he could barely cope. He left the couple with a "cold good night" and got "[s]carcely any sleep. ... I detest 'niece,'" he wrote fiercely as anything ever expressed in his diary in August 1933.

Then next day the drama continued. "In to wake Dicey. He is already up & gone (had taken salts, it turned out), or appears, though I have all sorts of ideas about him & 'niece.'" Randolph had a whiskey and went down to breakfast to find that Dicey had finished and was talking to a lady. "She teases him about 'niece'!! I'm cold & indifferent with him. Have awful morning."

Later they all reconnoitered with friends in the hotel and had highballs. "Dicey comes. Then all ok." They managed to be by themselves to have "lovely time in my room. *Wir kussen ful adieux,* which translates "we kiss goodbye" — even that small intimacy with a man catapulting him into another language, mostly German.

Dicey calmed Randolph's jealousy, naming the game he was playing. "'Women are necessary in our lives, but we understand,'" Dicey told him, "apropos of Marguerite, I think." That was Dicey's wife. For Randolph, the message was clear: women, wives, were to be used as "beards" to hide behind so no one would doubt their heterosexuality.

Dicey had to leave the next day. "In spite of complications I hate to see him go." Randolph felt bereft, expressing no regret at the women they might be betraying, something that many men chose (or felt) they were forced to do to keep up appearances in academia and society.[7]

Dicey had Randolph on a string, sometimes playing hard to get, once keeping his overcoat buttoned in the car when Randolph tried to touch him, granting him so little satisfaction that one wonders if Dicey had feelings for the older man or not. All we have of him are quotes by Randolph. Might Dicey have been using his physical attractiveness to get what he wanted? "Gay for pay" is how it is euphemistically termed today. At least there was no blackmail, which often happened to married men who made a pass at another male, who sometimes deliberately set up a trap.

Randolph was enamored. In one diary entry he recorded copying out poetry from *Love's Labour's Lost* and *Pippa Passes*. "Dicey comes in car. Give him poems. Marvelous [illegible] together." They had worked on school accounts before and then "Very charming & congenial. All sort of peter, scrotum, putting in other[?] Shakes my hand eagerly when I refer to our retiring [?] room in fixing up dormitory." This seems to imply that they were going to have a regular trysting spot, in one of the college's buildings, perhaps the men's dormitory — there were none for women in these years.

That was 1935; their working and sexual relations continued. In 1941, after doing his daily diligence to his diary, Randolph started on his walk from his house on Rutledge Avenue (nearly across from Ashley Hall) to the college, but suffered a stroke that left him paralyzed and unable to speak.

The college was in crisis, but, "[s]omehow," Nan Morrison notes in her history of the institution, Randolph "could communicate with his executive assistant" Dicey and a student. "Randolph and [Dicey] ... had enjoyed a close working relationship, a union seeming to prove that opposites attract," Morrison wrote cheekily. "Randolph was reserved, genteel and scholarly. Grice was loquacious and rough around the edges; he evinced little interest in scholarship. ... 'Dicey' ... frequently wore a green gambler's shade and smoked vigorously. The books on his shelves were written by Zane Grey." "The years from 1941 to 1945," she continues, "might be termed the Randolph-Grice years because Grice was running the day-to-day operations of the college, but according to a letter he wrote ... Grice consulted daily with Randolph."[8]

That was Dicey's real name: George Grice, one to become enmeshed in the institution's history: "because he was familiar with daily operations" and had "served as Randolph's assistant," Grice was appointed acting president and was recommended by his lover (it being "a source of satisfaction" to him) "for his executive ability and tact" to be his successor. Although the board prevaricated, many objected and one professor resigned. (Was the affair known? Or was it due to Grice's lack of experience, or his extreme right-wing views?) Grice was nevertheless named president of the College of Charleston in 1945. His ability, in Randolph's words, to put people, including Randolph himself, "in good humor" to get ahead had truly paid off.

While Randolph is often extolled for his contributions to the college, Grice has been excoriated for his disrespect of women, and his undeniable prejudice against African Americans; he was at the helm when the municipal institution became private to avoid integration. While Randolph saved the college, Morrison infers that Grice endangered its very existence, preferring to see it close rather than admit Blacks. An arch-conservative, he also may have had homophobic views. The Grass Roots League, a group Grice helped found in the 1950s, would take a stand against the evils of communism, integration, and homosexuality. (The membership list included a number of academics and dignitaries.)[9]

This casts Grice's motivation in returning the physical advances of the older man into question. Was it love? Was he gay or bisexual? Or was he just wrangling for a promotion any way he could? Or was it a combination of these? Both were married; Randolph and his wife did not have children. Grice and his wife did. Each still has a building named for them. The college's main building is called Randolph Hall; Grice is the name of the college's marine lab, established during his presidency.

How and why Randolph's diary survived is unknown. Randolph lived for nearly another decade after his stroke, naming Grice as an executor of his estate. Mrs. Randolph followed suit, Grice becoming her attorney in fact. Randolph also left Dicey some personal jewelry.[10] There was ample time for Randolph to destroy the evidence of their affair, which he did not do, raising the question of whether he wanted his truth to be known. Perhaps, mirroring the young college student, it might have been the last brave act of an academic to unmask himself, unveil secrecy, and help educate others to better policies. Or it could have been mere chance.

In this same era and city, Georgia Black also lived a secret, just as determined as Randolph and Grice to avoid detection. Both men died before their story came out. Black, however, was on her deathbed when her life became fodder for gossip, tabloids, and a national magazine.

"By every law of society, Georgia Black should have died in disgrace and humiliation and been remembered as a sex pervert, a 'fairy' and a 'freak,'" began the exposé in the October 1951 issue of *Ebony*, a mass circulation glossy magazine aimed at an African American audience. That it did not happen stunned the author of the piece and made the story newsworthy.

In Sanford, Florida during an era of racial segregation and animosity, even White citizens stood up and wanted to defend this African American woman, affording her respect despite the secret that was suddenly revealed.

All revered her as an upstanding member of the community, perhaps too good, too giving in her charity. The story that broke locally on the radio and in print made the locals angry at the physician who spread it. Black, aged 56, dying of cancer, had been taken against her will to see a doctor. And it was the physician who let slip that she was not what she seemed. Black was male and had been living as a woman for thirty years, a saga begun in Charleston sometime in the 1920s.

"Black," *Ebony* explained, "a seemingly normal boy, growing up on a small South Carolina farm, rejected his sex at age 15. ... For the rest of his life he lived a masquerade so perfect, acquired feminine mannerisms and interests so genuine that not even his closest friends suspected the curious secret. He became the 'girl friend' of one man, the 'wife' of two others, and the 'lover' of a number of men after the death of his two 'husbands.'"

Black had been born George Cantey (possibly in Greeleyville, South Carolina, called Galeyville in *Ebony*) and "rebelled" against the near slavery-like conditions of agricultural work in this small town. Black moved to Charleston for better opportunities.

"There he became a house servant in a mansion where a homosexual—a male retainer at the mansion—invited him to become his 'sweetheart.'" The only way this could have succeeded, the writer theorized, employing the old tropes of gay men "converting" youth, was due to the fact of Cantey being '[i]lliterate, untutored, and insecure, [and] having only a faint notion of right and wrong. ... Black's 'boy friend' dressed him in women's clothes, coached him in feminine actions and mannerisms."

The "masquerade became second nature. Even when his 'lover' forsook him, Black had become so accustomed to an unnatural way of life that he began to look for another man" — and apparently found several during the next decades. The story suggests that no one would ever want to dress or identify as someone of another gender, so George as Georgia was portrayed as a victim entirely. Certainly, Black was a minor, and that has to be factored in, but agency and free will have to be as well. Black seems to have made a choice and stuck with it. Her story can be seen as perversion and travesty, or it can read as a victory of a young Black person from the rural South taking charge of their own destiny.

Discovered to be anatomically male, Black dismissed the sex organs "as 'growths' [and] declared she had never had any emotional feelings for a woman." Her physician called the police. "At first we believed he might be a criminal in disguise," said the chief, but the story in South Carolina checked out, and the Florida townsfolk rallied in her defense. A White employer called her "wonderful" and another said she was "one of the best citizens in town." She died peacefully, and mourners of all races followed her casket to the cemetery.[11]

Two years later, *Ebony* revisited the story. "My Mother Was a Man" was the headline, but in a bit of grace rarely seen in these years, Willie Sabb, her adopted son, declared he was not ashamed in the least, "fearing neither ridicule or whispered gossip." He acknowledged Black's pronouns, something that would not be common practice until the 21st century. Throughout his story, he continued to "use the pronoun 'she' as that is the only way I can refer to my 'mother'." (It was the editors at *Ebony* who felt the need to supply quotation marks around them.) Sabb also refuted the charges of "weird, abnormal and freakish." His mother was "a fine, sensitive, decent human being. ... known to her neighbors as a generous soul who always helped her fellow man." "She was a tower of strength and a tireless worker for her church...."

Black assumed care of Sabb soon after his birth, taking full custody of him when he was about six, following her first husband's death. Of her second husband, who took the child in at Black's insistence, Sabb said, "Mama loved him very much. ... They were very affectionate towards each other. ... They slept together in a large bed in their bedroom and went to church together on Sundays." Widowed yet again, "[h]er womanly charms were admired by many of Sanford's citizens, not one of whom ever suspected that underneath her feminine ways, makeup and stylish dresses was the body of a man. Her voice was light and feminine, and I remember she could mimic men with ease and used to amuse the roomers with her imitations."

"Mother was a man all right," Sabb ended his piece. "But to me she was the most wonderful mother a man could want. For 30 of her 56 years she pretended to be a woman and as far as I'm concerned was a complete success. Some say she lived a lie. I don't." In finding her own truth, Sabb suggested, his mother found strength to share with others. "Georgia Black raised me to manhood and gave me tenderness and affection. I loved her with all my heart and shall cherish her memory as long as I live. She will always be 'Mom' to me."[12]

While some elite White men tortured themselves with abstinence, considered or committed suicide, or cowered in fear, Georgia Black defied expectations and lived bravely, loving many and being loved. In her "peaceful lovely life," she transcended the insults of pervert, fairy, or freak. Georgia Black is remembered, honored, and claimed on many trans sites as the heroine of a success story.

Chapter Thirteen

World War II and Following: Opening the Closet Door

If the Civil War had turned the town upside down, and World War I helped prompt the Charleston Renaissance, World War II changed Charleston just as radically, if only in the sheer number of people pouring in. The population grew a whopping 38 percent; hordes of servicemen and women, as well as war workers moved to the Lowcountry, LGBTQ people among them.

Some gay men stationed at the Army Air Corps base in nearby Myrtle Beach, finding strength in numbers, launched what scholars believe to be the first gay newspaper of any kind in this country: they called it *The Myrtle Beach Bitch*, filled with campy news stories of men they knew and what they were doing.[1]

While not as brazen and out, LGBTQ folks in Charleston and in the military were making their presence known. With as many as 7,000 servicemen coming to town every night, the sex industry was flourishing. Charleston had a reputation of corrupt cops in league with prostitutes and pimps, along with spiraling cases of venereal disease. Politicians and those in power tried to deny the facts, suggesting conditions were worse in other Navy towns, like Norfolk. The Navy strongly disagreed, and threatened to declare the entire city of Charleston off limits due to its flagrant tolerance of vice in bars and the red-light district. Undercover agents and plainclothes personnel spread out through the Market, along King Street, and to the dive bars on Folly Beach. The Market in particular was so notorious that it had the reputation as the one place in town where you get a tattoo, a beer, and a social disease all in the same afternoon. Details were amazing: prostitutes drugging men, sometimes into marriage, having sex in taxis, or even having liaisons in cars in auto repair shops, hoisted up from prying eyes on the hydraulic lifts.

The city's official answer was comical, blaming the problem on the forced movement of the red-light district after the Law and Order League's witch hunt. Before then, the argument went, everyone knew where the prostitutes were, and so the police could check on them. Now, however, they had dispersed. But the "Big Brick," notorious since before the Civil War, was still functioning on Fulton Street, and was so well known that two writers—Francis Colburn Adams, in the mid-19th century, and Richard Coleman, a hundred years later—set off-color stories there. It remained the place where young straight men went to lose their virginity.[2]

The evidence gathered of corruption and prostitution was compelling. While the main focus was on women propositioning men, or vice-versa, a small bit of evidence turned up the presence of young male prostitutes "engaged in degenerate practices" servicing gay and other servicemen. Twenty-four establishments were listed as "out of bounds to Navy personnel, because prostitution, gambling, degeneracy [read: homosexual and other sexual acts], dope, disease, unhealthy and unsanitary conditions prevailed there."

Mayor Henry Lockwood tried to suggest that the minutes of the meeting dedicated to solving the problem had somehow been altered, but the reports sent on to Washington were eventually read and retained by Senator Burnet Maybank of South Carolina, who demanded action.

In one Navy report of "CONDITIONS FOUND TO EXIST" at the Little Atlantic on Folly Beach, an undercover agent saw "a gang of young street Apaches, from 12 to 14 years of age, who seem capable of any violence. ... they use a great number of tricks to extort money from those they encounter."

This "confidential informant" went into a booth. "A boy of about 13 or 14 years of age came over ... sat down and started a conversation ... and the boy was asked if there were any women 'working' this establishment. He said there was none, but that they could very easily be picked up. ... He then said, 'There's some boys around here that'll suck you off for a couple of dollars.' He talked about this situation for a few minutes and the boy said, 'Hell, I've seen the time I'd do it myself.' This ragamuffin was definitely not homosexual, or at least none of the usual signs of such was evident. He indicated several times that he would engage in sodomy by the mouth for money — kept insisting that the informant take him for a ride. He mentioned that there were several boys around the beach like himself, and made LITTLE ATLANTIC a sort of headquarters; that they did a good business."

Again the issue of minors indulging in sex with those older and more powerful is disconcerting, but the informant's notes infer the boys were seeking sex voluntarily. That these tough kids did not seem to fit the confidential informant's image of what homosexuals should look or act like suggests a continuing reliance on trite stereotypes. He returned and saw young boys leaving with men and coming back with their friends and spending money. One infers that the sailors were gay, too, since sex with women was available nearly instantly.

The city was forced to prove that it was taking the charges seriously to avoid losing any cash being injected into the local economy. Arrests for illegal drinking, gambling, narcotics, and prostitution went up. Gay men in town went on the alert, and those in the era later spoke of picking up sailors for sex in local bars, while others offered free rides to men gathered at the bus stop on Marion Square, often detouring in the darkness of blackouts to indulge in sex. The poetry of Murray

Bennett suggests a sexual liaison between men in Marion Square being cut short by the police.[3]

Arrests did go up in these years, but the manner in which the numbers were aggregated makes them difficult to parse. In 1942, 108 people, the largest number yet, were arrested for prostitution, 28 listed as White males, 17 White females, 22 African American men, and 41 African American women. While statistics were kept on race, they weren't on other specifics. It's impossible to discern who was charged with what. Numbers were apparently what the city was trying to show the Navy.[4]

In 1944, local military police arrested Melvin Dwork of Kansas City, Missouri. He and his lover had joined the Navy Hospital Corps in 1943 in an attempt to stay together, but while Dwork was sent to Parris Island, south of Charleston, his lover went to New Orleans. Excelling in his work, Dwork was routed to officer candidate training, and sent to the Medical College in Charleston. Gay friends there cautioned him that purges were accelerating, and he needed to be discreet. He and his lover met once and kept up a correspondence, not in code, but openly. For years Dwork thought that's what triggered his waking nightmare.

"I had not taken many classes when the military police came for me," he recalled. "They took me to the brig originally, then the psychiatric brig. They kept me there for weeks. It was not pleasant I can tell you. The doctors were freakish. The psychiatrists were so stupid and asked such stupid questions. It was disgusting. They had no feelings for who I was and why I was there." The doctors declared him "deviant" and discharged him as "undesirable." Only years later, on his way to become a leading New York designer, did he realize that his lover had been arrested in New Orleans and had outed him to the military.[5]

Homosexuality awareness was on the rise, and numbers of arrests for buggery reflected it. There was one arrest in 1943, and in 1945, a man named George Chris was released on a $2,000 bond after being charged with buggery. Ronald Bender, a 21-year-old sailor, was arrested on the same charge, but pled guilty to assault and battery of a high and aggravated nature instead. There were 15 charges of buggery against one man in the next year, and he was found guilty on each. In 1949, Willie Williams was fined $500 and sent to jail for five years.[6]

But it was not all sordid, not all arrests and statistics of sodomy. The Charleston Museum's Laura Bragg had ratcheted up respect for gay men and lesbians earlier in the century and now LGBTQ life was beginning its slow creep out of the closet—if not exactly into the streets, then into parlors and drawing rooms. Two White men, partners for nearly 50 years, and great friends of Miss Bragg, helped usher in a new age of LGBTQ respect and visibility.

Neither Edwin Peacock nor John Zeigler was from Charleston. Peacock, born in Thomasville, Georgia, in 1910, had come to town around 1940 in the employ of the finance office at Fort Moultrie, an active military base on the barrier Sullivan's Island named for Florence O'Sullivan. Born in Marion, South Carolina, in 1912, Zeigler visited Charleston often as a child to stay with aunts and other family at 9 College Street. He had entered The Citadel, the state's all-male military academy, in 1928 because his mother was fond of the dances there, he said. He had sexual affairs with men, without any regrets, while one of his lovers, another cadet, considered suicide. Thankfully, he thought better of it, graduated, married, and had a family. Zeigler started *The Shako*, The Citadel's literary magazine. Peacock was interested in literature and music too, having befriended a girl, Lula Carson Smith, back in Georgia, encouraging her artistic pursuits.

Peacock introduced Reeves McCullers to her; Reeves and Smith married and she gained fame as the Southern writer Carson McCullers (1917–1967).

It was a cousin of Carson's who suggested that Zeigler and Peacock meet. In July 1940, Peacock, on a motorcycle borrowed to make a good first impression, drove over to Isle of Palms where Zeigler was summering. Zeigler and Peacock were each aware and unashamed of their attraction to men, and in a trip to the mountains, they became lovers and began a lifelong commitment. Zeigler would later celebrate their love in the *Edwin Poems* in 2007 and in his 2009 autobiography.

Knowing war was eminent, and wanting to stay together as long as possible, they headed west, living in New Mexico before sampling gay life in San Francisco and enlisting together. Now in the Navy, both were stationed in Alaska but at different bases. They kept in touch through coded letters and on leaves. Peacock was discharged from the Navy due to a hearing loss. (Carson McCullers would use him as the model for her deaf-mute central character in her first critically acclaimed, best-selling 1940 novel, *The Heart Is a Lonely Hunter*.) Zeigler saw action in the Pacific as a radio operator on a destroyer. They reunited in Charleston after the war and launched a bookstore called the Book Basement on the ground floor of Zeigler's aunts' house at College and Green streets, opening it on McCullers's birthday, February 19, 1946.

McCullers could not attend but would visit her Charleston friends in the coming years as she published books with gothic characters, misfits, freaks, and men with repressed homosexual desires. While she and some of her biographers hid the fact that she was a lesbian, McCullers has now been claimed by her community. The Book Basement became a center of culture and tolerance, welcoming all into the warmth these two men created between them. On Saturdays, they broadcasted the Metropolitan Opera on the radio, introducing classical music and opera to many.

The store became a sort of "gay underground railroad," not just for local men and women, but for visitors, too: Maurice Sendak (1928–2012), the famous children's writer, became a friend, stopping by the store while he summered on nearby Folly Beach. He befriended the artist couple William Halsey and Corrie McCallum, dedicating a book to their daughter Louise. African American author Langston Hughes (1901–1967) stopped by, too. Zeigler and Peacock had joined the NAACP early on, which very few Charleston Whites did in the 1940s. They welcomed Black students, librarians, and administrators on equal footing.[7] Their good friend, the gay artist Prentiss Taylor (1907–1991), who visited often, had illustrated works of Hughes and had been heavily influenced by a number of artists of the Harlem Renaissance, being a White artist himself.[8]

Zeigler had met Taylor in the 1930s in Washington, D.C., and Taylor, a friend of Josephine Pinckney's, had

Figure 26. Edwin Peacock and John Zeigler

previously visited Charleston, staying at one of the city's oldest structures, the early 18th century "Pink House" on Chalmers Street.[9]

> **Gay Art of the Renaissance?**
>
> Young and cherubic, pursued by such gay men as Aaron Copland, Prentiss Taylor also had a sly wit; he intertwined a unicorn and a steeple for the dust jacket design of Josephine Pinckney's *Great Mischief*. He appears to have pulled off another mischievous coup, a homoerotic riff in one of his Charleston lithographs. (If true, it stands as the only public homoerotic art of the Charleston Renaissance.) In his 1934 *Charleston Battery*, he did not choose to depict the fairly new Defenders of Fort Sumter monument with its large male nude dedicated two years before. Instead he took on the less imposing Sgt. William Jasper statue, celebrating the man who rescued the flag when it was shot down by the British in the Revolutionary War. As described by John R. Young in *A Walk in the Parks: A Guide to Those in the City*, "the statue clearly depicts Sergeant William Jasper in heroic pose … his right hand pointing across the harbor … his left holding the regimental flag." His sword at his hip trails behind him. And it was this unexpected and unusual point of view — the rear — that Taylor chose to pursue.
>
> In his rendition, he rounded Jasper's buttocks, and skewed the sword so that it curves suggestively between his legs, and not away from his body as it does in reality, perhaps a winking suggestion of a phallus, or the sword-like thrusts of "the long fleshen pole" shared by Thomas Jefferson Withers and James Henry Hammond. And as if about to accept it, Jasper braces forward. There is the vague suggestion of the buttocks of the gargantuan male defender of Fort Sumter monument in the background as well.
>
> The park in which they stand seems to have already become a cruising site for gay men, with "angels" on "fertile paths," and

The Real Rainbow Row

Figure 27. The Book Basement by Prentiss Taylor

Figure 28. Charleston Battery lithograph by Prentiss Taylor

hands sowing or bestowing "endless seed," as in the poetry of Murray Bennett. There is a bench in the lithograph, perhaps offering advice of where to sit, and in high prominence are the steps leading up to the elevated part of the seawall, possibly suggesting cruising would be more visible and successful up there. Obviously, the perspective an artist chooses determines everything, and the lithograph, as noted, is not named for Jasper, but for the Battery itself.[10]

Did he get away with it? A reviewer may have sensed what Taylor was up to, as an article mentioning him makes gratuitous mentions of art depicting men seeking sex with men: "Charleston WINS Art Show Praise," was the 1935 headline describing a gallery show in New York City that featured Charleston lithographs of Prentiss Taylor. "Ranked Among Best" referred to Taylor, and right under that was "'The FLEET'S IN' Again: Artist Who Angered Naval Officials Paints Rowdy Bohemian Scene." The critic explained how gay artist Paul Cadmus (1904–1999), "whose painting of drunken sailors *The Fleet's In* was angrily rejected by naval officers in Washington last spring." The image upset the top brass not just for men ogling women, but for one obviously gay man eyeing a sailor. The Charleston reviewer mentioned the scandal it caused, and deliberately sought out an exhibit where an etching of it was on view. From that, the writer immediately switched to Taylor and his work, hinting at a link.

One of the few critics in town sophisticated enough to do this was Rowena Wilson Tobias (1912–1975). In this same year, 1935, she was one of rare critics in the country to write a positive review of the novel *We Too Are Drifting* by Gale Wilhelm. While others uniformly condemned it because of its theme, Tobias called it a "frank and unashamed Lesbian love story," and "a thing of beauty and artistic distinction." In 1938, Tobias again went out of her way to drop Cadmus's name, not just as the creator of the sets for Lincoln Kirstein's Ballet Caravan then on stage in town, but once more as "the American painter

> who aroused such furore [sic] in government circles with *The Fleet's In*." She and others in her sophisticated set were not only accepting (and promoting) of gay men and lesbians, but counted them among their friends.[11]

Prentiss Taylor also contributed the design for the postcard used to advertise Zeigler's and Peacock's bookstore.

There customers saw two men, making no secret of their relationship, or their championship of civil rights and cultural causes in the city. Zeigler pursued his writing. National magazines published his poetry, but a novel of his with a gay subtheme never made it into print. Peacock gardened and handled the rare and out-of-print part of the business. Though they did not march, they were among the most visible gay couples in the city. They carried gay-related books in their store, which didn't sell especially well, but they mentored many and provided a safe space where all were welcome.[12]

While there were bars that admitted gay people, including Club 49, the Cove, or the Elbow Cocktail Lounge, Zeigler and Peacock chose to stay at home, entertaining straight and gay, young, and old, indiscriminately. Perhaps in the words of DuBose Heyward in his novel *Mamba's Daughters*, Peacock and Zeigler were "drawing room pioneers," living by example, raising respect and visibility for other LGBTQ people by simply living honestly in plain view.[13]

Zeigler in later life ridiculed the idea that there was any sort of bravery in this, inferring it was more dangerous to belong to the NAACP. While he and Peacock were called "the boys" by straight people, he did not see it as diminishing or pegging them as childish, or less than real men, although African American men know how the term "boys" can sting.

"I would like to emphasize," he wrote in 2009, "that among

about twenty-five gay couples whom Edwin and I knew intimately, almost all living in Southern cities, none had any problems with their identities as homosexuals. They were lawyers, teachers, doctors, architects, bankers, artists, and a couple of ministers. ... None actually came 'out of the closet', but ... their same-sex arrangements were obviously known."[14]

While they and their friends might have been spared discrimination, others of the era were not so lucky, especially those from less tolerant families, more restrictive religious backgrounds and upbringings, or in different types of jobs and of lower socio-economic status. Georgia Black, working as a maid and helper in White families, stayed disguised for 30 years, while other young Black men went to prison for buggery. Harrison Randolph and George Grice would have certainly been ostracized or fired if their relationship came out.

The fear of being recognized as gay was real. Years later, in 1966, in the so-called "Swinging Sixties," the president of the board at the College of Charleston would threaten to fire all homosexuals on the faculty. Even John Zeigler confessed in his autobiography that an acquaintance of his "outed" in Washington, D.C., shot himself at work, and many of the men he knew, described in *Jeb and Dash: A Diary of Gay Life, 1918 – 1945*, were closeted and unhappy.[15] Zeigler and Peacock may have felt secure because they were partnered, providing each other support; they also had access to a network of like-minded men for a safe harbor in a hostile world. Despite Zeigler's denial of heroism on his and his partner's part, whether it was easy or not, they were braver than many. Even straight men got in trouble for just suggesting the existence of homosexuality.

This very misunderstanding happened to Calder Willingham.

Born in Georgia in 1922, a descendant of the Baynard family of Hilton Head Island, Calder B. Willingham attended The Citadel from 1940–41, but left without graduating. His experience in that testosterone-fueled atmosphere became the basis for his first novel set in a southern city called Port George, and in an all-male military school called the Academy. One of its main characters is the sadistic cadet Jocko De Paris, and there are episodes suggesting sex, cruel hazing, and barely suppressed homosexuality. The cast includes one obviously gay, nearly flaming, cadet, Perrin McKee. The publication of *End as a Man* in 1947 brought Willingham an international reputation, with critics agog at his graphic realism, and his mastery of black comedy.

In Charleston, there was barely a peep. No local review was published in the paper, whose editors were dedicated to conservative values. There was a refusal to acknowledge even a fictional depiction of homosexuality, especially at The Citadel, that venerated bastion of White male power and supremacy.

Only one small article noting its publication and excerpting some gushing praise appeared. But with time, *End as a Man* gained traction, readers, and notoriety. The New York Society for Suppression of Vice brought charges of obscenity against the publisher, bringing the book more publicity while making Willingham's life a nightmare until the case was dropped. A dramatic adaptation under the same title was transferred to Broadway, where it electrified audiences with a stage full of Method actors. It launched the career of Ben Gazzara, who would later star in the role of the conflicted, possibly gay, character Brick in Tennessee Williams's *Cat on a Hot Tin Roof.* Just as it was getting too large to ignore, the local press finally acknowledged it.

"When a novel called *End as a Man* was published in 1947, many Citadel men were angry at what they registered as a slur on their alma mater," the editorial began. "The novel, written in the 'realistic' (some call it 'crude') style ... was about life in a military academy in the South. ... Now the story has been turned into a play and produced as an experimental stage group in Greenwich Village. New York Drama critics ... gave it serious attention in their reviews.

"While much of the theme is unpleasant it is not likely that the play will hurt The Citadel, any more than 'Mr. Roberts' hurt the Navy."

The editor noted regretfully, "These hard-boiled works have turned away from the romantic or academic styles of other periods. They may be in keeping with the age of Kinsey, Communism, and atomic warfare, when emphasis is on the animal rather than the spiritual aspects of the human race. Just as family [read: straight, heterosexual "lifestyles"] will survive the deviations [read: deviant, lesbian and gay behaviors] reported by Dr. Kinsey, institutions like The Citadel will continue to train and educate young Americans regardless of novels and plays that 'expose' the seamier aspects of barracks life."

The title of the editorial "Won't Damage Citadel" was meant to be reassuring. Indeed, it has proved prophetic over the years; for with the admission of women and having LGBTQ members of the corps of cadets out and proud, The Citadel today reflects more of this country's and the military's values. (In 1973, Citadel cadet and future author Pat Conroy would joke, "There are three things you can be when you graduate. One, an alcoholic, two, a sex maniac, three a homosexual, four, combination of all three.") In time there would be an organization of LGBTQ alumni and strong support within the administration and the student body.[16]

Back at the time of its publication, however, there was a danger in not obeying the party line of silence. "Have you read *End as a Man*?" queried a newspaper advertisement for the Book Basement. It listed a post-paid price including mailing for those too timid to purchase the book in person. But then a kindly Citadel librarian warned the men to remove the book from their display window; otherwise the school might retaliate and no longer do business with them.

The book vanished. But Calder Willingham went on to gain fame for novels and films, including *One-Eyed Jacks*, *Little Big Man*, and another black comedy of sexual hijinks, *The Graduate*.

His career in film began with his authoring the script for his novel, renamed *The Strange One*. After its release in 1957, it appears to have never been shown within Charleston city limits. It got as far as the Magnolia Drive-In, a few miles from The Citadel campus. Even though Sam Spiegel, the producer of the Academy Award-winning best picture of that year, *The Bridge Over the River Kwai*, had visited the school, and opined it would "be a wonderful film about The Citadel and Charleston," administrators nevertheless refused his request to film on site. Shot on location in Florida instead, *The Strange One* did not get Sam Spiegel's vaunted golden touch and was one of his least successful productions.[17]

Figure 29. Shower scene from *The Strange One*

Chapter Fourteen

Freedom and Fright: The 1950s

In the 1950s, LGBTQ people had more freedom than ever in the history of the city. The Kinsey Reports, *Sexual Behavior in the Human Male* (1948), and *Sexual Behavior in the Human Female* (1953), introduced gay men and lesbians into the sexual spectrum and into public consciousness and conversations. National news mentioned "homophile" groups like the Mattachine Society and the Daughters of Bilitis, meeting in big cities and advocating for acceptance. You could get physique magazines in plain wrappers through the mail, or purchase novels with cheesy covers of men and men and women and women at bus stations and newsstands. LGBTQ people saw themselves in movies such as *Rebel Without a Cause* and *The Strange One* (maybe with its racy shower scene intact), as well as in novels by Carson McCullers, Gore Vidal, and Truman Capote stocked at the Book Basement. There were also hints in *The Children's Hour* and plays by Tennessee Williams that would soon be filmed. While racial segregation was still enforced with signs on water fountains, waiting areas, and washrooms, the barriers for gay men and lesbians were becoming more permeable.

Meringue and Mustard Gas: One Man's View

At the popular Anchor Bar on Meeting Street, the owner, a tough-looking fellow, "muscled, [with] an arresting ugliness, befurred like a bear," let a few artsy types in to mix with the blue-bloods and debutantes.

Musicians played in a section of the bar resembling a terrace dubbed the Magnolia Room. In 1956, a talented jazz pianist, but less talented thief (he spent years in jail for petty larceny)

The Real Rainbow Row

Figure 30. The Anchor Bar on Meeting Street

wandered in. James Blake had hitchhiked to town and was staying at the Star Gospel Mission before chancing upon the bar and auditioning. Hired to play what he called "chic champagne music," he sometimes joined the bass and trombone players.[1]

While taking a break (the audience "made the air ache" with their "livid attention," Blake complained, mistaking him for a "Liberace or something"), he introduced himself to a couple of actors from the Dock Street Theatre. The older one, improbably called Julian Ravenal, "had a face ancient with weary satiety; his beautiful young companion a face of placid dreaming wickedness. There was not a doubt in my mind that we three could wind up in some piquant erotic arrangement," Blake sensed, but then the bar owner abruptly broke up their conversation. When the bar closed that night, the very macho "Dan Cooper" and Blake began a sadistic sexual affair, details of which Blake shared with friends. "What I feel is beyond shame or guilt, or even embarrassment: I know that his homosexuality is like my own, in that it is an attraction between two masculine minds, and not a tinsel thing in which one of them must pretend to be a woman."

Blake may have known his way around piano keys, but he was an even better wordsmith. Novelist Nelson Algren shared some of Blake's letters with French intellectuals Jean-Paul Sartre and

Figure 31. James Blake

Simone de Beauvoir, who promptly began to champion and compare him with literary master André Gide. The sophisticated *Paris Review* was printing Blake's writings while his affair with the "rugged-ugly" Cooper continued.

Cooper, brutal and controlling, made Blake a virtual prisoner on Pea Island, near Folly Island, taking him into town to work, and bringing him back each evening. Blake could not figure out what made the supposedly aristocratic Cooper tick, why there was "a vast uneasiness and torment in the man." Their meetings and trysts yielded "scorching, scalding merciless truth."

Blake felt that the man was trying to make him over into someone he was not. Later, upon publishing details of his life in Charleston, he returned the favor, making over his lover. For his boss was not an aristocrat named Dan Cooper, as Blake claimed, but the more humble Luther Brown. Brown was an ex-merchant seaman, father of two, a small criminal himself, who hid his homosexuality, a ruse Blake continued, keeping Brown/Cooper in the closet long after he died and Blake published their story. The affair burned itself out in the summer heat, especially after Blake took up with two musicians from the Navy base "who complicate[d] things." That ended his "Carolina caprice."

Having fled his lover, Blake wrote a farewell letter to the fellows at the Dock Street Theatre, thanking Julian Ravenal (a pseudonym, too, apparently) for making his "life in Charleston a little more interesting." Theirs, however, had been a poisonous posing scene, Blake believed, with the young men acting out stereotypical roles and poses "born of *Vogue*, *Fortune*, [and] *Harper's Bazaar* [magazines], dear Noel [Coward] … elbow patches, and (possibly) some fear.… Your attitude (it seems almost a way of life) is apparently compounded of pale green enamel, meringue and mustard gas.

"Seemingly you have marooned yourself on an arid island with a number of castaways (joyless and juiceless but oh utterly comme il faut) and there you sustain yourselves by nibbling on one another in modish cannibalism." He feared Ravenal and his friends, were like "harpies, who kill even the trees where they roost."

"So, a plea," Blake wrote in his moving envoi in farewell to the gay Charleston scene: "Less cleverness? More kindness? For the good of the breed such as it is?"

He signed it, "Fondly."

Not only was Blake somewhat masochistic, putting up with a man as crude and cruel as Calder Willingham's Jocko de Paris, but the artistic elite White men he met, the bluebloods, seemed damaged, too. Blake's book *The Joint* came out in 1971; no reviewer at the time, not even oral historian Studs Terkel who interviewed the author, mentioned Blake's open and uncloseted sexuality. Yet, it was his unhappy homosexual affair in Charleston that *Paris Review* chose to feature in an excerpt for its international audience, enforcing a dim view of gay life in America, and specifically in Charleston, in the 1950s.[2]

While single gay life was seen as depressing, men and women in couples had an easier time in the 1950s and beyond — even if the couples were not entirely monogamous. As for women, even in the public eye, Dorothy (or Dottie) D'Anna and her partner Carol "Kit" Lyons (1927–2011) survived scrutiny and thrived. Born in Buffalo, New York, D'Anna came to town in 1958 to become associate director of the Footlight Players, a local theatre group that staged its plays in the Dock Street Theatre. A few years later, Lyons, termed "her longtime collaborator" in D'Anna's 2012 obituary, moved down, and together they founded, ran, made costumes for, and directed the Little Theatre School for children.

Lyons and D'Anna were as different as day and night: D'Anna sporting short, cropped red hair, brusque and austere, and Lyons, feminine and gracious, always laughing and hugging. Together they ran their school for thirty years. D'Anna also directed plays for adults in which Lyons acted and sang, displaying her gift for drama and comedy. Newspaper photographs showed them collaborating, making no mention of anything beyond, but they entertained at their home, leaving no doubt of their relationship to anyone who participated in Dock Street Theatre cast parties. Perhaps the most visible female couple in town in these years, they were also drawing room pioneers, avoiding any suspicion of being untrustworthy with, or "recruiting" children. They enriched the theatrical culture in town immeasurably.[3]

There were other LGBTQ artists doing the same. Wilmer Hoffman, a sculptor, worked in Charleston in the 1940s. He restored and opened his home on Church Street filled with antiques to tours for the Historic Charleston Foundation. At his death in 1954, a letter to the editor recalled his blithe spirit, flawless taste, and "gay" conversation, lauding him for his attention to the cultural matters of the day. It was noted that he "valued his privacy more than most people."[4]

Aloof, and high in their flat in the Seargent Jasper apartment building were some other new arrivals: musical partners Russel Wragg (1891–1977) and Thuel Burnham (1875–1961). The latter had a career as a concert pianist with an adoring international fan base.

While back visiting in his native Midwest, Burnham was introduced to the younger pianist, who had come to him for advice. (It was at the suggestion of "a famous woman numerologist," that Wragg dropped the final "l" from his first name.)

"I played for him," Wragg wrote, "he played for me, and it was a toss-up which was more amazed. ... It was a revelation and an awakening and there was to be no turning back."

Indeed, when Burnham left Iowa, Wragg went with him. "I was engaged as his secretary and personal representative," he explained, using the same cover employed by Carleton Hildreth when he was swept up by Harry Hervey as his "secretary." The veneer of a professional relationship, which had some truth to it, lent the couples cover and legitimacy.[5]

They never separated. Wragg was present when Burnham injured two fingers on his left hand, forcing him to give up performing for a teaching career. Readers of Wragg's memoir have to wonder if he was being camp when he noted that one of his "minor accomplishments, picked up along the way, was the knack of massaging, learned in my boyhood at the Y.M.C.A." The "Y" was known even then as a meeting place for men.

Wragg also tried his hand at music, publishing a few pieces he composed, some based on Southern plantation melodies. About 1950 the men retired to Charleston where Wragg had relatives, intrigued by, but not entirely committed to, the community. "We find its inhabitants charming, friendly and courteous, but with our somewhat monastic mode of living, we prefer not to enter into any social activities," Wragg wrote.

Monastic indeed, for the biography Wragg wrote of Burnham has religious overtones replete with rhapsodic reverence for the older man. While his text employs the first person, it is not really an autobiography, but really a telling of Burnham's life. The title *Portrait Over My Shoulder: Personal Recollections of a Piano Virtuoso, Surreptitiously Gleaned by the Author* gives an idea of the contortions gone through to construct it in a way to hide their homosexuality.[6]

After Burnham died, Wragg became more involved in the cultural life of the city; one newspaper writer wondered if he was a musician, poet, or impresario. Wragg took to teaching piano, founding and running a successful chamber music series for the Carolina Art Association, and participating in the Poetry Society. He opened his home as a gathering spot for gay Citadel cadets and others seeking a safe and cultured place away from campus.

In the coming years John Zeigler, a mainstay of the local concert scene, would also publish a more honest narrative of his life with Edwin Peacock, bringing the number of same-sex couple memoirs in Charleston to three. There were many other prominent artistic couples in the city in these years: DuBose and Dorothy Heyward, writers Clements and Katharine Ball Ripley, Pat and Emmett Robinson of the Dock Street Theatre, and visual artists William Halsey and Corrie McCallum among them. But apparently none of them ever felt the need to write the truth about their own lives. While Ripley included details of her married life in her nonfiction, it was the not the main premise of her work. Dorothy Heyward's unfinished and unpublished autobiography was really more about *Porgy* and *Porgy and Bess* than anything else.[7]

Perhaps it was knowing how their official obituaries might eviscerate their lives, and bury their unsanctioned relationships with them that prompted Wragg, Surles, and Zeigler to pick up their pens to add (albeit sometimes in code) the stories of their loves to the annals of the city. Others, not so fortunate, ended up in police statistics, headlines, and decisions by juries.

On Halloween evening of 1958, children in the precincts of the Dock Street Theatre went shrieking "trick or treat" in an integrated neighborhood where people were accepted in the live-and-let-live sort of bohemian atmosphere. No one paid particular attention to the two quiet young men at 14 Queen Street, a pink building that had recently been converted to an attractive rental unit, making it part of a miniature rainbow row between the structure on its right, magenta, and the one on the left, sky blue. One of the young men had bought candy that day to give out to the masked ghouls and goblins.[8]

Both men had come to Charleston from smaller towns, seeking opportunity — economic, educational, emotional, and, no doubt, romantic. Jack Dobbins, born in Spindale, North Carolina, in 1928, finished his tour of duty in the US Air Force in the medical corps, and was now working as a finance accountant for a local drug company. His 30th birthday was coming up in less than three weeks. His roommate Edward Otey, five years younger, was a graduate student and PhD candidate in pharmacy at the Medical College. Otey had been born in Charlotte, but grew up in St. George, South Carolina. Together that night, to celebrate the one day in the year when it was permitted to dress up, dress down, assume a different persona, or claim your own, they went to an all-male party on Rutledge Avenue. Dobbins left to help tend bar at Club 49, a popular nightspot on King Street. Around 1 a.m. the fellows from the party came in to see Dobbins and have a nightcap. Otey went home to sleep.

Affable and outgoing, Dobbins, described as stocky and friendly-faced, with straight dark hair and horn-rimmed glasses,

Figure 32.
Club 49 matchbook

was working behind the bar and chatting up John Mahon, a young man in the Air Force out on the town with a pal from the base. The thin and pale Mahon was just 18, dressed in dungarees and a leather jacket (a costume of male hustlers of the day). Mahon's friend left to go back to the base, but Mahon lingered while Dobbins kept up the conversation, refusing to take the younger man's money for more beers. When Dobbins decided to leave, he suggested Mahon tag along, which he did happily. "Mr. Dobbins seemed like a pretty nice fellow," he said.

They went to the Cove, a bar on East Bay Street where straights and gays gathered. Then they tried the Elbow Room Lounge, but it had a dress code that Mahon did not meet. So they went to Dobbins's place on Church Street

Dobbins's roommate, Ed Otey, was upstairs asleep. Dobbins left the front door unlocked, with the keys dangling from the lock. Mahon put the keys in his jacket pocket, while waiting for his host, who came in from the back with two highball glasses of whiskey. After they drank, Mahon said, Dobbins made improper advances towards him.[9]

What happened next may never be known. Mahon claimed he was surprised that a man who had befriended him and had been buying him drinks all evening would suggest sex. The front door was unlocked, he had the keys in his pocket, but he did not leave. Instead, he said, he went upstairs to use the bathroom.

Back downstairs, he claimed, he found Dobbins undressed, though the next day, only Dobbins's underwear was there. The rest of his clothes were upstairs, the pockets of his trousers picked. "Come here, John," Dobbins said, Mahon testified, adding he ran back up the steps, panicked, and returned downstairs with one of a pair of Dobbins's prize possessions, a brass candlestick two feet tall, incised with figures of Jesus, Joseph, and Mary.

Mahon said he told Dobbins he wanted to leave, but Dobbins replied, "You aren't going anywhere yet." When Dobbins reached, Mahon bludgeoned him with the candlestick, two or three times, he reported (nine blows according to the coroner), resulting in three skull fractures, and blood spatters on the sofa and walls. With Dobbins crumpled to the couch, Mahon tossed the candlestick in his lap, grabbed his jacket and fled "as late Halloween revelers were winding up their activities."

The next morning Mahon bragged to his friends, one of whom had been with him briefly the night before, how he had punched out Dobbins and stolen his money. The friends would later be threatened with perjury charges when they changed their story, claiming Mahon had never said those things, and that Dobbins had voluntarily given cash and other trinkets to him. Only reading the papers about a nude body being found by the cleaning lady, a candlestick in the dead man's arms, did Mahon realize, he said, what he had done. He surrendered to police and his attorneys immediately called it justifiable homicide. He was charged with murder and theft.[10]

As the trial grew near, the tactic taken by defense attorneys George Campsen and W. H. Ehrhardt seemed to distill itself from the atmosphere. This was the 1950s when a fear of homosexuals, effeminacy, and loss of male American dominance beset the country. Communists were undermining capitalism, using Negroes to overturn the social order by infiltrating lunch counters and washrooms, and limp-wristed pansies were gaining visibility, recruiting children, and infecting masculinity. Demagogues of the Red Scare escalated hysteria to include a Lavender Scare as well, with vocal local support emanating from the press, hyped again by organizations such as George Grice's Grass Roots League: Homosexuals in government, liable to be blackmailed by communists, were seen as security risks; Negro men were lusting after White women, while White men under stress were hesitant in assuming their God-decreed macho roles as heads of families.

The press, alert to these fears, began to script a not-so-subtle attack, not against the accused, but the victim. Reporters described the offender Mahon as "boyish" and "clean-cut" in the announcement of his arrest, while another article the same day linked Dobbins, the victim, to more feminine things. "An admirer of fine paintings, with a flair for artistic home furnishing and antiques" is how he was described, the reporter using the ornate murder weapon itself in a character assassination of the victim. The pink stucco house was called "quaint" and "tasteful" and the dead man was tainted further by noting he often visited the nearby art museum.

In an article in *One* magazine, the publication of the Mattachine Society, a gay newsletter circulated nationally, an anonymous reporter called out the defense, proclaiming that it was the victim and his sexuality, and not the assailant, that was put on trial. The best prosecutor Theodore Stoney could muster was his comment "that it was known that some people preyed on persons of abnormal behavior to get money." In the 1860s, the city had arrested people for cross-dressing; now even "gender appropriate" apparel a gay man wore was used against him. Dobbins was described in court as "a man of artistic tastes and a meticulous dresser." Worse yet was the color of sheets Dobbins slept on: lavender. He had nude statues in his bedroom and only had men at his parties. His roommate, embarrassed at being described as sleeping on yellow and white striped sheets, produced a girlfriend and testified he had feared Dobbins had homosexual tendencies, and had thought of moving out. The "Charleston reporter" for the article in *One*, called Otey a Judas, betraying Christ, whose image was in fact on the murder weapon candlestick.[11]

"'Give back this mother her wonderful son,'" defense attorney Ehrhardt pled, after making sure Mahon's mother came to sit beside him throughout the trail. "Give back the Air Force its excellent soldier. Give back this young man his future and his self-respect,'" he said, making no mention of the other mother whose son was dead, inferring that being touched by a gay man might have cost this he-man his self-respect. Defense attorney Campsen cited a South Carolina law which, he said, "gave him [Mahon] the right to defend himself against improper advances." Campsen said the killing was justified. As scholar Santi Thompson argues, the press and Mahon's legal team had turned Dobbins into an ogre that society had to defend itself against, the horro of "the homosexual menace" personified.

The jury of twelve men, many of whom worked at the Navy Yard, owing their livelihood to the armed forces, retired to deliberate after Judge J. B. Pruitt gave them four alternatives. He listed them as (1) murder as charged carrying a mandatory death penalty, (2) murder, with recommendation of mercy, which carried a life sentence, (3) manslaughter, demanding a term from two to 30 years imprisonment, and (4) acquittal. About two hours later, the jury requested to see some photographs and rehear some evidence. After 10 p.m. Judge Pruitt got testy, upset at how long the deliberations were taking. Many in the courtroom believed a verdict should have taken less than an hour or been instantaneous. Five hours into deliberations, after midnight, Judge Pruitt called the jurors in. "'We've had this trial,' he told them, 'and you are here to get a verdict — the truth — in this case.'" The verdict had to come that night, he demanded. After a few minutes more of a lecture, the jury withdrew.

Eight minutes later they filed back in and announced their verdict. Not guilty. Acquittal. No penalty. The highly partisan group in the courtroom, including giggling teenagers, burst into applause. "Mahon smiled and laughed." His mother said she had never been worried. "The jury had awarded the airman quite a Christmas present," noted the reporter the next day. The Air Force added another:

"Mahon's top sergeant ... said Mahon would be allowed to go home to Michigan and remain throughout the holidays." It had been a bad Halloween for the clean-cut boy, but he was now going to have a Merry Christmas.

Solicitor Stoney said, "I have no quarrel with the verdict."[12]

LGBTQ people in the city, perhaps lulled into complacency by having been tolerated a bit, saw this as a wake-up call. A young gay boy growing up in town at the time realized his city would not protect him; he left for college and did not come back (or come out) for decades. Another gay youngster, a 15-year-old attending Catholic Bishop England High School, was distraught. Leonard Matlovich "heard all about the candlestick murder of Jack Dobbins, and heard people around him praising Mahon for being 'a hero for killing a queer.' When everyone said, 'Oh, that poor airman, being molested by a terrible creature," [Matlovich] only thought, 'My God, am I one of those terrible creatures?'"

At the Book Basement, military police asked Zeigler and Peacock if they had ever seen some other servicemen suspected of being gay, proof that the couple were known to be that way. They denied everything.

A Citadel professor, whose name was found in Dobbins's address book (Citadel cadets were known to have gone to the Queen Street parties), was quietly taken aside by President General Mark Clark, according to John Zeigler. Clark could have fired the man outright but just suggested he quietly submit his resignation and leave. He went to teach at another college that did not allow smoking and drinking, both of which he indulged in.

This was the message being delivered and received loud and clear by LGBTQ folks in town: To survive, it was best to act like someone you were not, or just leave. Dobbins's body was interred in a cemetery upstate, noting his military service that had not been brought up in court. A few years later Edward Otey died suddenly and mysteriously, no cause of death given, unmarried.[13]

Chapter Fifteen
Stonewalling: Into the 1960s

The year before the candlestick murder, a young White man serving five years for the crime of buggery was found hanging by binder twine at the Boykin State Prison Farm in Sumter County, an assumed suicide. An 18-year-old Black man was sentenced to 19 months for buggery in 1965. To avoid fates like those, some homosexual men left town or went into hiding. Many fled into the camouflage of assumed safety and respectability by what one witness called "getting married, having children, and living in a proper house downtown."

To protect themselves, those who remained single kept mum on their private lives. When asked if he were gay by someone he had known for years, one bachelor demurred, wittily quoting Tennessee Williams: "I have covered the waterfront."[1]

Charleston journalist Jack Hitt, reporting that response, called it quintessentially Charleston, being "discrete yet direct, informative but coy—but also something only someone from this generation of homosexuals might say." The very idea of gay "outness" offended closeted sensibilities in these years.

Tom Nall, a lieutenant commander in the Navy in Charleston agreed, noting, "In the 50s and 60s ... almost everyone lived 'in the closet,' and hiding behind the façade of a marriage of convenience was common." Years later Tom Lamme saw that gay men still "married for social reasons. ... you even ... [had] children because you were expected to." A boyfriend on the side was fine, as long as he did not live in the same city.

Bars also had understood rules, restricting what was allowed and what was taboo: "It was common to have piano bars and cocktail bars where the guys were expected to dress nicely in coat and tie. ... Most bars in Charleston were small, and of the 'neighborhood' type." One could not be too obvious or oblivious. "Bars, however, had to watch their Ps and Qs," Nall recalled, "so as not to be placed 'off limits' to military personnel" — like himself.

So, what was one to do to escape such suffocation?

"In those days, public cruising (especially at Battery Park) was much more evident," Nall explained, "and street cruising was a major pastime." Outside in a park or on the street, married or single men could claim they were just out innocently seeking a breeze, or smoking a cigarette before going to sleep. At the most visible spot in town, gay men could be out and closeted simultaneously.[2]

The Battery: Use It, Cruise It, Don't Abuse It

Other than Fort Sumter, no other geographic spot in Charleston may have witnessed more turf wars than White Point Garden at the Battery. Pirates were hanged at the low water mark in the early 1700s, and as the area developed, various factions fought to use the park as a badge of empowerment and visibility.

Before the Civil War, the encircling avenue and its "pleasure garden" offered elite Whites a place to parade and nod to each other; enslaved and free people of color were banished or needed a reason to visit. But after emancipation, freedmen and women staked their claim to the park, congregating, dancing, and celebrating in a previously forbidden place. In the years of Reconstruction, many Whites gave up the area entirely; but with the withdrawal of federal troops in 1877, the tide turned and Jim Crow laws and customs again made the Battery a White bastion. African American nursemaids, or Dahs, could bring their White charges down and supervise their play.

In the first half of the 20th century, various ethnic groups gathered in particular spots in late summer afternoons to catch a breeze. But with the advancement of civil rights, Whites again retreated on weekends in the 1970s and '80s as Black families gathered en masse, prompting police to set up roadblocks to keep drivers from constantly looping Murray Boulevard on the Ashley River. In the early 21st century, especially after the Confederate flag was removed from the South Carolina Statehouse grounds, the park at the Battery became a flashpoint where pro- and anti-Confederate flag contingents faced off, Stars and Bars taking on the Stars and Stripes. Flag defenders often parked a pickup with a flagpole and huge flag in front of the homoerotic Confederate Defenders monument, as others stood their moral high ground on High Battery, their signs protesting White supremacists. Black Lives Matter marchers gathered in 2020, while members of the Sons of Confederate Veterans and other Whites kept an eye on the monument, which was spray-painted with slogans a time or two.

The park has drawn its LGBTQ "protesters" as well, with gay men taking possession of it at night, and some more brazenly in the light of day, demonstrating their right to see and be seen (sometimes fighting off those who were out "rolling queers"). The bandstand in the center of the park once had public restrooms; they were locked for decades until the city lowered the building back to its original height to stop cruising. If Prentiss Taylor's lithograph of Sgt. Jasper's statue is the coded gay tribute it appears to be, that would mean the Battery has been a site of gay activity since at least the 1930s. In the 1980s, *Southern Exposure Magazine*, in its report of gay life in the South, featured a cover of drag queen Bryan Seabrook, known as Africa Brooks. In a hoop-skirt-like dress on the seawall across from the park, Seabrook was hoisting another battle flag of sorts, a Black man appropriating Confederate era drag to stake out his gay Black identity in the most public spot in the city.

Newspaper columnist Tom Hamrick attacked both Blacks and homosexuals for taking over White Point Garden, using "ghetto"

> as his code word for Blacks and "homo hand-holders" for gays, implying the park was really for straight White citizens only. But gay men refused to surrender their turf. In 1982, a gay columnist for *The Charleston Alternative* weighed in with this: "The Battery is ours and we are very fortunate to have one of the most beautiful sights [sic] in the world, but let's use it, cruise it, and don't abuse it." In 1993, the magazine *Steam* gave tips for best times and behaviors for cruising.[3]
>
> It remains one of the most iconic spots in the city.

In 1960, when Charlestonian Al Griffen was 13, attending a "special preparatory school downtown," he heard about the park. "My [straight] male classmates taught me how to cruise the Battery, the waterfront part at the tip of Historic Charleston, getting picked up by wealthy older gentlemen and being paid for sexual favors." He went there immediately, saying it was only money he was after, denying his own homosexuality. From sex in the park or parked cars, Griffen graduated to work as "a bellhop at one of the exclusive downtown hotels. It was there that I plied my trade as a hustler and—due to the restrictive liquor laws of the era—also bootlegging liquor for the local Mafia. This led to the opportunity to become a young bartender at Charleston's only transvestite-hooker bar, in the historic ... Market area. There I oversaw the comings and goings of many a drunk sailor paying to get his rocks off before heading back to the base."

Freeman Gunter, a sometimes Charleston resident who "covered the waterfront" for many gay magazines, later becoming a friend of the singer Peggy Lee, and a bit of a cult figure in New York City, witnessed similar high jinks. "Anyone who passed through the bars in the early sixties," he wrote, "will certainly remember the outrageous drag queen who called himself 'Cleopatra.' 'Cleopatra' used to hustle the sailors, many of whom were under the impression that 'she' was really a woman. More than once, Cleopatra's mother, who also did some hustling, would steal a trick from Cleopatra and her cries of 'motherfucker! motherfucker!' would follow the sailor out into the cobblestone street."

Yet it was in that dive of a bar that hustler Al Griffen faced the truth and broke through the self-deception and denial of social forces of the day. It was there he first "experienced man-to-man sex as a willing participant, instead of a bought commodity," realizing that sex did not have to be exploitive or seedy.

While Griffen managed to escape the trap of internalized homophobia, others could not. At Bishop England High School, Leonard Matlovich, the teen who had heard John Mahon praised for killing the queer Jack Dobbins, was in a quandary. "When I was in grammar school, they called me a faggot," he recalled. "Then when I was in high school, they did the same." In church and in school, Matlovich "was warned about a Catholic priest who was connected with the basketball team. Friends cautioned him to never sleep with the man on road trips, because he had a reputation for making sexual advances."

Not knowing where to turn, fearful of going to a bar or the Battery, he denied his homosexuality. Turning in on himself made him turn on others, fueling a true perversity. When Blacks came into his all-White neighborhood in North Charleston he and others "grabbed Confederate flags and rocks and chased them out." He screamed the N word as he passed through African American neighborhoods. "When [President Dwight] Eisenhower came to South Carolina to speak at The Citadel [in 1955], we hung [sic] him in effigy because we thought he was pro-black. And we held meetings to decide what to do if blacks tried to join the all-white Teen Club on the military base."

Only in retrospect did Matlovich realize the trap he fell into. "By picking on blacks, I thought I was making myself better than them. It meant that I [as a gay person and an outsider] was not the lowest person on the totem pole any more."[4]

Like the gay bachelor refusing to out himself, Matlovich and others were stonewalling, prevaricating, coming up with obstructions and obstacles to keep others (and themselves) from getting too close to whatever secret they were hiding.

But, despite the obstacles and stigma, a movement was growing. At bars and the Battery, in bookstores, and even on the streets, LGBTQ folks were becoming more visible, something some straight people in power found frightening. To clamp down on any positive push forward, the conservative *News and Courier*, famous for its strict segregationist views, began to warn about homosexuals and homosexuality too.

"It's Talked about in Whispers," an August 1965 headline teased, announcing the paper's new exposé. "Perversion isn't a nice topic of conversation," apologized city editor J. Douglas Donehue, "but parents need to know about it to protect their children." The tired trope of LGBTQ people as child molesters began the series.

Charleston, being a seaport, was vulnerable to homosexuals, Donehue believed. "And being a military town, it is a home-away-from-home for many lonely young men." Those elements "also bring the city her share of 'fags.'"

These "fags," Donehue argued, weren't local — but from "off," the oft-abused term for those not born between the Cooper and Ashley rivers or environs. More and more were arriving, causing problems like the "outside agitators" accused of riling up otherwise contented Blacks. As a public service to alert citizens to this menace, the paper was presenting a "thorough survey and penetrating analysis of a problem faced by our community."

"During World War II, Charleston was often plagued with homosexuals," the argument ran. And in peace, "[t]he problem diminished and the community breathed easier, thinking ... it had ceased to exist." Yet the 1960s saw the situation worsening. "What's more, homosexuals apparently are becoming bolder and bolder in their public activities." Donehue reported that on a recent evening, at an unnamed bar, "pallid faced young men stood by a jukebox ... [when] a thing called 'Baby Love' by The Supremes came on ... [giving him the opportunity to denigrate Black and LGBTQ culture simultaneously]. The two young men ... moved out onto the dance floor together. The one with the black hair [neatly swept into a prim ducktail] led. It was shortly after 11 p.m., on a Friday night in downtown Charleston. The other customers in the place hardly noticed." But the writer did, and reported that the black-haired fellow had "a limp hand."

Readers were told to imagine two young men walking hand-in-hand down a quiet street with church bells sounding. "Both strollers are dressed in tight-fitting trousers and they walk with a barely noticeable effeminate gait." One has the nerve to wear "a bright yellow polo shirt," the other "a red and white checked blouse which puffs at the shoulders."

While Charleston was hardly New York or San Francisco, it offered more opportunities than smaller southern towns. The city had "always been more open, more of a swinging town, than other cities in the area," gay journalist Freeman Gunter agreed. "In the most repressive eras, there was at least one or two gay bars flourishing with their attendant regulars and casts of characters."[5]

Both Jack Dobbins and his roommate Edward Otey had relocated to Charleston. So had John Zeigler, Edwin Peacock, Laura Bragg, Flora Belle Surles, Anne King Gregorie, Thuel Burnham, Russel Wragg, Dottie D'Anna, and Kit Lyons. Harrison Randolph had, as well, but the race-baiting George

Grice was a native, publicly condemning homosexuality in his Grass Roots League. The natives with families and "reputations" to uphold often kept lower profiles so it was the more out and obvious who were targeted by the series.

Donehue gave the obligatory nod to ancient Greece, saying homosexuality had been known for millennia and suggested "that such people cannot help being the way they are and might deserve compassion and understanding." Lesbians, unlike gay men, he added hopefully, could have normal lives and produce viable offspring and were not as prone to seducing children. Some even sought doctors to be cured: "Lesbianism, while it does exist in Charleston, is nothing more than a minor irritant to the public conscience," he somehow knew.

"There are no state or municipal laws dealing with lesbianism," Donehue noted, although local police kept tabs on some, aware of a few incidents regarding them. Straight men could save them "by having children," but gay men were doomed. "Once a homo, always a homo." With no drugs available to affect a cure, Donehue divided "homos" into three categories: (1) the latent, (2), the active, and (3) the sexless, "who manage to live out their lives without having their secret revealed." The number estimated to exist was "infinitesimal," he wrote. "But you can never be certain about the stranger sitting next to you on the train or bus," he concluded, abating and abetting fear simultaneously.[6]

While today such comments seem laughable, newspapers in 1965 could print them as truths, revealing the conditions under which LGBTQ people lived. Absurdly, the series continued with "The Policeman's Point of View."

Donehue interviewed both county and city police chiefs who agreed the area had "our share of difficulty with sexual perverts." Neither chief thought the issue acute, however, with Charleston Chief William F. Kelly articulating the theory that sexual "perversion" was behind many crimes such as "shoplifting, simple assault, arson, kidnapping, indecent exposure, and even trespassing." It also made people drive their cars too fast. Yet, despite these transgressions, he had to admit, "Records of sex deviants being involved in serious crimes in Charleston are few and far between." Yet Donehue felt compelled to bring up the kidnapping and murder of a 10-year-old boy named Johnny Robinson by a young man the year before. ("Homosexuals often prey on children because they are easy victims for sex deviates," was his belief.) The candlestick murder was referenced, yet the police chief said men in the military were "more often than not the victims, rather than the perpetrators, of homosexual incidents." Chief Silas B. Welch of the County Police spoke of "sex deviants being beaten up and robbed by normal men," something reported as "almost routine in Charleston." But that was okay; some of those homosexuals enjoyed being thrashed, he continued.

"As a rule," said Chief Welch, "homosexuals are creatures of the night. They roam the streets ... looking for their victims. They frequent dimly lighted bars, or places where you don't find respectable citizens." Comparing them to vampires and wolves, Welch reported that they often ran in packs of three or four and gave certain spots a bad reputation. "Some experts ... say the deviates speak a language all their own," Welch shared, showing his ignorance of camp and coded vocabularies, again equating LGBTQ and Gullah-speaking African Americans, hard to understand by the uninitiated. For some gay men, Charleston was similar to a "sundown town," the phrase used for cities that demanded Blacks exit by nightfall. Even if the police could not charge a suspected homosexual with a crime, cops would nevertheless tell him to leave immediately.[7]

The local military followed a similar aggressive policy. "Navy personnel spend a considerable amount of time checking on persons suspected of being homosexual." If they somehow managed to sneak in, it was the rule, a psychiatrist on the Navy base reported, not to rehabilitate the sailor, but to hustle him out of the service immediately. (Despite that, closeted Lieutenant Commander Tom Nall, quoted above, and Armistead Maupin, quoted below, managed to survive without detection, as did thousands of others in these years.)

One serviceman, readers were informed, managed to hide his sexuality for five years, but most were found out earlier. Homosexuals could infect a whole crew; they were bad for morale and posed security risks. "Nothing causes a military commander more headaches than having to deal with problems created by the presence of homosexuals." Those discovered were discharged, honorably or dishonorably, depending "on the extent of their homosexual tendencies or activities."

The only local allies of LGBTQ people seemed to be attorneys. Many interviewed by the newspaper reported having no qualms representing gay men (not mentioning lesbians at all). "An attorney who has represented several homosexuals in recent years, makes this observation: 'In my experience with these people, I have found them to be generally more law-abiding ... than other individuals. ... Homosexuals are more often victims of larceny and violence than they are perpetrators of them. Many avoid legal redress entirely, their fear of exposure described as 'fanatical.'" The attorney never suggested that the law that made them criminal might be unjust or unfair. It would take another 10 years for Conni Ackerman to protest discrimination against homosexuals and lesbians in a letter to the editor, perhaps a first for Charleston attorneys.

"These people can't help the way they are," an unnamed source continued. "I've had perverts come to me for legal assistance with tears running down their cheeks. They are like little children when they get into trouble and every one of them knows that he has two strikes against him. ... They know that they are condemned by normal people simply because they are homosexuals. Thus they quickly become victims of black despair when they run afoul of the law, or get into trouble of any kind."

Yet the attorney knew of one case where an employer went to bat for his homosexual employee charged unjustly with a crime. "The man's employer hired the best attorney he could find. ... In court, the homosexual was acquitted. He went back to his job the next day and was warmly greeted by his fellow employees."

This article was the most positive in the series, ending on the note, "A homosexual in need of legal assistance is like any other citizen in similar circumstances," with attorneys working to see that their clients "receive the full protection of the law."[9]

To prevent ending on too high a note, the editors reverted to the beginning trope that "Children Should Be Warned of Homosexuals." There was some consolation, however: "As a rule, homosexuals who are attracted to children are not overly aggressive."

"It isn't likely that the opinion and attitudes of Charlestonians towards homosexuals are going to change noticeably in the foreseeable future," Donehue wrote next. "The subject will continue to offend people and homosexuals must continue to hide."

Besides, he concluded, there were too many important things for the public to consider than to "bother with homosexuality." With that finding, one wonders why the *News and Courier* spent so much ink discussing it in the first place.[10]

Even with that, the editors would not abandon the topic. Soon the paper was reporting that the rate of homosexuality was rising among teenagers. In fact, "[h]omosexuality is becoming one of the most serious problems among young people today." A doctor "at the South Carolina Retarded Children's Habilation Center" felt that "[m]ost deviates have poor ego structure and a poor concept of themselves." (Why a physician at a "retarded children's facility" was considered an expert on homosexuality went not only unexplained, but unquestioned.) Another physician opined that homosexuality and that same "poor ego structure" could have something to do with appearances, "especially true if you become sloppy. You soon lose your sexuality and masculinity." The rest of the article veered to venereal diseases, perhaps now hitting on some real facts. South Carolina was ranked second to Florida in the number of VD cases treated annually.

Were LGBTQ numbers really rising, or were people just paying more attention—and were more people coming out? While only one man was reported arrested in 1960 for buggery, another case came in 1964, with five more men charged within a few days of each other in 1965, four of them involved in an incident in jail. Another case hit the papers in 1969 and more the next year, again involving forced sex in prison. In two 1972 cases, prisoners in the Charleston County Jail were again charged with "unnatural ... sex acts, and buggery on other prisoners." Prison rapes and beatings went on unchecked, the police doing nothing. Other buggery arrests followed two and three years later. In 1973, North Charleston proposed to outlaw obscene materials, including any representations of buggery with "mankind or beasts." (Depictions of cunnilingus and fellatio were outlawed, too.) In the 1830s, Charlestonians had looted the post office and burned abolitionist materials deemed obscene. More than a century later, vigilant citizens were still carrying out these duties.[11]

To alert locals of the growing menace, the February 11, 1965, issue of the newsletter *Conservatives, Inc.* coming out of the Grass Roots League, run by members of some of the oldest families in town, included an article about the Mattachine Society, a group of gay men and lesbians fighting for their rights, focusing on their activities in Washington, D.C.

The League of Women Voters, "the extremely liberal women's organization ... in Charleston, Columbia, Greenville, and Hartsville," was, amazingly enough, grouped with this homosexual advocacy group. "Testimony of the president of the Washington [League of Women's Voters] group indicates that homosexuals believe there should be no law against sex relations between men and women and animals." Readers were urged to get a copy of the hearings that supposedly proved the league had come out in favor of bestiality. Readers were also told that there was "no law in South Carolina to prevent homosexual lecturers presenting their views to the students at private or state-supported colleges," not that there was a great chance of that happening. (In 1988, the state would pass the South Carolina Comprehensive Sex Education Act, forbidding any mention of homosexuality except in the context of disease in health and sex education classes in public schools, and administrators would interpret it to mean that there could be no mention of LGBTQ subjects at all in any classrooms.)[12]

Not only were schools in danger, these conservatives brayed, but churches were, as well, with ministers accused of colluding with the enemy. The 1965 newsletter reported that in Washington, D.C., "The clergy of various denominations had given a 'sodomy ball' to promote 'dialogues' between homosexuals and church members."

The News and Courier series had failed to consider the religious point of view on the topic of homosexuality in its exposé, possibly assuming such behavior would be uniformly condemned by all denominations, as it had been by White churches back in the founding of the Law and Order League in 1913.

Millicent Brown, herself not gay, does not believe this was practiced in her church when she was growing up in the

1950s. She knew discrimination firsthand, being the daughter of J. Arthur Brown, president of the local NAACP, and she herself a litigant in integrating local schools. In her community, church members turned the other cheek, she said, spewing no hate against LGBTQ people. Many were aware of the sexuality of various Black teachers and leaders, and she had many gay and lesbian friends in high school clubs. The term used to describe them was "funny," and although there might have been some unkind comments, no one, Brown affirms, was excluded for being gay or lesbian. If anyone had something to contribute, they were allowed.

"White people did not exist for us; our lives were led in isolation," Brown reminisced. Facing discrimination from the larger community, she, her parents, and their contemporaries did not then turn around and inflict it on others the way White Leonard Matlovich at Bishop England High School had. "People led their lives," she reflected, "whatever went on behind closed doors did not make it out on the street." Some, like Burke High School teacher and civil rights leader Eugene Hunt, she thought, may have sublimated their sexuality to make things better for the next generation, giving up on personal happiness to teach, or preach and lead. The instinct among most of her group, she said, was just to grow up and get out of town. Of her graduating class at Burke, she guesses, at least half left the city for less prejudiced places, many gay men and lesbians among them. In his masterful book, *The Lavender Scare: The Cold War Persecution of Gays and Lesbians in the Federal Government*, David K. Johnson makes the case that some African American institutions, like the press, were much more favorable to the LGBTQ cause than similar White ones, viewing the gay and lesbian struggle as one for civil rights.[13]

Across the Cooper River, in a traditional African American Gullah community, White anthropologist Greg Day, soon to come out himself, found a similar tolerance toward sexual minorities. Black men who were passive partners in sex may have been called "faggots," but it did not carry the derisive sting or exclusion seen in urban society. Drag queens, in fact, were praised for their beauty, their dancing ability, and their sex appeal, and men were not judged, condemned, alienated, or isolated if they went off to have sex with a "faggot" or "screw 'um in the bukie." Elaborate shows staged in the late 1960s and early 1970s by the drag queen known as Shake-a-Plenty drew crowds from Six Mile, Hamlin, Phillips, and downtown. "Shake-a-Plenty can dance and sing," one woman told Day, calling the entertainer "beautiful ... a beautiful girl" and praising her clothes and her talent as a disc jockey. Everybody knew whose husband or brother Shake-a-Plenty was seeing. "It's ok to court a faggot around here?" Day asked of those with whom he was embedded in the basket-making community. "Sure," he was told, and he came to understand that "one of the cultural differences about the Gullah people is their strident inclusion of people who are different in age, physical and mental ability in all social activities. They are extremely polite, non-judgmental and don't shame or isolate others. Also their attitude about sex is positive, humorous and accepting." Many were lured to Shake-a-Plenty's juke joint at Remley's Point, not far from the Cooper River Bridge. "It's a dangerous place, the police don't come ... white and colored go there," Day was told. "It costs $3.50, but it's a good show." There was little hostility against homosexuality in this tight-knit community.[14]

But one of the first local ministers to attack LGBTQ people vocally and publicly was Apostle Helen Smith of the Cainhoy Miracle Revival Center, geographically close to some Gullah communities that respected gay people and lauded Shake-a-Plenty. The apostle's stance, however, was just about as far away as possible from that community's loving Christian charity.

"One Sunday night ... we were casting a Homosexual Demon out of a young man," she bragged. "While the young man confessed to us, God showed me for the first time that Homosexual Demon. A horrible monster that forced men and women to try to satisfy craves [sic] that could never be satisfied."

She knew of female teachers pulling knives on girls to compel them to have sex, was aware of women preachers seducing females, and practicing their lasciviousness in church, this somehow prompting hysterectomies. Though she herself was a woman minister, Apostle Smith countered this was not unnatural, nor was she. Smith went on to deride men in dresses who waited until their wives were exhausted so they could go at night to trap other men. She warned of homosexuals "in heat" who would prostitute themselves 15 times a day; they would "rape a baby, a dog, a cat." Nothing was safe from them.

But at her church, she was attracting homosexuals and lesbians from other African American "Holiness churches, bars and hospitals" and "curing" them, ministers among them. She painted pictures as horrifying and lurid as any Hieronymus Bosch painting, so that LGBTQ members in her congregation would be terrified into repenting, considering suicide, or leaving. But her apocalyptic vision for a world delivered and washed clean of same-sex desire, was just not going to come to pass, not even in Charleston, the Holy City.[15]

On June 28, 1969, while locals celebrated Carolina Day, the anniversary of a 1776 victory of Charlestonians fighting back the British, a similar strike against tyranny was playing out in a bar in New York City. Gay men and lesbians at the Stonewall Inn, tired of being picked on, deprived of their rights, turned back an attack by the police, who ran cowering back into the abandoned building.

In other cities, more groups had risen and marched for equality; but this incident caught the headlines and became national news. The local Charleston papers did not note it, just as they had tried to ignore the African American hospital workers striking for fair wages at the Medical College that same year. The only "Stonewall" mentioned at the time referred to a book by beloved local artist Elizabeth O'Neill Verner, *The Stonewall Ladies*, a sentimental series of interlocking stories of Southern women living in a retirement place similar to the Confederate Home.[16]

In 1861, just before the tumult of the Civil War, Charleston had hosted future LGBTQ activists Anna Brackett at Memminger Normal School and James Mills Peirce at the Unitarian Church. With a new age coming, the city again was home to LGBTQ revolutionaries.

Chapter Sixteen

Charleston and Change: Matlovich, Maupin, and Dawn Langley Hall

On September 8, 1975, a uniformed member of the armed forces appeared on the cover of *Time* magazine under the caption "I Am a Homosexual." For the first time in US history, an out gay person appeared on the cover of a national magazine. "To a movement still struggling for legitimacy, the event was a major turning point," noted author and activist Randy Shilts.

This new spirit of openness was soon visible in Charleston, too. On September 28, 1976, an announcement appeared in the morning paper: "The Charleston Gay Task Force will meet October 13 at 8 p.m. at the People Against Rape (PAR)

Figure 33. Leonard Matlovich, *Time* magazine

office... Discussion will include the need for support and consciousness-raising groups, possible national affiliation, and the law as it concerns homosexuals. Anyone interested is invited to attend." For such a positive squib to appear in the conservative anti-gay press was quite impressive, it perhaps being the first public call for LGBTQ people to stand up and organize in the city. But another news article followed, noting that the meeting had been postponed and was to be rescheduled. While clues about this precedent-breaking group are frustratingly few — was the meeting called off due to cold feet of the conveners, or PAR, or some other reason? — the group apparently worked on its mission and reportedly published a newsletter under the heading "The Task Force."

The group soon went even more public, featured in an advertisement for a radio interview with Dr. George Orvin, chief of adolescent psychiatry at the Medical University of South Carolina, and Dr. Oliver Bowman, "Head Psychologist at The Citadel." Included would be two members of the Gay Task Force. The discussion was titled, "Life Styles, homosexuality, the single man, the single woman, marriage, living together, [and] youth problems" — quite a full slate, especially for what seems to have been the first such open forum in the city.

Fay Solomon, interviewer and host of the show, knew that Orvin, well respected in town, took a dim view of homosexuality. He believed it was learned behavior, despite the American Psychiatric Association's removal of it as a diagnosis and disorder from its manual in 1973. She also knew that Bowman was gay and would present a contrasting view. Bowman told Orvin that while others may define homosexuals entirely by their sexuality, gay people themselves did not. If asked questions, a gay man or woman would likely respond with what they did for a living instead of what they did in bed. Bowman recalls that the members of the task force, a man and woman whose names are lost, were excellent on air. The man reported knowing he was gay from childhood on, which somewhat flummoxed Orvin. Like the uniformed Air Force officer on the *Time* cover, they were taking a brave public stand. In a way, these two events were linked because the officer in *Time* was none other than the local Leonard Matlovich, who, hiding his sexuality at Bishop England High School, had become racist to fit in.[1]

Born in Savannah in 1943 into an Air Force family, Matlovich moved around a lot as a boy before the family came to Charleston, which was "no place for gay people," according to his biographer. In May 1963, he enlisted in the Air Force, following his father. A decade later, he was teaching race relations classes, having roundly rejected the theories he previously embraced. He was so articulate and impassioned on the topic that the Air Force tapped him to lead workshops around the country. Eventually, Matlovich came to see that anti-gay prejudice was just as twisted, baseless, and senseless as that about race.

If he could help the service and his country defeat racism, he theorized, maybe he could help America combat homophobia, too. Working with national gay leaders like Frank Kameny and attorneys (his chief counsel was David Addlestone, from Sumter, South Carolina) in 1975, Matlovich hand-delivered a letter to his commanding officer declaring his sexual identity. When asked what it meant, Matlovich replied that this might lead to an eventual Supreme Court ruling similar to the *Brown vs. Board of Education* decree that had outlawed segregation in schools.

Matlovich, due to his superior service record, was the perfect test case to make the armed forces decide whether there was any reason, other than being gay, to discharge him or others like him. But homophobia ruled the day, and Matlovich was discharged the same year, the only reason being his homosexuality. He sued for reinstatement, but the Air Force delayed and played a waiting game, with no resolution until 1980 when it agreed to a settlement of back pay. In 1982, the military specifically banned all LGBTQ people from serving.

For his bravery Matlovich became a role model and a leader in the movement. He was arrested in front of the White House protesting President Ronald Reagan's non-response to the AIDS crisis.

He became ill with HIV himself and in May 1988, he spoke out on that issue in California, calling for love and unity. He died the next month and was buried in Washington, D.C. where his tombstone reads:

A Gay Vietnam Veteran

When I was in the military, they gave me a medal for killing two men and a discharge for loving one.

He had overcome the divisive lessons he had learned growing up gay in Charleston to become a spokesperson and leader for both African American and LGBTQ equality. In 2010, the military's Don't Ask, Don't Tell policy was overturned following Matlovich's lead. And in a further local twist, another Charleston veteran scored a similar victory the very next year.

In 2011, Melvin Dwork, the sailor who had been discharged from the service in Charleston in 1944 for being gay, sued. It was a landmark when he had his "undesirable" discharge overruled. According to the *New York Times*, this change to "honorable" made Dwork "the first veteran of World War II to have an 'undesirable' discharge for being gay expunged."

"It meant an awful lot to me," he said in 2014, "because I know I never did anything disgraceful or dishonest." Doing this, the Navy said was "in the interests of justice."[2]

Just like Leonard Matlovich and Melvin Dwork, Armistead Maupin went through transformative experiences in Charleston that later allowed him to come out and be a leader for equality.

Born just a year after Matlovich, Maupin grew up in a conservative, but more elite, milieu in Raleigh, North Carolina. Like Matlovich, he had a tour of duty in Vietnam, and outgrew his racist and conservative upbringing. Maupin was in the Navy from June 30, 1968 through July 18, 1969. Stationed in Charleston, he rented a small apartment downtown near the water. He had not heard of the heroics of LGBTQ people fighting at the Stonewall Inn in June 1969, but he engineered his own liberation at about the same time. It came one night at the Battery.

"I was sitting in the park, one of the most beautiful places in the world, in all innocence at not quite dead of night, watching the moonlight on the water. And a man ... walked by, rather heavily scented, and said, 'Have you got the time?' It was a total howdy-sailor routine. And I knew exactly what he was up to and said, 'I'm not what you're looking for.' And he left. And I sat there for another ten minutes and thought about it and finally said to myself, 'I'm exactly what he's looking for.'" Thinking he had discovered "the only other queer in the World," Maupin scoured the park and found the man, and in so doing, found himself.

It was a revelation that bore repeating. Another night, he had a brush with the police, discovered by a cop in a parked car with a drunk married man who had gone down to the Battery. The man had gotten drunk to get his courage up, but as Maupin ruefully discovered, that liquid courage had the reverse effect on getting something else up. Back on the base, Maupin saw a sailor "piped ashore" and discharged for homosexuality.

Despite the dangers, Maupin could not resist exploring his newfound self. "Charleston was such a sultry place," he

Figure 34. Armistead Maupin (center) and the cast of *Tales of the City*

recalled. "You felt sex oozing out of every corner of it." (In the 1920s, Harry Hervey had written of the carnal "flesh song" present in the city's streets in *Red Ending*, and in her 1973 novel *Nerves*, lesbian novelist Blanche Boyd observed that the city smelled of "sex and cabbage.")[3]

Upon leaving Charleston, Maupin went back to Vietnam, and he was processed out of the Navy in 1970. He returned to the Lowcountry to work as a newspaper reporter for the *News and Courier*, and again rented an apartment in the historic part of town, this time above the studio of Charleston artist Elizabeth O'Neill Verner. Maupin, while not cruising, wrote general interest stories about such things as the Salley, South Carolina, Chitlin' Strut Festival, and the local tourist attraction Boone Hall, which claimed it had been used in *Gone with the Wind*.

One day, in the Verner studio, Maupin saw a handsome man browsing her artwork. Their eyes met, and Maupin spoke to the man who was an actor visiting with a woman friend.

The three took off for Middleton Plantation, which for Maupin became "the perfect set for my first love story."

Maupin left Charleston in 1971, eventually landing a newspaper job in San Francisco where he began publishing a serial in the paper. *Tales of the City*, a nine-novel saga of entangled gay and straight lives, became as popular as it was trend-setting, one of the first best-selling depictions of a variety of LGBTQ people leading normal lives, for the most part, out and proud. Those books gave him a platform from which to speak, and the series helped raise visibility and normalize gays, lesbians, and trans people to millions of readers around the world. When *Tales of the City* was dramatized and shown on public television, it was censored and at first not allowed to be broadcast in South Carolina. Further, one of the most important characters in his saga was based, partially at least, on someone Maupin encountered locally. His character Anna Madrigal evolved from a real person who had intrigued him and countless others in the city and across the country: Gordon Langley Hall, who transitioned to Dawn.[4]

Perhaps no one could have been as different from Matlovich and Maupin than Hall. Born around 1922 in Sussex, England, and raised male, Gordon Langley Hall was the illegitimate child of servants on Vita Sackville-West's vast estate, Sissinghurst. Sackville-West and author Virginia Woolf had a brief intense relationship, and no one retelling Dawn Simmons's story has been unable to resist mentioning that Woolf's novella, *Orlando*, about a character who changes sex, was based on Sackville-West.

Hall eventually migrated to the United States, where he published numerous books, many of them sweet and sentimental tales, with some worshipful biographies of famous women thrown in. In New York, Hall befriended wealthy socialite and artist Isabel Whitney, who made Hall her heir. With his fortunes rising and an unhappy outcast past in the rear-view, Hall visited Charleston in 1961, and soon bought a house that needed restoration in the Ansonborough neighborhood, which was quickly being gentrified, gay men among the "pioneers." Ever an Anglophile city, Charleston took to the presentable young bachelor for his accomplishments, support of preservation, unerring good taste, social connections, and his English accent. While Hall always denied it, many gay men in town claimed Gordon was gay. What bothered some was Hall's affinity for Black men; it was so well known that African American delivery boys from the nearby corner grocery story were forbidden by their employers to enter the restored house.[5]

Sex across racial lines was well-known in Charleston, and the hypocrisy was accepted by many if it went in a certain direction. White men sleeping with Black women, by force or by consent, had been known in the city for centuries. Alarm bells had gone off in 1899 when Black and White men were found together in a brothel on Wentworth Street, just a block or two from where Hall had set up housekeeping. This behavior upset some gay men, a few of whom were overtly racist, but others who were more upset by Hall's not bothering to hide it. Bobby Tucker (apparently interviewed and quoted under the pseudonym Billy Camden by historian James Sears) said of Hall, "When he first came everyone accepted him. He was small framed, a very effeminate guy, with a thick English accent. ... But as soon as it got out what was going on — with all the blacks he entertained—that was the end of it! He would always be with a group of black screaming queens. Charleston people would have nothing to do with him." Tucker continued on to say, "He was an insult to the gay community."

Another neighborhood resident, under the pseudonym Jeremy Morrow, recalled, "Back then, gay men did not date blacks. ... Sex between black and white was always behind closed doors." This flagrant disregard of racial etiquette

Figure 35. John Paul and Dawn Langley Simmons at City Hall

upset many, even though their neighborhood sported a house dubbed the "Homo Hilton"—the hangout of drag queens, hustlers, and drug dealers.

In the late 1960s Gordon met and fell in love with a young Black man named John Paul Simmons. In September 1968, Hall had sex reassignment surgery at Johns Hopkins, something so rare then that it garnered national—and international—attention. Hall, never averse to publicity, returned to Charleston, renamed Dawn Pepita, and married Simmons on January 22, 1969. The news of the marriage was buried among the local paper's obituaries.

Reporter Jack Leland attended the ceremony along with a local television crew, and in his story he revealed the prevailing attitude to Blacks and gays. While specifically ridiculing Hall, he also made fun of the nervous behavior of Reverend William Singleton, of Shiloh African Methodist Episcopal Church, detailing his grammatical mistakes. Noting how Simmons had once been "lionized by the literary and artsy segments of the population and [had been] … the guest in the homes of a number of the city's social arbiters," Leland reported that her fall from grace had come when "Hall's taste for living with young Negro males became known," condemning her for her lack of prejudice and homosexuality. "Hall has been called a homosexual on several occasions," Leland stressed. Furthermore, "The presence of Negro youths ... became a neighborhood scandal ... and some neighbors protested to the police." (The neighborhood had been racially diverse for years, until gentrification flipped things.)

Not surprisingly, the outlaw couple lost status quickly. Simmons claimed with some justice that she was a martyr for her actions. She reported being terrorized and attacked, her dogs killed, and her house foreclosed on her illegally. Jack Hitt, a journalist who as a youth lived nearby, remembered it differently, recalling instead her running out of money, antiques being sold out of her house by friends of her husband, dog feces piling up inside, and the house being foreclosed and sold. When Simmons claimed rather astoundingly that she had delivered a daughter by natural birth, it became the stuff of jokes on the popular TV show *Laugh-In*. Years later, when assessing her, Hitt wondered if Simmons's gender had been misdiagnosed at birth, an anatomical anomaly called congenital adrenal hyperplasia. He visited her years later when she no longer lived in Charleston, but was still loyal to John Paul, eventually hospitalized for mental illness. Simmons moved back to Charleston with her daughter and grandchildren, her death in 2000 leaving a very conflicting legacy. Some of this was due to the sensationalist distortions of others, but Simmons did herself no favors by writing contradictory details of basic biological and biographical facts in her three different autobiographies — *Man into Woman: A Transsexual Autobiography* (1971), *All for Love* (1975), and *Dawn: A Charleston Legend* (1995).[6]

Even after her death, she continued to be fodder for tabloids, and the subject of the 2010 *Peninsula of Lies* by Edward Ball. Hitt's reminiscences of her, however, are the most poignant, he having known her personally. He concluded that, while some of her truths would never be known, that did not absolve Charlestonians from facing their own. "Ours," he wrote, of locals who ridiculed her, "were elaborated by unspoken terrors of exotic sexual tastes, transgression and miscegenation. ... If we were guilty of crafting an elaborate myth to protect us from the real Dawn Langley Hall, she was, in her own way, just as guilty." She dramatized herself and her martyrdom, spoke airily of non-existent social triumphs, while refusing "to accept the Dickensian misery of her birth and station."

When Hitt asked Simmons how she would like to be remembered, "I'll be satisfied," she replied, "if all they put on my tombstone is 'Dawn Pepita Simmons—Housewife.'"

While that is not likely, her legacy includes her impact on Armistead Maupin, as evidenced in his trans character Anna Madrigal, landlady at 28 Barbary Lane, the setting of the *Tales of the City* series. "I saw Dawn only once, buying popcorn in the lobby of a movie theater," Maupin wrote. "I'll always be sorry I didn't say hello, given the difference she made in my life by her mere example, her brave singularity. Dawn ... certainly opened my writer's imagination to the possibly of gender fluidity, an idea that still bordered on the fantastic back then."

Tales of Charleston

Other works reflecting LGBTQ lives by writers associated with Charleston appeared in these years. Blanche Boyd mentioned gay men in her 1973 novel *Nerves*. "All the queers go down to the Battery at night," a teenager says, and a friend finds it hard to believe "there were really any queers in Charleston." They speak as if it were the height of sophistication — exoticness, or "otherness" — to be queer; the character "could believe it about New York City, or some place like that, but not Charleston." In *Mourning the Death of Magic*, published in 1977, the first truly out gay novel set locally, Boyd showed her lesbian character Galley Rhett, her sister and a friend trying to live and make peace in a place haunted by homophobia, anti-semitism and racism. "This book is trash," was the predictable judgment of the *News and Courier*. Boyd went on to a distinguished career teaching and writing for the *Village Voice*, *Ms Magazine*, *Esquire*, and *Vanity Fair*, publishing five novels, and a book of essays, often focusing on the burden of racism and the complexities of life in the South and in Charleston. She impacted LGBTQ literary history not only by physically helping set type for the iconic lesbian novel *Rubyfruit Jungle* by Rita Mae Brown, but even more so with her own work. Boyd won the Lambda Literary Award and the Ferro-Grumley Award for Lesbian Fiction for her 1992 *The Revolution of Little Girls* and was nominated for the PEN/Faulkner Award for her 2018 *Tomb of the Unknown Racist*.

In 1978, another White writer, Ann B. Ross, stuck with stereotypes in her use of a twisted psychotic gay man as her villain in her Charleston-set novel, *The Murder Cure*. African American writer, Alice Childress, who left for New York as a youngster, depicted homosexuality in a completely different way in 1979, treating it tenderly and respectfully in her novel *A Short Walk*, partially set in Charleston. In it the main character's best friend is an out and proud Black man who attends the famous drag ball at the Hamilton, frequented by White Charlestonian Huger Jervey and his friends. Her 1989 young adult novel, *Those Other People*, again, would treat the topic respectfully.[7]

Chapter Seventeen
The Sophisticated(?) City

Charlestonians were no longer exempt from dealing with LGBTQ people and issues. Yet among some, the hope still lingered that comfortable old social customs could continue. If gays or lesbians were in town, maybe they would be respectful and not flaunt their sexuality. When Gertrude Stein had visited a generation before, her fame kept most from snickering or pointing. That pattern held for Gian Carlo Menotti (1911–2007). The composer charmed just about everyone when he arrived in 1975 in search of an American home for the cultural festival he had founded in Spoleto, Italy, in 1956.

He was, after all, Italian, handsome, a winner of two Pulitzer Prizes, and famous for his opera for children *Amahl and the Night Visitors*. In the more closeted times of the 1970s, his long-standing love affair with collaborator and composer Samuel Barber was not generally known. They did not travel together, and even when the Spoleto Festival eventually staged their co-written opera *Vanessa* and they stood raising their arms in victory on opening night, most in the audience knew nothing of their relationship. Besides, though not married, Menotti could speak of and introduce a son who did travel with him, a young handsome skater and dancer he adopted.

In the early discussions of bringing the festival to town, nearly everyone was enthusiastic, including bankers and socialites who saw Menotti's planned Spoleto as a huge plus for the city. The first opera in what became the US had premiered in Charleston, after all, and the first purpose-built theatre had risen on Dock (later Queen) Street in the 1730s. It seemed only natural to have Charleston revived as a center for the arts. In 1976, to get a taste and preview of the festival, a group of prominent and philanthropic Charleston sophisticates traveled to Spoleto.

According to one who witnessed the fallout, when banker "Hugh Lane returned to Charleston, he said he would have nothing more to do with it. He did not want to expose the citizens of Charleston to people dancing without clothes and felt that the people who would come to Charleston would be depraved [meaning] queers—and he offered to return all the money that people had donated to this effort." The social leader Nella Barkley "wrote a letter resigning," and Lane reiterated his position that he was not going to subject Charlestonians to be "a breeding place for undesirables," although those he put in that category—LGBTQ people—were not generally known for "breeding" in those years.

With pledges withdrawn, the city faced disaster and embarrassment, fueled by homophobia and fear. Meanwhile, Menotti himself was treated respectfully; it was those out, artsy, flighty types who were not wanted on the streets. Fortunately, the young new mayor in town, Joseph P. Riley, Jr., was a progressive who came to be credited by many as being a change agent on social issues. (In his predecessor's term, members on some city committees were flagged as Negroes or Jews.)

Riley turned to Theodore (Ted) Stern, president of the College of Charleston, whose support was key. Stern, a retired Navy commander who had many gay associates, came to the rescue. Having revived the college from some of the depredations of George Grice, he helped anchor Spoleto to the city and college, stepping in at a crucial moment. It was Stern who revealed that a few people's attitudes toward the avant garde and queers nearly lost Charleston one of its greatest cultural coups of the 20th century.[1]

International media covered the festival's successful opening and noted how it would inevitably change the city; later gay media did, too, including Freeman Gunter. In a 1982 issue of *Mandate*, he mentioned the many gay artists (including Tennessee Williams) then in town, proving how well founded the fears of the original backers just might have been. According to one witness, the city was "getting a whole influx of gay people who would come down for Spoleto, and bought houses down here. … It was becoming much more cosmopolitan thanks to the Spoleto Festival, and the people had much more progressive ideas."

For all the gay folks visiting and moving to Charleston, Gunter gave helpful directions on how to get to the end of Folly Beach to enjoy nude sunbathing where "an unmistakable gaggle of your gay brothers" would welcome them. "George Gershwin stayed here," he continued, "when it was deserted and he was engrossed in *Porgy and Bess*. I wonder what he would think of it now."

And one can't help wondering exactly what those who feared queers would have thought of Gunter's description of the festival's symphonic and firework finale at Middleton Place: "you haven't lived until you have strolled down by the river bank [to] meet a sweet honey and climaxed during the climax of the *1812 Overture* while leaning up against a tree … thousands of years old."

The tree, in reality, was only centuries old, but it was not hyperbolic to say that despite prejudicial attitudes, LGBTQ people in Charleston were becoming more visible and accepted through the 1970s and into the 1980s thanks to Spoleto and other changes. Coming back after years away, Gunter saw that the city was "less closeted and repressed at one extreme, and also less outrageous, more like that of any small city."

"During the Spoleto Festival the normal and considerable gay population swells with the influx of dancers, actors, and musicians, to say nothing of the male audience members who fancy them. Suddenly, during the two-week period, Charleston's gay life really springs to life." Gunter gave an obligatory nod to White Point Garden, "a gay cruising strip for decades" where "schoolboys, travelers and sailors can be seen on any evening strolling casually besides the bay...." He noted that no less than four gay bars were openly operating, one in particular tied specifically to Spoleto and Gian Carlo Menotti.[2]

Bars

While the exact date that LGBTQ-only, or predominately so, bars first opened in the city is not known (definitely by the early 1960s), there is one thing that is known: these safe zones fulfilled the same function churches did for African Americans, providing an escape from the prejudices and pressures of the predominant straight population. In bars, one could join peers, express oneself uninhibitedly, and share common beliefs. Just as the push for civil rights came out of African American churches, so the gay rights struggle emerged from bars like the Stonewall Inn, with the national groups like the Mattachine Society, Daughters of Bilitis, etc. paralleling the NAACP.

After the first 1899 reference to the male brothel on Wentworth Street, the next concrete reference dates to World War II at the Little Atlantic on Folly Beach, where gay activity was reported to authorities. Another Folly Beach hangout, where men could "mess around" in the dunes, known as the Tiltin' Hilton, became active by the 1960s. Charleston novelist Robert Molloy noted "a queer bar of sorts" across from the Charleston Hotel. That was the Hanover at 227 Meeting Street, which Josephine Pinckney seems to have used in a scene of a somewhat fey male character unsuccessfully trying to impress a very voluptuous woman in a bar called the Hangover in her 1946 novel *Three o'Clock Dinner*. Just a few blocks south was the Rathskeller on Courthouse Square. In the other direction, was the Y.M.C.A. on George Street. With rooms to rent for two or three bucks a night, complete with gyms and locker rooms, men cruised and indulged in sexual activity. Men could also be picked up at the Merchant Seaman's Club on East Bay Street, those in the know laughing at its name's double entendre. The Cove and the Elbow Cocktail Lounge were on East Bay, too. And apparently, which side of Calhoun Street a merchant marine favored walking home to the docks signaled if he wanted sex or not.[3]

Gay guides to bars and cruising sites, similar to Green Book travel guides used by African Americans to navigate friendly territory, appeared in 1964. But due to the fact that so many married men were gay, just about any public space could be a cruising scene, even the upscale and local favorite restaurant, Henry's.

Club 49, "The Gayest Spot in Town," where Jack Dobbins met his murderer, was still active in 1964, and the Anchor Bar at 101 Meeting Street where James Blake played piano, was too. More were clustered on Market Street: the Jewel Lounge at 104, the Rainbow Lounge at 102, and the Carriage House at 80. Listed as gay, it nevertheless advertised exotic dancers in tourist publications, suggesting that not all the sirens in feminine attire may have been women. Its claim of catering "to evry [sic] taste... to every mood ... of any and every moment" may be a clue.

336 King Street was the home of the Wagon Wheel, a dark place run by a "Goth" of a woman named Molly, who drove a Cadillac and walked with a limp. A White man entering it remembered a loud welcome from a Black drag queen. With new management, it morphed into Tucker's Tavern, it was briefly known as Cheeks, and finally Street Car, making it the site of a gay bar, mostly for men, but welcoming to women, for about 20 years (Whites and Blacks mixed easily, and most folks welcomed the few furtive Citadel cadets who

Figure 36. Carriage House matchbook cover.

darted in, promptly removing their uniform blouses.) Further south at 221 King, the New Yorker Tavern was listed as gay in the mid-sixties. In July 1965, a possibly gay-related murder took place there. The bartender separated two young men to no avail: 17-year-old Charles Kelly Bullock pulled a handgun and started shooting, sending patrons fleeing and leaving 18-year-old sailor Gary Richard Kock dead. While the press did not mention motive, at least one gay resident in town clipped the story.

On the southwest corner of King and Market Streets, the Ocean Bar and Grill beckoned, with another establishment called Pat's Lounge apparently accessed through it. A young college student drinking beer at the Grille, noted only men coming in. Leaving, he saw women. It was a transvestite bar, he realized: patrons entered in their street clothes and then changed. Behind Pat's on Market was the Bat Room, with a cracked cement dance floor, overrunning urinals, and quarter beer mandatory to purchase upon entering.[4]

In the 1970s, a new crop of bars popped up, including Basin Street South, at 16 Hayne Street. The Stardust Lounge, a few doors away, was run by a man dubbed "Nubs" for his amputated fingers. If you knocked but were a stranger, you might be told to kiss a man for proof you were qualified to be let in. Camelot, later the Lion's Head, entered through a brick archway at 81 Hasell Street, was two floors, and its management protected members in the military by locking up and hiding their papers. Nearby, a little person in glitter coveralls often presided at Club David, at 185 Market Street.

In the 1970s, the list expanded beyond bars. The Coffee Cup, open 24 hours a day, at the corner of Wentworth and Meeting streets, served all and welcomed those when bars closed. Immediately to the north, the Midnight Sun, later the Silver Dollar, became listed as a gay pickup spot, too.

Club Bacchus was listed in 1977 at 135 Calhoun. The Dolphin snack bar, on Wentworth between King and Meeting (the same area of the 1899 bordello) was, too, but it does not appear in city directories. In 1979, the Love Inn restaurant (another double-entendre?) was touted for after hour pickups off the peninsula, at 1668 Highway 171. And further away was the Virgo Social Club at 2052 Hampton Avenue, in North Charleston.[5]

In 1972, the Zebra Supper Club, north of the city limits at Mt. Pleasant Street, advertised dining, go-go boys, and "hunky" bartenders. Just a few years earlier, it had advertised for go-go girls. The owner, a "member of the Baptist faith," apparently felt no compunction in the LGBTQ tilt of his property; and there were those, avoiding bars, who rampantly recruited young boys for hanky panky in churches of various denominations.[6]

Many bars stayed open for a few years and then disappeared, some no doubt existing off the radar. The most acclaimed one of all, the King Street Garden & Gun Club, becoming the place for LGBTQ people to be seen, looms legendary and mythic in many a Charlestonian's memory.

On a sultry night in May 1978, people gathered in front of an empty JCPenney department store on King Street. Folks in jeans stared at those in black tie; jeweled ladies with swept-up hair looked askance at men with long hair and earrings. Few of those pouring in when the doors opened could have realized they were witnessing a tipping point in Charleston's social history. The opening of the disco ushered in a new democratic era in the city's diversity. Beforehand, blue bloods went to the Yacht Club; college kids went to noisy bars on George Street or the Merchant Seamans Club; African Americans, Navy base employees, and gay men and lesbians all favored spots where they felt welcome. Now the Garden & Gun Club had become the first place in Charleston where all could go, and where it might actually be considered cool to be queer.

The genius behind the place, the ringleader who'd mix all social classes of Charleston just as his handsome bartenders mixed drinks, was Richard N. "Dick" Robison. A native of South Bend, Indiana, he had been managing the box office at the Arena Stage in Washington, D.C. The Potomac had frozen two winters in a row, sending Robison south "in search of palm trees." His yacht entered Charleston harbor in March 1977. Seeing only palmettos, he stayed, having accepted the management of Spoleto's box office, nervous if there'd be a reaction to one of the very first earrings to be seen in a man's ear since pirates had walked the streets.

After working all day, and attending performances at night, Robison and the diva of Spoleto's first operatic production wanted to dance; the only disco nearby was dank and seedy. He looked around and saw world-class performers in dives, and that triggered the idea.

With $11,000 "burning a hole in my pocket," and access to the old department store building, where Charleston Place Hotel now stands, Robison had a place. He also had friends: volunteer carpenters were still hammering on the dance floor five minutes before the grand opening. Terry Fox, pressed into a service as bartender, got through the first few weeks, he says, with a drink-mixing guide in hand.

The plan was for the venue to remain open only during the Spoleto Festival, but it proved so popular that it stayed open for

Figure 37. Mr. & Ms. G&G Club
pageant contestants

Figure 38. Garden & Gun Club bar coupon

years. The space was large, airy, and untraditional in a tradition-bound city. Robison said the name came to him as way of welcoming all — the garden club set, the gun club set, men and women, elites and egalitarians, blue collar, and bluebloods, grand dames and drag queens. Nevertheless, rumors soon grew that the logo of one G upright next to another upside down suggested "69" of sexual activity. (And it's of no little irony that the name has been appropriated for a magazine catering to Southerners and others with large disposable incomes. Few turning the slick pages of *Garden & Gun* realize its debt to an Indiana gay man opening a place for all colors, creeds, classes, and identities.)

At 14,000 square feet, the club had a long bar, a dance floor, and a mezzanine. "At the Garden & Gun Club, differences were checked at the door," Maura Hogan remembered. "This is a mixed club," began the membership rules one had to sign; it was a pledge of allegiance to be respectful of differences. Membership grew to 4,000.

That large number, and the peaceful nature of just about every evening, suggested a new era dawning. And by the time it closed in a new location, due to a sudden pushback by a religious group, it was almost too late to matter. For in the words of cultural critic Hogan, "the ever joyous nightclub … dramatically altered Charleston's cultural and social landscape."

Another writer made comparisons to Camelot, stating, "It seemed that for one brief instant the city was deluded into believing that race, gender, social standing, religion, politics, sexual orientation, and money did not matter"—no small accomplishment in a city that had been as stratified as geological layers for 300 years. When posing the question how Spoleto and the 1970s transformed the city, *Post and Courier* columnist Edward Gilbreth wrote, "It was the sudden awareness of the gay community" that helped to clinch it. And as for what expressed the "spirit of the moment better than any other ... [t]he single best answer, of course, would be the Garden & Gun Club."

"It worked because of the members," Robison averred, "because they wanted it to work; the members of the club, gay and straight, White and Black, made it."

It was liberating, it was energizing, and it was about time: the social changes that had been rocking major metropolitan areas were finally being felt, like delayed and overdue aftershocks, in Charleston. At the Garden & Gun Club, it came with the disco's insistent beat, winding down each evening with its sign-off song, a tribute to the dance "the Charleston." Within its walls, many LGBTQ people found a sense of unity, empowerment, and self-respect, all necessary for a stronger, visible, and more vocal community. [7]

Invisible History

If the local LGBTQ community was literally becoming more visible, it was not just due to burgeoning opportunities to be seen in bars, on the Battery, at Spoleto functions, or the beach; but now photography of the community by the community was coming of age, too. Before the 1970s, while images of individual gay men and lesbians existed, publicly displayed images were rare. This was not due to a lack of pride but due to well-founded fears that such graphic evidence could be used for blackmail. So pictorial evidence of Charleston gay life is rare in these years, much rarer, in fact, than photos of African Americans, whom had been subjects of photographers since the invention of the medium in the mid-19th century.

Figure 39. Early 1950s drag photo

Figure 40. Gay men at a private party, ca. 1960

One of the earliest to document the local queer community was Greg Day. Born in Alabama in 1944, Day came to the Lowcountry as a graduate student in anthropology to study the Gullah basket-making community, where he learned of its acceptance of same-sex attraction and the drag queen Shake-a-Plenty. "The basket makers taught me a process of integrating art into every aspect of life," he reflected. Moving to New York in 1975, he put that philosophy to work documenting the "burgeoning queer art community." His photography of gender-bending "gutter art" and street performer Stephen Venable was acclaimed for its importance when Venable was rediscovered in the 21st century. Meanwhile, in 1976, Day returned to Charleston to continue his work on his PhD, while also using his "keen eye for documenting ephemeral culture as it flourished" on the local gay scene.

Day became director of the Folk Art Media Project at the Charleston Communications Center, while also taking pictures of his lover Leonard Robinson dancing in decaying buildings and on rooftops on his own time. But he focused mostly on one of the most out and outrageous figures in the local gay community: Bryan Alston Seabrook, known as Africa Brooks.

Day took images of Seabrook at Charleston's most iconic gay spot, White Point Garden at the Battery, which appeared on the covers of *Southern Exposure* and *RFD* magazines. This gave locals the first glimpse of themselves or members of their community lionized in publications that went beyond the Lowcountry. Day also used the newly developed medium of home video. The aim of the Communications Center was to enable citizens to document local folk cultural communities; in his words, "some [men and women] formed the … Gay video team to document drag performances at Charleston's Garden & Gun Club." And the flickering black-and-white images that exist, thanks to him, afford a view of ephemeral and exultant performances that otherwise would have been lost.

Day worked for civil rights, and Seabrook/Africa intrigued him. Being Black, gay, and one of the most visible members of the LGBTQ community, Seabrook had become an activist by default, facing down prejudice, including that directed at African Americans by White drag queens. Day remembered how, facing a hostile crowd, "Miss Africa, aged 19, ignored them all and gave a stellar performance as Glenda the Good Witch in *The Wizard of Oz*. His mother, who made his dresses, was present as were many fans. His performance brought the audience, both Black and White, to their feet screaming. Africa won the title [of Miss Gay Charleston in 1978, the first African American to do so] and the city that had once championed slavery and started the Civil War was forever changed," Day believed. That Day filmed it, and the films exist, marks another turning point in Charleston's LGBTQ history.

Figure 41. Greg Day's photo of Bryan Seabrook as Africa

"The Miss Gay Charleston Pageant was an annual event that drew contestants from South Carolina, Georgia, and other places. It was their 20th anniversary the year Africa won," Day recalled, adding, "That year the audience voted for the winner. ... Sometime after 1979 Africa departed Charleston for Atlanta, where she performed on a red velvet swing at the Sweet Gum Head, a club frequented by young straight and gay couples."

Seabrook also caught the eye of Charleston artist and filmmaker David Boatwright. With an NEA grant to document local gospel music, Boatwright caught Seabrook and some of his friends hanging out and clowning around on Meeting Street for his small vignette of a film, *Charleston*, some of the earliest moving pictures known of gay Charleston.

Literally personifying the subject of Black and gay prejudice, Seabrook continued to defy each, gaining not just respect but credit, screen credit, in what may be one of the best films to come from Charleston, *The Corndog Man*, released in 1999.

Robin Shuler, who moved to Charleston from Florence, South Carolina after visiting the Garden & Gun Club in high school, was involved in the production, as was her husband Gil, who knew many of the creative team. The script called for a drag queen, and Shuler, knowing Africa as one of her "family" at the Garden & Gun Club, tracked her down at the Brooks Motel on Morris Street, one of the few hotels for African Americans in the once segregated city, and moved him into her home for the duration of the shoot. Shuler's casting of an African American and Africa's performance have made *The Corndog Man*, never widely released, into a powerful piece of art. Racism and homophobia — twin demons which have menaced the Lowcountry for years, and which still haunt — dominate the film. Bryan Seabrook, born in 1958, died in 2004, leaving many powerful images behind him.[8]

Chapter Eighteen
"An Obligation to Be Proud:" The Eighties

While founded in 1670, Charleston waited until 1732 for a regular newspaper, providing local news, worldviews, and a sense of being bound up in common destiny. African Americans found their voice in Reconstruction and in later papers, including *The Chronicle*, which started publishing in 1971. The Charleston Gay Task Force is said to have produced a few publications called *The Task Force* in the mid-1970s, but no copies have been located. It was not until 1981 that the LGBTQ community got its own news source.

Its founder, like many other agents of change, was not a native. George Holt's father was in the Navy, his mother Spanish. He was born in Madrid; the Navy brought the Holts to the Lowcountry when he was 15. At 17 he entered a gay bar, "astonished" and "blown away" at what he saw. He attended the College of Charleston and left for Chicago. Upon his return to town, he went through a "starving artist" phase, before finding his métier as a distinguished non-traditional builder focusing on craftsmanship and aesthetics on a small livable scale.

In Chicago, Holt had discovered national and local gay publications and thought Charleston could benefit from something similar; he gathered a few friends, drew a picture of Drayton Hall for the cover, and launched *Gay Charleston* in February 1981. Seeking counsel, Holt telephoned Armistead Maupin. The well-known author's advice was to get the paper typeset, crucial for its look. This is exactly what Holt did, incurring the paper's major expense. The fledging paper, first

Figure 42. The second issue of *Gay Charleston*

distributed for free, and later sold for 50 cents, called itself a statewide journal and a "magazine of the southern gay celebration." While it lasted for over a year (with no complete run known to survive), LGBTQ Charlestonians no longer had to rely on publications from large cities, or the local paper with its condemnation of "homos" and "queers."

"Charleston is a proud city" began an unsigned letter in the inaugural issue. "I feel however, that the community of gay people, cannot be so characterized. ... it does not yet possess that concept of 'we' which ... is important ... for a healthy community."

"Gay people form a unique minority," the anonymous author (possibly Holt himself) continued, a minority "which transcends all traditional social boundries [sic] — ethnic, political, religious, class, so on and so on." The newspaper was seen as "a first step to a more hopeful future."

"Among the individuals each of us knows personally in the gay community, most are reasonably successful in their respective fields. This is an extremely important point — that we are an elemental part of the Charleston area. In a sense, we have an obligation to be proud, since we contribute so much. Yet since we hide in the shadows, whom do we celebrate and identify with? Who are our achievers — in the professions we respect, in business, politics, and the military? Where are our artists — poets, writers, and musicians to describe our experience?"

These questions were not rhetorical — and they would be answered in the coming years. Gay realtors would be the first to organize and advertise; Linda Ketner, Charlie Smith, and others would run for political office; Holt himself would become a leader in his new field. Visual artist William van Hettinga would edit *Poor William's Omnibus*, an eclectic arts paper, and his designs would stamp businesses around town; the piano duo Delphin and Romaine would be artists in residence at the College of Charleston. In 1992 writer Blanche Boyd would win a Lambda Literary Award for best lesbian novel, *The Revolution of Little Girls*, and I would win for best gay male novel, *What the Dead Remember*, both with Charleston settings. In the next generation, Joel Derfner would gain fame for his books *Gay Haiku*, *Swish: My Quest to Become the Gayest Person Ever*, and *Lawfully Wedded Husband: How My Gay Marriage Will Save the American Family*; he'd wed legally, the ceremony broadcast on a cable television series in 2010, and work as a composer. Other successes were coming.[1]

Sons of the City

As the first gay publication appeared around town, a gay male African American couple was in the public eye. "Pianists Wilfred Delphin and Alfred Romain, named artists in residence at the College of Charleston in 1979, began their partnership in 1968 as students at Xavier University in New Orleans. Upon graduation both went on to earn master's degrees from Southern Illinois University, and doctorates from the University of Southern Mississippi."

"The duo made its professional debut in 1977 as soloists with the Symphony of the New World in New York's Carnegie Hall. Since then, they have appeared as guest artists with some of America's finest orchestras. ... Each season, Delphin and Romain tour extensively throughout the United States and abroad." They lived together, toured together, appeared on stage together, and in 1987, in a program narrated by Ted Stern, the men were adopted together as "True Sons of the City." The format included a special *This is Your Life* tribute where their stories were told and details shared, except perhaps the most important one of all, the fact of their loving relationship. Had they come out publicly as not just piano partners, as many in the city knew them to be, it's possible they would have never succeeded in their musical careers.

Sadly, in 1995, no longer living in Charleston, Romain died from complications of AIDS. Local and other obituaries spoke of renal failure. In 2016, Delphin received a Lifetime Achievement Award "for his meaningful contributions to the field of the performing arts," especially for students at his alma mater, Xavier University. "Noting a 'separation in audiences,' Delphin now feels a duty to help other artists, minority artists, in particular," a journalist wrote then, continuing that "Delphin laments at the lack of recognition some minorities receive when he feels their talent is worthy of more recognition," a remark that can be construed to apply to not just African American musicians, but LGBTQ ones as well — perhaps a nod and acknowledgment of the real story of Delphin and Romain.[2]

Figure 43. Delphin and Romain

The opening words of *Gay Charleston* were not just prophetic, but truly revolutionary. Despite the temperate tone, for the first time in a public forum, "gay" (the umbrella term for LGBTQ at the time) and "pride" were linked, and once the concept was abroad in the humid Lowcountry air, there was no turning back. The author urged the formation of organizations to sponsor events so diverse voices could be heard, and people could forge a community. "[A]ll the bars are private clubs," the writer noted, and not sufficient for people's needs. Lest the skittish fear, however, the author assured readers that there was no "need to envision parades down Broad [Street] ... or outlandish demonstrations on the Battery." (These too would come with time.) "We are not going to achieve ... a San Francisco, a New York, not even an Atlanta," he wrote. Yet a "group ethic ... would provide a better climate for people in Charleston."

Figure 44. Advertisement for the Streetcar bar

"We are a people. We have a history. And we most definitely have a future," Scott Doonan declared in issue number two.

A College of Charleston student disagreed, disgusted at a flier for *Gay Charleston* found on a table in Maybank Hall. In a letter to the editor he wrote, "You should not bring your gay shit and put it out at a school. Keep it away from normal people. ... I know about certain places that homosexuals go to, which is all right with me, but do not leave your materials on school ground [sic] to contaminate everybody with."

There were now, according to *Gay Charleston*, at least four of those "certain" places where LGBTQ people could go, including:

"Franny's [sic] 11 Fulton Street (formerly Judy's). Mostly women. Mostly gay. Pool tables; entrance at top of steps. Only Lesbian bar in Charleston—casual—look for 'Shari's Lounge' sign. All types, all ages." The King Street Garden & Gun Club had become so popular by then that the reviewer called it "very mixed and mostly straight," a charge refuted in a later issue. Then there was "Les Jardins—private club 36 Market.

Men 70%, women 30%. Very few straight. Not disco. [Which it was.] All types all ages, jeans to suits." It was run by Richard Little, who wanted to give gay men and lesbians a more private place to congregate away from the glare of the Gun Club. And finally, there was "Streetcar—public bar 336 King. Mostly men, mostly gay, never a cover, beer and wine only. All types. Cruise bar. Jukebox. All ages. 18 up in all."

Local news coverage included the story of the gay-friendly vintage clothing shop Grocery Store Chorus Girls closing. Advice was given if arrested for buggery: call the American Civil Liberties Union. The question was asked if women could be arrested, too. A cheerleading letter was contributed by Bryan Seabrook, aka Africa, the city's reigning drag queen.

To spread the message even further, *Gay Charleston's* founders took to the airwaves. A gay friend invited Holt for an interview, and he and Joanne Seraphin agreed, assuming a sympathetic ear on *Open Mike*, a call-in show on WQSN radio Friday evening, March 6, 1982.

The radio host turned unexpectedly hostile and "consistently attempted to equate homosexuality with ... child molestation, murder and rape." Holt and Seraphin countered, and a gay caller fought back, too. Yet the host went on blustering against lesbians leading the fight for equal rights for housewives and other "normal" women, demonstrating how to many gay rights and women's rights were linked.[3]

Gay Rights and Women's Rights

Back in 1975, attorney Conni Ackerman (soon to come out herself) had chided *The News and Courier* for its editorial attacking the National Organization for Women (NOW) for going too far. "The implication," Ackerman wrote, "that lesbians are not 'normal, respectable women' is one that NOW strongly disagrees

> with. Our position on lesbianism is that people should not be discriminated against on the basis of their sexual preferences ... any more than people should be discriminated against because of their race, color, religion or sex."
>
> *Gay Charleston* gave great space covering the activities of the local chapter of NOW. As the two civil rights movements matured over the years, there were some rough spots, especially in 1997 when the Center for Women demanded the removal of the word "lesbian" from one of the groups it hosted, to avoid alienating funders. The questions Ackerman asked still held true: "Why are you so afraid to allow homosexuals the same freedom from legal discrimination and personal harassment that we promote for all other groups?"[4]

Discrimination was what Holt and Seraphin were countering on the radio, so enflaming their audience that Holt received threats after his appearance. Yet he and his volunteer staff soldiered on. Charleston Police Chief Reuben Greenberg, when queried about harassment of gay men at the Battery, replied that he had no issue with men and women holding hands and kissing, but suggested those cruising favor the more public, water side of the park, and not disturb those living along the street. This was quite different from the views expressed by police in the local paper's 1965 series.

Good news continued. Two women announced they were getting married (certainly not legal), and right on cue, George Exoo, a minister at the Unitarian Church, began performing same-sex weddings in Georgia and South Carolina, while Stan Harris, pastor of Metropolitan Community Church (MCC), was doing the same locally. Nineteenth-century gay advocate James Mills Peirce had occupied the pulpit at the Archdale Street church just before the Civil War, and now some 120 years later, Exoo was in charge. His congregation, with its full-page ad in *Gay Charleston* inviting LGBTQ attendance, became the first welcoming and affirming congregation in town before the term took on its current meaning.

Born in Ohio in 1942, Exoo, a graduate of Emerson College and Harvard Divinity School, with a doctorate in music history from the University of California, Berkeley, arrived in town in 1977. Now, as reported in *Gay Charleston*, he was holding "rap sessions" at the bar Les Jardins to "provide another opportunity for our scattered community to come together...." He also opened the Unitarian Church's Gage Hall to LGBTQ groups.

In June 1982, Exoo announced the launch of "a new group for gay men and women involved in business or professional work to be called Metropolitan Professional Organization ... to lend support to gay interests, foster community awareness and encourage social interactions." While it had other aims, it was primarily for networking and non-bar social meetings.[5]

By then, Lambda of Charleston, founded in February 1981, was also functioning as a "supportive network of gay men and women" offering, "[t]houghtful conservation [sic], socials, education, [and] counseling." The twice a month meetings, coordinated by a young man named Chris Dhose, attracted an average of 10 to 15 men and women.

The founding and flourishing of these groups began to answer the call voiced in *Gay Charleston*'s first issue for new, non-bar outlets and activities: there were covered dish socials, discussions, and religious gatherings in people's homes, in bars, Gage Hall, and often at Jackie's Café Espresso on Pinckney Street.

The Unicorn, a new and short-lived women's bar, opened for business on Wentworth Street; men could accompany women, and its management hosted a gay and lesbian pride week in 1983, the same year a gay pride picnic was sponsored by the MCC. A congregation had been established locally after Fred Williams, the MCC minister from Columbia, had come down to speak to locals to gauge interest. Almost immediately afterwards, in July 1981, an MCC congregation was launched. Pastor Stan Harris, a native Australian, began holding services in Club Tango on Society Street. "Most people don't know we're here because we keep it pretty quiet," Harris commented. "We avoid the political, because that's not where the Charleston people are at," he said. "The other churches pretend that we're not really here, but when someone in their church has a [gay related] problem, they send him or her to us."[6]

Two new organizations led by George Exoo, The University Club and E None of the Above, both primarily social groups consisting of university educated professionals, appeared.

It's impossible to determine if *Gay Charleston* by its presence was calling these new groups into being, or if it was just the vehicle publicizing them. With so much going on, a social calendar appeared, and Holt and his team exhausted themselves keeping up with reporting. There were repeated calls for volunteers to keep the paper with an estimated audience of 3,600 functioning.

The paper's demise came when the management of Les Jardins found *Gay Charleston* a little too gay for its lobby, a further example of social standards trumping activism. With the loss of sales there, the newsletter folded.

But, proving just how much the community had been galvanized with new ideas and attitudes, and attesting to its value, the paper was resurrected almost immediately, under a new name, *The Charleston Alternative,* proving, too, the power of language, "Alternative [now] including gay men, lesbians, bisexuals, transvestites, transsexuals, and people who are undecided."

Its founder, Barry Kohn, and his wife, Alice Matusow, had hosted a fundraiser for *Gay Charleston* at their Sullivan's Island home, and now he was taking it on. Newly arrived from Philadelphia, Kohn, Matusow, and mutual friend Cheryl Keats had gained

Figure 45. Cover of *The Charleston Alternative*

national attention on the *Phil Donahue Show*, the pre-eminent television talk show of the day, discussing the book *Barry and Alice: Portrait of a Bisexual Marriage*, in 1980. Having crisscrossed the country, the "'normal' couple with a very unusual marriage" talked about their open relationship, and attorney Kohn, a charismatic man with a head of curls and a deep commitment to social change and sexual experimentation, had become a local spokesman for LGBTQ rights, chafing under the restraints of conservative Charleston.[7]

"I know the South is about ten years behind the North," he editorialized, focusing on the psychological damage of the closet, lamenting "the toll ... these secrets exact in our daily lives." Being out in the city was "like being on a desert island with a few close friends around the issue of gay activism. ... I suggested to my activist friends that we approach the mayor, asking him to declare Gay Pride Week in Charleston. Everyone just laughed at me."

"He has been many things to many people, all in the name of elevated awareness," a journalist wrote of him. Kohn saw,

Figure 46. Masthead of Barry Kohn's column in *The Charleston Alternative*

as Holt had, the similarities between LGBTQ people and other minorities: "Blacks and women felt the same [reluctance] about asking for their rights," Kohn reported, but now those groups were outdistancing the LGBTQ community.

Another newcomer to town, the journalist J. Edward Parham who wrote of Kohn, was shocked at the local acceptance of segregation; he had been taken to a local "key club" that issued keys only to Whites even though the restaurant was in a Black neighborhood. Whites and elites were in charge in Charleston, he was told. "They can do whatever they want here."

"For gays, the attitude leans more towards tolerance than acceptance," Parham reported. "The more identifiable you are as a gay, the more trouble you are likely to have here. ... Charlestonians prefer to look the other way and ignore what they do not want to know. It is not a subject for polite conversation among the proper below Broad [Street] set. The opinion is largely that if you are gay, then fine, as long as you do it quietly, without calling any attention to it whatsoever." Employing a powerful simile, Parham wrote that, "While much of the country is heard letting out squeals of sexual self-esteem, gay Charlestonians are rather like rowdy teenagers, hushed by the imposing finger of an ancient librarian." In the January 1983 newsletter, in "ON THE OTHER HAND—A WOMYN'S TURN," the anonymous author estimated that although there were at least 2,000 lesbians in the city, four bars, and two homophile organizations, too many were still paralyzed by fear or apathy.

Change may have come, but not enough for the likes of Holt, Kohn, and Parham, outsiders all. MCC was meeting in a bar with less than 20 attending; LGBTQ Charleston remained a backwater, lagging behind other parts of the country. Locals did not feel the same urgency as newcomers. Parham quoted a "42-year-old merchant, who has frequented Charleston bars for the last 20 years and a lifelong resident." He was happy with the status quo, saying, "'To me, it's a very liberal city by virtue of its interest in the arts. I haven't found that my being gay here has barred me from anything. This is a great environment for gays, and it's an exciting small city.'"[8]

But many found Charleston much too conservative. That was the reason, Kohn believed, it was chosen by the American Association for Personal Privacy as the site of its semi-annual conference in November 1982. With a mission to reform all laws restricting sexual conduct between consenting adults, the group had come "because South Carolina still has a sodomy statute which makes it a felony to have sexual relations with someone of the same sex. ..." Anxious for more dramatic changes, Kohn did see reasons to hope.

A Lambda oyster roast event drew 80 attendees, and over 50 came to a cookout Kohn hosted. But just then, he reported on something whose impact no one could yet guess. In January 1983, Kohn passed along a tidbit gleaned about an odd new gay cancer. The same issue also carried an advertisement for sessions he was leading on sex between men, intimacy, trust, toys, anal sex, and S and M. The next month, an article naming AIDS and its "seven deadly symptoms" appeared. There were three confirmed cases in South Carolina, with as many as eight suspected. Tom Lamme, a transplant with a view from the bars where he worked, saw infection spreading from those who partied in Atlanta and New York City.

The community responded, hosting AIDS and herpes discussions. A fundraiser was held at Streetcar in June. Rumor soon had it that six people had died in Charleston, and more people were being diagnosed. Almost immediately after, *The Charleston Alternative* ceased publishing.[9]

People began to fear. AIDS cases grew to 21 in the state in 30 months, and by 1986, Charleston County accounted for 20 of the 71 cases in South Carolina. Alarmingly, 92 of 412 of bisexual and gay men tested in the county health department proved positive for HIV. All too soon, Kohn became news himself. A 1987 issue of *Newsweek* on "The Face of AIDS" included his photo, noting his death from the disease.

With the *Alternative* gone, the community had only *The News and Courier* to cover LGBTQ and AIDS issues. "The local media have certainly done nothing to advance, or even acknowledge, the considerable gay population," was Parham's critique. "When the subject does appear in local papers, it is either an Associated Press wire story about gays elsewhere or the object of attack." On August 30, 1983, it published syndicated columnist Jeffrey Hart's article "Homophobia," which he seemed to endorse. He informed his readers that an active gay man would average 1,600 partners in his lifetime, noting, as Apostle Helen Smith had, that, "it is not unusual for a homosexual to have a dozen sexual encounters in the course of an evening." Frank Gilbreth, who had once laughed at Gertrude Stein laughing at him, wrote that if once people felt "what homosexuals do to each other is none of our business" that was no longer the case. For "anything that destroys public morals is our business. And now that AIDS is a serious epidemic, the matter is not only our business but a matter of vital concern."[10]

The LGBTQ community now had two battles to confront: one against a devastating disease, and the other against the backlash of homophobia rising.

Chapter Nineteen
HIV and AIDS

By March 1985, 28 HIV cases had been diagnosed in South Carolina, with 14 deaths. Dr. Robert Ball, an infectious disease physician, may have encountered the first patient in the state some three years earlier, a fellow who "was so weak that he couldn't lift his head off a pillow ... [and] had to be helped to clean the saliva from his mouth." Ball disagreed with statistics seeming to suggest Charleston's rate of disease was below the national average, saying instead, "I think we are dealing with under-reporting. ... My impression is that Charleston is actually on par with the rest of the nation." He theorized that "Charleston's rate is higher than the rest of the state for two reasons. First, Charleston has more gay people than most other cities in the state. Second, the Medical University serves as a referral center (and therefore reporting place for patients from other state regions)."

The Medical University of South Carolina (MUSC) would reflect both the best and worst of the response to the epidemic, repeating and repudiating some of its troubled history. Founded in 1824, it had deliberately relied solely on Black bodies for anatomical dissections and advertised itself as a place peculiarly adept at teaching about Negro diseases, a skill doctors needed to keep slaves working. Its dental school discriminated against Jews in the mid-1950s; in the 1960s, a White patriarchal system denied equal pay for Black women nursing assistants. While outright racial discrimination had eased by the 1980s, those LGBTQ could encounter prejudice, misunderstanding, and lack of sensitivity among some staff and physicians at MUSC—as well as other local hospitals.

Medical students had to sit through lectures from professors who spoke of gay men inserting gerbils up their rectums. One student was picked on by a professor for treating an AIDS patient at the Charleston County Hospital kindly; staff there "in particular were pretty brutal to people who tested positive. It was a pretty hideous thing to walk in and see someone in a hallway, or all the identifying information outside of their room that they had had AIDS."[1]

When Richard Little, proprietor of the gay bar Les Jardins, decided to enter medical school, he was roundly rejected for his out identity and his association with the bar and the community. He attended the new rival medical school begun in Columbia, South Carolina instead, and was elected national president of the American Medical Student Association. In a distinguished career at the National Institute of Health, Little became an AIDS/cancer specialist, encountering men who had once danced in his club now coming to him for help.

But there were many physicians and researchers at MUSC who were early pioneers against the disease. "In 1984, the same year that scientists discovered the virus that caused HIV/AIDS, MUSC was one of six institutions in the world chosen to do a pilot experiment that tested a therapy to prevent pre-AIDS from progressing to AIDS," reports Kymberly Mattern in her thesis on the history of LGBTQ sites in the city. "Dr. H. Hugh Fudenberg and Dr. Kwong Tsang were two of the key leaders in this HIV/AIDS research." The next year, "MUSC used 100 gay and bisexual male volunteers to research early detection and treatment of AIDS. ... Dr. Mariano F. LaVia, Professor of Laboratory Medicine ... was heavily involved with this research," which helped develop, "a treatment for HIV/AIDS patients before protease inhibitors became widely available."

Mattern continues: "In 1988, Dr. Peter J. Fischinger, who was the former director of the National AIDS Program Office in Washington D.C., accepted the position as Vice President of

Research at MUSC. ... Under Dr. Fischinger's direction, MUSC held a health fair about AIDS and other illnesses at the [historically Black] Cannon Street Y.M.C.A. in 1988. A panel discussion, 'AIDS in the Black Community,' answered questions ... and disproved myths about AIDS. In 1989, MUSC also hosted an HIV/AIDS outreach and educational event [as] ... a response to a lack of a national strategy to AIDS prevention and treatment."

This was the era of President Ronald Reagan not mentioning the word AIDS, and George Bush not allocating sufficient funds to fight the disease. Closer to home, South Carolina US Senator Strom Thurmond (who, after his death, was outed for his sexual improprieties, impregnating an African American servant in his family and keeping their daughter a secret), stood by coldly as Michael Boyle, a key African American member of his staff, came out as gay and HIV positive. In 1963, Thurmond had tried to discredit the March on Washington for African American Civil Rights by outing its gay leader, Bayard Rustin. His homophobic and racist maneuver did not work, however, and every year until he died, Rustin sent Thurmond a red rose on the anniversary of the march to remind him of it. Boyle maintained his loyalty to Thurmond. But all the Senator did was attend his staffer's funeral, never changing any of his anti-gay votes or policies. Upstate US Congressman Bob Inglis was even more pointed, saying people with AIDS deserved it. "I have no tolerance for gays and lesbians," he said. "I do not represent you."

While the nation fumbled, states had to come up with their own policies. Locally, Dr. Robert Ball, in many people's opinion, became the hero (and the victim) of the AIDS epidemic in the medical community. "Those of us who have been working with projects ... have been very frustrated indeed with the poor response of the Charleston community," he said in an October 1985 interview. "Unfortunately, the straight community has looked upon AIDS with blindness... and has done very little in the work of overall research. I would like to say to the gay community that unless gays start internally policing themselves, we are going to see a tremendous backlash."

He was right, probably never realizing that he'd become a victim of the backlash aimed at those he was treating. "I became a pariah," he recalled years later. "For the first time I learned discrimination and prejudice to a high degree. At least a third, maybe up to a half, of my patients left because they didn't want to be in the same waiting room as 'those people.'"

"One local hospital—unnamed—refused to admit patients for a while because of the fear among medical staff. Parents were abandoning their gay children and not paying medical bills and they were going broke and suffering. That was '83, '84, '85. By '85 I was 'the AIDS doctor,' although a few other infectious disease doctors were also seeing a few other patients here and there, but I was sort of the hit man and struggling.

"... Two items ... were my coup de grace: my two on-call partners, older internists, refused to see my patients and take call with me because they didn't understand the lifestyle; they disagreed with it.... [In]1987. ... I ended up being on call all the time, 24/7, working 100-plus hours a week and barely earning a living."

At 42, unable to support himself practicing medicine, Ball moved to Columbia to earn a master's in public health at USC, which led to employment at the South Carolina Department of Health and Environmental Control (DHEC). In 1990, he led the team that came up with a statewide plan to counter AIDS, helping DHEC win federal funding the next year under the Ryan White Act to put into action South Carolina's response to the disease.

If a straight, White, church-attending, seventh-generation physician of impeccable pedigree could face such discrimination for his mere association with people with AIDS, one can imagine what those with the disease were facing. *Post and Courier* Columnist Frank Gilbreth sounded serious in 1992 when he wrote that people with AIDS should be tattooed. He suggested that maybe they should only "be tattooed in the vicinity of their sexual organs. No one but the sufferer himself would be able to see this, except his or her doctor, and — here's the important thing! — a prospective sex mate."

Ideas like his stoked panic and fear. When a chocolate shop on King Street hosted an AIDS fundraising event, the owners had to cover the windows to protect sympathetic donors from being seen, fearing they would be ostracized for merely wanting to help. Similarly, some longtime customers stopped frequenting the popular, gay-run restaurant, the Hungry Lion, on George Street.[2]

In the LGBTQ community, two ministers heeded Ball's call for self-policing. Reverend James Martin of MCC warned against anonymous sex in restrooms, adult bookstores, and the Battery, which locals had protested for years. Bathrooms were locked at White Point Garden in 1975, and the World War II era bandstand in Marion Square, with its lavatories, was torn down entirely. But it was a rest area on Interstate 26 that concerned George Exoo, then chairman of the South Carolina Christian Action Council's AIDS Response team. At least 2,000 sexual "incidents of hanky-panky" occurred monthly, he said, at the rest area near Ladson. One frequenter reported visiting rest stops for years and contracting AIDS, yet refusing help, not identifying as gay, since he had a wife and children. Ball likened this type of sex to fast food, and Dr. Mariano LaVia agreed, calling for HIV posters and condoms in rest areas. Republican Governor Carroll Campbell refused, fearing it would "appear to condone illicit sexual activity," calling instead for police. "If they engage in arresting and entrapments, then we're going back to the Middle Ages," Exoo replied, noting it would drive activity further underground, assisting spread of the disease.

(Years after he left the area, Exoo traveled to Ireland to assist a woman without a terminal diagnosis end her life, garnering international attention. By his death in 2015, he claimed to have helped over 100 people with suicide, the focus of the documentary *Reverend Death*. The unsettling film omits his AIDS work, with no mention of his attempt to keep people from dying before their time.)

In Exoo's absence, the state continued to blame victims, and deaths mounted. Barry Kohn had been dead since 1987. Two years later the city lost William van Hettinga, who left his imprint in his fish prints and artistic logos for businesses around town. His *Poor William's Omnibus*, if not a gay paper per se, was nevertheless stamped with a camp, carefree sensibility; van Hettinga also printed many of Elizabeth O'Neill Verner's etchings, creating new imagery while perpetuating iconic ones. Even in death, some were victims of homophobia. The local paper's editorial policy often balked at including the names of surviving partners, only printing names of relatives who sometimes had disdained and disowned the dying.[3]

The epidemic was widespread and devastating to, the African American community, historically underserved in health care and public spending. Jenny Turner, a White lesbian social worker, got a phone call at work one day from a doctor. "She said, 'Look, the head of PALSS [Palmetto AIDS Life Support Services] called me and said, 'No one here in town wants this baby. ... He was born with AIDS. His parents have AIDS. "None of the adoptive families used by the Department

Figure 47. William van Hettinga

Figure 48. Cory Jerome Glover

of Social Services would take him, and nobody in the AIDS Supportive Services would take him because they were afraid ... of this disease, that their children could play, or they could be bitten by this child, all kinds of things. I said, 'That's crazy.' She said, 'Well, call me back. Let me know.' I called her back within the hour and said, 'Yeah, we'll take him.' I became a mother like that."

In the state of South Carolina, it was then illegal for gays or lesbians to foster children, but because Turner and her partner were known to the social services network, and because there was no other option, the system suspended its prejudices and the boy went home with them.

"We went to the shelter, and the lady pretty much said, 'Here, here's your baby, and by the way, this box full of medicine goes with it.' I thought, 'Oh my God, how are we going to do this?' .... That first night we ended up in ... the NICU [neonatal intensive care unit] because he had pneumonia. ... Every few weeks or so, we would end up at the NICU with him."

But against all odds, the little boy thrived. "Cory was a delightful child. He was a happy boy. We can only assume what happened ... that probably he had been left in a back room in a crib or something because he didn't know how to walk or talk. ..."

"I carried, back then, two beepers, one for work, and one for Cory. I'd get a call, and I'd have to leave work, and they understood. There are a lot of happy memories, and of course, many of those calls meant I had to take him or we had to take him to the doctor or to the hospital. What he couldn't say he could sign to a limited degree. He started to speak, and he started choking one day. I realized he wasn't choking; he was learning to laugh. That was very good. He learned to laugh with us. He learned to walk with us. ... He was a happy boy. God knows, we had medicine going into him in any form of ice cream, cookie, whatever he would take. Sometimes it would come right back out."

Cory made friends and was part of a family. One summer day he was in the hospital. "I was just talking to him, and then I realized something was wrong, and I went to the nurse. ... She came in, and she said, 'Do you want to hold him?' ... He was dying in my arms. I held him during that time for about 45 minutes, and I talked to him as he passed on from this world. So glad I was able to do that. That was a precious time. I feel like that was a gift for me. ... We had DSS contact the family, and ... had the funeral for him. They took care of that, which was also a blessing. The family had nothing. The grandmother wanted to do things, but she didn't even have a telephone. She did acknowledge Cory, and we had the viewing at the funeral home, and the burial. I was allowed to come up front with the family there. I had quite a hard time between anger and loss. ... It was hard. It was just hard."

Cory had not quite reached his third birthday. It took years but Turner made sure he was remembered, his brief life recalled by a tombstone above the tiny grave in Monrovia Cemetery.

Like Turner, Mark Gray had moved to Charleston from elsewhere and had initially been taken by the place's charm. "I just thought, well, there's something about this town, and the spirit of this town. ... I could see young gay men flitting and flirting around King Street, going to bars ... Nobody bothered them. In the many years that I've lived here, I've never heard of anybody getting hurt." In his chocolate shop, he and the others in his group of friends fascinated young gay adolescents such as future author Joel Derfner and Tom Myers, whose father would establish a gay youth organization, We Are Family. In search of models and mentors, the youths were taken with Gray and his coterie, living out and having fun while being professionals.

Seeing so many unmet needs as the disease spread, Gray and other gay men left light-hearted pursuits behind them. He, Peter Milecewz, Michael McLaughlin, Tom Lamme, and Don Watson came together to discuss what needed to be done. There was "a lot of fire, a lot of urgency, a lot of willingness to help, a lot of, 'I don't give a damn, we're going to take care of these people.' We had to do what we had to do, and we did it. Sitting with people who were dying, trying to reason and help families get through it, educating ourselves, educating other people ... you've got Gay Men's Health [Gay Men's Health Crisis] up there in New York. We're starving for information down here, because we're in the South and all this bullshit that you have to put up ... with religion and segregation."

They founded an organization they called Helping Hands, which did a little bit of everything: "Advocating, getting people to [doctors] — we would just network it, calling each other. This was way before the Internet. We were phone calling each other. ... And a lot of times we met over on the Isle of Palms. ... about six o'clock, and we might get a mass of people anywhere between fifty to one hundred people. At that time, Susan Pearlstine ... was living in San Francisco ... So, she saw firsthand what was going on .... She came back to Charleston, and ... she was a great firebrand ... quick to get the movement going, and ... in a very silent way of donating money. ... Helping might mean paying a hospital bill, helping might mean to pay for a funeral. That's just what you did. And eventually, Helping Hands went into an organization known as PALSS, Palmetto AIDS Life Support Services."

Under the directorship of Bill Edens in Columbia, the agency was coordinating a response around the state, training volunteers to be "buddies" to help those with AIDS with shopping, medicine, transportation, and companionship.

Locally, the response to the crisis was so pronounced with the amount of money raised, that many thought funds raised in Charleston should stay in the Lowcountry and not go to Columbia. Joe Hall (1958–2020), who spent part of his high school years upstate, and who was then working in Charleston in substance abuse counseling, was hired at a nominal sum to coordinate services in the Lowcountry.

It was a natural fit with Hall's skillset, but the fact that he was gay — and out — was seen as problematic due to stereotypes promulgated by local and national media, suggesting that gay men were irresponsible, and if they were responsible for anything at all, it was only for spreading the virus. Even among friends, supporters, and allies, Hall perceived "a general distrust of an organization whose public profile was a gay man."

Confounding the issue further was the fact that "nothing like the AIDS epidemic had ever brought into focus and into such sharp relief all the different social issues and prejudices and forward thinking and backwardness of this time and era ... I mean it was issues of women and what women faced. It was issues of African Americans and racism ... and homophobia, but racism with[in] the gay community [too] and internal homophobia that was almost as destructive as any other force we faced."

Some people with AIDS would not seek help, fearing they would be treated like the social outcasts newspaper columnist Frank Gilbreth said they were; others feared getting tested because they did not trust the South Carolina testing authority. If not tattooing, some leaders were discussing quarantine, the talk intensifying when a developmentally challenged young woman was diagnosed with HIV. And in mounting prejudice, in 1984 two gay men were kidnapped at gunpoint on the Battery.

But this younger generation of leaders, most of them in their 20s or 30s and from other cities, were much more in step with national trends. "We were gay, and we were out, and we wanted to talk about being gay," Hall recalled despite being told, "You can't have gay leadership in this organization if you're going to serve women." Complicating it more, "there were gay people in town who didn't want to be involved in a gay agency" for fear of being stigmatized with the label, as well as fearing the agency would fail. Most South Carolina lawmakers were not empathetic, and instead of providing more funding, they publicized cases of HIV transmission and passed a law penalizing those who transmitted the virus knowingly.

With Edens focusing on the state, Hall assumed leadership of Lowcountry PALSS, which soon created its own board that decided to separate fiscally and in other ways from the larger organization. "What was created was something pioneering ... a case management system that was actually motivated by or dictated by the needs of the patient ... and that actually took into account all of his or her psychosocial needs and their medical care and helped point them in the [right] direction and [began] to be the access point that could leverage all these different things." Lowcountry PALSS, working through volunteers such as therapist Suellen Hawkins, attorney Susan Dunn, local philanthropist Linda Ketner, and countless others, was soon offering legal clinics, support groups, food banks, buddy training, and even volunteer pharmacies.

To help fund and expand services, Hall adapted an idea from Greensboro, North Carolina, when he launched the Dining with Friends program, "which meant ... we would get as many people as we knew to have dinner parties, and people would bring donations and we would provide the invitations and a unifying theme and we'd invite everyone to a central location for dessert."

The idea was brilliant and well suited to a city that loved to party. Hosts could say to themselves, "'I'm going to have a dinner party and I'm going to let my friends know that I care about AIDS,' or 'I'm going to let my friends know how liberal I am' or 'I'm going to do something nice because my hairdresser told me to do it.' ... It was hot, and people loved to go to the after party ... in different places like the site of the old museum" and the maritime center. The first one brought in about $7,500, then considered an astonishing amount "for a single fundraiser in Charleston, South Carolina, for something that wasn't ... Ducks Unlimited." Eventually an annual event, it raised tens of thousands of dollars as hosts, guests, and the restaurant and hospitality industries united in a common cause.

A real tipping point, one whose importance cannot be overestimated, came, Hall stressed, when Lowcountry PALSS was granted United Way agency status, a legitimacy never before conferred on any other local LGBTQ nonprofit. This was a milestone not just for PALSS but also for the community, an achievement that would lead to other organizations being funded — and founded. Previously, "[t]he gay community had not had its own philanthropic institutions or institutions it could give to, and nobody knew how to do it unless they had a history of giving to other things." Ketner, taking her first steps towards LGBTQ leadership, supported the cause generously in challenge grants, prompting a literal buy-in from the community.

Still, as the organization stabilized there were tensions. "We were being called upon by certain quadrants of the gay community to be more gay, and to be more out and concerned about gay rights," Hall recalled, while at the same time, "We were being pressured ... by the wealthier components of the gay community, that we were just getting too gay. ... In the same breath were concerns because the majority of our clients were African American and there was a significant number of women, and there were donors who really just wanted to help their friends."

Nationally, disruptive protests were being staged by organizations like ACT UP calling for mass rallies, grabbing media attention with dramatic actions. In Columbia activists staged a "kiss-in" in front of the State House in 1989, while Charleston's most public action resulted from a tip-off that Governor Carroll Campbell, wanting to fund another project, sought to cut the state program that paid for home care for AIDS victims. Noticing that a governor's conference was being held at Patriot's Point, a maritime naval history museum across the harbor from Charleston, Hall and his supporters took action. With an image of a bloody hand on the face of

Figure 49. AIDS activists' handbill

Governor Campbell, they started photocopying and phone calling. As various governors' limousines drove by to the USS *Yorktown*, volunteers lined the way, chanting that Campbell was cutting Medicare and killing people; the limousines slowed, windows went down, and the occupants were passed the handbills. Campbell's legislative policy was abandoned in the glare of national publicity.

Many religious leaders had to be educated and brought along just as surely. "No church or organization wanted a big association with AIDS," Hall realized from the start. "There was an African American church-related institution that got a lot of grant money to do AIDS outreach but that also ran a shelter that would not admit people who were HIV positive."

To counter that, Harry Burns became outreach director to the African American community. One of his achievements was the staging of Gospelfest in 1992, a gathering of over 30 local and grassroots gospel groups to help spread the word and to bring Black churches into the fold of AIDS education. "The church is the heart of the black community," Burns acknowledged, himself Black, "and we're hoping to get the message across about the danger of the virus. It's running rampant ... and it doesn't discriminate.'"

Unable to find a church base (or basement) for her work, volunteer Sybil Schroeder thought she'd fail in her outreach until Hall handed her a key, allowing her to facilitate a group for HIV positive African American women in the PALSS office at the corner of East Bay and Cumberland streets. The suite had received a makeover by a volunteer interior designer, and Hall, a smoker, gave up the habit once he realized he was in the health care providing field. But try as they might, the staff could never quite vanquish the smell of oyster shells from the restaurant that had once occupied the ground floor.

The pressure to please everyone while avoiding censure weighed heavily on Hall, who had to keep up a delicate balancing act, "always walking down the breach between the African American community, the White gay community, the White establishment" and his staff who "were always trying to navigate" complexities in their mission to deliver care for everyone in need.

In October 1992, the board of Lowcountry PALSS announced a legal separation from the Columbia-based operation and changed its name to Lowcountry AIDS Services (LAS). "That was kind of a coming out of the closet," Hall thought. "Just claiming that and owning that ... There was no longer any confusion about what we did."

And although the success of the organization was due to a variety of constituencies, there was no confusion as to who was responsible. Reflecting years later, Hall concluded with pride that, "We fucking were a gay agency ... gay people can take care of African American women and straight men, and so what? Had it not been for gay people, none of this would ever have happened. The urgency and the immediacy of the AIDS epidemic happening to us is what sparked this, and there were many straight allies, but it was a bunch of gay men that started PALSS, and that's that." Continuing, Hall said, "And one thing, I have to say, the backbone of the volunteer program was always lesbians. That was the backbone of the Gay Men's Health Crisis. Lesbians, lesbians, lesbians ... anybody training was 70 percent gay women. Our board was chocked full of gay women ... And lesbians took care of their gay friends, and frankly, they taught us some lessons about community and banding together. I don't know if that's written into the history books, but somebody needs to talk about it...."

Abandoning the closet and refusing the concept of stigma, gay men and lesbians banded together to help themselves and their straight, Black, and White brothers and sisters who were suffering. The realization that they could step out of the shadows and take charge of their own destiny was transformative and empowering.[4]

Chapter Twenty
The Gay Nineties

In August 1990, a group of men and women founded the Lowcountry Gay & Lesbian Alliance (LGLA), with the stated goal of "ending prejudice and discrimination against gays and lesbians through public education and service to the Charleston-area gay and lesbian community." As its name suggests, the founders were deliberately being more inclusive, making sure that men and women equally shared power and responsibility. LGLA relied entirely on volunteers to chair committees, handle finances, plan events, and put together a calendar and publish news. Operating as a 501 (c) 4 instead of a 501 (c) 3, it did not qualify for tax-deductible donations, and as a result, it would struggle financially.

Joseph Sass and Birgit Pols were co-chairs in 1990 and 1991. Other later leaders included Allen Reardon, Kevin Campbell, Margaret Loos, Kathy Hartman, and Michael Schwarzott. Presidents included Frances Wright, Trish Bender, Dick Latham and, again, Allen Reardon.

Membership was diverse, varying over the years. One list has 121 members receiving the newsletter; 150 were mentioned in 2001, but in 1993, when press reported a murderer possibly attacking gay men at a West Ashley adult cinema close to the 35th anniversary of the Halloween candlestick murder, LGLA leaders said they could warn 700 gay men "not to take any chances when meeting strangers."

Members met monthly to discuss business and share a meal in a private dining room at Ryan's Steak House on St. Andrew's Boulevard, objected to by a group of self-identified Christians who threatened to boycott the business for allowing such sinners to assemble, albeit separately. Other events, including book discussions and lectures, took place at the more welcoming

Figure 50. Lowcountry Gay & Lesbian Alliance logo

public library founded decades earlier by Laura Bragg. For its dedication to community service, LGLA participated in the statewide Adopt a Highway program, with members cleaning litter from public roads, and in hopes of gaining visibility. But it was troubling to some as to just how public LGLA should be. It was not unheard of in these years for people to lose jobs and housing due to sexual orientation. Members had the option of using first names only at meetings, in articles written for the newsletters, or in other services contributed, a practice many abandoned as time went on. When LGLA compiled a first-ever list of lesbian and gay businesses offering members discounts, the guide was only circulated internally.[1]

The same sort of balancing act was also a feature of Metropolitan Community Church, which offered its members a first name only worshipping opportunity, reflecting the growing pains of a conservative city. A member of both LGLA and MCC recalled that more people attended the latter than the former, suggesting a hierarchy of member needs (more religious than political) in the Lowcountry. Tellingly, when interviewed on TV about a local gay bathhouse being denied a license in North Charleston, LGLA leader Michael Schwarzott said he faced more negative feedback from some in his organization than from straight strangers who hailed him on the street. He became one of the most visible gay people in town at the time, interviewed often when newscasters sought a gay view on Don't Ask, Don't Tell or other issues.

Kevin J. Campbell, LGLA co-chair, was vocal, too. In a letter to the editor of the *Post and Courier*, he chided the paper for its homophobic rhetoric, "polarizing the state and trying to pit heterosexual against homosexual ... the all too similar stand your newspaper took against black Americans." Campbell also led a protest against religious conservative Pat Robertson when he spoke in the city.

On October 5, 1991, LGLA, along with the South Carolina Gay and Lesbian Pride Movement took another step forward in co-sponsoring a very public Coming Out Rally at the Custom House in Charleston. LGLA always sent a contingent from Charleston to wherever the state Pride organization paraded, the first one in Columbia in 1990.

In 1992, LGLA participated in the city's first communal observance of World AIDS Day. The candlelight rally, hosted by Lowcountry AIDS Services, consisted of a march from Washington Park to the Custom House. More organizations would join in the coming years, including, among others, the Reid House of Christian Service, Christian Service Hospice, the Charleston Interfaith Crisis Ministry, the Catholic Diocese, Catholic Charities, Hotline, the Trident Health District, MCC of Charleston, St. Stephen's Episcopal Church, a mission church that embraced its LGBTQ members wholeheartedly, the Volunteer Center of the Lowcountry, and the Charleston Area Arts Council. In 1997, the march starting at Marion Square ended at Emanuel AME Church. In that same year, as part of the Piccolo Spoleto festival, LGLA's Schwarzott and a cadre of volunteers successfully brought the Names Project's AIDS Quilt to town, and exhibited it at the State Ports Authority Terminal, with profits supporting local food banks and AIDS work.

In further service to the community, LGLA maintained a telephone line to answer queries about LGBTQ events, bars, health and legal issues, sometimes responding to hundreds a month, this in an era when even listing an LGBTQ phone number was new. In 1998, at the instigation of the Trident Knights, LGLA amended its bylaws to embrace bisexuals in those it represented. Trans people were eventually included too, reflecting growing unity and growth of vocabularies.[2]

The newsletters, under a variety of names including *Gay Daze*, *Rainbow Times*, and *Rainbow Times Newsource* noted their activities and those of other groups, such as the Trident Knights. Known for "bringing men, women, and leather together for fun and meaningful experiences," it was founded by four men in 1993 and grew to include women, billing itself as "a Lowcountry leather organization working for hospitality, comradery and educational issues viable for the community." It held monthly meetings, published a newsletter, *The Knight Times*, and worked

Figure 51. LGLA newsletter

to "promote sexual diversity, HIV/AIDS awareness," and supported "local organizations such as Sue Kuhlen's Camp for Kids, Lowcountry AIDS Services, and others."

LGLA partnered with the Knights and other groups, both flourishing and fledgling. There was now a local chapter of Parents and Families of Lesbians and Gays (PFLAG), a newly launched gay Alcoholics Anonymous, a series of women's issues meetings, a Friends Unlimited Bowling League, as well as the Gay and Lesbian Alliance at the College of Charleston, and an annual Lesbian and Gay Film Festival at that institution's Communication Museum. (In the next few years, The Citadel would support a gay and lesbian online group, and T Sisters, an early trans support group, would be founded, both in 2003.) In fact, so many LGBTQ organizations were popping up that it just might be appropriate to call this decade Charleston's real gay nineties. The community's story was no longer a saga of isolated individuals, but of institutions and issues.

In 1997, LGLA hosted the first annual Outfest at James Island County Park. More than 300 people attended. Coming out had become a national phenomenon with celebrities and sports figures sharing their identities. But there was a new complication as well: the fiercely debated, hot-button issue of outing people, prominent or not, against their will. It was the subject of the popular Kevin Kline film *In and Out*, released in September. And as if on cue, exactly two days before Charleston's first October Outfest was scheduled to take place, the city was rocked by a nasty outing that became national news.[3]

White, and born in Charleston in 1956, David Schwacke graduated from the College of Charleston, an outstanding student and president of the student body. At graduation, just as a female recipient of an award presented her cheek to be kissed by President Theodore Stern, Schwacke had presented his, too, prompting Stern to pull away and say, "You can tell he's going to be a lawyer and not a politician."

There was nervous laughter, but Schwacke eventually proved Stern wrong. After practicing as an attorney, he ran for and was elected solicitor for Charleston and Berkeley counties in 1992, and was re-elected four years later. Married with children, he was forced unwillingly into the limelight when fellow Republicans outed him to the local press, accusing him of using office computers to download gay pornography, a charge he vehemently denied and which was never proved. "This being deepest Dixie and deepest Bible-Belt country and, more recently, deepest Republican country, Charleston is politically and socially conservative — more conservative, many Charlestonians like to boast, than any other American city," opined the *New York Times* in its coverage of the story. The outing unexpectedly gave Schwacke the distinction of being the only known gay Republican in an elected position in the South, and one of the few in the country. "I've done my job, done it right and well," he told reporters. Refusing the call to resign, he said he was "a victim of homophobic Republicans, most of them hard-core members of the Christian Right, the most powerful and rapidly growing force in South Carolina politics in recent years."

In response, LGLA co-chairs Mike Schwarzott and Kathy Hartman participated in a two-hour radio show to discuss the issue. "Coming out is a very personal and private matter and should not be forced onto any individual against their wishes, or for any political agenda," Schwarzott said to the press.

Letters to the editor, both for and against Schwacke, filled a whole page of the local paper. A woman wrote, "Homosexuals can shatter the mutual commitment of married partners; destroy the sanctity of the family; twist people's mental well-being and spread disease." She spoke of sexual sin and referred the solicitor to verses in Romans, Corinthians, and Leviticus. Several accused the Republicans and Christian Right of smear tactics, and a 32-year-old South Carolinian living in Los Angeles declared he could never return to the Lowcountry due to its fear of diversity. "Try taking out the word 'gay' in any of the comments made about Schwacke and insert the word 'black.' Do that and realize how scary S.C. leadership resembles its predecessors."

Many gay people defended Schwacke, but Joe Hall, still in HIV/AIDS work, now in Nebraska, brought up another side of the argument. "It is neither brave nor particularly principled to come out of the closet as a means of political damage control. In a state notorious for its right-wing demagogues and legislative enmity towards gays and lesbians, David Schwacke's powerful disclosure does not absolve him of his role as collaborator. South Carolina's elected Republicans continue to be among the most vociferous, mean-spirited homophobes in the country. He cannot possibly be surprised that they turned on him." Hall closed with the hope "that Schwacke will use his sudden notoriety to unmask the entrenched operatives of hate with whom he has colluded and who ultimately forced his hand."

When re-election time rolled around in 2000, Republican Ralph Hoisington ran against Schwacke in the primary, using coded language like "family values" while noting in his TV ads that he would be tough on child molesters. In the only debate, the first question lobbed at Schwacke focused on sexual predators, the inference being that since gays were known to do such things, he would let such criminals off lightly.

The Loop, the next iteration of Charleston's gay paper, reported the outcome: "The people in Charleston County voted overwhelmingly for Schwacke. The people in Berkeley County (where Hoisington's family resides) had a close race between the two candidates. The Hoisington campaign had to outspend the Schwacke campaign almost 4 to 1 to win the race. Schwacke came within approximately 270 Republican votes for winning the primary." Hate, homophobia, and conservatism ruled.

In continuing to defend LGBTQ rights, LGLA joined with numerous other agencies in trying to defeat the South Carolina constitutional amendment defining marriage as a union between a man and a woman. Targeting Republican state senator George E. "Chip" Campsen, who voted for the amendment, LGLA President Richard Campbell called for an economic boycott of Fort Sumter Tours and Spirit Line Cruises, Campsen's family-owned businesses that took visitors around the harbor, a service which many gay organizations had used. (Campsen's father had been one of the attorneys who defended the man who killed Jack Dobbins on Halloween 1958.) African American state senator Robert Ford, a supporter of gay rights, disagreed with the boycott, calling it "regrettable."[4]

LGLA was not alone in its fight for LGBTQ rights in the Lowcountry; two other organizations also founded in Charleston's gay 90s joined in. Unlike LGLA, which did not outlast the first decade of the 21st century, We Are Family (WAF) and the Alliance for Full Acceptance (AFFA) are still extant, educating, and serving the Lowcountry.

The changes in LGBTQ Charleston were obvious to Steven Willard, who returned after being forced out the decade before. As a teenager seeking LGBTQ information, the only source available to him had been libraries; yet he still believed that because he was gay, he'd develop AIDS automatically. When his parents discovered his sexuality, he had to leave home—quickly—and fled to New York City. Now back, he realized the "90s [in Charleston] were much different. People were just much more out by this point, and ... I think activism around AIDS did a lot of this, because you were literally fighting to be alive. So, I think a lot of us were like, 'You know what? Fuck you. Yeah. I'm queer, and I exist. Deal with it.'"

Youngsters and teens, however, still did not have that luxury, confidence, or power. South Carolina's 1988 Comprehensive Health Education Act had a chilling effect on youth especially, only allowing public schools to discuss homosexuality in the context of disease, prohibiting teachers and administrators from mentioning it any way across the entire curriculum. By not mentioning homosexuality, the school systems demonized it. What else could students believe? So no one protested when a Mount Pleasant gay teen was physically beaten in school, or when a Summerville school administrator said abuse like that was to be expected; at the same time in Goose Creek, a girl was called a dyke by an assistant principal.

For those who might have wanted to help, the idea of reaching out to gay youth brought up the old stereotype of lecherous men and lascivious women seducing children, and many educators, adults, and parents were uncomfortable with the idea of adolescent sexuality. And so, it might have been inevitable that only someone straight, completely above suspicion, could take on the issue.

Tom Myers, Jr. (1940-2016) fit the bill perfectly. Of a prominent old family, having attended the Gaud School, Phillips Andover, Sewanee, and Harvard Business School, he returned to his ancestral city, with memberships in exclusive and prestigious organizations like the St. Andrew's and St. Cecilia's societies. But when his son, Tom, told him he was gay and was having trouble in school, Myers, like Dr. Robert Ball, and Judge J. Waties Waring (who, although White and elite, a generation before, had become an advocate for racial equality) chose social justice over the charms of society.

Wanting to help, Myers was unsure how to proceed: "I had absolutely no model to go by because most leaders of the gay and lesbian groups are gay or lesbian. ... Since I was straight, I was viewed as neither fish nor fowl. Many straight people were suspicious of me and began to think I was gay.

They reasoned, why else would I give up everything and dedicate my life to this if I were not gay."

Starting simply with a theme, "We help families stay together," and a bumper sticker that said "Hate is not a Family Value," Myers set to work in 1993 at his dining room table, first identifying those places and people questioning LGBTQ youth could contact for support. He sent positive information to churches, schools, youth activity centers, and counselors. Once supportive sources were identified, Myers would direct those in need to the appropriate agency.

By 1997, his program named We Are Family had outgrown his dining room and moved to rented office space on Spring Street once occupied by the NAACP. Myers recruited Warren Gress, a gay ex-Catholic priest who had moved to Charleston with his partner, Jim Redman. Gress had been working part time at St. Stephen's Episcopal Church, once a historically Black congregation that had become a nexus for acceptance, evolving into a larger more vital congregation with significant LGBTQ membership. Gress, with an interest in youth counseling and impressed with the "near miracle" that Myers had pulled off keeping the organization alive, signed on as executive director.

No longer just educating the public, the nonprofit began providing a safe space for LGBTQ youth. When a newspaper reporter attended one of the weekly meetings, she found about 20 young people ranging in age from 16 to 23 discussing experiences which included being urinated on, sleeping on the street, coming out to parents, and being tested for HIV. One young man talked of drugs and suicide. He and others affirmed this was the one place they felt safe, and the one time they looked forward to all week. "Parents think gay only means sex, and not emotions like love," one participant volunteered, and another young man in "an electric blue jumpsuit" reported he no longer saw himself and others as victims. "I happen to think the world is a beautiful place and this is a great organization for people to be able to talk openly about their feelings and to help each other."

"Gay kids go to school and get picked on and tormented and they come home to parents that look a whole lot more like their tormentors than they do about people who have anything in common with them," Charlie Smith, a volunteer at the organization saw, "and they learn you have to keep it bottled up. That's what you learn."

WAF became a life-saving force for solitary youths and families who had been searching for help. Myers's board included religious and community leaders, and while its impact was great, its finances were not. "It's very difficult to raise money for this organization," board member Steve Steinert admitted, and Myers himself wistfully noted, "If we had $100 or $150 a year from everyone who has reacted positively to what we are doing, we would have no troubles financially." As for other numbers, the organization had a database of 48,700 individuals, its website was registering 1,000-plus hits a month, and staff had direct contact with at least 500 youths, there

Figure 52. Marching in the 1998 Pride parade

being an estimated 5,000 to 8,000 LGBTQ youth in the area between the ages 14 and 23. In 1998 and 1999 at the Circular Congregational Church, WAF, with other groups such as LAS and LGLA, sponsored Growing UP Gay Conferences.[5]

Impressed and moved by this, local closeted philanthropist Linda Ketner could only ruefully recall her own unhappy youth in small town North Carolina. While she had been generous in issuing challenge grants in support of AIDS work, she had remained in the closet. But now, seeing the impact enlightened leadership could have, she decided to come out, forgoing the advice of a colleague from one of the nonprofits on whose board she served. He told her it would hurt both her profile and that of the organization if she made her sexual orientation known. Having served as president of the Charleston Interfaith Crisis Ministry, and chair of the Mayor's Committee on Homelessness and Affordable Housing among other things, she realized that although she had supported other causes, still, "I've never been an activist for my own issue." With characteristic humor and insight, she noted, "I had been so deeply in the closet, I was a garment bag."

Figure 53. Linda Ketner

As in earlier work, she committed herself to this new cause wholeheartedly. "It has taken me decades of emotional and spiritual work to repair and heal my childhood wounds," she reflected, "decades to erase the messages of shame, and to root out my internalized homophobia. Today I can live openly, lovingly and proudly."

These were the words and ideas many did not want to hear. In 1998, the *New York Times* noted how difficult life was for LGBTQ activists in South Carolina due to the tide that had overtaken Schwacke in the rise of fundamentalist Christianity, and its alliance with the Republican Party, all targeting gay pride and visibility. Ketner sought out LGLA, the most active LGBTQ organization in town, but she was dismayed at how some still chose anonymity.

"I went to one of the meetings and … it was in the back of a Ryan's Steak House, and it was like a funeral," she recalled. "Everybody was so glum, and it was so sad, and I thought, 'If I'm going to be an openly gay person I can't be this kind of openly gay person.'"

Since Tom Myers had been so successful with We Are Family, she turned to him for advice. "I didn't know gay people," she confessed. "I said to him, 'Okay, what I need from you is the names of LGBT people and allies, but they need to be emotionally healthy and they need to be intelligent and have kind of a thirst for activism.'"

Tom Myers was quick with recommendations, and so, not for the first or last time, one LGBTQ organization in town assisted in the birth of another. Myers's advice led Ketner to "some of the most fantastic people on the planet. I feel like it was a gift from God," she enthused; "they are, and they were then, just tremendous people. We had Warren Gress who later became our executive director, now he's Warren Redman-Gress, because he married our treasurer, Jim Redman-Gress, and he had been a former priest. Then we had ... Lynn Moldenhauer, who I affectionately call Nun with a Gun, because she had been a former nun. So, we had an ex-priest and an ex-nun, [who] was now chief agent of Probation and Parole for the county ... she was fabulous. And we had Charlie Smith."

Smith also had a religious background of sorts, having served as senior warden at Trinity Episcopal Church in Miami, Florida. He had grown up in South Carolina, graduated from the College of Charleston, and had returned to check out the city following the death by AIDS of his partner, Carlos Guillermo Rodriguez-Mendez. Smith volunteered for LGLA, writing for its newsletter, and like Ketner, he was amazed at the success of We Are Family.

"I was so floored that there was a straight man that had an organization that parents allowed gay kids to come to from the age of thirteen to twenty-three that the thought of that happening and him not being accused of something blew me away."

Smith immediately saw a connection between the bias against African Americans and that against gay people, especially youth. But there was one striking difference: "When Black children go to school and they get picked on and tormented, they go home to Black parents who understand, because they had it done to them when they were children too," Smith reasoned. Now the tragedy was that gay children, going home from school, often found their families tormenting them as well. (Gee Smalls, growing up on James Island in the 1980s, before We Are Family, found himself the subject of both racism and homophobia. The son of a White mother and a Black father, "called 'faggot-ass half-breed' for my light bright skin, soft curly afro, freckly face and feminine ways ... I was an outsider," to all groups, he recalled in *Black Enough, Man Enough*, his memoir autobiography.)

Smith was encouraged to see not just an organization or two moving forward but a whole city capable of change, something he attributed to progressive and openly supportive Mayor Joseph P. Riley, Jr. He and others believed the time was ripe for the fight for LGBTQ rights to be more public, and for smaller towns and cities to take up the cause. Charleston was attracting more and more people, like the couple Carolyn Newkirk and Linda Gwillim, who agreed.

A new day and a new organization were beginning.

Chapter Twenty-one
The Last Straw

Linda Ketner and the people around her tapped into that zeitgeist, and the new friends came together to envision an entirely new organization. LGLA had sported the motto, "changing the world one opinion at a time," and *Gay Charleston* had set its sights, not on the masses, but only on "opinion makers." For Ketner and crew, it was all or nothing. Alliance for Full Acceptance (AFFA) was the name ultimately chosen.[1]

"Linda called the meeting and it was at [The Inn at] Middleton ... I believe it was August of 1998 and it didn't include people who were from here. It was really outsiders or people who had only been here for a short period of time," Smith recalled. He felt that was necessary because "we didn't get anchored into this old, closeted society [that existed in Charleston.] We had all new ideas and we were willing to do them whether anybody went along with us or not, and if it was just us, we were fine with that."

But organizations, Ketner knew, even those founded with enthusiasm and good intentions, often foundered. Other skill sets were necessary, and she could provide them, for Ketner was a co-founder and principal of a consulting firm that specialized in assisting organizations and individuals in the development of leadership and management skills, with a full roster of satisfied national and international clients behind her.

"So we had that meeting and ... Linda was really, really good at ... getting non-profits to examine themselves and see what their mission is and see if what they're doing really aligns with their mission or if they're really accomplishing what they're supposed to be accomplishing or just blowing people's money...

and that's what we did that weekend," Smith reminisced. "We worked on what we all perceived were the issues that were important to the LGBT community, what the problems were, what was achievable and what our next step needed to be."

According to Smith, "It was Linda who taught the rest of us what leadership was and what commitment was. We recognized in the first weekend that we spent together exactly what it was that had caused other groups to fail ... mostly backbiting and not keeping commitments. She made us understand and commit that if we had a problem with someone, that if we didn't take it directly to the person we had a problem with first, that we could not be part of the group. There was simply no opportunity for backbiting within the group, and frankly, I really don't remember there being much cause for it, other than folks who came after ... who did not really share the same vision and passion for what we were doing. Those folks tended to be short termers on the board. ...

"The commitment, trust and vulnerability part of that experience has stayed with me every day of my life since then," Charlie Smith reflected. "Linda knew that the community needed to learn that, and she made it available to us, even if we could not afford it.

"I also remember a meeting at her house when there was a real vision disagreement that brought out exactly what the problem ... was at the time ... and exactly what our overriding goal needed to be ... building a healthy LGBTQ community. There was simply not much about the community ... that was healthy. We thought poorly of ourselves for the most part, and we operated that way. AFFA's mission became as much about improving our own self-image and sense of self-worth as much as changing the hearts and minds of the non-LGBTQ public."

Perhaps there was a little bit of the LGLA ethic present in AFFA, after all, for changing themselves one person at a time allowed the founders to build a board able to work for the betterment of all.

They agreed upon the process "Education without Alienation." Smith explained, "Some of us were so damn angry after coming out of the AIDS crisis and everything else we had been through in the 80s and 90s that we had to realize that the anger had to go if we were going to be effective. I was at the front of that line," he confessed, "and it was Linda who made me realize that I had some personal work to do ... and I did it." Many in the group, from divergent religious backgrounds and beliefs, shared the feeling that if not turning the other cheek, they, at least, were going to be polite in their battle for equality; they were not going to descend to the same level of hate and vitriol often spewed by many of their enemies, religious institutions included. Incorporating as a 501 (c) 3 tax-exempt organization, affording donors tax-deductible credit for contributions, was another tactic differentiating AFFA from past LGBTQ groups in the city.

As the members of the small group educated themselves and continued to plan, events escalated, prompting action. That summer of 1998, at the 13th Lambeth Conference, the Anglican Church found "homosexual practice incompatible with scripture," creating a split in the Anglican communion that had lasting effects on LGBTQ people around the world and in the city, discouraging and angering this new group, grounded as many were, in religion and spirituality. In May of that year, Mark McBride, the mayor of Myrtle Beach, tried to keep the ninth annual South Carolina Pride Parade from succeeding. And even closer to home, in July, Harold Koon, a beloved gay neighborhood leader, who had been rewriting LGLA's bylaws to make the organization more open, had a heart attack while jogging. Smith believed that it was fear of AIDS that kept onlookers from providing Koon help while he lay on the concrete, bleeding profusely, though one brave man did intervene, getting him to the hospital, where he eventually perished.

The last straw came in October as the local paper printed an advertisement sponsored by the East Cooper Baptist Church, railing against homosexuality. According to the Reverend Conrad "Buster" Brown, "for a Christian who has a homosexual tendency, the only alternatives are to become celibate in their sexuality or to ask the Lord to give them a heterosexual desire within the confines of holy marriage."

The ad featured a "former" lesbian who encouraged gays to give up sin and enter conversion therapy. (Growing up in that church, Tanner Crunelle would later become an LGBTQ advocate at the College of Charleston, on a scholarship given by Linda Ketner, goaded to action by the church.) "It was a full-page ad of nothing but lies," Smith recalled. "Just lies about the gay community. And it was just so offensive to us. We weren't really ready to hit the ground, but we said if we're going to do anything, we can't sit still for this. So when that came out the next day, we had a meeting over at a member's [Carolyn Newkirk's and Linda Gwillim's] house on James Island and we decided that we were going to take a full-page ad and that we were going to write that content ourselves. We sat there for hours and we hammered out a full-page ad for the *Post and Courier* and we printed it and it knocked the living hell out of these religious conservatives, because nobody had ever said boo to them.

"They could get away with whatever they wanted to with impunity and nobody ever said a word because anybody who said a word would be destroyed, and we set ourselves up in a way that they couldn't do that to us, and we said boo and they ran. We have never had another full-page ad in the paper again against the gay community in this city. It ended." And it was done with a half page ad, apparently, a larger one costing too much money.

"I'm living proof that the Truth can set you free," the caption under the "former" lesbian began. "If you really love someone, you'll tell them the truth," was its end. In "A Letter to the People of Charleston" published Sunday, October 11, 1998, the Board of AFFA replied in kind. "The truth is ... we are your children, your friends, your mothers, your fathers, your sisters, and your brothers. ..." it began. "The truth is ... we can be silent no longer."

"The truth is," the letter continued, "it is immoral to have the Bible misused to hurt us ... it is immoral to reduce people of character and kindness to stereotypes ... love is good and moral [and] gays and lesbians are as diverse and complex as heterosexuals."

Like a declaration of independence from religious and prejudicial tyranny, "a group of gay, lesbian and heterosexual South Carolinians concerned with the elimination of prejudice against gay men and lesbian women," later to include trans people and others, stood up for their rights in a glare and blare of publicity.[2]

PALSS had first found it necessary to equivocate about its LGBTQ core to gain support in the 1980s. In the 1990s, We Are Family, by its very nature, was an out organization, and LGLA was tending that way. While the latter and AFFA co-existed for a few years, AFFA would eventually replace LGLA as the primary LGBTQ civil rights organization in the Lowcountry.

"It was definitely an 'us' and not a 'me,'" Ketner wrote, recalling the early years. "Truthfully! ... Our small founding group ... really was different ... What we shared in common was: our belief in the work, a trust in one another that built over time and was rock solid, our desire to make important change and make it quickly; everyone had a great work ethic, took responsibility for their work and took pride in doing it exceptionally well.

"We did not have paid staff until the 4th or 5th year. Before that, each board member put in a minimum of eight hours each week, some of us 40, and we met frequently together each month. The ideas for the ... training programs ... all came from this group. Our monthly meetings had every national leader ... of the LGBT movement and artists like Rita Mae Brown, Andy Tobias—also Howard Dean, Mayor Riley, etc. Our monthly meetings generally had 75-125 people attend. ... And, although we weren't a membership organization, it was donations from our cohort that comprised a large part of our budget. We did healing-internalized-homophobia workshops, hours of dialogue with the likes of Rocky D on his [local conservative radio] show, made frequent trips to the State House, birthed South Carolina Equality etc., etc.—all before [having] a paid staff member."

Due to the criticism of homosexuality in many congregations, AFFA founders and members now found new challenges in approaching their own religion and spirituality. "There was some division on the board about whether or not this is something to take on," Lynn Moldenhauer (Ketner's "nun with a gun") explained in an interview. "But truthfully ... we knew that we could not ignore the religious element in our lives." With a mission "to champion faith-based respect for LGBT persons," AFFA created A Dialogue on Religion and Sexual Orientation (ADORASO) which hosted conversations on theology, sexuality, and related issues in which clergy, individuals, and interested parties could participate in a respectful atmosphere. "[W]e plant seeds at these formal meetings," Moldenhauer explained, "and ... we just entrust the seed planting to go forward...." Musing on the issue, she wondered, "do we want to have tolerance? We don't like the word 'tolerance;' 'acceptance' is a little harder to achieve, but as a beginning, let's work on respecting each other. It's a very important first step."

Another program AFFA pursued was sponsoring pro-LGBTQ billboards on busy stretches of Interstate 26, at accesses and exits to and from the city. The first billboard, set up in 1999, declared, "Lesbian and Gay People Valued Members of this

Figure 54. AFFA program

Community." "That seems like the most innocuous phrase even now," Chase Glenn, the second director of AFFA, reflected years later. "The day that billboard went up, hate mail started coming in, the phone started ringing. People were irate. ... It really spoke to sort of the revolutionary ... work that was happening at that time." People driving by couldn't believe the positive and visible messaging after literally centuries of negativity and lies. Some drivers exited the highway, turned around, got back on, and gawked.

The second billboard had even more impact. When Melissa Moore, a youth in high school forced into a damaging conforming identity stereotype, saw it, it was revelatory. "I was driving down I-26 and I saw a billboard and it said, 'Homosexuality isn't the problem, prejudice is.'"

"That was one of the first times it had occurred to me that I should fight for my right to be who I am rather than trying to quit this like a drug. ... I saw that billboard and it just stuck with me. I looked at that website address and I contacted

The Real Rainbow Row

Figure 55. Melissa Moore

them and asked how I could get involved." Moore abandoned thoughts of suicide, later reflecting, "that in a perfect world, it would not have taken a billboard to help me understand that I didn't need to kill myself." But religious institutions did not agree. A Baptist minister sent out an open letter to Charleston clergy urging them to unite against AFFA's "unholy assault." His battle cry was "Prejudice isn't the problem, sin is."

Moore began attending AFFA events, the youngest person present. "I started working with AFFA [and] then I went on to work with SC Equality during the marriage amendment campaign." When other states were sanctioning gay marriage, South Carolina's reactionary politicians instead led a movement to amend the state's Constitution to define marriage as only between one man and one woman.

To combat this, AFFA helped birth the South Carolina Equality Coalition (SCEC) and Moore became key to the organization's workshops, advertisements, and grass roots campaigns. Although the amendment passed in 2006, Moore was energized, continuing to work for social justice, first for abortion access and eventually homelessness and city planning. When Moore became director of We are Family (resuscitating and supporting it with personal funds) events had come full circle: Tom Myers, the leader of We Are Family had helped launch AFFA, and now Melissa Moore, an AFFA veteran and activist, was leading We Are Family. Moore laid the plans for a thrift store to help fund the organization and, in August 2019, We are Family, AFFA and Charleston Pride would move to one location on Reynolds Avenue in North Charleston, creating the first LGBTQ hub in the Lowcountry.³

Continuing its messaging, AFFA fought billboard companies giving in to homophobic pressure and institutions threatening to pull their advertising. In 2003, the 900 member organization faced similar resistance from a local television station that refused to air the half-hour documentary it had commissioned. Interviewing locals aged 24 to 84, Steve Lepre and Mark McKinney had assembled a positive portrait of LGBTQ life in the Lowcountry that Lepre defined as "a tapestry for all different kinds of people." The station's general manager, who had previously been glad to take AFFA's money for 30-second commercials, now balked at broadcasting the *We Are Your Neighbors* documentary on Sunday morning before religious programming. AFFA prevailed and the documentary aired, demystifying men and women who many were trying to demonize and portray as frightening, evil, and alien.

In 2006, in "a move viewed as both controversial and historic" AFFA worked to debut "Charleston's first radio show geared towards the gay community." Patricia Estes, a pastor at North Palm Ministry Center in North Charleston, objected. "Any show that goes against the word of God," had to be condemned, she said, painting the LGBTQ community as one that destroys families, relationships and societies.

Unfazed, the first "Equal Time" program was broadcast at 9:30 a.m. Saturday, January 21, 2006. Dozens more followed, with much of the show's success due to interviewer Wilhelmina Hein. Born in the Netherlands and raised in

Australia, living for a while as a married gay man, Hein emigrated to the United States after transitioning. She served as a minister for the Metropolitan Community Church. In 2000, she came to Charleston to pastor the local congregation, which had been granted full commission status in 1987.

Since its first worship service on July 3, 1981, under pastor Stan Harris, the congregation had moved services from a bar to various borrowed churches, and rented sanctuaries before purchasing its own building on Dorchester Road in 1997. They catered to LGBTQ people shunned by their own churches and denominations, providing a spiritual home, and serving the area through volunteerism and outreach. Hein left MCC in 2003, and with many who followed, helped organize the Open Door Congregation, Charleston's second predominantly LGBTQ church. On her radio show, running for over a year, discussions focused on politics, race, HIV and AIDS, Don't Ask, Don't Tell, profiles of leaders and members of the community and other topics. Hein made quite an impact before returning to her native Netherlands and continuing her spiritual journey by converting to Judaism, part of her ancestry.[4]

Figure 56. Wilhlemina Hein

While radio shows, billboards, TV commercials and documentaries raised visibility and promoted acceptance, AFFA simultaneously zeroed in on more focused groups and needs, such as workshops aimed at educating the police. In 2000, Linda Ketner asked Solicitor Ralph Hoisington, who had replaced David Schwacke, to add the category of sexual orientation to his department's non-discrimination policy, and he agreed. Then Schwacke asked Hoisington to stop the Charleston and Mount Pleasant police departments from asking questions about homosexuality and sexual orientation in their pre-employment interviews and polygraph tests. Hoisington ducked the request, saying it was not "his role to dictate to local police departments and suggested that would be a matter for AFFA to address."

Mount Pleasant authorities backed down immediately, but Charleston's Police Chief Reuben Greenberg dug in his heels. "Greenberg maintained that 'sodomy' and 'buggery' were a felony in the state of South Carolina and that he would not hire anyone who was committing a felony." Off camera, he also said that the South Carolina Department of Criminal Justice Police Academy would not accept homosexuals. When asked, its spokesperson and the one for State Law Enforcement Division (SLED) both denied following those anti-gay policies.

In response to Greenberg's intransigence, Ketner went directly to Mayor Joseph P. Riley, Jr., who, in turn, went to Greenberg. "Under pressure from a Lowcountry gay rights group, the Charleston Police Department is no longer asking job applicants whether they have participated in homosexual activity," the *Post and Courier* reported on March 14, 2001, marking another AFFA and LGBTQ victory. Once changed, the police department adapted swiftly, eventually employing an out African American trans officer on the force and an out lesbian as its chief recruiter.

The Loop, the newest LGBTQ paper to appear in the city, was reporting on these and other issues. The idea for the paper had come one evening when Daryl Crouse and "friends were sitting around watching *Will and Grace*. Crouse mentioned how many times he had missed a Gay/Lesbian-themed movie in Charleston. Some of the other people in the group discussed how often times an event would occur with low attendance. To keep people informed, to represent all and not just 'gay white boys' and to raise funds for LGBTQ organizations, *The Loop* was born!" The first issue appeared in September 2000, the final one in 2003.

It featured columns by Schwacke and reported, among other things, on the large number of gay sailors being discharged from the Navy; astonishingly, 81 sailors or 24 percent of the Navy's discharges under Don't Ask, Don't Tell policy came locally. "'The numbers from Charleston are alarming,' said [C. Dixon] Osborn," executive director of the Servicemembers Legal Defense Network. "'While we do not know the precise reason so many Navy personnel were discharged from that installation, we do know that service members come out for a reason. Those reasons most often include unchecked harassment, inadequate training and a failure of leadership.'" *The Loop*, incidentally, had done one article on LGBTQ history, based on the memories of a Navy lieutenant colonel, who had led a closeted gay life in Charleston in the 1960s. He had not been removed from the service.

In 2001, *The Loop*, advertising the Freedom Parties that for a while included Charleston in their circuits, also did a survey of its readership. When asking if gay men and lesbians felt comfortable holding hands in public, 23 percent expressed fear of physical harm or verbal abuse; 27 percent said they had no problem with such displays of affection, while 8 percent admitted being embarrassed. The largest percentage, 42 percent, said they would not "hold hands out of respect for those Charlestonians who do not see the relationship as being acceptable."

Back in the 1980s, Lambda of Charleston had conducted a survey of its own. Tabulated, its participants included one person who identified as straight, 11 as bisexual, and 50 as gay, making a total of 62; but another question reflected 67 respondents. Of that latter number, 43 were male, 23 were female. Forty said they were generally comfortable in their identities, but only 27 said "always." Six reported being closeted with everyone, eight with most of their friends, 34 with their parents, 27 with their employers, and 16 said they were totally out. Most reported religion as unimportant, with about half saying their denominations made them feel guilty. When asked about discrimination, 17 said they faced it in employment, one faced it in housing, five in legal situations, 25 socially, and five in other ways, showing that about half faced prejudicial treatment.

All those answering the question noted they wanted places other than bars to meet. The vast majority wanted better health services and more LGBTQ friendly counseling opportunities. Over two-thirds saw the need for more political action.[5]

If those who took that survey back then were still around, they'd have lived to see many of their dreams achieved: there were more LGBTQ organizations, spaces and opportunities, and more health professionals sensitive to community needs. AFFA had impacted the police and hiring policies, but most political programs, like fighting for marriage equality, had gone down in defeat. But the era for out LGBTQ people running for political office was fast approaching.

Chapter Twenty-two
"It's time": Politics and Pride

Charlie Smith was the first to throw his hat into the ring. In 2002, he announced his running for seat 119 in the South Carolina House of Representatives in the West Ashley district and neighborhood of Charleston. He ran against GOP incumbent John Graham Altman, III, an outspoken critic of what he called the militant homosexual agenda. When David Schwacke had been outed, Altman accused him of actions "the Bible calls sin and state law calls a felony." As for any statute that protected gays, Altman called it "pedophile protection."

Altman lived in an old house across from the South Windemere Shopping center, famous for the sagging portico and plastic pink flamingoes on his lawn, spawning political buttons for Smith with a diagonal line across a flamingo. Before gaining statewide office, Altman had served on the local school board, where, according to *Charleston City Paper* columnist Will Moredock, "he spent 20 years bullying and demeaning his fellow board members."

"He belligerently opposed school busing and on one occasion proposed a white history month." Once in the legislature, first elected in 1996, Altman "spoke defiantly against an MLK holiday, against interracial marriage, and in favor of keeping the Confederate flag flying above the Statehouse." He blamed women for staying in abusive relationships and tried to get Charleston County to secede from the state of South Carolina. While he was condemning others, he was jailed for failing to pay child support, and admitted to gambling on sports in defiance of state law.

In opposing him, Smith, with a degree in city planning and experience in Miami Shores, Florida, took the high road; he stuck to the facts, spoke about equality, controlling growth, and other issues, following the AFFA idea of education without alienation. Altman, saying he'd defend "family issues," a coded phrase used to alert supporters to the sexual identity and orientation of his opponent won 60 percent of the vote. The next time Smith challenged him in 2004, Smith garnered 46 percent, unable to dislodge a long-time politician who in the words of columnist Will Moredock, "was a demagogue and a fear-monger who used his considerable powers of persuasion to mislead a frightened and gullible public. He could quote scripture at one moment and lash out at blacks, gays, atheists, liberals, and the media at the next. To understand Altman is to understand why Southern politics remain so mean, divisive, and ineffective." Altman served in the South Carolina House for 10 years.

Smith, non-plussed, went back to his real estate career, also serving as a Charleston County Planning Commissioner and as a member of the West Ashley Revitalization Commission. Philosophical over defeat, he noted that it was Linda Ketner who had prompted him to run for office, something she soon took to heart. In 2008, she announced her candidacy against Republican Henry Brown, US Congressman from South Carolina's First District, including Charleston and much of the Lowcountry. Brown, in office since 2001, was a solid conservative boasting support of the National Rifle Association, a Right to Life Campaign PAC, a Veterans of Foreign Wars PAC, and other groups ranging from Focus on the Family to the US Chamber of Commerce.

Ketner addressed the issues of homelessness, healthcare, education, seniors, energy independence, equity for all, arts, and the timely issue of the war in Iraq. As an out lesbian and a newcomer, running in a district no Democrat had won since the 1990s, she had an uphill battle, which she fought with honesty and integrity. Polls reflected her newfound popularity, some suggesting a gap of just single digits between the candidates before the election. But the Friday before the vote, *Time* magazine released an online story of a group of wealthy Democrats it dubbed the Gay Mafia focusing on members' financial support of liberal candidates. Seeing Ketner's name on the list prompted others to weaponize it. Unknown opponents printed, photocopied, and distributed the article in church parking lots that Sunday in conservative Horry County, which Ketner had expected not to carry. She lost it by larger percentage points than predicted. Incumbent Brown managed to hang on to his seat, against Ketner's capture of 48 percent of the vote, the closest race in the district in some 20 years. Brown declined to run again in 2010, and Ketner did as well, choosing to do what she did best: focusing her energies on acceptance for all and social justice.

Despite these losses, the era did see LGBTQ political victories, from a younger generation that had come of age in a changed world.[1]

In 2006, Lane Hudson, a 2001 graduate of the College of Charleston, who had interned in President Clinton's White House, caught the national spotlight through a controversial act of outing. Working for the Human Rights Campaign Fund (from which he was eventually fired) and knowing of Florida Congressman Mark Foley's inappropriate sexual advances to young male pages, Hudson first reported the story anonymously on a blog dedicated to stopping sexual predators. What made the Foley story compelling was the congressman's high rank in the Republican administration, his vociferously anti-gay rhetoric, and his avid sponsorship of anti-gay legislation. In the ensuing controversy, Foley was forced to resign from Congress; and similar charges of inappropriate sexual actions were lodged against another Republican leader. Cover-ups at the highest level in the Republican Party were suggested, with the inference that Congressional leaders knew of Foley's gross misbehavior and were complicit in both condoning and keeping it a secret. Some political analysts suggested that Foley's resignation in September 2006 helped instigate the Republicans' loss of control of Congress in the November general elections, sweeping in the Democrats. Hudson himself eventually was "outed" as the source of some of Foley's inappropriate emails.

Two years later, another College of Charleston student, Nick Shalosky, also created a political impact. Born in 1987, in Conway, South Carolina, he had come out in high school and was majoring in Political Science when he found a topic for an independent research project. Wanting to study the impact of the Internet on local elections, he discovered a vacant school board seat that had not attracted any candidate a scant two weeks before the election. Online, Shalosky established himself as a moderate, employing Facebook to promote himself and his candidacy. "I thought it would be interesting to see how students could use social networking sites to get one of their own elected," he noted, spending not one cent on his campaign.

Shalosky's victorious election to the seven-member school board came from his landslide tally of all votes cast (22), having no opposition. He represented downtown Charleston's 20th district for a four-year term, starting in November 2008.

While a fluke, it was nevertheless something for the record books, with Shalosky then being the first and only openly gay elected official in South Carolina, and also the youngest in the country. *The Advocate* magazine included Shalosky in its "Forty under 40" feature focusing on upcoming LGBTQ "Pioneers who never knew a time before Stonewall."[2]

Shalosky had been inspired by his College of Charleston professor of American History, Tom Chorlton, an oversize presence on campus and on the national political scene. Weighting in at 360 pounds, and looking a lot like Santa Claus, Chorlton called himself "the world's largest gay vegetarian hymn-singing agnostic." Not only did he talk the talk in classes on contemporary political issues, American government, and the political issues of the American Revolution, he had walked the walk, having had a national profile before coming to Charleston.

In Washington, D.C. in 1975, he had worked on the staff of Congressman Melvin Price (D-Illinois), chair of the House Armed Services Committee. From 1982 to 1987, Chorlton served as the founding executive director of the National Association of Gay and Lesbian Democratic Clubs (the forerunner of today's national Stonewall Democrats). In 1988, he ran for a seat on the City Council of the District of Columbia. He taught his students that democracy will survive only through participation, and he opened the door to engagement to his students before his death in 2014. "The College was lucky to have him," another student, Tony Williams, said. "He was kind of a mentor in the early days." Williams "had a couple of lunches and dinners with him and picked his brain about a lot of things, especially when it came to PRIDE and getting that up and off the ground and staying involved." Williams would do web work for the city's first Pride event, would later serve as liaison with vendors, and eventually become CEO of Pride.

Besides Chorlton, there were others helping to turn the tide of homophobia that had once been prevalent in the administration of George Grice, the era when the board had called for the firing of gay faculty. Among them was Dr. James Sears, a distinguished professor who had written much on LGBTQ Southern and Charleston history. He lived in Charleston and taught a few courses at the college in the 1990s.

Times were changing. Back in 1975, transsexual Paula Grossman had been ridiculed by the staff of the college's yearbook; she was mistakenly called a transvestite, and the write-up reported she "spoke on how it felt to have things jiggled around," showing no understanding or empathy. Although gay and lesbian students had been meeting on campus since the 1980s, with a formal alliance formed in 1991, it had faced pushback. Cathy Evans of the Communication Museum also got negative comments from donors for her hosting of an annual LGBTQ film festival.

The year 2003 saw an expanded film series, along with a variety of classes touching on LGBTQ topics. Now, many believed, was the time to start a minor in Lesbian and Gay Studies, which the *Post and Courier* noted "could be a first for South Carolina, long considered a conservative bastion. ... 'Charleston is somewhat different from the rest of the state,'" a professor told the reporter. Organized religion had often been a foe, but now, on hearing the news of what professors were proposing, a spokesperson for the South Carolina Christian Action Council affirmed the idea, saying that "people learning about other people" was a good idea; "the more we know, the greater is our understanding."

But Robert Baker, the Catholic Bishop of Charleston, a denomination and diocese soon to face a major sex scandal, ignored the separation of church and state by immediately articulating an argument designed to stop the project. "I'm surprised," he said, "that a state-operated university would offer a course that does not reflect the sentiment of most of the taxpayers of South Carolina in its moral content. ..." Creating such a course of study "would not be intellectual freedom, but intellectual tyranny." He thought "a course on the history of stable, monogamous heterosexual marriages," would be better for everyone (except, of course, for an assumed celibate clergy).

So, the understanding hoped for by the Christian Action Council became grandstanding instead. John Graham Altman, who had criticized gay Republican David Schwacke and gay Democrat Charlie Smith, rose up in protest. Altman called for a meeting with Lee Higdon, president of the College of Charleston, who previously had been an advocate for diversity, especially on African American issues. The next day, however, without consulting the faculty, Higdon and provost Elise Jorgens rejected LGBTQ issues as being a valid topic of academia. "The College of Charleston has no minor in gay and lesbian studies and there is no minor in any stage of formal review process," they wrote in a letter to the paper, surrendering completely and sacrificing LGBTQ interests to a politician—granted, one who threated to control purse strings. "Talk of C of C Gay, Lesbian Minor Squelched," the headlines read succinctly. Many professors and students protested the head-spinning decision to abandon the plan knowing full well that if similar tactics had been taken on African American or Jewish or other minorities' studies there would have been a huge outcry. But diversity on the college campus (and in the state legislature) had not yet grown to include the LGBTQ community. "It is not, for a number of reasons, in the overall best interest in the college," Higdon wrote tersely.[3]

Altman, threatening to cut off state funding to the institution, had gotten his way, and the legislature continued to meddle in College of Charleston affairs. Trouble began brewing again in 2014 when The College Reads! Committee chose *Fun Home*, an autobiographical graphic novel by acclaimed lesbian author/artist Alison Bechdel for a book to be read and discussed by incoming freshmen.

College of Charleston board members disavowed and decried it; comments came in that the book was a "recruiting" manual for lesbians, and the State Legislature cut funds it erroneously assumed had paid for the books and for Bechdel to visit and speak. The money actually stemmed from student activity fees, not state appropriations. Making the scandal worse were the hurtful statements made by some of the college's board of trustees when they testified before the state legislature, saying the values of *Fun Home*, the story of a young woman discovering herself in college as her father faced his own homosexuality differently, were not the college's. Many on the board chose to ignore a significant portion of their student body, soon to be estimated as nearly one in five based on the college's own statistics, to maintain their board seats.

But faculty and students and staff of the college turned the defeat into victory. The novel was adapted as an off-Broadway play, and, working through Dr. Todd McNerny of the Theater Department, the entire original cast consented to come to Charleston to stage a protest. Along with them, sacrificing major fees and royalties, came author Alison Bechdel, playwright and lyricist Lisa Kron, and composer Jeanine Tesori.

On April 21, 2014, in an incredible show of esprit de corps and professionalism, with just a few hours to rehearse an entirely new format, the authors and actors staged two shows to whistling, screaming, and foot-stomping audiences in Memminger Auditorium (the school at which lesbian feminist Anna Brackett had taught before the Civil War). The original show went on to win an Obie Award, and when it was later produced on Broadway, with most of the cast that had performed in Charleston, it won five Tony awards, including Best Musical, while Bechdel won a MacArthur Fellowship genius grant. In this swift succession of events, the world got a glimpse of how forward-thinking and backward-looking the same institution could be. Money to help pay for expenses had come from the Samuel and Regina Greene family fund created by two Holocaust survivors (this author's parents) to fight intolerance, with the legislature's homophobia deemed an example of it.

At this time except for a marker on the Society Street, home of Dawn Langley Hall Simmons, calling her a "hermaphrodite" the city's Holocaust monument in Marion Square, dedicated in 1999, was the sole other public place in town noting the existence of LGBTQ people. An explanatory plaque listed gay people, along with Jews, Jehovah Witnesses, Gypsies, and Seventh Day Adventists, as victims of Nazi policies. That a city filled with monuments, markers, and plaques had not yet acknowledged its massive role in the slave trade and the toll of human misery during slavery, but could build a memorial to European carnage had not gone unnoticed. No one, however, commented on the fact that prejudice against LGBTQ people in Europe was also memorialized, even as it was being tolerated a few blocks down the street.

In 2009 a plaque was installed on a short plinth in front of the old Book Basement building to honor John Zeigler for his gifts to the school (nearly a million dollars in music scholarships). It was where Zeigler and Edwin Peacock had loved and lived and served as out examples for decades. But officials timidly crafted language that failed to tell the truth, inferring that Peacock and Zeigler had just been business, and not life, partners. Compounding that injustice was the memorial's propinquity to the building where Harrison Randolph and George Grice had engaged in their hidden sexual affair, which ultimately led to the latter man, a closeted homophobe leading the institution.[4]

Across town, other state supported schools were also dealing with LGBTQ issues. The Citadel, South Carolina's military institution, had been following the policies of Don't Ask, Don't Tell, but as soon as the laws were changed and the military adopted a pro-gay policy, the school complied, and the legislature had to bow to Federal mandates. (The outcry over admitting women in the 1990s had created a much greater scandal than admitting LGBTQ students), and to its credit,

The Citadel had never articulated statements against gay men in the corps; in its manuals, it just repeated the language of the state statute against buggery. Although there was a zero-tolerance policy on homosexuality and drugs in the 1960s, still, Citadel President General Hugh P. Harris knew both existed. When he asked Professor Oliver Bowman, who was known to be gay, what to do, Bowman suggested creating a counseling center to help cadets deal with such things. Students learned that certain rules governed their life on campus, but not necessarily elsewhere. Bowman recalls that gay cadets found safe zones and welcoming places like the Book Basement and musical salons held by Russel Wragg. Cadets began to rent places on Folly Beach and elsewhere to do the things verboten on campus.

The school's Human Relations policies protected employees from any discrimination based on gender or sexual identity. Over the years the experiences of LGBTQ students and faculty varied, some meeting very little prejudice and gaining acceptance from their peers. Others, however, had to remain closeted, and a few faced homophobia and its consequences. Somewhat similar to the secret society dramatized in Pat Conroy's fictional *The Lords of Discipline* (1980) set at The Citadel, LGBTQ students came together to create something much more benevolent: a word-of-mouth support group, with LGBTQ alumni mentoring cadets and distinguished members of the military coming to speak. (But when Paramount Pictures wanted to film *The Lords of Discipline* on the campus, administrators declined, following the example of *End as a Man* some 25 years before.) A Gay and Lesbian Alliance, with a subsequent name change to the Citadel Pride Society, was founded in 2008. Inevitably, a gay male romance based on Citadel cadets, titled *Knobs*, appeared in 2016.

The Medical University of South Carolina was also making great strides in adapting to new attitudes, and like The Citadel, one's acceptance varied, both for students and faculty. While some applicants, like Richard Little, had been turned down for being gay and others had to behave discretely in those years, eventually it became easier. Yet new arrivals to town were sometimes shocked at the antiquated views of physicians on staff about LGBTQ health issues, and sought less-prejudiced doctors elsewhere. It was by no means across the board, however. MUSC has a longstanding Gay/Straight Alliance, called the MUSC Alliance for Equality, an organization of students of all orientations and identities coming together "for anyone whose real or perceived sexual orientation, gender identity, or alliance may put them in an at risk minority group." Goals include educating all on LGBTQ and related issues, both students and policymakers, while the group provides connections to a national network of LGBTQ health professionals. Overcoming past prejudices and building on its history of AIDS and HIV research, in 2016 MUSC Health was recognized as a "Leader in LGBT Health Care Equality" by the Human Rights Campaign Foundation, the educational arm of the country's largest LGBTQ civil rights organization.

The area's other institution of higher learning, Charleston Southern University, founded as the Baptist College in 1964, was on the "Shame List" maintained by Campus Pride, mostly due to its 2014 receipt of an exemption to Title IX, allowing the school to accept federal funding even while discriminating against students for sexual orientation, gender identity, and on other issues as marital status, pregnancy, or having had abortions. Yet a posting on the Internet suggests that LGBTQ students at Charleston Southern have sought out each other for comfort, if not to confront the rules. Views expressed by Lynn Moldenhauer a decade before were still proving true: some organized religions continued to resist acceptance and make life harder for LGBTQ people in Charleston and the larger society.[5]

While a few organizations and individuals remained retrograde on sexual identity and civil rights issues, more and more people held increasingly liberal attitudes. In 2009 the City of Charleston expanded ordinances on housing to protect discrimination against sexual orientation and gender identity. Laws eventually included protections of LGBTQ people in areas of municipal employment and public accommodations, with the nearby municipalities of Mount Pleasant and Folly Beach having similar statutes. In 2017 Charleston would be recognized as one of only two cities in the state with a passing grade by the Human Rights Campaign on protections for its LGBTQ citizens, scoring a 72. Columbia followed closely with a 71, with both scoring higher in 2020. The Sun Belt continued its appeal to retirees, but younger people were also intrigued, discovering the amenities of the beach, good cuisine, and other opportunities in the Lowcountry. Lynn Dugan was one of the many.[6]

Born and raised in New York City, Dugan came out young, and eventually came to know some of the men and women who participated in the Stonewall Riots; she continued her activism as she lost friends to the HIV plague ravaging the city. In 2003, when visiting a brother in Rock Hill, South Carolina, she searched for a place that could offer "art, and music, and culture, a close airport, and [be] kind of gay-friendly." (Sue Groff had come to town earlier in search of a state and a city allowing lesbians the rights of adoption. Relocating, she worked as an attorney in employment law and social justice.)

The Pride Parade took place in Columbia the year Dugan was visiting. She went and met Charlie Smith, who offered her a ride in his convertible in the parade. Dugan explained she was looking to relocate. "'Why don't you come check Charleston out?'" he asked.

"So, I came down ... and he introduced me around. And everyone was so friendly ... I knew as soon as I got here ...

that there was a community. It was strong, hidden ... but definitely here."

In 1670 Native Americans of varying gender expressions saw European outsiders arrive to inject poisonous ideas and condemn them for the open way they lived. But for at least a century, the pattern slowly reversed. More and more enlightened outsiders were arriving to challenge the homophobic attitudes that had taken root and been endemic for years.

In 2003 Dugan moved to town and immediately started the Charleston Social Club for lesbians "so that we could socialize ... it was so people could come out to see who's gay." She realized many women were isolated. Not liking the bar scene, they much preferred and welcomed the new opportunity to gather for concerts, boating, kayaking, house parties and movie nights. Within a couple of years hundreds of women were involved. "I remember women crying that they were so happy they found Charleston Social Club," Dugan said in her oral history. The gatherings grew and an annual celebratory party called Lezz Fest took root in North Charleston. For the club's 10th anniversary, "[w]e had music ... We had games, we had booths set up. We had people coming in from everywhere." Men came, too. Over 1,000 attended with very little pushback from the community.

In 2009, making her annual trek to the Pride Parade, again in Columbia, Dugan had an idea. "I thought, 'Why in God's name am I driving all the way up here, dragging everything, trying to get people to represent Charleston Social Club? ... Why don't we have something in Charleston?"

"So, after I came home, I said, 'That's it. I'm going to get this going. I have no idea what I'm doing. I have no idea how it can be done, but I'm just really determined.' So, I started calling the city about permits, where we could have it, would they allow us to have it?"

The response from the city of Charleston was testy at best, with a city employee responding, "'You'll never have a Gay Pride here.'" Dugan thought to herself, "Okay, we'll see about that."

There had been Outfests sponsored by LGLA at Brittlebank Park and Folly Beach; gays and straights had marched in AIDS vigils; in 2008, when the marriage amendment failed on the ballot in California, hundreds of Charlestonians massed and marched from Liberty Square on the Cooper River to City Hall to voice protests. But there had never been anything like this — a Pride Parade, not protesting or mourning, but celebrating the joy and visibility of being LGBTQ. Back in 1981, the first gay newspaper in town had preached that there was an obligation to be proud, as if encouraging individuals to do their duty. Now Dugan sensed it bursting from the community.

"It's time," she told *The City Paper*. "It's really way overdue." And that was her theme: "It's Time to Bridge the Gap," showing a logo of a rainbow over the iconic Ravenel Bridge connecting the peninsula of Charleston to the mainland. It would not just link Mount Pleasant and Charleston, the beaches, West Ashley and North Charleston, but all groups and citizens. It would also serve as a bridge from the past to what the future could be; "that concept of 'us' ... important …. for the health of community" found lacking in 1981 had been overcome. In the three crucial decades since the founding of *Gay Charleston*, in organizing socially and politically, in fighting AIDS, in taking care of others, in nurturing its youth, creating self-respect and demanding it from others, lesbian, gay, bisexual, transgender, queer and questioning people had become a force in the Lowcountry.

The City Paper, a weekly alternative to the standard press, realized the significance. "Indeed, Charleston's gay community has been loosely organized amongst nonprofit and support groups like Alliance for Full Acceptance, but education and advocacy programs took priority over the time-consuming proposition of a pride event." There was CATS, Charleston Area Transgender Support, run by Lee Ann Leland (whose father had written acidly of transsexual Dawn Langley Simmons), We Are Family, MCC, AIDS organizations, straight and gay alliances, and welcoming congregations — but all were responses to problems or issues. Dugan saw a parade as a chance to bring all populations together to revel and celebrate, a sort of a vast centuries-in-the-making coming-out party.[7]

A few were unsure. Police had not solved a three-year-old murder of a gay teacher from First Baptist School who had probably been cruising the Battery. The survey done by *The Loop* a few years before revealed the qualms many felt even just holding hands in public; most LGBTQ candidates had gone down in defeat; the state legislature kept demeaning laws on the books and passed new ones against LGBTQ equality.

As if enforcing those homophobic views, the Charleston city official continued to resist Dugan's request for a parade permit. Dugan was firm, yet relentless, and so the official conceded, but only to a march "down East Bay [Street], or towards Liberty Square, near the Aquarium," a space literally on the margins of the city, the one space the community had occupied for centuries. Dugan saw it as demeaning and settling for less, so she deferred, insisting on nothing less than a permit that would grant respect, legitimacy, and admit LGBTQ presence into the very heart of Charleston. She demanded the traditional route down King or Meeting streets.

But the official would not budge.

Dugan then looked a little afield and met with Keith Summey, mayor of North Charleston. "He was more than welcoming. ... He couldn't have been more supportive. And, believe me, he got a lot of pushback. ... I think he told me 47 ministers came to complain. ... He was really welcoming," Dugan reported.

"This is not in any way saying that I am supportive of their lifestyle," Summey qualified to the press. "Though I do not agree with everyone's lifestyle, I firmly believe in everyone's equality," he said. And Dugan, ever gracious, dubbed Summey a "visionary."

With a venue and date, there were now deadlines to meet. The first fundraiser was held on Johns Island — an oyster roast in the pouring rain. But nothing dampened the enthusiasm of Dugan and her volunteers, who met in a local coffee shop and divided up chores and duties. Further fundraisers were held every third week, but with only four months to plan, the effort was rigorous. Sensing the importance of what they were doing, meeting after work, people did not sleep, and gave up their weekends.

"It was really exhausting, but it came together. And people, the community supported us. They finally got that, yeah, this was really going to happen. ... By the time February and March rolled around, they were just supporting the heck out of us. So, without the team, and without the support of the community, it wouldn't have happened."

They raised $28,000 with AFFA acting as fiscal agent. Dugan's "Team Pride" crew included Annie Sheehan, Amy Sloane, Brannon Montgomery, Cheryl Glenn, Dominic Kelly, Isabel Alexander, Julianne Suchy, Karen Allen, Melissa Bridges, Misty Brady, Paul Rakoczy, Reba Parker, Sharen Mitchell, Joseph Fennell, and Tera Mabe.

The date was May 15, 2010, a cusp for the community, a chance to succeed. The day dawned hot, and the route was long—stretching from Park Circle to Riverfront Park. Dugan was nervous, but cautiously optimistic; the event's website had gotten over 60,000 hits.

The Real Rainbow Row

Fourteen people, including co-organizers Paul Rakoczy and Joseph Fennell were in line, and Dugan thought, "Okay this is it. This is really happening." She hoped at least 400 people would show up.

Fifty floats were in line representing institutions and groups.

"There is no gesture more loving than to allow others to know who you are," the program decreed, listing the reasons "WHY WE MARCH... It is a matter of trust. A token of respect. And honor bestowed."

And with that in mind, the parade started.

There were "lots of families by the side of the road," Dugan saw, as well as individuals and institutions. Many churches joined in support; "whether you were straight or gay, it didn't matter." Not 400, but 4,000 people attended that day with straight allies, Dugan believed, "vital to the success." People danced, laughed, and cried, most never thinking they would live to see the day that LGBTQ people could march proudly hand-in-hand, in groups, in families, in drag, or in clothes

Figure 57. LezzFest Guide

claiming one's identity in the middle of the day, in the middle of the street.

With people along the way cheering.

This was important: "People came in from all over ... Columbia supported us, as well. Savannah, Florida, Myrtle Beach, Augusta. ... The young people were jumping up and down of course. This was something new, but it was the older folk that were emotional because they couldn't imagine that this would happen here in this town ... I had one woman come up to me crying because she was so happy to be part of it and blessed."

Dugan and others feared the attendance of Fred Phelps, whose Westboro Baptist Church in Topeka, Kansas, lambasted LGBTQ people, blaming them for national catastrophes, and praying for their agonizing deaths. He was in the Lowcountry that day, but for whatever reason, he did not appear, and none of the local anti-LGBTQ churches showed up either. After hundreds of years of stops and starts, hopes, and fears, there were celebrations and cheers.

Four years later the Pride Parade made its way down King Street, threading through the heart and soul of the old city.

Figure 58. Lynn Dugan

Figure 59. 2010 Pride Parade program

At the end of the first march that hot day, there were speeches and a rally, with another celebration that evening. Dugan had succeeded in booking The Citadel's Johnson Hagood Stadium for the official after-the-rally Pride Party. People poured in to dance and hear the rapper Jipsta perform. Costumes were encouraged — sailor, construction worker, police officer, pirate, princess, or whatever, but the only cowboy allowed that night was Randy Jones of the Village People, recreating his part in the iconic disco group of the 1970s. Jones had been prevented by homophobes from performing in the Pride Parade at Myrtle Beach in 1998, but now there was no stopping him.

The festivities lasted till midnight, and when they were over, everyone knew there would be no going back. LGBTQ people had arrived, with pride, and with power, to claim their rightful place with a victory party.

Leaving, revelers looked up and Dugan stopped, amazed. "[W]e flew flags over The Citadel, the rainbow flags, and everybody was just blown away."[8]

Epilogue
After the March: A Summary

In a book dedicated to a community's coming of age and coming to terms with itself, any ending date is, of course, arbitrary, but the first Pride Parade may be as good as any. Changes and challenges inevitably continue; this brief summary suggests how the community has kept up its momentum. In the decade since that march down a Lowcountry street, it has grown in numbers, in visibility, in power, and in addressing the nature of its diversity and intersectionality, a word not in vogue in previous years.

In 2010, the Rev. Robert Arrington arrived, the first openly gay African American pastor in the state, shepherding his flock at his Unity Fellowship Church, eventually sharing space with Metropolitan Community Church. A Black Pride group with founders including Regina Duggins, one of the few minorities or women on the Charleston Pride board, separated itself from the latter organization in 2019. The purpose was to fill a need felt in the African American community for more representation in leadership and for programming in accessible places on more relevant topics. This move, it was suggested, was not so much a fracturing as a focusing on specific demographic needs. In 2021, as if in response, AFFA hired its first person of color and first female director, Holly Whitfield, replacing Chase Glenn. He had served as AFFA's first transgender leader and went on to head LGBTQ+ Health Services and Enterprise Resources at MUSC.[1]

Transgender empowerment and visibility grew in the community. In 2014 Charleston Area Transgender Support, under the continuing guidance of Lee Ann Leland and others, began the sad necessity of conducting an annual Transgender Day of

Remembrance, with support from such diverse groups as the Circular Congregational Church, the Unitarian Church, and the reform Kahal Kadosh Beth Elohim Synagogue, showing a shift in many religions' points of view. (The Secular Humanists of the Lowcountry were sponsors, too, and the Charleston Jewish Federation came out in support of Pride Marches, and the civil rights nature of LGBTQ issues. A schism appeared in the Episcopal Church, however, over ordination of women and LGBTQ marriage, breaking up congregations and families.) Hot button topics such as gender-neutral bathrooms in schools, and trans students on sports teams were debated locally as fiercely as they were nationally, as many organizations, such as the College of Charleston, created new "chosen name" policies, allowing individuals to discard names dead to each of them.

Violence against transgender people, especially trans women of color escalated dramatically. In 2019 Denali Berries Stuckey, murdered on Carner Avenue in North Charleston, not far from the Equality Hub on Reynolds Avenue, was one of the three such fatalities in South Carolina that year. In response to a similar attack, the Charleston Police Department, which had initiated gender identity training in 2018, held a town hall to hear people out. In 2020 it became the first police department in the state to create a Safe Space program, working with businesses identifying themselves through logos as supportive places for victims of harassment or violence. The next year, 2021, LGBTQ protections were stripped from language in proposed legislation going forward in the General Assembly for a Hate Crimes bill, but the ensuing public outcry was so dramatic that legislators reinstated the wording. The House passed the bill but several Republican senators objected and it did not come up for a vote, leaving South Carolina and Wyoming the only states lacking such legislation.[2]

Charleston City Council passed its own hate crime legislation in 2018; the city was perceived as the most LGBTQ accepting place in South Carolina. The fact was shockingly revealed when a man upstate, finding out his son was gay, drove him to the Lowcountry and put money in his hand. "'If you want to be gay, you can be gay in Charleston,' the father said. 'You're an embarrassment to us. No one wants you back.'"

In a 2018 report on needs of the LGBTQ community, a survey by AFFA, the College of Charleston, and the MUSC College of Health Care Professionals, the obvious need for extended outreach to LGBTQ youth was one of the recommendations. Improvements in health care were suggested, too, along with an expansion of strategies to counter bias and prejudice. Findings also stressed the need to help people navigate the system to access support programs, and to elevate and address issues of minorities and intersectionality. Half of those interviewed reported not being able to come out at work or at home, and one quarter had considered suicide.

Palmetto Community Care's (PCC) survey of 1,700 people in the tri-county area identified 23 new AIDS cases in 2018, up from 20 the year before. Seventy percent of the cases were people under 30, more than half were African American, and 90 percent were men who had sex with men. PCC enrolled people in its PrEP program, which provides a daily pill to reduce the chance of infection. In its outreach, the Roper St. Francis Hospital System opened a free-standing Ryan White Wellness Center for those living with HIV in 2016, eventually offering a variety of health, dental, wellness, vision, and counseling services under the direction of Kimberly Butler Willis.[3]

In 2019 the *Post and Courier*, now no longer an enemy of LGBTQ people and issues, broke the story of McKrae Game —founder and leader of the one of the largest conversion therapies programs in the country, centered in Spartanburg, South Carolina—coming out as gay, quoting his apologies and his acknowledgment of the fraud Hope for Wholeness had always been. (His 2015 book, *The Transparent Life: Learning to Live Without a Mask*, might be the most ironically titled of all the aforementioned LGBTQ autobiographies.) While the state, unlike most others, refused to outlaw such "therapies," the city of Columbia did.

In 2020, South Carolina took a giant and excessively belated step forward, not just in sex education, but in education (and free speech) in all its public primary, middle, and high schools, through an action prompted by Charleston teens. A lawsuit was filed on behalf of the Gender & Sexuality Alliance of LGBTQ and allied youth, headed by articulate young activist Eli Bundy at Charleston County's Magnet School of the Arts. They came together to fight the South Carolina Comprehensive Health Education Act, which had been in effect statewide since 1988. That law forbade any mention of homosexuality except in the context of disease in sex-education classes. It stifled discussion, encouraged discrimination and ignorance, made pariahs of the community, and a laughing stock of the state for being one of the last in the union to still have a "no promo homo" law on the books. There was a very swift ruling by the courts, and State Superintendent of Education Molly Spearman, acknowledging the unconstitutionality of the law, abandoned it. The victory had come at the behest of teenagers, many of whose parents had not even known a time before Stonewall. A new group whose members did remember it and had lived through that era, had now also organized: Prime Timers celebrated receiving its charter in November 2018, bringing gays of a certain age together for socials, outings, and meetings.[4]

That generation was witnessing changes never dreamed possible. In 2012 the Charleston Blockade Rugby Football Club became South Carolina's first and only gay sports team. Maria Rivers published *Beau*, a short-lived, full-color LGBTQ quarterly magazine launched in 2014, as drag brunches became the rage, with once-ostracized drag queens now paragons of popularity, many taking up political causes. At least one restaurant in town offered two Sunday brunches to accommodate the after-church crowds. Similarly, Gay Bingo grew enormously popular as a new funding strategy for Palmetto Community Care, again entertainment supplied by drag queens.[5]

Like the rest of the county, the local community was transformed and heartened by the arrival of marriage equality decided by the Supreme Court Judgment of *Obergefell vs. Hodges* on June 26, 2015. The event's celebration was muted in Charleston, it coming not long after the racist murder of nine African American congregants in Bible Study at Emanuel AME Church, plunging the city and the country into mourning. Earlier, in November 2014, Federal Judge Richard Gergel decreed South Carolina's ban on gay marriage unconstitutional. Nichols Bleckley and Colleen Condon promptly took out the first marriage license issued in the state at the Charleston County Probate Court, and on the 19th of the month, Kayla Bennett and Kristin Anderson's marriage in Charleston was the first legal same-sex union recorded. Countless others followed, making Charleston an LGBTQ destination wedding city.[6]

The visibility and power of LGBTQ people progressed even further in the hotly contested election of 2020, which culminated in the presidency of Joe Biden, who included LGBTQ people and issues in his embrace of a diverse America and its values. Thirteen counties out of the state's 46 had supported him, with Charleston's vote coming in at 55.5 percent for Biden. While the state went for Donald Trump, locally, lesbian Kristin Graziano defeated her male boss Al Cannon, a politically seasoned incumbent who had held the position of Charleston County Sheriff for years. Graziano's sexuality had not been an issue in the campaign; the public elected a candidate based on her integrity, ideas, and ideals, and her wife Elizabeth was fully acknowledged in her victory.[7]

Another milestone came in October, the month set aside for celebrating LGBTQ history. In recognizing progress, the importance of the past, and the contributions of organizations like LGLA, AFFA, We Are Family, and Charleston Pride, Mayor John J. Tecklenburg congratulated the community and affirmed the city's commitment to its LGBTQ citizens and its dedication to "inclusiveness, and mutual respect." He set his hand and seal on a document acknowledging the community's experience, the strides it had made, and the civil rights achieved.

But in November 2021, in a great lapse backward, Republican Governor Henry McMaster launched a call to remove LGBTQ gender-sensitive books from school libraries, calling them obscene. He also signed legislation to ban transgender children from playing on girls' or women's teams in the state's public schools and colleges the next year. That's when, finally, those who had been convicted of sodomy no longer had to register as sex offenders, even though the Supreme Court had overturned South Carolina's sodomy convictions in 2003. Then, in June 2022, the state's newly passed "Medical Ethics and Diversity Act" gave health care providers the power to deny treatment to trans, LGBTQ, or other people if it conflicted with their religious or ethical beliefs. And earlier, in 2021, as Charleston City Council debated the creation of a committee to deal with the effects of racism, LGBTQ issues were added only as an afterthought.[8]

The past is important to the city of Charleston, and so it must be to members of the LGBTQ community. In keeping faith with those who came before, whose labors helped achieve current liberties, the community remains vigilant. Its future is promising, but it remains to be seen if the story of its past, told here, will stand as a cautionary tale or as a valedictory.

Acknowledgments

Books have their own chronologies as to what called them into being. This one, built upon the work of predecessors and enriched by contemporaries and peers, is no exception. I gratefully acknowledge the assistance of those who were part of the evolution of a work which transitioned from a hazy idea into its current reality.

If credits are listed chronologically, a very important date came in 2016. That is when historic preservation graduate student Kymberly Mattern came into Special Collections at Addlestone Library to research her thesis investigating the possible nomination of local LGBTQ sites to the National Register of Historical Places. It was revelatory to see that a student of a younger generation naturally assumed that any archives supporting an academic institution, especially one with significant primary resources on local elites, as well as Jewish and African American lives, would also house materials on the LGBTQ community. Alas, this was not the case, and as an archivist, I was excited by her assumptions and prompted to action. Kerri Forrest of the Gaylord and Dorothy Donnelley Foundation was extremely receptive to the idea of a grant proposal to help remedy that oversight. Her help and that of Drs. Cara Delay and Beth Sundstrom in shaping the proposal led to its successful funding. It's no exaggeration to state that this book would not have been possible without the accumulation of archival materials and oral histories that the largesse of the Donnelley Foundation made possible.

Nor is it an exaggeration to say that the aforementioned Drs. Delay and Sundstrom and their students helped immeasurably. But the real success of the project is attributable to Rebecca Thayer and Brandon Reid. Each took it to heart, and, with passion and professionalism, went beyond the bounds of expectations and job descriptions to turn the idea into a reality, becoming trusted friends in the process. Donors, especially major contributors such as Linda Ketner, Harriet MacDougal, and Dr. Jim Phillips (the full list of donors is on our website https://speccoll.cofc.edu/lgbtq), made the extension of the project possible, enabling further research and outreach. Losing Rebecca for lack of funding was a major blow, but Brandon, despite professional commitments elsewhere, has continued to ensure the project's survival. Hopefully, more funding will be found, and institutional support will be forthcoming along with the establishment of an LGTBQ College of Charleston alumni affinity group. Rebecca and Brandon are the future of LGBTQ history.

They found collections, made contacts, and helped create the oral histories now accessible via the Lowcountry Digital Library (https://lcdl.library.cofc.edu/content/south-carolina-lgbtq-oral-histories-archives-and-outreach-project/). The narrators who shared their stories, including those cited in the text, all made valuable contributions of their time to keep history from disappearing. Oral histories referenced in the pages include those of Robert Ball, MD, Terry Cherry, Tanner Crunelle, Lynn Dugan, Terry Fox, DeLesslin George-Warren, Mark Gray, Sue Groff, Wilhelmina Hein, George Holt, K. J. Ivery, George Thomas Lamme, Dick Latham, Richard Little, MD, Linda Ketner, Michael Lott, MD, Melissa Moore, Pat Patrick, Tzipi Radonsky, Mike Schwarzott, Jack Sewell, Douglas Seymour, Gil and Robin Shuler, Charlie Smith, Jenny Turner, Steven Willard, and Tony Williams. A special note of gratitude goes to Andre Saade for allowing the extensive quotations from the oral history of his husband Joe Hall, whose premature death many of us are still mourning.

All of our narrators' stories, quoted or not, are important, as are those stories contained in the archival materials donated to Special Collections by various institutions and individuals.

The footnotes and bibliography of the book reveal the part these donors played in rescuing a past in danger of going undocumented. I thank you, and future historians do, too.

The oral history, archival and outreach project very fortunately caught the attention of Eileen Waldron of community-based WOHM radio. After interviewing me, Eileen spoke to her husband Michael Nolan, executive editor of Evening Post Books, proving again that it is not just what you know, but whom you know that matters. It was Michael who first suggested the possibility of a book. Astonished and flattered, I immediately demurred; the gaps in the historical record seemed insurmountable and the challenges too great to do the subject justice.

I was involved in Special Collections' 2014 launch of a website on local LGBTQ historical sites that had appeared under Dr. Sandy Slater's inspired title, "The Real Rainbow Row." The inspiration for the website itself had come from The College Reads! committee's equally brilliant choice of Alison Bechdel's *Fun Home* as the book to be discussed by incoming freshmen; the furor that it fueled on the college campus and in the state's halls of power (discussed in the text) was an impetus to prove to all that, despite what might be said, LGBTQ people and values had enriched the city for years.

After some reflection, it seemed to me that the online tour could serve as a template for a book, if not a narrative, then a guide to Charleston's LGBTQ sites. That prompted more research and reading; Liza Gadsden, Chris Nelson, and Brandon Lewter of Addlestone Library's Interlibrary Loan Department were heroic in assuaging my appetite and feeding my greed. A Writer's Retreat (begun by the late Dr. Consuela Francis and by Dr. Lynn Ford, who had chaired The College Reads! committee) offered an opportunity for a week of uninterrupted research and reading. After more work nights and weekends, it seemed that a narrative history might be possible. I thank Addlestone Library Dean Dr. John White, Dr. Suzanne Austin, provost of the

College of Charleston, and the committee that granted me a sabbatical to pursue its completion.

In the process of my work, numerous friends and colleagues shared their expertise on Charleston, LGBTQ, and local LGBTQ history. I also rediscovered notes jotted down from as long before as the 1970s, and recalled information shared with me over the years by those long deceased. While the living and the dead are attributed in footnotes, their contributions deserve elevation here. I gratefully acknowledge the help provided by David F. Addlestone, Beth Bilderback, David Boatwright, Rick Bodek, PhD, Oliver Bowman, PhD, the late Laura Bragg, Millicent Brown, PhD, Nic Butler, PhD, Lucas Carpenter, PhD, Marianne Cawley, the late Robert Cuthbert, Greg Day, Taylor DeBartola (who also worked valiantly to assure funding), Frank Deese, Susan Dunn, Terry Fox, Henry Fulmer, Mae Gentry, David Halsey, Louise Halsey, the late Jerry Hayes, Lisa Hayes, the late David Heisser, Steve Hoffius, Susan Hoffius, Lahnice Hollister, my late partner Olin B. Jolley, MD, Jonathan Ned Katz, Louise Knight, PhD, Barbara Lieu, the late Clifford (Kip) Milton, Alexander Moore, PhD, Alyssa Neely, Rose Norman, the late Edwin Peacock, Nancy Phelps, the late Dick Robison, Tina Rogonia, Dale Rosengarten, PhD, Wendy Salinger, Michelle Schohn, Howard Stahl, Barry Stiefel, PhD, Nancy Thode, Lish Thompson, Gene Waddell, John White, PhD, Susan M. Williams, PhD, and the late John Zeigler.

Charlie Smith and Linda Ketner were nothing but grace and generosity in their responses to my constant questions on contemporary LGBTQ history, they themselves having played key roles in the city. Tom Lamme also answered my every query. Friend, scholar, and mentor beyond compare, Stephanie Yuhl, PhD, vetted the entire text, doing her best to keep me from mistakes, missteps, and misperceptions. She vastly improved the manuscript; the mistakes in sins of omission and commission that no doubt dot the text are mine alone.

Staff at the College of Charleston, including Sam Stewart in particular, and staff at the South Carolina Historical Society including Virginia Ellison and Molly Silliman were most helpful in providing illustrations. At Evening Post Books, I'd like to thank Michael Nolan, Elizabeth Hollerith, Plum Champlin, John Burbage, and Pierre Manigault.

And if this book's chronology is to be true, I can't overlook those who prepared me for the task. My father, Samuel Greene, and most especially my mother, Regina Kawer Greene, survivors of the Holocaust, did their best within their means to raise a son open to intellectual pursuits, driven to meet goals, and to work, even in his scholarly way, against discrimination and prejudice. My beloved partner Olin B. Jolley, MD, who died at 33 of AIDS, altered my life for the better, and my loving husband Jonathan D.A. Ray, often over my protests for, lo, these many years, kept up the battle to give me a life in the present, despite the lures and the traps of the past. I would not be who I am, or this book what it is without his love and devotion and the contributions of all mentors, colleagues, and friends mentioned above.

And finally, of course, there are those whose stories I have tried to tell. Here's to them, and those whose lives are lost to us; may such human tragedy and discrimination never happen again.

Notes

Abbreviations:
The Charleston Alternative, CA
Charleston County Public Library, CCPL
Charleston Evening Post, EP
Charleston Library Society, CLS
Charleston *News and Courier*, NC
Charleston *Post & Courier*, PC
Gay Charleston, GC
South Carolina Historical Society, SCHS
South Carolina Historical Magazine, SCHM
Special Collections, Addlestone Library, College of Charleston. SCCofC
URLs for *South Carolina Encyclopedia* articles, for the most part, have been omitted.
Unless noted otherwise, all web citations were accessed September through December of 2021.

Chapter One

1. For information on Laudonniére and others' LGBTQ contacts, see Megan E. Springate (ed.) *LGBTQ America: A Theme Study of Lesbian, Gay, Bisexual, Transgender, and Queer History* (National Park Service, 2016), 5, https://www.nps.gov/subjects/lgbtqheritage/upload/lgbtqtheme-nativeamerica.pdf See also: Jonathan Ned Katz, *Gay American History: Lesbians and Gay Men in the U.S.A.* (New: Thomas Y. Crowell, 1976).

2. Ed Madden, "South Carolina," in Chuck Stewart (ed.), *Proud Heritage: People, Issues, and Documents of the LGBT Experience* (Santa Barbara, CA: ABC-Clio, 2105), vol. 3, 1170; William Benemann, *Male-Male Intimacy in Early America: Beyond Romantic Friendships* (New York: Routledge, 2012), 8.

3. Springate, *LGBTQ America*, 7, 6.

4. Oral history of DeLesslin George-Warren, SCCofC.

5. Quotes and information on O'Sullivan are from Patrick Melvin, "Captain Florence O'Sullivan and the Origins of Carolina," *SCHM*, 76, 4 (October 1975), 235-249. The sole source for the daughter (arriving a decade later) is Agnes Leland Baldwin, *First Settlers of South Carolina, 1670-1700.* (Easley, S.C: Southern Historical Press, 1985), 28.

6. Sheila R. Morris (ed.), *Southern Perspectives on the Queer Movement: Committed to Home* (Columbia, SC: University of South Carolina Press, 2018), xi.

7. Thomas Cooper (ed.), *The Statutes at Large of South Carolina Edited Under Authority of the Legislature* (Columbia, SC: A. S. Johnston, 1837), vol. 2, 465.

8. For a history of sodomy laws in South Carolina, see George Painter, "The Sensibilities of Our Forefathers: The History of Sodomy Laws in the United States: South Carolina" https://www.glapn.org/sodomylaws/sensibilities/south_carolina.htm

9. Cooper, *Statutes at Large*, vol. 2, 465.

10. For more on the topic see B. R. Burg, *Sodomy and the Pirate Tradition: English Sea Rovers in the Seventeenth Century Caribbean* (New York: New York University Press, 1995).

11. Walter J. Fraser, Jr., *Charleston! Charleston! The History of a Southern City* (Columbia: University of South Carolina Press, 1989), 12-13, 33-6. For Bonnet in women's clothes, see: https://www.postandcourier.com/350/articles/october-25-1718-pirate-stede-bonnet/article_8baf9760-122d-11eb-8f2a-b73d982cac37.html accessed May 1, 2021.

12. Reuben Greenberg and Arthur Gordon, *Let's Take Back Our Streets*! (Chicago: Contemporary Books, 1989), 67-9; Bentley Waterbush (pseud.), "Harassment on the Battery," *CA,* 1,1 (November 1982), 7.

Chapter Two

1. William Benemann, *Unruly Desires: American Sailors and Homosexualities in the Age of Sail* (self-published, 2019), 153, 53. For Abbott in Charleston, see his diaries published in *SCHM*.

2. Benemann, *Unruly Desires*, 36, 260; Lorri Glover, *Southern Sons: Becoming Men in the New Nation* (Baltimore, MD: Johns Hopkins University Press, 2007), 130. For mariner societies in Charleston, see C. C. Chichester, *Historical Sketch of the Charleston Port Society For Promoting the Gospel Among Seamen, with the 63d Annual Reports and List of Officers and Members* (Charleston, SC: News and Courier Book Presses, 1885).

3. [Managers of the Charleston Port Society], *Second Annual Report of the Board of Managers of the Charleston Port Society Read Monday, 21st March, 1825* (Charleston, SC: C. C. Sebring), 4; Benemann, *Unruly Desires,* 60. Chichester, *Historical Sketch,* 26-7.

4. Jack Hitt, "The Legend of Dawn," *GQ*, 68, 12 (October 1998), 275; Josephine Pinckney, *Sea-drinking Cities* (New York: Harper & Brothers Publishers, 1927).

5. Benemann, *Unruly Desires,* 96-151 passim, 117-18, 99.

Chapter Three

1. Leon Huhner, "Francis Salvador: Prominent Patriot of the Revolutionary War," *Publications of the American Jewish Historical Society*, 9, (1901), 107-22.

2. Huhner, "Francis Salvador" quotes John Drayton's *Memoirs of the American Revolution*, 111. Benemann, *Male to Male,* 12, 11.

3. "An Original Character," Obits and Death Notices, Abbeville County South Carolina, http://genealogytrails.com/scar/abbeville/obits_n-r.htm Mary Katherine Davis, "The Feather Bed Aristocracy: Abbeville District in the 1790s," *SCHM,* 80, 2 (1979), 147; Benemann, *Male to Male*, 1.

4.. J. H. Easterby, *History of the St. Andrew's Society of Charleston, South Carolina,1729-1929* (Charleston, SC: The Society, 1929), 44.

5. John Faucheraud Grimké, "Order Book of John Faucheraud Grimké. August 1778 to May 1780 (Continued)," *The South Carolina Historical and Genealogical Magazine* 14, 4 (October 1913), 220; Benemann, *Male to Male,* 64.

6. Benemann, *Male to Male,* 93-220 passim. For the Hamilton/Laurens letters, see Jonathan Ned Katz, *Gay American History,* https://www.outhistory.org/exhibits/show/rev/j-laurens

7. Ron Chernow, *Alexander Hamilton* (New York, Penguin Press, 2004), 95. E-mail communication from Lisa Hayes, CLS, December 11, 2020. Re *Roderick Ransom,* see Mark Mitchell and David Leavitt (eds.), *Pages Passed from Hand to Hand: The Hidden Tradition of Homosexual Literature in English from 1748 to 1914* (Boston: Houghton Mifflin, 1997), 1-15; Benemann, *Male to Male,* 128, 129. Chernow, *Hamilton*, 95.

8. "Out History: Alexander Hamilton and John Laurens: 1779 -1782," https://www.outhistory.org/exhibits/show/rev/hamilton-laurens-letters Benemann, *Male to Male,* xii. Chernow, *Hamilton,* 95.

9. "Out History: Alexander Hamilton and John Laurens: 1779 -1782," https://www.outhistory.org/exhibits/show/rev/j-laurens Chernow, *Hamilton,* 95; John C. Miller, *Alexander Hamilton: A Portrait in Paradox* (New York: Harper and Row, 1959) quoted in "Out History: Alexander Hamilton and John Laurens: 1779 -1782" (see footnote 8 above).

10. Katz, *Gay American History*, 452-56. Re the elder Francis Kinloch, see "18th Century Pride: The Sexuality of John Laurens https://www.18thcenturypride.com/the-sexuality-of-john-laurens/ and "As sincerely as a Republican can be to a Royalist," https://revolutionary-demosthenes.tumblr.com/post/616294221008224256/letter-francis-kinloch-to-johannes-von-m%C3%BCller

11. Re younger Francis Kinloch, see estate papers, 12-160-18/23 Middleton papers, SCHS. George W. Greene, US consul in Rome, mentions the two young men attending Kinloch. On July 25, 1840,

to Kinloch's sister, he wrote, "You have the assurance that tho in a foreign land, your brother has not died among strangers & that his last look was upon faces familiar & dear to him." The author thanks Alex Moore for this information. Benemann, *Male to Male*, 189, 191.

Chapter Four

1. Re Ashley Hall, Nicholson, and Duncan, see E. Milby Burton, February 1946 typescript history "The Patrick Duncan House" and Nic Butler's notes in vertical files, 172 Rutledge Avenue, SCHS; Douglas Egerton, Robert L. Paquette, Stanley Harrold, and Randall M. Miller. *The Denmark Vesey Affair: A Documentary History* (Gainesville, FL: University Press of Florida, 2017), 280-81. (The editors may be mistaken in their reference to the garden of a Duncan on Bull Street. It is not likely the enslaved would have conspired on a city street, but rather here, beyond city limits, where Blacks had more freedom.)

2. Martin Duberman's "Writhing Bedfellows" was first published in *Journal of Homosexuality*, 1980-1981, Fall-Winter, 6, (1-2), 85-101.

3. William Kauffman Scarborough, *The Allstons of Chicora Wood: Wealth, Honor, and Gentility in the South Carolina Lowcountry* (Baton Rouge: Louisiana State University Press, 2011), 80; Benjamin Allston to "Charly" Alston, March 9, 1861, R. F. W. Allston Papers, SCHS, 12-17-9; Anthony Q. Devereux, *The Life and Times of Robert F.W. Allston* (Georgetown, SC: Waccamaw Press, 1976); Benjamin Allston to "My Dear Father," December 5, 1849, R. F. W. Allston Papers, SCHS, 12-2-20; Benjamin Alston to "Charly," March 9, 1861. The "W" in R.F.W. Allston is for "Withers", as in Thomas Jefferson Withers, Hammond's bedmate.

4. Charles P[etigru] Allston to "Dear Mama," April 21, 1861, R. F. W. Allston Papers, SCHS, 12-14-3.

Chapter Five

1 Benemann, *Male to Male*, 64, 42-4. GC notes local NOW history, March 1981, and has an advertisement, June 1982; CA lists it among local resources.

2. Christina Snyder, "The Lady of the Cofitachequi: Gender and Political Power among Native Southerners," in Marjorie Julian Spruill, Valinda W. Littlefield and Joan Marie Johnson, *South Carolina Women: Their Lives and Times*, (Athens: University of Georgia Press, 2009) vol. 1, 11-25; Margaret Sankey, "Coming, Affra Harleston," *The South Carolina Encyclopedia*; Karen J. Blalock, "Hume, Sophia Wiginton, *The South Carolina Encyclopedia*; Chapter 5: "Loose, Idle and Disorderly: Slave Women in the Eighteenth-century Charleston Marketplace" in David Gaspar and Darlene Clark Hine, *More Than Chattel: Black Women and Slavery in the Americas* (Bloomington: Indiana University Press, 1996), 97-110. The author thanks Louise Knight for her insight on the Grimké imagery. Arkee Escalera, "Harlem Renaissance at 100: Angelina Weld Grimké: Lesbian Poet Laureate," http://www.newnownext.com/ harlem-renaissance-at-100-angelina-Grimké-lesbian-love-letters-poems/02/2020/ Thomas L. Johnson, "King, Susan Dupont Petigru," *The South Carolina Encyclopedia*.

3. For Whitman on Simms see *Emerson's United States Magazine*, June 1857, in *The Complete Prose Works of Walt Whitman* (New York: G. P. Putnam's Sons, 1902), vol. 6, 174. Gloria Rudman Goldblatt, *Ada Clare, Queen of Bohemia*: http://digital.lib.lehigh.edu/cdm4/nysp_viewer2.php?col=-clare For information on Menken and Clare, see Noreen Barnes-McLain, "Bohemian on Horseback: Adah Isaacs Menken," in Robert A. Schanke and Kim Marra (eds.), *Passing Performances: Queer Readings of Leading Players in American Theater History* (Ann Arbor: The University of Michigan Press, 1989) 63-79; quote, 76.

4. Buzzard (pseud.), "Charleston Correspondence, Charleston, October 24, 1859," *National Police Gazette*, November 12, 1859; and in the same publication: "Charleston Correspondence, Charleston, S.C., Nov 28th, 1859," December 17, 1859; "Charleston Correspondence. Charleston, July 2, 1859," July 16, 1859.

5. Pink, "Charleston Correspondence, Charleston, S. C., April 20, 1861," *National Police Gazette*, May 11, 1861. William S. King, in *The Newspaper Press of Charleston, S.C.: A Chronological and Biographical History, Embracing a Period of One Hundred and Forty Years* (Charleston, SC: E. Perry, 1872), 145, notes the "Pink"s: J. W. Kennedy and L. Israels. Pink contributed a column to the

Charleston paper called "New York Correspondence" and wrote his Charleston columns for the New York press, which the local paper did not reprint. Pink did report on Ada Clare (the stage name of local Jane McElhenny) whose "*nom de plume* is, or ought to be well known in your latitude," "Correspondence of the Courier, New York, March 31, 1860," *Courier*, April 4, 1860.

Chapter Six

1. Charlotte Myers Griswold's commonplace book, SCCofC.

2. See Joy Bayless, *Rufus Wilmot Griswold: Poe's Literary Executor* (Nashville: Vanderbilt University Press, 1943) and Rufus Griswold, *Passages from the Correspondence and Other Papers of Rufus W. Griswold* (Cambridge, MA: W. M. Griswold, 1898.)

3. His review of *Leaves of Grass* appeared in *The Criterion*, November 10, 1855 https://whitmanarchive.org/criticism/reviews/lg1855/anc.00016.html

4. Cynthia Lee Patterson, "'Hermaphroditish Disturbers of the Peace': Rufus Griswold, Elizabeth Oakes Smith, and Nineteenth-Century Discourses of Ambiguous Sex," *Women's Studies*, 2016, 45:6, 513-33.

5. All references are from his *Statement of the relations of Rufus W. Griswold with Charlotte Myers (called Charlotte Griswold) Elizabeth F. Ellet, Ann S. Stephens, Samuel J. Waring, Hamilton R. Searles, and Charles D. Lewis; with particular reference to their late unsuccessful attempt to have set aside the decree granted in 1852 by the Court of common pleas of Philadelphia County, in the case of Griswold vs. Griswold* (Philadelphia: H. P. Ashmead, 1856).

6. Griswold, *Statement of the Relations*, 13.

7. Charlotte Griswold's version is summarized in "Dr. Rufus W. Griswold's Divorce," Cleveland, Ohio *Leader*, January 8, 1856, and other papers of the day. Griswold quoted the comparison to a French novel in Griswold, *Statement of Relations*, 19.

8. Griswold, *Statement of Relations*, 28. Even feminist scholars aware of Griswold's misogyny take his view of Charlotte as fact. See Patterson, *Hermaphroditish Disturbers*, 517.

9. For Caroline's writing career, see Mary T. Tardy (ed.), *Living Female Writers of the South*, (Philadelphia: Claxton, Remsen & Haffelfinger, 1872), 505.

10. Death record card files, South Carolina Room, CCPL.

11. Bayless, *Rufus Wilmot Griswold*, 106. Griswold, Passages, 9, 10. "Don Juan," canto 2, stanza 194. Bayless, *Rufus Wilmot Griswold*, 33. Bayless, on why Hoffman never married, suggests it was due to having an amputated leg.

12. Nic Butler, "Under False Colors: The Politics of Gender Expression in Post-Civil War Charleston" https://www.ccpl.org/charleston-time-machine/under-false-colors-politics-gender-expression-post-civil-war-charleston#:~:text=Annual%20Report-,Under%20False%20Colors%3A%20 The%20Politics%20of%20Gender,in%20Post%2DCivil%20War%20Charleston&text=In%20the%20 spring%20of%201868,they%20do%20such%20a%20thing%3F

13. X, "Charleston Correspondence, Charleston, S.C. Nov. 28, 1859," *National Police Gazette*, December 17, 1859. "A Female Sailor," December 2, 1848, notes a woman dressed as a male, caught on a ship to Charleston. The Captain, was going to "restore… her to a proper sense of the responsibilities of her sex."

Chapter Seven

1. "Anna C. Brackett, 'Charleston, South Carolina (1861)'" in Jennie Holton Fant (ed.), *The Travelers' Charleston* (Columbia: University of South Carolina Press, 2016), 321-9.

2. Debbie Bloom, "'An Abiding Mark': The Charleston Students of Anna C. Brackett," *Carologue* (A Publication of SCHS), Winter 2016, 20-3. The poem is quoted in Dorothy G. Rogers, *America's First Women Philosophers Transplanting Hegel, 1860-1925* (London: Continuum, 2005), 82; the book contains information on Brackett and Elliott.

3. "City Intelligence," *Charleston Courier*, January 28, 1860. Jonathan Ned Katz, *Love Stories: Sex Between Men Before Homosexuality* (Chicago: University of Chicago Press, 2001), 308-16.

4. For Brackett's article, see Fant, *Traveler's Charleston*, 321-9. Meredith Martindale and Pamela Moffat, *Lilla Cabot Perry, an American Impressionist* (Washington, D.C: National Museum of Women in the Arts, 1990). Katz (footnote above) notes Peirce and Perry.

5. For information on Badeau (and Booth) see "Adam Badeau (1831 — 1895)" https://outhistory.org/exhibits/show/badeau/badeau. The author thanks Jonathan Ned Katz for bringing them to his attention. Goldblatt, *Ada Clare*, 104. The attack by Booth in the Planters Hotel is told in the standard biographies and referenced here: https://www.nps.gov/places/dock-street-theatre.htm.

6. For Joseph Adrian Booth, see New Gallery: Joseph Adrian Booth | LincolnConspirators.com; See Mordecai's diaries, Thomas J. Tobias Collection, SCCofC, 1029-5-9 and 1029-5A-10, the latter available: https://lcdl.library.cofc.edu/lcdl/catalog/lcdl:31741 James Traub, *Judah Benjamin: Counselor to the Confederacy* (New Haven: Yale University Press, 2021).

7. Michael Bronski, *A Queer History of the United States* (Boston: Beacon Press, 2011), xix.

8. T. J. Johnson, *The War Apart* (Hard Title Publishing, 2008) and *The War Ahead* (Hard Title Publishing, 2008). Kellie Granier, "Carolina Interlude," *Prologue of Seduction: Sexy Stories Collection* (Xplicit Press, 2014), 1-15.

9. Julien Green, *South: A Play* (New York: Marion Boyars, 1991).

10. Mark Brown, "New Unearthed ITV Play Could Be the First Ever Gay Television Drama," (The Guardian Friday, March 15, 2013). https://www.theguardian.com/film/2013/mar/16/itv-play-gay-television

11. William Furtwangler, "Actors' Theatre Presents Play with Different View of Old South," *PC*, October 9, 2004.

Chapter Eight

1. https://www.carolana.com/SC/Documents/South_Carolina_Constitution_1868.pdf For South Carolina sodomy laws, see: https://www.glapn.org/sodomylaws/sensibilities/south_carolina.htm

2. For "Negro laws," see David J. McCord, *The Statutes of South Carolina: Containing the Acts Relating to, Charleston, Courts, Slaves and Rivers* (Columbia: A. S. Johnson, 1840). Charleston, SC city statutes also had many such restrictive dress codes.

3. For information on Jehu Jones, see *The South Carolina Encyclopedia*.

4. W. Craft, *Running a Thousand Miles for Freedom, or The Escape of William and Ellen Craft from Slavery*. (London: William Tweedie, 1860); Butler, "Under False Colors," footnote 4. City of Charleston Police Records, MSS 366, vol. 2, December 1861-March 1865, CLS.

5. Butler, "Under False Colors."

6. Harlan Greene (ed.), *Porgy and Bess: A Charleston Story* (Charleston, SC: Homehouse Press, 2016).

7. DuBose Heyward, *Mamba's Daughters* (Garden City, NY: Doubleday, Doran & Co., 1929), 28; Dorothy and DuBose Heyward, *Mamba's Daughters: A Play* (New York: Farrar & Rinehart, 1939), 19. "B.D. Woman's Blues" lyrics by Lucille Bogan https://www.jiosaavn.com/lyrics/b.d.-womans-blues-lyrics/QxEaUEJCcwc See also: https://timeline.com/lesbian-blues-harlem-secret-f3da10ec2334

8. Dorothy Heyward, 180.01.03.04 (C) 04-23, Dorothy Heyward Papers, SCHS.

9. Ethel Waters with Charles Samuels, *His Eye Is on the Sparrow* (Garden City, NY: Doubleday, 1951), 150, 247, 250. For the television version see: https://eyesofageneration.com/fascinating-photo1939-nbc-presents-mambas-daughters-staring-ethel-waters/

10. Butler, "Under False Colors," note 15; *Yearbook City of Charleston: 1895* (Charleston, SC: Walker, Evans & Cogswell Co, 1896), 183; *Yearbook City of Charleston: 1902* (Charleston, SC: Walker, Evans & Cogswell Co., 1903), 121; Butler, "Under False Colors," note 16.

Chapter Nine

1. Gary Scharnhorst, et al. *Oscar Wilde in America: The Interviews* (Urbana: University of Illinois Press, 2010), 162-65. Also: https://www.oscarwildeinamerica.org/lectures-1882/july/0707-charleston.html accessed December 2, 2019.

2. Richard Ellmann, *Oscar Wilde* (New York: Alfred A. Knopf, 1988), 197.

3. *EP*, April 6, 1895, April 11, 1895, April 27, 1895, and May 25, 1895.

4. "Oscar Wilde on Trial," *EP*, April 11, 1895; "Two Years for Wilde," *EP*, May 25, 1895; "Wilde Has Friends," *EP*, April 30, 1895; "The Case Against Wilde," *EP*, April 27, 1895; "Wilde Under Arrest," *EP*, April 6, 1895; "Two Years for Wilde: And English Justice is Again Vindicated," *EP*, May 25, 1895.

5. "Was Never Popular," *EP*, April 13, 1895. An article, April 15, 1895, *EP*, notes burning of Wilde's books by the Newark, NJ public library.

6. The poem is quoted in a transcription of the *Blue Book* in Mark R. Jones, *Wicked Charleston, Volume 2: Prostitutes, Politics and Prohibition* (Charleston, SC: The History Press, 2006), 112.

7. "A Vile Resort," *EP*, May 22, 1899. The article immediately above it, "In the Police Court," lists the names of the Black offenders and their sentences again.

8. "An Appeal Taken," *EP*, May 26, 1899.

9. "An Appeal Taken," *EP*, May 26, 1899; "Before the Recorder," *EP*, May 27, 1899.

10. The case papers, part of the records of the Recorder's Court at CCPL, present in the early 2000s, are now missing.

11. For charges against a Gus Green see the *EP*: threatening to cut S. Banov, August 8, 1895; cutting someone, January 27, 1896: stealing from Sinclair White, "Police Court," January 21, 1896; larceny, "Before the Recorder." July 7, 1898; and for fighting, August 31, 1899. Ed Drayton, charged in the brothel with Green, is referenced again as "disorderly" and "vile," "Before the Recorder," January 13, 1904. "Disorderly" was often used, as in running a "disorderly" house, but "vile" suggests a further level of disgust. They are not called "colored" in these articles, while some others are, or called "coons." There is a later mention of Gus Green, colored, "In the Police Court," November 15, 1915. The articles relating to the shootout near where a Gus Green also was involved, are "Shooting on Marion Square," *EP*, April 9, 1901; and "A Remarkable Case," *EP*, April 16, 1901; his death record card at the South Carolina Room, CCPL, notes age, occupation, date of death, etc. Recorder records in the Archive, CCPL, also contain other charges against a Gus Green.

12. https://www.findagrave.com/memorial/86339753/huger-wilkinson-jervey

13. For the South's fascination with classics, etc., noting Charlestonians and Thomas Grimké, see Edwin A. Miles, "The Old South and the Classical World," *The North Carolina Historical Review*, 48, 3 (July 1971), 258-275. J. H. Easterby, *A History of the College of Charleston, Founded 1770* (Charleston, SC: The Trustees of the College of Charleston, 1935), 169.

14. Benjamin E. Wise, *William Alexander Percy: The Curious Life of a Mississippi Planter and Sexual Freethinker* (Chapel Hill: University of North Carolina Press, 2012), 48, 50, 51, 221.

15. *Yearbook City of Charleston: 1899* (Charleston, SC: Walker, Evans & Cogswell Co., 1900), 136. John Hammond Moore, *Carnival of Blood: Dueling, Lynching, and Murder in South Carolina, 1880-1920.*(Columbia: University of South Carolina Press, 2006), 76-8.

16. "Before the Recorder," *EP*, January 22, 1895. He is not referred to as "colored", the custom then for Blacks charged with crimes. But a "colored" man was listed as charged with buggery in the *City of Charleston Year Book: 1895*, 181. "The Criminal Court," *EP*, November 5, 1898, 8; "Are Accused of Riot," *NC*, March 2, 1901, 8.

17. Law and Order League Records, SCHS, 43-0024. *EP* advertisement "The Law and Order League of Charleston," May 21, 1913, 9; "Law and Order League, Searchlight No. 1: The Road to Memminger," May 28, 1913, 8; "The Law and Order League Announces the Discontinuance of Their Search Light Series in its Present Form," June 14, 1913, 2; "Law and Order Auxiliary," December 3, 1913. "Mayor Grace's Annual Review," in *Yearbook City of Charleston:1923* (Charleston, SC: J. J. Furlong and Son, Charleston Printing House, 1924), xxxii-xxxv. *Special Report of the Law and Order League of Charleston, S.C. 1913*, 24-5.

18. Unknown author's manuscript notes, Law and Order League Records, SCHS, 43-0024.

Chapter Ten

1. Louise Anderson Allen, *A Bluestocking in Charleston: The Life and Career of Laura Bragg* (Columbia: University of South Carolina Press, 2001) is the source of information in this section.

2. James T. Sears and Louise A. Allen, "Museums, Friends and Lovers in the New South: Laura's Web, 1909-1931," *Journal of Homosexuality*, 40, 1 (2000), 105-44, 106.

3. Henry James, *The American Scene* (London: Chapman and Hall, 1907), 417.

4. Allen, *Bluestocking*, 203, 222. Lillian Faderman, *Surpassing the Love of Men: Romantic Friendships and Love between Women from the Renaissance to the Present* (New York: Quality Paperback Book Club, 1994), 297-313, passim; Jenn Shapland, *My Autobiography of Carson McCullers* (Portland, OR: Tin House, 2020), 20-1.

5. Helen McCormack to Laura Bragg, August 1, 1928, July 19, 1928, and December 4, 1928, Laura Mary Bragg Papers, SCHS, (11/80/11-12); Allen, *Bluestocking*, 222. See footnote 2 above for the journal article reference.

6. Allen, *Bluestocking*, 222. Miss Bragg made the author one of her "boys" with a ceremony of ice cream, pound cake and a glass of Strega, which she introduced to Charleston.

7. Harlan Greene, *Master Skylark: John Bennett and the Charleston Renaissance* (Athens: University of Georgia Press, 2001), 141-2. "Dr. Huldah J. Prioleau: Negro Woman Physician, 60 [sic], is Buried Here," *NC*, December 17, 1940, 2. (A birthdate of July 4, 1866 is on her tombstone in the Unity and Friendship Cemetery, and the 1870 census, misspelling her name as "Prieaulean," lists Josephine, her middle name, as age four. The author thanks Lahnice Hollister for this information.) Dr. Huldah J. Prioleau, *Fair View Industrial Home Columbia, S. C.*, (no printer, no date), SCHS. The author thanks Susan Hoffius, past curator of the Waring Historical Library, for help on this issue.

8. "School Children at Playgrounds," *NC*, January 19, 1925, 7; "Field Meet Monday," *NC*, June 18, 1927, 10; "Fall Playground Sports Schedule Outlined in Meeting of Recreational Center Directors — Program is Varied," *NC*, September 24, 1937, 9.

9. Theodore Jervey to Huldah Prioleau, Jervey letter book, SCHS 28-257/1-2; "Colored Playground," *EP*, September 24, 1923, 11; *Yearbook City of Charleston: 1924* (Charleston: Walker, Evans & Cogswell Co., 1926), 147; "Dr. Huldah J. Prioleau: Negro Woman Physician, 60 [sic], is Buried Here," *NC*, December 17, 1940, 2. The 1940 City Directory lists Crawford as a nurse and a City Playground employee.

10. "Red Cross Work Has Been Heavy," *NC*, May 12, 1931, 12. See the letterhead in Prioleau's letters to John Bennett, John Bennett Papers, SCHS.

11. Legal announcement, *EP*, December 28, 1940, 10; "Realty Transfers," *NC*, September 19, 1942, 9. "Worthless Father Neglects His Wife and Six Children," *NC*, December 24, 1942, notes Crawford donating a dollar. Charleston City Directories note the lodgers. "Nursery Anniversary," *EP*, April 29, 1944. "Seek Support to Day Nursery Here," *Jackson* [MS] *Advocate*, September 9, 1944, 2.

12. When Eugene Hunt was interviewing Dr. Joseph Hoffman regarding early African American physicians in Charleston, the latter mentioned a Dr. Prioleau on Spring Street as "one of the three colored people on our block." He did not think she was a native, nor did he cite her first name, that being the only mention. Joseph Hoffman oral history transcript, Avery Research Center for African American History and Culture, 25. Her letter appears in "Good Work Done by R. C. Branch: Dr. Huldah Prioleau Tells of Service Given — Appeals for Members," *EP*, February 19, 1923, 5; "Allen University Announces Plans For Mammoth Founder's Day Here," Columbia, SC *Lighthouse and Informer*, January 21, 1950, 4. While online sites refer to Prioleau's contributions, no mention are made of Crawford or their relationship https://discovering.cofc.edu/items/show/19?tour=2&index=6 and https://www.ccpl.org/charleston-time-machine/10-progressive-women-early-20th-century-charleston

13. For information re the Mickey, Harleston and Jenkins families, see Edward Ball, *The Sweet Hell Inside: A Family History* (New York: William Morrow, 2001), passim; quotes re Ellen: 230-1, 347-8; and re Edward, 335; April 27, 2021 email communications from Mae Gentry, whom the author thanks, discuss Ellen's affair with a minister's wife and notes how family members believed Edmund Jenkins was gay;

the Mickey newspaper wedding announcement is printed in *EP*, October 1, 1926, 24. Ball mentions Laura Bragg and Harleston, but see also Susan V. Donaldson, "Charleston's Racial Politics of Historic Preservation: The Case of Edwin A. Harleston" in James Hutchisson and Harlan Greene, (eds.), *Renaissance in Charleston: Art and Life in the Carolina Lowcountry, 1900 – 1940* (Athens: University of Georgia Press, 2003), 176-98. Ball describes Edmund Thornton Jenkins passim; for his planned and abandoned wedding proposal (and a more focused view on Jenkins), see Jeffrey P. Green, *Edmund Thornton Jenkins: The Life of an American Black Composer, 1894-1926* (Westport, CT: Greenwood Press, 1982), 133.

14. For Clements, see Allen C. Abend, *Gabrielle DeVeaux* [sic] *Clements: Etcher, Painter, Muralist, Teacher* (Self-published, 2012); for Hale, see Claire Angelilli (ed.), *Inked Impressions: Ellen Day Hale and the Painter-Etcher Movement: January 26-April 14, 2007* (Carlisle, PA: Trout Gallery, Dickenson College, 2007); J. Franklin Burkhart, "Unitarian Church in Charleston," *EP*, May 6, 1924, 38.

15. Elizabeth O'Neill Verner, "Lines in Perspective" typescript, Verner papers, SCCofC. Martha R. Severens, *The Charleston Renaissance* (Spartanburg, SC: Saraland Press, 1998), 35-6.

16. For Jennings, see Allen, *Bluestocking*, passim, and Harlan Greene, *Why We Never Danced the Charleston* (Charleston, SC: The History Press, 2005), 119-27. See also Sears and Allen, "Museums, Friends and Lovers." This author does not agree that Jennings and puppeteer Tony Sarg were lovers, as claimed. The 1929 Charleston City Directory lists Sellers (1911-1971) as occupying the Broad Street studio with Jennings. His parents lived nearby at 101 Meeting Street; a few years later, he left Charleston, married, and died in 1971, "Robert B. Sellers" obituary, *EP*, February 2, 1971, 7.

17. Greene, *Mr. Skylark*, 216-17, 334 (note 53).

18. A failed love affair with a woman was suggested as a reason for suicide. Some suggest Nan Shan Ball, with whom he corresponded, but the finding aid to her papers, SCHS, suggests Julia Ball instead. See also the summary of the Gibbes Museum of Art's exhibit on Ned Jennings which does not mention his sexuality. http://www.tfaoi.com/aa/7aa/7aa753.htm

19. Gamel Woolsey, "*The Collected Poems of Gamel Woolsey* (Norfolk, UK: F. Crowe & Sons, 1984), 114; also: "In Memoriam: E. J." dedicated "To Ned Jennings of Charleston, who killed himself," 171. For Woolsey, see Gamel Woolsey, introduction by Barbara Ozieblo, *Patterns in the Sand* (Sherbone, Dorset, UK: The Sundial Press, 2012), i-vii.

20. The source for Hervey is Harlan Greene, *The Damned Don't Cry – They Just Disappear: The Life and Works of Harry Hervey* (Columbia: University of South Carolina Press, 2017).

Chapter Eleven

1. Barbara L. Bellows, *A Talent for Living: Josephine Pinckney and the Charleston Literary Tradition* (Baton Rouge: Louisiana State University Press, 2006), 43. Frank Durham, *DuBose Heyward: The Man Who Wrote Porgy* (Columbia: University of South Carolina Press, 1954), 26. James A. Lundy, *A History of the Poetry Society,* (Self-published, 2021), 91; an earlier draft in the author's possession notes that no local would host Millay. James T. Sears [sic], *Edwin and John: A Personal History of the American South* (New York: Routledge, 2009), 16. While the book is credited to Sears, John Zeigler made insistent claims as to his authorship. Sears annotated and footnoted it extensively. Henceforth, citations will note it as edited by Sears. Zeigler also stated that the propositioned woman was his bridge partner, Sara Simons (Mrs. C. Norwood) Hastie. "George Dillon: Poet's Own Requiem," *NC*, May 27, 1968, 10.

2. Bellows, *Talent for Living*, 50-4; Greene, *Mr. Skylark*, 181.

3. "Gertrude Stein Here Next Week," *NC*, February 4, 1935, 10; "'Poetry and Grammar': Subject is Announced for Gertrude Stein Lecture," *NC*, February 10, 1935, 14.

4. Nicholas Hobbes, "Adventures Among the Literati," *The Shako*, 3, 2 (Spring 1935), 31-3; Ashley Cooper, pseudonym of Frank B. Gilbreth, "Doing the Charleston," *NC*, January 23, 1953, 4. Philip R. Dillon, "After the French," (letter to the editor), *NC*, February 21, 1935, 5. Frank B. Gilbreth, "Who is the Best Writer Alive? 'I Am,' Says Gertrude Stein," *NC*, February 15, 1935, 3.

5. Frank B. Gilbreth, "Who is the Best Writer Alive? 'I Am,'" *NC*, February 15, 1935, 3. Ashley Cooper, pseudonym of Frank B. Gilbreth, "Doing the Charleston," *NC*, January 23, 1953, 4; February 26, 1953, 4; January 18, 1968.

6. "Frances Frost Well Received," *NC*, April 4, 1935, 2; Bellows, *A Talent for Living*, 149; "Frances Frost," in Steele, *Those Intriguing Indomitable Vermont Women* (Vermont State Division of the American Association of University Women, 1980), 52-4.

7. "Mr. Sam Gaillard Stoney Weds Miss Frost, Poet, at Peterboro," *NC*, September 19, 1933, 5. Pinckney, *A Talent for Living*, 149-151; Greene, *Mr. Skylark*, 234; Steele, "Frances Frost," 54. Sam Stoney would later joke that he was the father-in-law of God because his step daughter, Jean, as a nun in the order of St. Joseph, was married to Jesus.

8. Pinckney's affair was with Thomas R. Waring, editor of the *NC*, Bellows, *A Talent for Living*, 113-15, 161-2. Margaret Edwards, "Frances Frost, 1905-1959: Sketch of a Vermont Poet," *Vermont History*, 58, 2 (Spring 1988), 102-111, 105. Steele (in "Frances Frost," 53) notes that Frost "made a household with a journalist friend, Norene Carr Grace".

9. For Surles's life, see dust jacket copy of her biography of Gregorie and the finding aid for her collection of letters to Rankin, Arthur and Elizabeth Schlesinger Library on the History of Women in America at Harvard's Radcliffe Institute: https://snaccooperative.org/view/12356309. See also Walker Scott Utsey, *Who's Who in South Carolina: A Standard Biographical Reference Book of South Carolina*. (Columbia: Current Historical Association, n.d.), 465. For Gregorie, see Roberta VH. Copp, "Of Her Time, Before Her Time: Anne King Gregorie, South Carolina's Singular Historian," *SCHM*, 91, 4 (October 1990), 231-46. Copp sums up Surles's role in Gregorie's life in a footnote, calling her a "co-worker, close friend, and companion for twenty-nine years" (231, footnote 1). Flora Belle Surles, *Anne King Gregorie*. (Columbia: Printed for the author by R. L. Bryan Co., 1968), 147, 152-3.

10. Anne King Gregorie Papers, SCHS, 1254, 28-1-4. The author thanks Brandon Reid for bringing this to his attention. Her tombstone is in Christ Church Cemetery, Mount Pleasant, SC. https://www.findagrave.com/memorial/32602266/flora-belle-surles

11. Schuyler Livingston Parsons, *Untold Friendships: 60 Years with a Famous Host and his Famous Friends* (Boston: Houghton Mifflin Company, 1955), dust jacket text.

12. Tom Nall and Bobby Tucker, "Charleston's Changing Bar Scene," *The Loop*: 4, (December 2000), 9. Lee Hall, *Betty Parsons: Artist, Dealer, Collector* (New York: Harry N. Abrams, Inc. 1991),18-19, 178 ("Courtship, Wedding, Marriage": notes 2, 3, 4 and 5). Rauschenberg first came to Charleston in 1952 and photographed pedestrians, including a tall very fit sailor; he returned in the 1980s, later using Charleston images in collages and paintings. Sara C. Arnold, *Rauschenberg in Charleston* (Charleston: The Gibbes Museum of Art, 2019).

13. Parsons, *Untold Friendships*, 152-64, passim.

14. "Charleston Actor Says His Three-Legged Dog Got Him Role In Tennessee Williams Prize Winning Play," *NC*, August 19, 1956, 35; "S.C. Poetry Society Hears Broadway Actor at Meeting," *NC*, October 13, 1957; "S.C. Poetry Society To Hear Readings By Murray Bennett," *NC*, October 17, 1948; Jean Bosworth, "Over the Teacups," *NC*, October 14, 1954, with information on Bennett and Millay. Murray Bennet, *Invisible Pursuit* (New York: The Ram Press, 1961), 23.

15. Bennett, *Invisible Pursuit*, 27, 39, 42, 45. G[irdler]. B[rent]. Fitch, review of *Invisible Pursuit*, *NC*, December 17, 1961, 55. John Zeigler, ("Murray Bennett's Poetry Well Received," *NC*, January 12, 1962.) noted the poet "tell us, but not too explicitly, what he wishes us to know."

16. For Murray Bennett's papers, see https://library.syr.edu/digital/guides/b/bennett_m.htm Henry Timrod is referenced as the name of a literary society dealing with out gay writers in Felice Picano, *The Book of Lies* (Los Angeles: Alyson Publications, 1999).

Chapter Twelve

1. Photocopies in the author's possession. The author thanks a descendant for generously allowing the publication of these excerpts.

2. For information on Randolph and his impact on the College, see Easterby, *History of the College of Charleston*, 167-211, and Nan Morrison, *A History of the College of Charleston, 1936-2008* (Columbia: University of South Carolina Press, 2011), 8-37, passim.

3. Diaries of Harrison Randolph, January 30, 1935, January 31, 1935, January 30, 1935, Harrison Randolph Papers, SCCofC. The author thanks Gene Waddell for bringing this to his attention.

4. Diary of Harrison Randolph, May 5, 1934. Harrison Randolph Papers, SCCofC. German is used in the entry of August 23, 1933, Italian on February 2, 1935; both appear throughout.

5. "Acquit Powell in Murder Case," *NC,* November 19, 1930, 5; "Three Plead Guilty, Hear Sentence," *NC,* September 15, 1928, 3; "Court News," *NC,* June 10, 1937, 5; "Bound Over," *EP,* March 6, 1945, 9.

6. Diary of Harrison Randolph, May 5, 1934; March 4, 1935; January 30, 1935; February 2, 1935; Harrison Randolph Papers, SCCofC.

7. Entries mention the niece on August 22, 1933 and conclude on the 23rd, diary of Harrison Randolph, Harrison Randolph Papers, SCCofC.

8. Diary of Harrison Randolph, March 3, 1935, Harrison Randolph Papers, SCCofC. Morrison, *College of Charleston,* 29, 30.

9. Letter of Harrison Randolph to Judge Paul M. Macmillan, June 18, 1942, Harrison Randolph Papers, SCCofC; Morrison, *College of Charleston,* 37, 59-81, passim; "'Grass Roots' Citizens Club To Be Formed Here Tuesday," *NC,* January 24, 1952. For homophobic mentions see "Conservative, Inc." Newsletter, Bulletin No. 32, (February 11, 1965), Emily Ravenel Farrow Papers, Box 33, SCCofC. Besides President Grice and Professor Horatio M. Hughes at the College, others on the mailing list included US Senator Strom Thurmond, Charleston Mayor J. Palmer Gaillard, First Baptist Church minister John Hamrick, Star Gospel Mission's Rev. Ernest Dugan, Episcopal ministers Edward B. Guerry and Marshall E. Travers, Citadel President General Mark Clark, Clemson University President Dr. Robert C. Edwards, Medical College of SC Professor George Orvin, Ashley Hall Headmistress Mary V. McBee, and faculty from the University of SC, Clemson, Newberry, Furman, and Presbyterian College, Emily Ravenel Farrow Papers, SCCofC, Box 31, folder 4.

10. Estate Papers, Harrison Randolph Papers, 2019 Accession, SCCofC.

11. "The Man Who Lived 30 Years As A Woman: Georgia Black married twice, even 'mothered' devoted son," *Ebony,* VI, 12 (October 1951), 23-6. For a radically different story of gay sex as a servant in Charleston, see Roger Edmonson, "I Once Had Two Masters: Bob McNair Reflects On His Life as S-M Slave," *The Advocate,* issue 532 (August 29, 1989), 36-7.

12. Willie Sabb, "My Mother Was A Man: Philadelphia steelworker tells intimate story of how he was reared by Georgia Black, the man who lived as a woman for 30 years in Florida," *Ebony,* VIII, 8 (June 1953) 75-8, 80, 82.

Chapter Thirteen

1. "Teaching American History in South Carolina," *A Costly Prosperity: South Carolina in World War II* (scetv.org); Allan Bérubé, *Coming Out under Fire: The History of Gay Men and Women in World War II* (Chapel Hill: University of North Carolina Press, 2010), 105. For more on the *Myrtle Beach Bitch* and the men who went to prison for publishing it, see Allan Berube, *My Desire for History* (Chapel Hill: University of North Carolina Press, 2011), 113-24, passim.

2. Fraser, *Charleston! Charleston!,* 390-1. Vice reports are in Senator Burnet Maybank Papers, SCCofC, Box 44, folder 15. For Francis Colburn Adams, the best source (which omits his novel *An Outcast* linking Black and White slavery) is Harold Woodell, "Justice Denied in the Old South: Three Novels by F. Colburn Adams," *The Southern Literary Journal,* 11, 8 (Fall 1978), 54-63; Richard Coleman, "The Infamous Mansion," *Story: The Magazine of the Short Story,* XXXI, 123 (November-December 1947), 15-23.

3. For the Little Atlantic and other bars, see Senator Burnet Maybank Papers, SCCofC, Box 44, folder 15. City reactions are in "Minutes of the Conference… October 1, 1941…" in the same file. See also John White, "Un-'Holy City': Vice in Charleston, South Carolina, 1941 – 1943," unpublished typescript in author's possession; Charleston Chamber of Commerce, *1934 Guide Book, Fort Moultrie Camps, Fort Moultrie, S.C.: Regular Army National Guard Organized Reserves* (Charleston, SC: J. J. Furlong & Son, 1934), 19. "Marion Square," Bennett, *Invisible Pursuit,* 23.

4. *City of Charleston Year Book: 1942* (Charleston: Walker Evans and Cogswell Co., 1943), 130.

5. "Melvin Dwork, cast from Navy in WWII for being gay, dies" https://www.sfgate.com/nation/article/Melvin-Dwork-cast-from-Navy-in-WWII-for-being-8310554.php "Melvin Dwork,

The Real Rainbow Row

94, Once a Navy 'Undesirable' Dies," *New York Times,* June 17, 2016. Dwork had a notable career in interior design. See also Sears (ed.), *Edwin and John*, 105, re homophobic accusation against another soldier in Charleston.

6. "County Police Report Made," *EP*, January 18, 1943, 5; "Bound Over," *EP*, March 6, 1945, 9; "Lodged in Jail," *EP*, October 26, 1945: "Grand Jury Returns 49 True Bills as Criminal Court Opens," *NC*, December 4, 1945, 5; "Sessions Court Convicted 83, Exonerated Three Last Month," *EP*, October 7, 1946, 2.

7. For John Zeigler and Edwin Peacock see *Edwin and John* edited by James Sears. (See footnote 1, Chapter 11, above.) For "Nicky Bowen," see Ina D. Russell, *Jeb and Dash: A Diary of Gay Life, 1918-1945* (Boston: Faber and Faber, 1993.) See also John Zeigler, *The Edwin Poems* (self-published: Xlibris Corp., 2007). The book dedicated to Louise Halsey is Maurice Sendak, *Very Far Away* (New York: Harper & Bros., 1957).

8. While Taylor was depicting African American life in Charleston, he also collaborated with Langston Hughes, protesting for African Americans' civil rights. Taylor, the subject of Van Vechten photographs, photographed Black gay artists, sometimes as "Baxter Snark," including the sculptor Richmond Barthé (1901- 1989), who had an affair with Richard Nugent (1906-1987), an out Black artist in the Harlem Renaissance. Nugent toured for years in DuBose and Dorothy Heyward's play *Porgy*. For Barthé's and Nugent's relationship see: https://africanah.org/portrait-of-a-friendship-2-richmond-barthe-and-richard-bruce-nugent Images of Barthé by "Baxter Snark," donated by John Zeigler, are at the Avery Research Center for African American History and Culture at the College of Charleston. .

9. Bellows, *Talent for Living*, 148-9.

10. John R. Young, *A Walk in the Parks* (Charleston, SC: Evening Post Books, 2010), 39-43. R. Ingrid Rose, Roderick S. Quiroz, and Patrice La Liberté, *The Lithographs of Prentiss Taylor: A Catalogue Raisonné* (Bronx, NY: Fordham University Press, 1996) lithograph number 35, p. 84.

11. "Charleston Wins Art Show Praise," *NC,* December 16, 1934. Jonathan Ned Katz, *The Daring Life and Dangerous Times of Eve Adams* (Chicago: Chicago Review Press, 2021), 88. The author thanks Jonathan Ned Katz for bringing this to his attention. Rowena Wilson Tobias, "Filling Station Ballet Big Hit," *NC*, April 30, 1938, 5.

12. One of the people Zeigler and Peacock influenced was a young customer named John Dunning who eventually opened a bookstore in Colorado. He authored best-selling mysteries involving rare books and sellers. *The Bookman's Promise* (2004), referencing Charleston, revolves around the 19th century explorer Richard Burton (1821-1890), who wrote the longest text to that time on homosexuality, experiences he may have shared. (Burton's theorized areas he called the Sotadic Zones where gay behavior flourished; little of Europe was included, but all of North and South America were.) See the John A. Zeigler, Jr. Papers at SCCofC, Box 4, folder 19 and Sears (ed.), *Edwin and John*, 108.

13, Heyward, *Mamba's Daughters*, 231-2.

14, Sears (ed.), *Edwin and John*, 113-14.

15. Morrison, *College of Charleston*, 101; Sears (ed.), *Edwin and John*, 31.

16. Calder Willingham, *End as a Man* (New York: Vanguard Press, 1947); Ben Brantley, "Calder Willingham Is Dead; Novelist and Screenwriter, 72," *The New York Times*, February 21, 1995; Sears (ed.), *Edwin and John,* footnote 1, chapter 3, 129; "Former Citadel Cadet Author of First Novel," *NC*, February 24, 1947, 13; "Won't Harm Citadel," *NC*, September 22, 1953, 4. Letter of Pat Conroy to Anne Head Morse, 30 November 1973, courtesy of Morse's daughter Nancy Thode, whom the author thanks for access. For later gay life at The Citadel, see Steve Estes, "The Long Gay Line: Gender and Sexual Orientation at The Citadel, *Southern Cultures*, 16, 1, (Spring 2010), 46-64. See also the oral history of Douglas Seymour, SCofC. John Zeigler also discusses The Citadel in Sears (ed.), *Edwin and John*.

17. For the advertisement and Zeigler's comment, see the John A. Zeigler, Jr. Papers at SCCofC, Box 4, folder 19, and Sears (ed.), *Edwin and John*, 14. "1st Showing in Charleston," *NC,* July 16, 1957, 6; "Hollywood Producer Will Film Willingham Novel: Portions To Be Shot At The Citadel," *NC,* February 12, 1956, 14.

Chapter Fourteen

1. James Blake, *The Joint* (Garden City, NY: Doubleday & Company, Inc. 1977), 125-52, passim.

2. For Luther Brown's identity, see the letters of James Blake, Morgan Library and Museum; the return address is "Pea Island, Box 232, Folly Road, Charleston, SC." Blake refers to "Lew" (short for Luther) in letters of November 10 and 18, 1956, and calls him his "Carolina Island squire" (February 12, 1957). Luther Brown's obituary also calls him "Lou." ("L.W. Brown Dies at 43; Rites Pending," *NC*, August 18, 1959, 9). City Directories list him as the Manager of the Anchor Bar, and an article ("Anderson Rites for L. W. Brown," *NC*, August 19, 1959, 11) notes his 13-year management. He had daughters and was a Merchant Marine. Another article ("Three Forfeit Bail," *NC*, September 8, 1955, 6) gives Brown the alias James Monroe. Blake (letter, March 24, 1957) mentions a clipping from a Charleston paper sent by a "malicious Charleston acquaintance… telling how the government is demanding $45,000 in cabaret taxes from Lew, my island laddie." A news article mentions a tax lien for $35,077.04 against Brown "doing business as the Anchor Lounge. ("Notice Of Tax Lien Filed Against Brown," *NC*, September 7, 1956, 15.) These letters, mostly unpublished, offer a candid and somewhat rueful view of the love life of a gay man in jail and his rejection of guilt or shame. The Studs Terkel interview: https://studsterkel.wfmt.com/programs/james-blake-pianist-author-and-petty-thief-talks-about-his-book-joint James Blake, "The Happy Islanders," *The Paris Review*, Number 52, 107-27.

3. For more on Lyons and D'Anna, see their papers, SCCofC. For the obituary, in the *PC*, August 7 & 8, 2012, see: https://obits.postandcourier.com/us/obituaries/charleston/name/dorothy-d-anna-obituary?pid=159017877 The author's personal knowledge informs the text.

4. Harold Meltzer, "William Hoffman," Letters to the Editor, *NC*, May 24, 1954, 4. A memorial exhibit of his work was held at the Gibbes Museum in November of that year, and the Charleston Museum showcased his snuff box collection. A photograph of Hoffman is in the Betty Bonner scrapbook at SCHS, 34-0696. John Zeigler told the author that Hoffman was gay.

5. Thuel Burnham souvenir post card, author's collection. Ashley Cooper (pseudonym of Frank Gilbreth), "Doing the Charleston," *NC*, February 17, 1958, 12; Russel Wragg, *Portrait Over My Shoulder: Personal Recollections of a piano virtuoso, surreptitiously gleaned by the author* (Charleston: Walker, Evans and Cogswell Company, 1952), 24.

6. Wragg, *Portrait*, 44, 132; for sexual activity at Charleston's Y.M.C.A. see the oral history of Jack Sewell, SCCofC. "Wragg Does Well In Book of Verse," *NC*, October 24, 1930, 12, mentions relatives in the city. Charlotte Walker, "Russel Wragg: Musician? Poet? Impressario [sic]?" *NC*, March 8, 1963, 17; "Russel Wragg, Noted Pianist-Composer, Dies," *NC*, February 25, 1977, 11; see also articles in the Preservation Society of Charleston newsletter, such as "Ansonborough's 'Off-Broadway' Restorations," *Preservation Progress*, X, 2 (March 1965), 4-6; Wragg and cadets: telephone conversation of author and Oliver Bowman, February 4, 2021.

7. John Zeigler also wrote a cycle of poems about their relationship, *The Edwin Poems* (self-published: Xlibris Corp., 2007). Dorothy Heyward's unpublished autobiography, SCHS, also exists as Elizabeth Hanna, "'Tiptoeing in Their Footsteps': Dorothy Heyward's Unpublished Autobiography" Thesis (M.A.), Graduate School of the College of Charleston, 2005.

8. For details re the incident and aftermath, see: Santi Thompson, "'Offending Decent People': Murder, Masculinity, and the (Homosexual) Menace in Cold War era Charleston" Thesis (M.A.), University of South Carolina, 2008, and Dustin Waters, "A Slow Burn: The Sensational Candlestick Murder Trial of 1958 Struck Fear in Charleston's Gay Community," *Charleston City Paper*, 23, 6 (September 11, 2019), 18-20, 22-24. See also: A Charleston Reporter, "The Hallowe'en Party," *One*, 7, 5 (May 1959), 17-19. David Halsey (b. 1944) speaks of neighbors accepting the roommates as gay in his oral history, SCCofC. "Former Bakeshop Becoming Attractive City Residence," *NC*, February 4, 1957; William Chapman, "Jack Dobbins Was Liked By Neighbors, *NC*, November 3, 1958, 13.

9. Chapman, "Dobbins Liked"; "Edward Stanforth Otey" obituary, *Orangeburg* [SC] *Times and Democrat*, January 8, 1969; "Airman Held for Grand Jury In Slaying Here," *NC*, November 8, 1958, 1; Otis Perkins, "Airman Held in Killing," *NC*, November 3, 1958, 1; "Dobbins Murder Case Given to Jury Here," *NC*, December 12, 1958, 17. (The latter describes Mahon's dress; its being the costume of "male prostitutes on the make" is in Reporter, "Hallowe'en," 19.)

10. "Dobbins Murder Case Given to Jury Here," *NC*, December 12, 1958, 17; William Chapman, "Queen Street Man Murder Victim," *NC*, November 2, 1958, 1; Glenn Robertson, "Candlestick Plays Big Role in Murder Case," *NC*, December 11, 1958, 21; "Conflicting Tales Told By 2 Trial Witnesses," *NC*, December 11, 1958, 21; Otis Perkins, "Airman Held in Killing," *NC*, November 3, 1958, 1.

11. Otis Perkins, "Airman Held in Killing," *NC*, November 3, 1958, 1. William Chapman, "Jack Dobbins Was Liked By Neighbors, *NC*, November 3, 1958, 13. "Dobbins Murder Case Given To Jury Here," *NC*, December 12,1958, 17; Reporter, "Party," *One*, 7, 5 (May 1959), 17-19; "Candlestick Murder Trial Gets Underway, *NC*, December 10, 1958, 15.

12. "Dobbins Murder Case Given to Jury Here," *NC*, December 12, 1958, 17; Thompson, "'Offending Decent People;'" "Candlestick Murder Trial Gets Underway," *NC*, December 10, 1958, 15; Otis Perkins, "Jury Acquits Young Airman of Halloween Killing Here," *NC*, December 13, 1958, 9.

13. The late David Heisser told the author of his fraught childhood memories of the murder. Mike Hippler, *Matlovich: The Good Soldier* (Boston: Alyson Publications, Inc., 1989), 14; Sears (ed.), Edwin and John, 105.Thompson, "'Offending Decent People,'" 20; conversation of the author and John Zeigler, January 17, 2009. For tombstone and death certificate, see: "Edward Stanforth Otey" obituary, *Orangeburg Times and Democrat*, January 8, 1969.

Chapter Fifteen

1. "The Day's Log," *NC*, September 16, 1965, 16; (his name was Leroy Wright). Jack Hitt, "Legend," 268-78, 275, 274; Jay Rumph, quoted about the waterfront, was befriended by Richard Schreadley, executive editor of the *NC* who consistently expressed negative views on LGBTQ issues; yet he wrote kindly of Rumph, whom he called "Choo-Choo" who "would shimmy and shake the night away" in Istanbul, where apparently it was fitting. Schreadley gave a friend a pass on gay behavior elsewhere but did not condone it in others in Charleston. R. L. Schreadley, Editorial, *PC*, June 17, 2013, 11.

2. Hitt, "Legend," 274-5; Nall and Tucker, "Charleston's Changing Bar Scene;" oral history, George Thomas Lamme, SCCofC; Nall and Tucker, "Charleston's Changing Bar Scene."

3. *Southern Exposure*, 16, 3 (Fall 1988); another image appeared on the cover of *RFD: A Country Journal for Gay Men Everywhere*, No 59 (Fall 1989); Tom Hamrick, "Charleston Line by Line," *Lowcountry News and Review*, 2, 31 (October 11-18, 1977) and 2, 35 (December 6-27, 1977); "Harassment on the Battery," *CA*, 1, 1 (November 1982), 7; Southern Gent, "Charleston, South Carolina: Fortress of the Old South," *Steam: A Quarterly Journal for Men*, 1, 2 (Summer 1993), 114-15.

4. Al and Lew Griffen-O'Connell, "The Rise from Rascals," in Alfred Lees and Ronald Nelson (eds.), *Longtime Companions: Autobiographies of Gay Male Fidelity* (Binghampton, NY: Harrington Park Press, 1999), 159-67; it contains Al Griffen's "Life as a Charleston Hustler," 160-2. Freeman Gunter, "Doing the Charleston," *Mandate: The International Magazine of Entertainment and Eros*, 8, 8 (November 1982), 75-9, 78. (Gunter is profiled in the April 2011 *New York Magazine*: https://nymag.com/realestate/features/apartments/freeman-gunter-2011-4/?mid=streeteasy); Hippler, *Matlovich*, 13-15. The link between racism and homophobia is often abused. When the College of Charleston LGBTQ archives tried to acquire the papers of conservative White James Bessinger (a self-described gay pagan and the head of the Secessionist political party, with planks legalizing marijuana and gay marriage), the archives was attacked for soliciting racist documents. Even when Bessinger called out Confederate memorialist groups as race-baiting and misogynist and disbanded the party, a young straight White academic ignored the LGBTQ nature of the materials and published an attack, exacerbating conflict between minorities. See: Aaisha Haykal, Barrye Brown, and Mary Jo Fairchild, "Between Accession and Secession: Political Mayhem and Archival Transparency in Charleston, South Carolina," in Andrea Baer, Ellysa Stern Cahoy, Robert Schroeder, and Jonathan Cope (eds.), *Libraries Promoting Reflective Dialogue in a Time of Political Polarization* (Chicago: Association of College & Research Libraries, 2019), 235-54.

5. The series title was "It's Talked About In Whispers," *NC*, August 1, 1965, 1. It was probably prompted by the much more positive five part series on homosexuality in the *Washington Post* in January 1965. Two years earlier, on December 17, 1963, the *New York Times* ran a front page

article (by Robert C. Doty) "Growth of Overt Homosexuality in City Provokes Wide Concern;" J. Douglas Donehue, "Homosexuality: A Problem Swept Under the Rug," *NC*, August 2, 1965, 1, 2; Gunter, "Doing the Charleston," 78.

6. J. Douglas Donehue, "Homosexuality Described As 'Incurable,'" *NC*, August 3, 1965, 1, 2; Mary Jo Smith Fetzer's papers, with a mention of M. E. Van Dyke, known as a couple to the author, are housed in SCCofC.

7. J. Douglas Donehue, "Sexual Perversion Plays A Part In Many Crimes," *NC*, August 4, 1965, 1, 5; "little Johnny Robinson," the murdered child, was also invoked in the first article, Donehue, "Homosexuality Described." James Blake wrote that on his first night in Charleston, he was "picked up on suspicion," Blake, *The Joint*, 128.

8. J. Douglas Donehue, "The Military Won't Tolerate Homosexuals," *NC*, August 5, 1965, 1, 2; Nall and Tucker, "Charleston's Changing Bar Scene."

9. J. Douglas Donehue, "Most Attorneys Give Legal Aid to Homosexuals," *NC*, August 6, 1965, 1, 2.

10. J. Douglas Donehue, "Children Should Be Warned Of Homosexuals," *NC*, August 7, 1965, 1.

11. Beth Brown, "Homosexuality Reported Rising Among Teen-Agers," *NC*, March 27, 1969, 7; "General Sessions Court True Bill," *NC*, September 15, 1960, 7; "The Day's Log," *NC*, December 9, 1964, 11; "4 Sentenced To 2 Years For County Jail Incident," *NC*, September 18, 1965, 11; "The Day's Log," *NC*, September 16, 1965, 16; Stewart R. King, "3 Plead Guilty to Armed Robbery," *NC*, September 12, 1969, 17; "7 Jail Inmates Charged With Sex Perversion," *NC*, September 28, 1971, 2; Clyde Johnson, "Six Inmates Ordered Held For Assault," *EP*, June 10, 1972, 11; Stewart R. King, "Grand Jury Investigating County Jail, *NC* August 17, 1972, 1, 2; Donald Fishburne, "Kidnap Incident Probed," *EP*, June 6, 1974; Mari Maseng, "Inmate Reports Sexual Assault at County Jail," *EP*, July 7, 1975, 1; Ernie Locklair, "Land Added By North Charleston," *EP*, August 11, 1973, 2; Fraser, *Charleston! Charleston!*, 213.

12. "CONSERVATIVES, INC.," Bulletin No. 32, February 11, 1965, 2, Emily Ravenel Farrow Papers, SCCofC, Box 33; Jenna Schiferl, "Federal Judge in SC strikes down law that bans LGBTQ sex ed unless it's about STDS," *PC*, March 11, 2020, updated September 14, 2020 https://www.postandcourier.com/news/federal-judge-in-sc-strikes-down-law-that-bans-lgbtq-sex-ed-unless-it-s/article_68dbaed4-63ac-11ea-a51c-c3c1c012e4ae.html "The law, passed in 1988, made it illegal for public school teachers to discuss 'alternate sexual lifestyles from heterosexual relationships' except in the context of sexually transmitted diseases. Teachers who disobeyed the law — whether by including LGBTQ issues in their curriculum, answering a student's question or allowing classroom discussion — could be fired." https://www.nbcnews.com/feature/nbc-out/s-carolina-law-banning-lgbtq-sex-ed-unconstitutional-judge-rules-n1156501

13. Telephone conversation of the author and Millicent Brown, May 22, 2020. The Eugene C. Hunt Papers are at the Avery Research Center for African American History and Culture, College of Charleston. The only mention of a gay issue is an undated and unfilled out, but saved, survey of "Gay persons as viewed by Chairpersons in English", Box 5, folder 5. David K. Johnson, *The Lavender Scare: The Cold War Persecution of Gays and Lesbians in the Federal Government* (Chicago: University Press of Chicago, 2004), 200.

14. Field Notes of Greg Day, "Saturday Evening January 11, 1972," copy in possession of the author who thanks Mr. Day for his assistance. Other comments come from Day's email communication, September 14, 2020.

15. All quotes are from Helen Smith, *What God Has to Say About the Gay Parade: Homosexuality* (Charleston: John J. Furlong & Sons, 1974).

16. For the bar closing, see the oral history of Jack Sewell, SCCofC. Elizabeth O'Neill Verner, *The Stonewall Ladies* (Charleston: The Tradd Street Press, 1967), initially published in 1963.

Chapter Sixteen

1.*Time Magazine*, 106, 10 (September 8, 1975); Randy Shilts, *Conduct Unbecoming: Gays & Lesbians in the U.S. Military* (New York: St. Martin's Press, 1993), 227; "Gay Task Force," *NC*, September 28, 1976, 6; *NC*, October 13, 1976, 20; J. Edward Parham, "The Discrete Charm and Conservatism of

Charleston, SC," *The Advocate*, Issue 366 (April 28, 1983), 26-8, 30; advertisement, *NC*, March 29, 1977; telephone conversation with Oliver Bowman, February 4, 2021. Orvin was a member of the Grass Roots Citizens Club, Emily Ravenel Farrow Papers, SCCofC, Box 31, folder 4.

2. Hippler, *Matlovich*, 14; 31-43, passim, 48, 155, unpaginated photograph, last in the volume; "Melvin Dwork, Once Cast From Navy for Being Gay, Dies at 94," *New York Times*, June 16, 2016 https://www.nytimes.com/2016/06/17/obituaries/melvin-dwork-once-cast-from-navy-for-being-gay-dies-at-94.html

3. Patrick Gale, *Armistead Maupin* (Bath, Somerset, UK: Absolute Press, 1999), 30-1, 32; Harry Hervey, *Red Ending* (New York: Horace Liveright, Inc., 1929), 13; Blanche Boyd, *Nerves* (Plainfield, VT: Daughters, Inc., 1973), 65.

4. Armistead Maupin, *Logical Family: A Memoir* (New York: Harper Collins, 2017), 131-6, passim; Karen Everhart, "With 'Tales of the City,' public TV earns extremes of scorn and praise," *Current*, January 31, 1994: https://current.org/1994/01/with-tales-of-the-city-public-tv-earns-extremes-of-scorn-and-praise/

5. Simmons wrote three autobiographies. Edward Ball's biography of her is *Peninsula of Lies: A True Story of Mysterious Birth and Taboo Love* (New York: William Morrow, 2010). "V. Sackville-West Is Visitor Here," *NC*, April 11, 1933, 8; she and her husband Sir Harold Nicolson stayed at the Ft. Sumter Hotel; Hitt, "Legend," 271.

6. James T. Sears, *Lonely Hunters: An Oral History of Lesbian and Gay Southern Life, 1948-1968* (Boulder, CO: Westview Press, 1997), 171. "Billy Camden" seems to be Bobby Tucker, who ran Tucker's Tavern; "Heyward", his partner, is most likely Howard Hemley; "Russell" and "Tool" appear to Russel Wragg and Thuel Burnham; "Nicky" is John Zeigler, called Nicky in *Jeb and Dash;* his partner "Tom" is Edwin Peacock. (The chapter on Charleston, full of LGBTQ history, has some errors: the Brooks Motel, the site of the Simmons wedding reception, for instance, did not mysteriously burn, but was razed in the 1990s to be redeveloped.) For Jack Leland's report, see Aubrey Hancock Papers, SCCofC. According to Leland's widow, the local paper would not publish it, but Leland sold it to other sources, see: Sears, *Lonely Hunters*, 179; Mark Jones, "Gordon Langley Hall," https://markjonesbooks.com/tag/gordon-hall/

7. Hitt, "Legend," 277, 278; Maupin, *Logical Family,* 134; Boyd, *Nerves,* 14; Fen Montaigne, "'Mourning the Death of Magic': A Novel About Charleston," *NC,* December 11, 1977, 76; See also: "Blanche McCrary Boyd Responds to Criticism," *NC,* December 13, 1977, 4; Blanche Boyd oral history, SCCofC. Ann B. Ross, *The Murder Cure* (New York: Avon Books, 1978); John Craddock, "'The Murder Cure' Set in Charleston," *NC,* January 7 1979, 39; Alice Childress, *A Short Walk* (New York: Coward, McCann & Geoghegan, 1979); Alice Childress, *Those Other People* (New York, Putnam Publishing Group, 1989).

Chapter Seventeen

1. Barry Singer, "Changing Fortunes," *Opera News,* 71, 1 (July 2007), 7.; Marley Seaman, "A Funny Man of Good Report," *Northwestern: For Alumni and Friends of Northwestern University* (Winter 2005). https://www.northwestern.edu/magazine/ winter 2005/ alumni/news/close-ups/colbert.html Sidney Hetzler, "Two Town Festivals: Signs of a Theater of Power," Thesis (Ph. D.), Emory University, 1990, 222-33, passim; the author thanks Gene Waddell for bringing this to his attention. Ca. 1969 list of committees, including Citizens Advisory Committee, Subcommittee on Minority Group Housing, Subcommittee on Relocation Housing and Subcommittee on Home Financing, City of Charleston Records Management files, copy in the author's possession; the author thanks Nancy Phelps for bringing this to his attention.

2. While Stern and Worthington were certainly in each other's lives (Worthington moved to North Carolina to help manage Stern's property there), there is no evidence of this in the words or writings of Stern himself. Worthington, however, did speak to the issue. On October 14, 2012, John Zeigler, an employer and mentor of T. J. Worthington, told the author that Worthington and Stern had an intimate relationship that lasted for years. Worthington, Zeigler related, had met Stern when he was making a delivery from the Book Basement. Wendy Salinger, another friend of Worthington's, confirmed this in a conversation with the author, February 19, 2019. According to a February 25, 2019 email from Lucas Carpenter, Worthington's papers were "mistakenly destroyed by the earliest heirs to reach his house." Oral history of George Thomas Lamme, SCCofC; Gunter, "Doing the Charleston," 78.

3. Folly Beach: Jack Sewell oral history, SCCofC. Robert Molloy Papers, South Caroliniana Library, University of South Carolina; Josephine Pinckney, *Three o'Clock Dinner* (New York: The Viking Press, 1945), 65; Rathskeller: conversation with John Zeigler, October 14, 2012, and Sears, *Lonely Hunters,* 171; Y.M.C.A.: Jack Sewell oral history, SCCofC; Merchant Seaman's Club: Hitt, "Legend," 275; The Elbow Cocktail Lounge and the Cove were visited by Jack Dobbins and John Mahon before the candlestick murder: "Dobbins Murder Case Given to Jury Here," *NC,* December 12, 1958, 17; Calhoun St: George Thomas Lamme oral history, SCCofC.

4. "Gayest": advertisement on matchbook, author's collection; Club 49, the Jewel Box, the Rainbow, and the Wagon Wheel are listed in Directory Services, *Guide 43* (Minneapolis, MN, 1964), 52, while *Guild Guide 1964* (Washington, DC: The Guild Press, 1964), 75, lists The Anchor, the Carriage House, Club 49, the Rainbow Lounge and the Wagon Wheel; "Goth": Jack Sewell oral history, SCCofC; "visitor": telephone conversation with Greg Day, January 12, 2021; Tucker's Tavern: personal knowledge of the author; Cheeks: Dick Latham oral history, SCCofC; Street Car: back page advertisement, *Gay Charleston,* issue one (February 1981); Streetcar, according to the *CA,* 1, 1 (November 1982), 2, moved to 346 King Street, later the site of the bar Dudley's; New Yorker: *Damon's Bar Guide 1964,* with local listings for other years: https://www.mappingthegayguides.org/map/ Aubrey Hancock clipped gay related items including the article by Robert Red Jann, "Sailor Is Shot To Death in King Street Tavern," *NC,* July 3, 1965, 1, his papers, SCCofC. Pat's (associated with the Ocean Bar and Grill in Charleston City Directories) is listed by 1970: https://www.mappingthegayguides.org/map/ transvestite reference: telephone conversation with Howard Stahl, September 17, 2021; Bat Room: Terry Fox oral history, SCCofC.

5. Gale, *Armistead Maupin,* 32; Basin Street, Club David, Lion's Head and Coffee Cup descriptions: personal knowledge of the author; Stardust: transcript of Pat Patrick oral history, SCCofC; Camelot, Coffee Cup, Club David, Midnight Sun, Silver Dollar, Dolphin, Love Inn, and Virgo Social Club are listed at https://www.mappingthegayguides.org/map/ Mapping the Gay Guides Site. Reynolds Avenue, near the Navy Base, Folly Beach, and the Battery or White Point Garden are also listed for cruising in these years. The SCLGBTQ Oral History, Archives and Outreach Project, SCCofC, maintains a spread sheet of bars, etc.

6. The Zebra and Stardust appear in 1973: https://www.mappingthegayguides.org/map/ the former with go-go boys, advertised in Henry C. Godley, and Mark W. Riley, *David* (Jacksonville, Fla: David Publications, 1972) 2, 7 (May 1972), 37; "Ernest M. Mitchum," obituary, *NC,* April 18, 1973, 12; an advertisement re go-go girls appears in *NC,* August 3, 1968, 4; see also help wanted ads, March 1, 1968, 27, and March 2, 1968, 18, with others these years. Michael Lott oral history, SCCofC. When the Carriage House was listed in a gay guide, it is also advertised in the tourist publication as "Charleston's Finest Supper and Night Club", with photos of six women, *Gateway Magazine,* 9, 3 (March 1964), 13; *Gateway Magazine,* 2, 1 (January 1957), 6; Mike Schwarzott oral history, SCCofC.

7. Details re the Garden & Gun Club are from the author's experience, a telephone interview with Dick Robison and several conversations with Terry Fox. Maura Hogan, "How the Garden & Gun Club upended Charleston's starched social order in just a few years," *Charleston City Paper* https://www.charlestoncitypaper.com/story/how-the-garden-and-gun-club-upended-charlestons-starched-social-order-in-just-a-few-short-years?oid=25672282 Richard Little oral history, SCCofC; Edward Gilbreth, "The Garden & Gun Club and Its Spoleto Legacy," undated clipping, unknown newspaper, Steven Small Collection, SCCofC. Julian Gabriel Colado, *Hiding Among the Palmettos* (greatunpublished.com, Title No. 3, 2000), 27.

8. Email communications from Greg Day, September 14, 2020; Greg Day's artist statement for a Stephen Varble Exhibit was attached to his email, December 19, 2020, as was his statement re the Folk Art Media Project. The photographs are in the Greg Day Papers, SCCofC. (For citations of the cover art, see footnote 3, Chapter 14.) The description of the Miss Gay Charleston pageant, which Day believes was the 20th anniversary, was written for the Face Exhibit at the San Francisco Queer Cultural Center's 1998 National Queer Arts Festival, email to the author, July 14, 2021. Email from David Boatwright to the author, January 31, 2021, see: https://nam11.safelinks.protection.outlook.com/?url=https%3A%2F%2Fvimeo.com%2F200030172&data=04%7C01%7Cgreeneh%40cofc.

edu%7C9883f9337d3f4dc59cdb08d8b7dad211%7Ce285d438dbba4a4c941c593ba422deac%7C0%7C0%7C637461497755683341%7CUnknown%7CTWFpbGZsb3d8eyJWIjoiMC4wLjAwMDAiLCJQIjoiV2luMzIiLCJBTiI6Ik1haWwiLCJXVCI6Mn0%3D%7C1000&sdata=KRW3wyHsWT1R6vK-KMUd3%2B15v0lfLcRPB%2Brhoi1MBvWs%3D&reserved=0 Oral history of Gil and Robin Shuler, SCCofC. Seabrook's death notice: PC, May 31, 2004; Bryan Alston Seabrook was born August 21, 1958 and died May 28, 2004. (For information on the mis-numbering of *The Charleston Alterative*, see note 5, Chapter 18, below.)

Chapter Eighteen

1. Parham, "Charm and Conservatism," 28. According to Greg Day, the Task Force also created anti-Anita Bryant tee shirts for her lecture in Charleston, email to the author, February 1, 2021. Day also stated the Task Force protested the 1977 Miss USA contest in Charleston and supported a counter contest wherein "a cute gay man" was chosen "Mr. USA." People Against Rape (PAR) helped found the Gay Task Force and worked with the Women's Advocacy Center on a "tribunal on crimes against women," a protest against Miss USA, "PAR Report," NC, April 20, 1977, 25. George Holt oral history, SCCofC. Charles Street: Witold Rybczynski, *Charleston Fancy: Little Houses & Big Dreams in the Holy City* (New Haven, CT: Yale University Press, 2019), 38-9. The first issue is noted "complimentary"; penciled prices of later issues are at SCHS; anonymous, "Gay Say," *Gay Charleston*, issue 1, February 1981, 3; Holt, in his oral history, could not recall the author of the piece signed "F". He notes that George Exoo wrote under many different pseudonyms as did Keith Griffith, later to write for the gay press and produce a sex-centered publication in San Francisco. A complete run of GC is not known. Holt's copies were lost in a December 2015 house fire; Frank Deese, who wrote for the paper, lost his in "the thousand year" rain event, October 2015. Derfner wed Mike Combs in Iowa on the Sundance Channel Reality Series, *Girls Who Like Boys Who Like Boys*.

2. Ken Burger, "Charleston to 'Adopt' Duo Pianists," September 24, 1987 clipping from unknown paper, CofC vertical files SCCofC. "Local pianist Romain dies at 44," PC, May 23, 1995 clipping, Aubrey Hancock Papers, SCCofC; Timothy David Ray, "Achievement vs. Service: Dr. Wilfred Delphin — Lifetime Achievement Reward Recipient," *The New Orleans Age*, January 27, 2016, https://myemail.constantcontact.com/Achievement-vs--Service--Dr--Wilfred-Delphin---Lifetime-Achievement-Award-Recipient.html?soid=1011087220895&aid=aFC0EaeqQ78

3. Anonymous, "Gay Say" and T. Walker in "Letters to the Editor," GC, 1 (February 1981), 9, 2; one wonders if the disgusted college student was aware that one of the certain homosexual spots he knew was in the men's room of the College's library, right across from Maybank Hall, listed in gay guides and referenced in Michael Lott's oral history, SCCofC; Scott Doonan, "Dear Gay Say Editor," *Gay Charleston*, 2 (March 1981), 3; "Gay Guide to Bars: South Carolina," GC, 1 (February 1981), 5; letters to the editor, GC, 2 (March 1981); "Grocery Store Chorus Girls To Close," 7, and "'Whosoever Shall Commit The Abominable Crime,'" 6, are both in the first issue; the letter from "Africa" is in GC, 3, (April 1981), 15, as is the article on the local radio show, "Around Town," 3; see also oral history of George Holt, SCCofC.

4. Conni Ackerman, "'Fair Play' for Lesbians," letter to the editor, NC, November 19, 1975, 7. "We Trace The History of Charleston N.O.W.," *Gay Charleston*, 2, March 1981 7, 12; email communications to the author from Charlie Smith and Linda Ketner, April 23, 2020.

5. Bentley Waterbush (pseud.), "Harassment on the Battery," CA, 1, 1 (November 1982), 5, 7; Marriage announcement of Cathy Mengarelli and Michel Zimmerman, CA, 2, 4 [sic] (July/August 1983), 9. [There is an error in the numbering of some issues of CA: the two 1981 issues of volume 1 (November and December) are numbered correctly, as are the first two 1983 issues (January and February); but the March 1983 issue also appeared as "VOL 2, NO 2" instead of volume 2, number 3; May/June, numbered as 3, should be 4; July/August, numbered as 4, should be 5. From here forward "[sic]" will be used to denote issues incorrectly numbered.] David Kromer, "Metropolitan Community Church," CA, 1, 2 (December 1982), 7, 11; advertisement for Unitarian Church, GC, 3 (April 1981), 23. Paul J. Nyden, "Assisted-suicide advocate Exoo dies," Charleston, WV *Gazette-Mail*, June 1, 2015; "Rap Sessions," GC, 2, (March 1981), 12; "Around Town," GC, 3, (April 1981), 3. "New Group For Gay Professionals," GC, 6 (June 1982), 5.

6. Parham, "Charm and Conservatism," 28; "Community Resources," *CA*, 1, 1 (November 1982), 2; Barry S. Kohn, Esq., "Editorial," *CA*, 2, 2 [sic], (March/April 1983;), 2; Unicorn, pride week, MCC picnic: "Community Resources" and "Calendar of Events," *CA*, 2, 3 [sic] (May/June 1983), 9, 5; "MCC," *GC*, 3 (April 1981), 10; "Metropolitan Church of Charleston — History," SCCofC vertical files; Parham, "Charm and Conservatism," 28.

7. "Community Resources," *CA*, 1, 1 (November 1982), 2; e None of the Above "October Poop Sheet" and University Club materials (1983-85) in the author's possession; George Holt oral history, SCCofC; advertisement, *GC*, 1, 1 (February 1981), 8; Richard Little oral history, SCCofC; Barry S. Kohn, "Editorial," *CA*, 1, 1 (November 1982), 2; "A thank you note," *GC*, 6 (June 1982), rear cover; Barry S. Kohn, "The Bisexual Window," *CA*, 1, 1 (November 1982), 8; Barry Kohn and Alice Matusow, *Barry and Alice: Portrait of a Bisexual Marriage* (Englewood Cliffs, NJ: Prentice-Hall, Inc., 1980).

8. Barry S. Kohn, "Editorial," *CA*, 2, 4 [sic] (August 1983), 2; J. Edward Parham, "Barry Kohn And The Charleston Alternative," *The Advocate*, issue 381 (November 24, 1983), 43-5, 43; Barry S. Kohn, "Editorial, *CA*, 2, 4 [sic] (August 1983), 2; Parham, "Charm and Conservatism," 26-7; Parham, "Barry Kohn," 43; Diana, "ON THE OTHER HAND: A WOMYN'S TURN," *CA*, 2, 1 (January 1983), 7; Parham, "Charm and Conservatism," 28.

9. Barry S. Kohn, Esq., "Editorial," *CA*, 1, 2 (December 1982), 2; Barry S. Kohn, Esq., "Editorial" *CA*, 2, 4 [sic] (August 1983), 2; *CA*, 2, 1 (January 1983) 2; Jo Jo, "Sodom and Gonorrhea" and "Sex Between Men" advertisement, *CA*, 2, 1 (January 1983) 9, 7; *CA*, 2, 2 (February 1983), 5; George Thomas Lamme oral history, SCCofC; "Lambda Events" and "Calendar of Events" " *CA*, 2, 3 [sic] (May/June 1983), 5; "Charleston AIDS: Acquired Immunity Deficiency Syndrome (AIDS): An Update." *CA*, 2, 4 [sic] (July/August 1983), 10.

10. Prentiss Findlay, "MUSC Seeks Volunteers For AIDS Study," *NC*, March 1, 1985, 8A; Barney Blakeney, "Goals In Tri-County AIDS Fight Reviewed," *NC*, May 14, 1986, 12B; Peter Goldman, "The Face of AIDS," *Newsweek*, August 10, 1987, 22-31, 34-6, with Kohn's image on page 36 captioned as "Barry Kohn, 44, *Lawyer Philadelphia*, He worked in the Peace Corps, then for the poor back home," omitting any mention of his LGBTQ life and work. Parham, "Charm and Conservatism," 27-8; Hart is quoted in Kymberly Natasha Mattern, "Outing the National Register: Including Lesbian, Gay, Bisexual, Transgender, and Queer (LGBTQ) Sites On The National Register Of Historic Places" thesis (M.A.), Clemson University and the College of Charleston, 2017, 94-5; Ashley Cooper (Frank Gilbreth), "Doing the Charleston," undated clipping from the *NC,* Aubrey Hancock Papers, SCCofC.

Chapter Nineteen

1. For history of the Medical College see Harlan Greene, "'Nowhere Else': South Carolina's Role in a Continuing Tragedy," in Ilisa Barbash, Molly Rogers and Deborah Willis, (eds.) *To Make Their Own Way in the World: The Enduring Legacy of the Zealy Daguerreotypes* (Cambridge, MA: Peabody Museum Press, 2020), 259-78; for antisemitism in Dental School, see Gordon Stine oral history, Jewish Heritage Collection, SCCofC; for the strike, see Claudia Smith Brinson, *Stories of Struggle: The Clash over Civil Rights in South Carolina* (Columbia, SC: University of South Carolina Press, 2020), 211-76; Frank Jarrell, "AIDS: Doctors answer the questions of what, who and how," undated clipping, Aubrey Hancock Papers, SCCofC; Sue Groff oral history, SCCofC; the gerbil story was related to the author by the late Olin B. Jolley, MD, a medical student at MUSC, ca. 1987; Michael Lott, MD oral history, SCCofC.

2. Richard Little oral history, SCCofC; Mattern, "Outing the National Register," 96-8; "Aide to Strom Thurmond dies of Aids," AP News, August 8, 1993 https://apnews.com/article/7d-02de-9135ec0204298080dcad7c36d4 James Kirchner, *The Secret City: The Hidden History of Gay Washington,* (New York: Henry Holt and Company, 2022), 281-82, 288. Bob Inglis: *Gay Daze* 6, 8, (August 1995) 2; Mattern, "Outing the National Register," 101; Robert Ball, MD, oral history, SCCofC; Robert Ball, MD Papers, SCCofC. "Ashley Cooper" (Frank Gilbreth), "Doing the Charleston," *PC*, November 1, 1992, 21; the status of leper resonates with homosexuality, it being the name of Menotti's one act opera on intolerance. Mark Gray oral history (Cacao's Chocolate), SCCofC; Jack Sewell oral history (The Hungry Lion), SCCofC.".

3. David W. MacDowell, "Highway rest stops: the bathhouses of the heartland," *NC*, July 2, 1989, 5. For destruction of public restrooms, see Mattern, "Outing the National Register," 85- 93; Andy Brack, "State trying to halt sex at rest stops," *NC*, March 21, 1990, 1; David W. MacDougall, "14 minutes and 4 seconds: A brief, dangerous liaison at the side of Interstate 26," *NC*, July 2, 1989, 5; MacDowell, "Highway rest stops;" Brack, "State trying to halt." Born in 1938, William Lance van Hettinga taught in universities and was a visual artist. He was recalled in the paper he founded ("A Picture Paper for People who can Read") as "a rare bird ... a multi-talented, quixotic, garrulous and, occasionally contentious artist, raconteur, and friend," undated clipping, author's possession. See also his and Reeves van Hettina's papers, SCCofC; Charles W. Smith oral history, SCCofC. Not listing partners of the deceased varied over the years: Charlie Smith notes rejection in the mid-1990s; the obituary of Daniel Stevens (*NC*, September 5, 1986) does not list his partner but that of Michael S. (Shan) Whittle (*NC*, April 5, 1992) notes a "companion," clippings, Aubrey Hancock Papers, SCCofC.

4. Jenny Turner oral history, SCCofC. For the story of a lesbian who moved to South Carolina to adopt, see the Sue Groff oral history, SCCofC; Mark Gray oral history, SCCofC; for Derfner's description, see *Swish: My Quest to be the Gayest Person Ever* (New York: Broadway Books, 2008), 77-8. Joe Hall oral history, SCCofC. In 2016 Lowcountry AIDS Services became Palmetto Community Care. For a summary of HIV laws in SC, see: Dorothy Givens, "Churches educating public about AIDS," *NC*, April 2, 1992, 74. See also Joe Hall Papers, SCCofC.

Chapter Twenty

1. LGLA bylaws and member list, LGLA Records, SCCofC; Miriam Wilchanovksy, "Up-to-the-Minute Minutes," *Rainbow Times Newsource*, 5, 11 (November 2001), 2; David W. MacDougall, "Gay men warned after 2 slashings," *PC*, October 27 1993, 13, 16; "Ryan's Steak House targeted by right-wing opposition," *Rainbow Times* 2, 2 (March/April 1998), 1; library meetings are noted throughout the (incomplete) run of newsletters and first names are appended to articles, etc.; the author attended and witnessed meetings. "LGLA Wins Award!" *Gay Daze*, 6,8 (August 1995), 1; Miriam Wilchanovsky, "Up-to-the-Minute Minutes," *Rainbow Times Newsource* gay guide, *Rainbow Times*, 5, 1 (February 2002), 3; for the business guide, see LGLA Papers, SCCofC.

2. Mike Schwarzott oral history, SCCofC; Kevin J. Campbell, "Gay Rights," letter to the editor, *PC*, July 17, 1993, 14; "Rally," *PC*, July 18, 1993, 24; "Coming Out Rally," Events Calendar, *PC*, October 3, 1991, 66: while in the calendar, news coverage of the event has not been found. "Get Back in Step," advertisement by Lowcountry AIDS Services, *PC*, November 28, 1993, 98; *Rainbow Times*, 1, 4 (November/December 1997), 10; Lynne Langley, "Lowcountry walk, program recognize World AIDS day," *PC*, November 30, 1994, 6; Mike Schwarzott oral history and papers, SCCofC; "Dear Members and Friends," *Rainbow Times*, 3, 8 (November 1999), 1; "Member Notes: August Monthly Meeting," *Rainbow Times*, 2, 4 (October 1998), 2; LGLA bylaws, LGLA Records (folder 206-1-8), SCCofC.

3. "Leather in Charleston? Indeed," *The Loop*, issue 1, September 13, 2000, 4; PFLAG appears in *PC* "Support Group" list in 1994; its meetings and the bowling league are noted in *Gay Daze*, 6, 8, (August 1995); for AA and women's issues, see *Gay Daze*, 7, 1 (January 1996). GALA, founded January 15, 1991, sparked controversy (College of Charleston *Comet*, vol 68, 1991, 61, 216); for the film festival, see *Rainbow Times*, 1, 3 (September 1997), 2, 4 (October 1996) and 5, 3 (March 2001); for The Citadel, see the publication 6, 9 (September 2003); for T Sisters, 6, 6 (June 2003), and "Outfest," 1, 4 (November/December 1997).

4. "Schwacke Takes Three Awards," *Newsletter: College of Charleston*, XXVI, 2 (August 1978, 2-3; B. Drummond Ayres, Jr. "Gay Prosecutor Reluctantly Goes Public," *New York Times*, October 26, 1997, 16; Kristina Torres, "Gays blast pressuring an 'outing' personal: At Sunday's 'Outfest,' many gays expressed disappointment in Schwacke's forced outing," *PC*, October 13, 1997, 3B; "Readers speak out about Schwacke's controversy," Letters to the Editor, *PC*, October 18, 1997, 23; "Republican Party Out of Sync?" *The Loop*, issue 1, September 13, 2000, 2-3; John Frank, "Gay alliance to boycott tour company: Senator backs ban on same-sex unions," *PC*, April 12, 2005, 1B.

5. Steven Willard oral history, SCCofC; Thomas Engelhard Myers, Jr., obituary, *PC*, April 28, 2016 https://obits.postandcourier.com/us/obituaries/charleston/name/thomas-myers-obit-

uary?pid=179816192; Dottie Ashley, "Support group started out of love for son," *PC*, May 7, 2000, 10G; "Teenagers find support — and a place to feel safe," *PC*, May 7, 2000, 1G; "Out of the shadows," *PC*, May 7, 2000, 1G; "Gay Teen Survey," *PC*, May 7, 2000, 11G.

Chapter Twenty-one

1. Linda Ketner oral history, SCCofC; see also her oral history in Morris (ed.), *Southern Perspectives*, 71-81; Kevin Sack, "Gay Rights Movement Meets Big Resistance in S. Carolina," *New York Times*, July 7, 1998, 1. Jim and Warren Redman-Gress oral history in Morris, *Southern Perspectives*, 121-36; Charles W. Smith oral history, SCCofC; Gregory Smalls, *Black Enough, Man Enough: Embracing My Mixed Race and Fluid Sexuality* (Atlanta, GA: Juan & Gee Enterprises, LLC, 2019), dust jacket text; email from Charlie Smith to the author, April 15, 2020; LGLA motto is in *Rainbow Times*, 1,1 (June 1997); "Gay Say," *GC*, 2 (March 1981), 3.

2. Charles W. Smith oral history, SCCofC; LGLA leaders also called for an end to "petty ness" [sic], *Rainbow Times*, 1,1 (June 1997); email of Charlie Smith to the author, April 6, 2020 and April 15, 2020; the Myrtle Beach affair is covered in Sack, "Gay Rights Movement;" Eric Frazier, "Religious leaders divided on homosexuality," *PC*, October 19, 1997, 15 E; Tanner Crunelle oral history, SCCofC; Charles W. Smith oral history, SCCofC. The advertisement "I'm living proof that Truth can set you free….. Sponsored by the Christian Life Committee and Your Friends At East Cooper Baptist Church" ran in *PC*, October 5, 1998; for a printed version of the letter to the *PC*, "October 1998" see AFFA Papers, SCCofC.

3. "Local Gay Summit Held," *The Loop*, 5 (January 2001) 1; email of Linda Ketner to the author, April 6, 2020; radio interview of Lynn Moldenhauer, March 11, 2006, Equal Time Interviews, AFFA Records, SCCofC; Chase Glenn comments, Charleston PRIDE's State of the Community Symposium, September 20, 2018, recording, SCCofC; Melissa Moore oral history, SCCofC; "AFFA Hires Executive Director," *The Loop*, 11 (August 2001), 1, 5; Rickey Ciapha Dennis, Jr., "First LGBTQ-dedicated hub in Lowcountry to open in North Charleston Saturday," *PC*, August 6, 2019, 2.

4. Sarah Lundy, "Gay, lesbian group strike deal for billboard on I-26," *PC*, May 26, 2002, 1B; Prentiss Finlay, "WCBD undecided about airing documentary on gays in Charleston," *PC*, July 12, 2003, 1 F; Michael Gartland, "Criticism precedes show — Gay rights group airs on radio," *PC*, January 19, 2006, 3B; Wilhelmina Hein oral history, SCCofC; "Metropolitan Church of Charleston — History," SCCofC vertical files.

5. AFFA's records, SCCofC, detail many of their programs. "Hoisington Speaks to AFFA," *The Loop*, 7 (March 2001), 1; "Police Discrimination," *The Loop*, 7 (March 2001), 3; Jason Hardin, "Police scrap sex question for applicants: Charleston Police Department criticized for asking about homosexual activity," *PC*, March 14, 2001, 3B; see oral histories of police officers Terry Cherry and K. J. Ivery, SCCofC; "We're Coming Out," *The Loop*, 1 (September 13, 2000), 1; "Military Investigation Underway," *The Loop*, 10 (July 2001)1, 5; Nall and Tucker, "Charleston's Changing Bar Scene"; "In the Closet…On the Street," *The Loop*, 7 (March 2001), 5,7; Daryl Crouse, "Freedom Weekend Was Fun," *The Loop*, 11 (August 2001), 1, 7. The ca. 1982 Lambda Program, featuring a lecture by therapist Diane Hamrick, dinner and music, gave time to fill out the survey before discussing "future plans," SCHS vertical file 30-12-95.

Chapter Twenty-two

1. Charles W. Smith oral history, SCCofC; Will Moredock, "So Long, John Graham Altman," *Charleston City Paper*, November 13, 2013, https://www.charlestoncitypaper.com/story/so-long-john-graham-altman?oid=4810418; see political materials (and buttons), Charles W. Smith Papers, SCCofC Linda Ketner Papers, SCCofC; telephone conversation with Ketner, September 30, 2021; John Cloud, "The Gay Mafia that's Redefining Liberal Politics," October 31, 2008 http://content.time.com/time/subscriber/article/0,33009,1855344,00.html or *Time*, vol. 172 (November 19, 2008), 52-5; Robert Behre, "Day later, Brown wins," *PC*, November 5, 2008, https://www.postandcourier.com/politics/day-later-brown-wins/article_b57af1e9-01aa-57c3-9685-953679cd0594.html

2. Greg Hambrick, "Blogger Lane Hudson exposes hypocrisy," *Charleston City Paper*, September 5, 2007 https://www.charlestoncitypaper.com/story/blogger-lane-hudson-exposes-hypocrisy?oid=1111322 Ben Adler, "From outing Foley to out of a job," *Politico*, July 14, 2008 https://www.politico.com/story/2008/07/from-outing-foley-to-out-of-a-job-011738 Hudson worked

briefly for Charlie Smith, telephone conversation with Smith September 29, 2021; Matt Comer, "College junior becomes S.C.'s first openly gay official," *Q notes*, March 7, 2009, https://goqnotes.com/1843/college-junior-becomes-scs-first-openly-gay-official/ "Forty Under 40: Nick Shalosky," *The Advocate*, issue 1027/1028 (June/July 2009), 90.

3. Liz Foster, "CofC professor Chorlton had a passion for politics," *PC*, March 14, 2014 https://www.postandcourier.com/features/faith_and_values/c-of-c-professor-chorlton-had-a-passion-for-politics/article_1197a056-6cdc-5d38-a1c5-455b32060161.html; Thomas Patrick Chorlton obituary, *PC*, January 11&12, 2004 https://obits.postandcourier.com/ us/obituaries/ charleston/name/thomas-chorlton-obituary?pid=169023343 B. D. Redmond, ed., *The Comet 1975* (Charleston, SC: The College of Charleston, 1975), 53; Tony Williams oral history, SCCofC. For the College's Gay and Lesbian Alliance, see footnote 3, Chapter 20, above; files of Cathy Evans, Charleston Communications Museum, SCCofC; Morrison, *College of Charleston*, 236-7; Seanna Adcox, "C of C weighs minor in gay, lesbian studies," *PC*, September 4, 2003, B1; Moredock, "John Graham Altman;" Seanna Adcox, "Talk of C of C Gay, Lesbian Minor Squelched," *PC*, September 12, 2003, 1B.

4. Dave Munday, "Play stirring up political drama," *PC*, July 11, 2014, 4; Report of the Joint Legislative Committee to Screen Candidates for College and University Boards of Trustees, March 13, 2004 https://www.scstatehouse.gov/CommitteeInfo/Universities&CollegesScreening Committee/ScreeningReports/Screenings%20Transcripts%20For%20March%202014.pdf (John Busch, testimony shown here, and Toya Pound, another objector to *Fun Home*, were named as board members charged with diversity, equity and inclusion issues, email from President Andrew T. Hsu to College of Charleston faculty, staff and students, April 9, 2021.) The information is further based on the author's knowledge of the event. For the Zeigler/Peacock plaque, see: https://discovering.cofc.edu/items/show/2

5. Estes, "The Long Gay Line," 46-64; telephone conversation with Oliver Bowman, February 4, 2021; "Joan Alden," https://winningwriters.com/people/joan-alden see the Douglas Seymour oral history, SCCofC, for his fairly benign experience at The Citadel; Pat Conroy, *The Lords of Discipline* (New York: Houghton Mifflin Harcourt Publishing Co., 1980); Scotty Cade, *Knobs* (Dreamspinner Press, 2016); Richard Little oral history, SCCofC; Sue Groff oral history, SCCofC; Tzipi Radonsky oral history, SCCofC; "Alliance for Equality," https://education.musc.edu/students/spsd/diversity/multicultural-organizations/alliance-for-equality ; "MUSC Health Named A Leader in 'LGBT Health Care Equality,'" https://web.musc.edu/about/leadership/ institutional-offices/communications/pamr/news-releases/2016/musc-health-named-a-leader ; "Charleston Southern, 'Worst List: The Absolute Worst Campuses for LGBTQ Youth,'" https://www.campuspride.org/worstlist/ ; Charleston Southern University Pride, https://www.facebook.com/Charleston-Southern-University-Pride-1604841693166356/ about/?ref=page_internal

6. "Gay Wisdom," White Crane Institute, "Today in Gay History," November 23 (2009), via an email by Greg Day, November 23, 2021; Christy Mallory and Brad Sears, *Research that Matters: Discrimination Against LGBT People in South Carolina* (UCLA School of Law Williams Institute, July 2019), 11 https://williamsinstitute.law.ucla.edu/publications/lgbt-discrimination-sc/ for city rankings on The Human Rights Campaign Municipal Equality Index see https://hrc-prod-requests.s3-us-west-2.amazonaws.com/MEI-2020-Charleston-South-Carolina.pdf?mtime=20201202124450&focal=none

7. Sue Groff oral history, SCCofC; Lynn Dugan oral history, SCCofC; "Charleston gay rights advocates to join national protest," *PC*, November 13, 2008 https://infoweb-newsbank-com.nuncio.cofc.edu/apps/news/document-view?p=AWNB&t=favorite%3APAC%21Post%2520and%2520Courier%2520Collection&sort=YMD_date%3AD&fld-base-0=alltext&maxresults=20&val-base-0=amendment%20%22city%20hall%22%20&fld-nav-0=YMD_date&val-nav-0=01/01/2008%20-%2001/01/2009&docref=news/163067DCA27551D0 "Gay Say," *GC*, 1 (February 1981), 3. Greg Hambrick, "North Charleston hosts the Lowcountry's first gay pride event," *Charleston City Paper*, May 12, 2010, https://www.charlestoncitypaper.com/story/north-charleston-hosts-the-lowcountrys-first-gay-pride-event?oid=1968201

8. Glenn Smith, "Nearly 7 years later, police are little closer to knowing who killed Clifton Harris," *PC*, March 15, 2013 https://infoweb-newsbank-com.nuncio.cofc.edu/apps/ news/document-view?p=AWNB&t=favorite%3APAC%21Post%2520and%2520Courier%2520

Collection&sort=; YMD_date%3AD&maxresults=20&f=advanced&val-base-0=%22clifton %20 harris%22%20%20murder%20&fld-base-0=alltext&docref=news/163075734E989A50 the case file 0616614 is available at https://www.charleston-sc.gov/DocumentCenter/View/1272/ Clifton-Harris-Jr?bidId= Lynn Dugan oral history, SCCofC; Hambrick, "Lowcountry's first gay pride event;" Lynn Dugan oral history, SCCofC; Anonymous, "Gay Say," *GC*, 1 (February 1981), 3. Tony Williams oral history, SCCofC; "Team Pride" and "Why We March," *It's Time to Bridge the Gap* (Charleston: Charleston Pride Organization, May 15, 2010), 24, 14. Charles W. Smith oral history SCCofC; Lynn Dugan oral history, SCCofC.

Epilogue

1. Rev. Robert Arrington oral history, SCCofC; Kalyn Oyerjipsta "Chas. Black Pride branches off from organization," *PC*, September 8, 2019, 3; Sam Spence, "Alliance for Full Acceptance announces new leader," *Charleston City Paper*, September 20, 2021; Sam Spence, "AFFA's Chase Glenn to head up LGBTQ+ resource office at MUSC," *Charleston City Paper*, March 26, 2021 https://charlestoncitypaper.com/affas-chase-glenn-to-head-up-lgbtq-resource-office-at-musc/

2. The Fifth Annual Charleston SC Transgender Day of Remembrance (November 15, 2018) lists sponsors, LGBTQ vertical files, SCCofC; email communication from Judi Corsaro, Charleston Jewish Federation, November 11, 2018; email from College of Charleston Brian McGee "for Use of a Preferred Name," July 29, 2018, SCLGBTQ vertical files, SCCofC; Stephen Hobbes, "'We don't have to be another name on the list'," *PC*, November 21, 2020, 5; Gregory Yee, "How Charleston Police are using gender identity training to serve the LGBTQ community," *PC* January 22, 2019 https:// www.postandcourier.com/news/how-charleston-police-are-using-gender-identity-training-to-serve-the-lgbtq-community/article_92771aa6-18fa-11e9-897b-0f0d4512ea49.html Angie Jackson, "Man arrested in transgender woman's attack: Charleston Police hear community concerns," *PC*, September 4, 2018; Paola Trista Arruda, Live Five News, February 7, 2020, "Charleston Police Department first in State to implement 'Safe Space' program," https://www.live5news.com/2020/02/08/charleston-police-department-first-state-implement-safe-place-program/ James Lovegrove, "LGBTQ protections added back to hate crimes bill," *PC*, March 16, 2021 https://www.postandcourier.com/ politics/lgbtq-protections-added-back-to-sc-hate-crimes-bill-as-it-advances-to-house-floor/article_4aed2b0e-8689-11eb-b85e-17c415526b1e.html Seanna Adcox, "SC legislative session ends with business leaders encouraged by progress on hate crimes law," *PC*, May 13, 2021 https://www.postandcourier.com/politics/sc-legislative-session-ends-with-business-leaders-encouraged-by-progress-on-hate-crime-law/article_115b31aa-b3fd-11eb-b8f9-7bb98426c5d5.html

3. Ricky Ciapha Dennis, Jr., "Struggles continue for LGBTQ community," *PC*, December 1, 2019, 1-2F; Ricky Ciapha Dennis, Jr., "New leader takes helm of North Charleston's LGBTQ advocacy group," *PC*, July 10, 2021 https://www.postandcourier.com/news/new-leader-takes-helm-of-north-charlestons-lgbtq-advocacy-group/article_56a65942-df4a-11eb-9fc9-73b51f3ee5fa.html Jerrrel Floyd, "Palmetto Community Care records 23 new HIV-positive cases in the Lowcountry," *PC*, January 24, 2019 https://www.postandcourier.com/ health/palmetto-community-care-records-23-new-hiv-positive-cases-in-the-lowcountry/ article_9ecfe646-1fe6-11e9-b71e-3510b69757d.html for Roper St. Francis Ryan White Wellness Center, see https://www.ryanwhiteofcharleston.org/

4. Michael Majchrowicz, "Conversion therapy leader for 2 decades, McKrae Game disavows movement he helped fuel," *PC*, August 30, 2019, updated May 18, 2021; Liam Knox, "S. Carolina law banning LGBTQ sex ed is unconstitutional, judge rules," ABC News, March 12, 2020 https://www.nbcnews.com/feature/nbc-out/s-carolina-law-banning-lgbtq-sex-ed-unconstitutional-judge-rules-n1156501 *Charleston Prime Time News*, December 2018, copies in SCLGBTQ; see also note 12, Chapter 15; copies in SCLGBTQ vertical files, SCCofC.

5. On the rugby team, see http://charlestonblockaderugby.org/about/ Lainey Millen, "Gay bingo moves to convention center," *Q Notes Carolina*, July 12, 2019 https://qnotescarolinas.com/gay-bingo-moves-to-convention-center Tabbuli restaurant advertised two seatings for Sunday brunch https://www.facebook.com/events/the-house-of-tabbuli/drag-brunch-at-tabbuli/723787041129196/

6. Jennifer Berry Hawes, "State's gay marriage ban struck down; Charleston's gay marriage ruling generates plenty of talk," *PC*, November 11, 2014 https://www.postandcourier.com/features/faith_and_values/states-gay-marriage-ban-struck-down-charlestons-gay-marriage-ruling-generates-plenty-of-talk/article_f3354a71-1535-595a-ae35-100389a84338.html Jennifer Berry Hawes, "Joy, uncertainty for gay couples: Two federal rulings open door to gay marriage in South Carolina," *PC*, November 18, 2014 https://www.postandcourier.com/archives/joy-uncertainty-for-gay-couples-two-federal-rulings-open-door-to-gay-marriage-in-south/article_1ee68531-c974-5340-bac3-7c8f4e467a0e.html

7. "Donald Trump won in South Carolina. South Carolina presidential results," *Politico*, January 6, 2021, https://www.politico.com/2020-election/results/south-carolina/ Gregory Yee, "Kristin Graziano wins Charleston wins Charleston County Sheriff's race, unseating longtime leader, Al Cannon," *PC*, November 4, 2020, https://www.postandcourier.com/politics/kristin-graziano-wins-charleston-county-sheriffs-race-unseating-longtime-leader-al-cannon/article_f2b37460-1e88-11eb-8564-6b7c74da7d60.html

8. City of Charleston Proclamation, LGBTQ History Month, October 28, 2020, SCLGBTQ vertical files, SCCofC; Libby Stanford, "Gov. McMaster calls on SC education department to investigate 'obscene' books in school," *PC*, November 10, 2021   Jeffrey Collins, "McMaster signs transgender sports ban bill into law in SC," *PC*, May 18, 2022, A5; Steve Garrison, "Status for conviction under anti-sodomy law challenged," *PC*, December 24, 2021, A5. Jocelyn Grzeszczak, "No sex-offender status for men convicted under anti-sodomy law," *PC*, April 23, 2022; Tom Corwin, "Advocates: Law will be excuse for bias," *PC*, 21 June, 2022, A1; Emma Whalen, "Push for commission to address racism faltering," *PC*, January 30, 2022, 1, 6.

Select Bibliography

Primary Sources
Alliance for Full Acceptance Papers, SCCofC
R. F. W. Allston Papers, SCHS
Nan Shand Ball Papers SCHS
Robert Ball, MD, Papers, SCCofC
John Bennett Papers, SCHS
James Blake Papers, Morgan Library and Museum
Laura Mary Bragg Papers, SCHS
Charleston, SC death record cards, CCPL
Charleston, SC police records, 19th century daily reports, CLS
Charleston, SC Recorder Court Records, CCPL
College of Charleston Communications Museum Administrative Files, SCCofC
Greg Day Papers, SCofC
Emily Ravenel Farrow Papers, SCCofC
Jo Fetzer Papers, SCCofC
Anne King Gregorie Papers, SCHS
Charlotte Myers Griswold Papers, SCCofC.
Joe Hall Papers, SCCofC
Dorothy Heyward Papers, SCHS
Eugene C. Hunt Papers, Avery Research Center for African American History and Culture, College of Charleston
Theodore D. Jervey Papers, SCHS
George Thomas Lamme Papers, SCCofC
Law and Order League Papers, SCHS
Lesbian and Gay Alliance Papers, SCCofC
Carol Lyons and Dorothy D'Anna Papers, SCCofC
Burnet R. Maybank Papers, SCCofC
Middleton Family Papers, SCHS
Robert Molloy Papers, South Caroliniana Library, University of South Carolina
Hortensia Mordecai Diaries, Thomas Tobias Papers, SCCofC
Harrison Randolph Papers, SCCofC
Mike Schwarzott Papers, SCofC
Steven Small Papers, SCCofC
Charles W. Smith Papers, SCCofC
South Carolina LGBTQ Oral Histories, Archives and Outreach Project files and oral histories, SCCofC
Elizabeth O'Neill Verner Papers, SCCofC
John A. Zeigler, Jr. Papers, SCCofC

Published Primary Sources
Charleston Alternative (Charleston, SC)
Charleston City Paper (Charleston, SC)

Charleston Prime Time News (electronic newsletter; Charleston, SC).
Conservative Inc. (Newsletter Bulletin of the Grass Roots League, Charleston, SC).
Cooper, Thomas (ed.). *The Statutes at Large of South Carolina Edited Under Authority of the Legislature.* Columbia, SC: A. S. Johnston, 1837.
Directories, City of Charleston, various years and imprints.
Evening Post (Charleston, SC).
Gay Charleston (Charleston, SC).
The Loop (Charleston, SC).
Lowcountry Gay and Lesbian Alliance newsletters (various names, Charleston, SC).
Lowcountry News and Review (Charleston, SC).
McCord, David J. *The Statutes of South Carolina: Containing the Acts Relating to Charleston, Courts, Slaves and Rivers.* Columbia: A. S. Johnson, 1840.
National Police Gazette (New York, NY).
News and Courier (Charleston, SC).
Post and Courier (Charleston, SC).
Yearbooks, City of Charleston, various years and imprints.

Monographs, publications, dissertations, and theses
Abend, Allen C. *Gabrielle DeVeaux* [sic] *Clements: Etcher, Painter, Muralist, Teacher.* Self-published, 2012.
Allen, Louis Anderson. *A Bluestocking in Charleston: The Life and Career of Laura Bragg.* Columbia, SC: University of South Carolina Press, 2001.
Angelilli, Claire (ed.). *Inked Impressions: Ellen Day Hale and the Painter-Etcher Movement: January 26-April 14, 2007.* Carlisle, PA: Trout Gallery, Dickenson College, 2007.
Arnold, Sara C. *Rauschenberg in Charleston.* Charleston: The Gibbes Museum of Art, 2019.
Baldwin, Agnes Leland Baldwin. *First Settlers of South Carolina, 1670-1700.* Easley, S.C: Southern Historical Press, 1985.
Ball, Edward. *Peninsula of Lies: A True Story of Mysterious Birth and Taboo Love.* New York: Simon & Schuster, 2004.
—. *The Sweet Hell Inside: A Family History.* New York: William Morrow, 2001.
Barbash, Ilisa, Molly Rogers and Deborah Willis (eds.). *To Make Their Own Way in the World: The Enduring Legacy of the Zealy Daguerreotypes.* Cambridge, MA: Peabody Museum Press, 2020.
Bayless, Joy. *Rufus Wilmot Griswold: Poe's Literary Executor.* Nashville, TN: Vanderbilt University Press, 1943.
Bellows, Barbara L. *A Talent for Living: Josephine Pinckney and the Charleston Literary Tradition.* Baton Rouge, LA: Louisiana State University Press, 2006.
Benemann, William. *Male-Male Intimacy in Early America: Beyond Romantic Friendships.* New York: Routledge, 2012.
— *Unruly Desires: American Sailors and Homosexualities in the Age of Sail.* Self-published, 2019.
Bennett, Murray. *Invisible Pursuit.* New York: The Ram Press, 1961.
Bérubé, Allan. *Coming Out under Fire: The History of Gay Men and Women in World War II.* Chapel Hill, NC: University of North Carolina Press, 2010.
— *My Desire for History.* Chapel Hill, NC: University of North Carolina Press, 2011.
Blake, James. *The Joint.* Garden City, NY: Doubleday & Company, Inc. 1977.
Boyd, Blanche. *Nerves.* Plainfield, VT: Daughters, Inc., 1973.
Brinson, Claudia Smith. *Stories of Struggle: The Clash over Civil Rights in South Carolina.* Columbia, SC: University of South Carolina Press, 2020.
Bronski, Michael. *A Queer History of the United States.* Boston, MA: Beacon Press, 2011.

Burg, B. R. *Sodomy and the Pirate Tradition: English Sea Rovers in the Seventeenth Century Caribbean.* New York: New York University Press, 1995.

Cade, Scotty. *Knobs.* Dreamspinner Press, 2016.

Charleston Chamber of Commerce. *1934 Guide Book, Fort Moultrie Camps, Fort Moultrie, S.C.: Regular Army National Guard Organized Reserves.* Charleston, SC: J. J. Furlong & Son, 1934.

Charleston Port Society, Managers. *Second Annual Report of the Board of Managers of the Charleston Port Society Read Monday, 21st March, 1825.* Charleston, SC: C. C. Sebring.

Charleston Pride. *It's Time to Bridge the Gap.* Charleston: Charleston Pride Organization, 2010.

Chernow, Ron. *Alexander Hamilton.* New York: Penguin Press, 2004.

Chichester, C. C. *Historical Sketch of the Charleston Port Society for Promoting the Gospel Among Seamen, with the 63d Annual Reports and List of Officers and Members.* Charleston, SC: News and Courier Book Presses, 1885.

Childress, Alice. *A Short Walk.* New York: Coward, McCann & Geoghegan, 1979.

— *Those Other People.* New York, Putnam Publishing Group, 1989.

Colado, Julian Gabriel. *Hiding Among the Palmettos.*greatunpublished.com, Title No. 3, 2000.

College of Charleston. *The Comet,* vol 68. Charleston, SC: The College of Charleston, 1991.

— (B. D. Redmond, ed.). *The Comet 1975.* Charleston, SC: The College of Charleston, 1975.

Collins, Andrew. *Fodor's Gay Guide to the USA.* New York: Fodor's Travel Publications, 1996.

Conroy, Pat. *The Lords of Discipline.* New York: Houghton Mifflin Harcourt Publishing Co., 1980.

Craft, W. *Running a Thousand Miles for Freedom, or The Escape of William and Ellen Craft from Slavery.* London: William Tweedie, 1860.

Damron Bob. *Bob Damron's Address Book '72.* San Francisco, CA: Bob Damron Enterprises, 1971.

— *Bob Damron's Address Book '82.* San Francisco, CA: Bob Damron Enterprises, 1981.

— *Bob Damron's Address Book '88.* San Francisco, CA: Bob Damron Enterprises, 1987.

— *Men's Travel Guide.* San Francisco, CA: Damron Co., 1999.

— *Men's Travel Guide.* San Francisco, CA: Damron Company, 2007.

Derfner, Joel. *Swish: My Quest to be the Gayest Person Ever.* New York: Broadway Books, 2008.

Devereux, Anthony Q. *The Life and Times of Robert F.W. Allston.* Georgetown, SC: Waccamaw Press, 1976.

Durham, Frank. *DuBose Heyward: The Man Who Wrote Porgy.* Columbia, SC: University of South Carolina Press, 1954.

Easterby, J. H. *A History of the College of Charleston, Founded 1770.* Charleston, SC: The Trustees of the College of Charleston, 1935.

— *History of the St. Andrew's Society of Charleston, South Carolina,1729-1929.* Charleston, SC: The Society, 1929.

Edgar, Walter B. (ed.). *The South Carolina Encyclopedia.* Columbia, S.C: University of South Carolina Press, 2006.

Egerton, Douglas, Robert L. Paquette, Stanley Harrold, and Randall M. Miller. *The Denmark Vesey Affair: A Documentary History.* Gainesville, FL: University Press of Florida, 2017.

Ellman, Richard. *Oscar Wilde.* New York: Alfred A. Knopf, 1988.

Faderman, Lillian. *Surpassing the Love of Men: Romantic Friendship and Love Between Women from the Renaissance to the Present.* New York: William Morrow and Co., 1981.

Fant, Jennie Holton Fant (ed.). *The Travelers' Charleston.* Columbia, SC: University of South Carolina Press, 2016.

Fraser, Walter J., Jr. *Charleston! Charleston! The History of a Southern City.* Columbia, SC: University of South Carolina Press, 1989.

Gale, Patrick. *Armistead Maupin.* Bath, Somerset, UK: Absolute Press, 1999.

Gaspar, David and Darlene Clark Hine. *More Than Chattel: Black Women and Slavery in the Americas*. Bloomington, IN: Indiana University Press, 1996.

Gateway Magazine, 2, 1 (January 1957).

Gateway Magazine, 9, 3 (March 1964).

Glover, Lorri. *Southern Sons: Becoming Men in the New Nation*. Baltimore, MD: Johns Hopkins University Press, 2007.

Godley, Henry C. and Mark W. Riley. *David*. (May 1972). Jacksonville, FL: David Publications, 1972.

Granier, Kellie. *Prologue of Seduction: Sexy Stories Collection*. Xplicit Press, 2014.

Green, Jeffrey P. *Edmund Thornton Jenkins: The Life and Times of an American Black Composer, 1894-1926*. Westport, CT: Greenwood Press, 1982.

Green, Julien. *South: A Play*. New York: Marion Boyars, 1991.

Greenberg, Reuben and Arthur Gordon. *Let's Take Back Our Streets!* Chicago: Contemporary Books, 1989.

Greene, Harlan *The Damned Don't Cry – They Just Disappear: The Life and Works of Harry Hervey*. Columbia, SC: University of South Carolina Press, 2017.

— *Master Skylark: John Bennett and the Charleston Renaissance*. Athens, GA: University of Georgia Press, 2001.

— (ed.). *Porgy and Bess: A Charleston Story*. Charleston, SC: Homehouse Press, 2016.

— *Why We Never Danced the Charleston*. Charleston, SC: The History Press, 2005.

Griswold, Rufus W. *Passages from the Correspondence and Other Papers of Rufus W. Griswold*. Cambridge, MA: W. M. Griswold, 1898.

— *Statement of the relations of Rufus W. Griswold with Charlotte Myers (called Charlotte Griswold) Elizabeth F. Ellet, Ann S. Stephens, Samuel J. Waring, Hamilton R. Searles, and Charles D. Lewis; with particular reference to their late unsuccessful attempt to have set aside the decree granted in 1852 by the Court of common pleas of Philadelphia County, in the case of Griswold vs. Griswold*. Philadelphia, PA: H. P. Ashmead, 1856.

Guide 43. Minneapolis, MN, 1964.

Guild Guide 1964. Washington, DC: The Guild Press, 1964.

Hall, Lee. *Betty Parsons: Artist, Dealer, Collector*. New York: Harry N. Abrams, Inc., 1991.

Hanna, Elizabeth. *"Tiptoeing in Their Footsteps": Dorothy Heyward's Unpublished Autobiography*. Thesis (M.A.), College of Charleston, 2005.

Hervey, Harry. *Red Ending*. New York: Horace Liveright, Inc., 1929.

Hetzler, Sidney. *Two Town Festivals: Signs of a Theater of Power*. Thesis (Ph. D.), Emory University, 1990.

Heyward, Dorothy and DuBose. *Mamba's Daughters: A Play*. New York: Farrar & Rinehart, 1939.

Heyward, DuBose. *Mamba's Daughters*. Garden City, NY: Doubleday, Doran & Co., 1929.

Hippler, Mike. *Matlovich: The Good Soldier*. Boston, MA: Alyson Publications, Inc., 1989.

Hutchisson, James and Harlan Greene (eds.). *Renaissance in Charleston: Art and Life in the Carolina Lowcountry, 1900 – 1940*, Athens, GA: University of Georgia Press, 2003.

James, Henry. *The American Scene*. London: Chapman and Hall, 1907.

Johnson, David K. *The Lavender Scare: The Cold War Persecution of Gays and Lesbians in the Federal Government*. Chicago: University Press of Chicago, 2004.

Johnson, T. J. *The War Ahead*. Hard Title Publishing, 2008.

— *The War Apart*. Hard Title Publishing, 2008.

Jones, Mark R. *Wicked Charleston, Volume 2: Prostitutes, Politics and Prohibition*. Charleston, SC: The History Press, 2006.

Katz, Jonathan Ned. *The Daring Life and Dangerous Times of Eve Adams*. Chicago: Chicago Review Press, 2021.

— *Gay American History: Lesbians and Gay Men in the U.S.A.* New York: Thomas Y. Crowell, 1976.

— *Love Stories: Sex Between Men Before Homosexuality*. Chicago: University of Chicago Press, 2001.

King, William S. *The Newspaper Press of Charleston, S.C.: A Chronological and Biographical History, Embracing a Period of One Hundred and Forty Years*. Charleston, SC: E. Perry, 1872.

Kirchick, James. *Secret City: The Hidden History of Gay Washington*. New York: Henry Holt and Company, 2022.

Kohn, Barry and Alice Matusow. *Barry and Alice: Portrait of a Bisexual Marriage*. Englewood Cliffs, NJ: Prentice-Hall, Inc., 1980.

Lees, Alfred and Ronald Nelson (eds.). *Longtime Companions: Autobiographies of Gay Male Fidelity*. Binghampton, NY: Harrington Park Press, 1999.

Lundy, James A. *A History of the Poetry Society of South Carolina, 1920-2021*. Self-published, 2021.

Martindale, Meredith and Pamela Moffat. *Lilla Cabot Perry, an American Impressionist*. Washington, D.C: National Museum of Women in the Arts, 1990.

Mattern, Kymberly Natasha. *Outing the National Register: Including Lesbian, Gay, Bisexual, Transgender, and Queer (LGBTQ) Sites on The National Register of Historic Places*. Thesis (M.A.), Clemson University and the College of Charleston, 2017.

Maupin, Armistead. *Logical Family: A Memoir*. New York: Harper Collins, 2017.

Michael's of Florida Travel Guide. Ft. Lauderdale, FL: Michael's of Florida, n.d.

Mitchell, Mark and David Leavitt (eds.). *Pages Passed from Hand to Hand: The Hidden Tradition of Homosexual Literature in English from 1748 to 1914*. Boston, MA: Houghton Mifflin, 1997.

Moore, John Hammond. *Carnival of Blood: Dueling, Lynching, and Murder in South Carolina, 1866-1920*. Columbia: University of South Carolina Press, 2006.

Morris, Sheila R. (ed.). *Southern Perspectives on the Queer Movement: Committed to Home*. Columbia, SC: University of South Carolina Press, 2018.

Morrison, Nan. *A History of the College of Charleston, 1936 – 2008*. Columbia, SC: University of South Carolina Press, 2011.

Parsons, Schuyler Livingston. *Untold Friendships: 60 Years with a Famous Host and his Famous Friends*. Boston, MA: Houghton Mifflin Company, 1955.

Picano, Felice, *The Book of Lies*. Los Angeles: Alyson Publications, 1999.

Pinckney, Josephine. *Sea-drinking Cities*. New York: Harper & Brothers Publishers, 1927.

— *Three o'Clock Dinner*. New York: The Viking Press, 1945.

Rogers, Dorothy G. *America's First Women Philosophers Transplanting Hegel, 1860-1925*. London: Continuum, 2005.

Rose, Ingrid, Roderick S. Quiroz, and Patrice La Liberté. *The Lithographs of Prentiss Taylor: A Catalogue Raisonné*. Bronx, N.Y: Fordham University Press, 1996.

Ross, Ann B. *The Murder Cure*. New York: Avon Books, 1978.

Russell, Ina D. *Jeb and Dash: A Diary of Gay Life, 1918-1945*. Boston, MA: Faber and Faber, 1993.

Rybczynski, Witold. *Charleston Fancy: Little Houses & Big Dreams in the Holy City*. New Haven, CT: Yale University Press, 2019.

Scarborough, William Kauffman. *The Allstons of Chicora Wood: Wealth, Honor, and Gentility in the South Carolina Lowcountry*. Baton Rouge, LA: Louisiana State University Press, 2011.

Schanke, Robert A. and Kim Marra (eds.). *Passing Performances: Queer Readings of Leading Players in American Theater History*. Ann Arbor, MI: The University of Michigan Press, 1989.

Scharnhorst, Gary, et al. *Oscar Wilde in America: The Interviews*. Urbana, IL: University of Illinois Press, 2010.

Sears, James T. *Lonely Hunters: An Oral History of Lesbian and Gay Southern Life, 1948-1968.* Boulder, CO: Westview Press, 1997.

Sendak, Maurice. *Very Far Away.* New York: Harper & Bros., 1957.

Severens, Martha R. *The Charleston Renaissance.* Spartanburg, SC: Saraland Press, 1998.

Shapland, Jenn. *My Autobiography of Carson McCullers.* Portland, OR: Tin House, 2020.

Shilts, Randy. *Conduct Unbecoming: Gays & Lesbians in the U.S. Military.* New York: St. Martin's Press, 1993.

Simmons, Dawn Langley. *All for Love.* London: W. H. Allen, 1975.

— *Dawn, a Charleston Legend.* Charleston, SC: Wyrick, 1995.

— *Man into Woman: a Transsexual Autobiography:* New York, Macfadden-Bartell, 1971.

Smalls, Gregory. *Black Enough, Man Enough: Embracing My Mixed Race and Fluid Sexuality.* Atlanta, GA: Juan & Gee Enterprises, LLC, 2019.

Smith, Helen. *What God Has to Say About the Gay Parade: Homosexuality.* Charleston, SC: John J. Furlong & Sons, 1974.

Special Report of the Law and Order League of Charleston, S.C. 1913.

Springate, Megan E. (ed.). *LGBTQ America: A Theme Study of Lesbian, Gay, Bisexual, Transgender, and Queer History.* National Park Service, 2016.

Spruill, Marjorie, Valinda W. Littlefield, and Joan Marie Johnson. *South Carolina Women: Their Lives and Times.* Athens, GA: University of Georgia Press, 2009.

Stewart, Chuck. *Proud Heritage: People, Issues, and Documents of the LGBT Experience.* Santa Barbara, CA: ABC-Clio, 2015.

Surles, Flora Belle. *Anne King Gregorie.* Columbia, SC: Printed for the author by R. L. Bryan Co., 1968.

Tardy, Mary T. (ed.). *Living Female Writers of the South.* Philadelphia, PA: Claxton, Remsen & Haffelfinger, 1872.

This Week with David. Fort Lauderdale, FL: David, n.d.

Thompson, Santi Thompson. "*Offending Decent People*": *Murder, Masculinity, and the (Homosexual) Menace in Cold War era Charleston.* Thesis (M.A.) University of South Carolina, 2008.

Traub, James. *Judah Benjamin: Counselor to the Confederacy.* New Haven, CT: Yale University Press, 2021.

Utsey, Scott. *Who's Who in South Carolina: A Standard Biographical Reference Book of South Carolina.* Columbia, SC: Current Historical Association, n.d.

Waters, Ethel, with Charles Samuels. *His Eye Is on the Sparrow.* Garden City, NY: Doubleday, 1951.

Whitman, Walt. *Complete Prose Works of Walt Whitman.* New York, NY: G. P. Putnam's Sons, 1902.

Willingham, Calder. *End as a Man.* New York: Vanguard Press, 1947.

Wise, Benjamin E. *William Alexander Percy: The Curious Life of a Mississippi Planter and Sexual Freethinker.* Chapel Hill, NC: University of North Carolina Press, 2012.

Woolsey, Gamel. *The Collected Poems of Gamel Woolsey.* Norfolk, UK: F. Crowe & Sons, 1984.

— (with an introduction by Barbara Ozieblo). *Patterns in the Sand.* Sherbone, Dorset, UK: The Sundial Press, 2012.

Wragg, Russel. *Portrait Over My Shoulder: Personal Recollections of a piano virtuoso, surreptitiously gleaned by the author.* Charleston, SC: Walker, Evans and Cogswell Company, 1952.

Young, John R. *Walk in the Parks.* Charleston, SC: Evening Post Books, 2010.

Zeigler, John. *The Edwin Poems.* Self-published: Xlibris Corp., 2007.

— (James T. Sears, ed.). *Edwin and John: A Personal History of the American South.* New York: Routledge, 2009.

Articles (excluding news articles, encyclopedia entries, etc.)

Blake, James. "The Happy Islanders." *The Paris Review.* Number 52, 107-27.

Bloom, Debbie. "'An Abiding Mark': The Charleston Students of Anna C. Brackett." *Carologue* (A publication of the SCHS), Winter 2016, 20-3.

Charleston Reporter, A. "The Hallowe'en Party." *One,* 7, 5 (May 1959), 17-9.

Cloud, John. "A Gay Mafia." *Time.* vol. 172 (November 19, 2008), 52-5.

Coleman, Richard. "The Infamous Mansion," *Story: The Magazine of the Short Story.* XXXI, 123 (November-December 1947), 15-23.

Copp, Roberta VH. "Of Her Time, Before Her Time: Anne King Gregorie, South Carolina's Singular Historian." *South Carolina Historical Magazine,* 91, 4 (October 1990), 231-46.

Davis, Mary Katherine. "The Feather Bed Aristocracy: Abbeville District in the 1790s." *The South Carolina Historical Magazine* 80, no. 2 (1979), 136-55.

Day, Greg. (cover photograph). *RFD: A Country Journal for Gay Men Everywhere.* No 59, (Fall 1989).

Day, Greg. (cover photograph). *Southern Exposure,* 16, 3 (Fall 1988).

Donaldson, Susan V. "Charleston's Racial Politics of Historic Preservation: The Case of Edwin A. Harleston" in James Hutchisson and Harlan Greene, (eds.), *Renaissance in Charleston: Art and Life in the Carolina Lowcountry, 1900 – 1940.* Athens: University of Georgia Press, 176-98.

Duberman, Martin. "Writhing Bedfellows." *Journal of Homosexuality,* 1980-81, Fall-Winter, 6, (1-2), 85-101.

Edmonson, Roger. "I Once Had Two Masters: Bob McNair Reflects on his Life as S-M Slave." *The Advocate,* issue 532 (August 29, 1989), 36-7.

Edwards, Margaret. "Frances Frost, 1905-1959: Sketch of a Vermont Poet." *Vermont History,* 58, 2 (Spring 1988), 102-11.

Estes, Steve. "The Long Gay Line: Gender and Sexual Orientation at The Citadel." *Southern Cultures,* 16, 1, (Spring 2010), 46-64.

"Forty Under 40: Nick Shalosky." *The Advocate,* issue 1027/1028 (June/July 2009), 90.

Goldman, Peter. "The Face of AIDS." *Newsweek,* August 10, 1987, 22-3, 31, 34-6.

Grimké, John Faucheraud. "Order Book of John Faucheraud Grimké. August 1778 to May 1780 (Continued)." *The South Carolina Historical and Genealogical Magazine* 14, no. 4 (1913), 219-24.

Gunter, Freeman. "Doing the Charleston." *Mandate: The International Magazine of Entertainment and Eros,* 8, 8 (November 1982), 75-9.

Hitt, Jack. "The Legend of Dawn." *GQ,* 68, 12 (October 1998), 268-78.

Hobbes, Nicholas. "Adventures Among the Literati." *The Shako,* 3, 2 (Spring 1935), 31-3.

Huhner, Leon. "Francis Salvador: Prominent Patriot of the Revolutionary War." *Publications of the American Jewish Historical Society,* 1901, 107-22.

"Man Who Lived 30 Years As A Woman, The: Georgia Black Married Twice, Even 'Mothered' Devoted Son." *Ebony,* VI, 12 (October 1951), 23-6.

Melvin, Patrick. "Captain Florence O'Sullivan and the Origins of Carolina." *The South Carolina Historical Magazine,* 76, 4 (October 1975), 235-49.

Miles, Edwin A. "The Old South and the Classical World." *The North Carolina Historical Review,* 48, 3 (July 1971), 258-75.

Parham, J. Edward. "Barry Kohn And The Charleston Alternative." *The Advocate,* issue 381 (November 24, 1983), 43-5.

— "The Discrete Charm and Conservatism of Charleston, SC." *The Advocate,* Issue 366 (April 28, 1983), 26-8.

Patterson, Cynthia Lee. "'Hermaphroditish Disturbers of the Peace': Rufus Griswold, Elizabeth Oakes Smith, and Nineteenth-Century Discourses of Ambiguous Sex." *Women's Studies,* 2016, 45, 6, 513-33.

Sabb, Willie. "My Mother Was A Man: Philadelphia Steelworker Tells Intimate Story of How He Was Reared by Georgia Black, the Man Who Lived as a Woman for 30 Years in Florida." *Ebony*, VIII, 8 (June 1953) 75-8, 80, 82.

"Schwacke Takes Three Awards." *Newsletter: College of Charleston*, XXVI, 2 (August 1978), 2-3.

Sears, James T. and Louise A. Allen. "Museums, Friends and Lovers in the New South: Laura's Web, 1909-1931." *Journal of Homosexuality*, 40, 1 (2000), 105-44.

Singer, Barry. "Changing Fortunes." *Opera News*, 71, 1 (July 2007), 7.

Southern Gent. "Charleston, South Carolina: Fortress of the Old South." *Steam: A Quarterly Journal for Men*, 1, 2 (Summer 1993), 114-15.

Steele, Dorothy. "Frances Frost." *Those Intriguing Indomitable Vermont Women*. Vermont State Division of the American Association of University Women, 1980, 52-4.

Waters, Dustin. "A Slow Burn: The Sensational Candlestick Murder Trial of 1958 Struck Fear in Charleston's Gay Community." *Charleston City Paper*, 23, 6 (September 11, 2019), 18-20, 22-4.

Woodell, Harold. "Justice Denied in the Old South: Three Novels by F. Colburn Adams." *The Southern Literary Journal*, 11, 8 (Fall 1978), 54-63.

Internet Sources

Adler, Ben. "From outing Foley to out of a job." *Politico*, July 14, 2008 https://www.politico.com/story/2008/07/from-outing-foley-to-out-of-a-job-011738

Aruda, Paola Trista. "Charleston Police Department first in State to implement 'Safe Space' program." Live Five News, February 7, 2020 https://www.live5news.com/2020/02/08/charleston-police-department-first-state-implement-safe-place-program/

Brown, Mark. "New Unearthed ITV Play Could Be the First Ever Gay Television Drama." *The Guardian*, March 15, 2013 https://www.theguardian.com/film/2013/mar/16/itv-play-gay-television

Butler, Nic. "Under False Colors: The Politics of Gender Expression in Post-Civil War Charleston" https://www.ccpl.org/charleston-time-machine/under-false-colors-politics-gender-expression-post-civil-war-charleston#:~:text=Annual%20Report-,Under%20False %20Colors%3A%20The%20Politics%20of%20Gender,in%20Post%2DCivil%20War%20Charleston&text=In%20the%20spring%20of%201868,they%20do%20such%20a%20thing%3F

Comer, Matt. "College junior becomes S.C.'s first openly gay official." *Q notes*, March 7, 2009 https://goqnotes.com/1843/college-junior-becomes-scs-first-openly-gay-official/

Cooper, John. Oscar Wilde's 1882 Lecture Tour | Charleston (oscarwildeinamerica.org)

"Donald Trump won in South Carolina. South Carolina presidential results." *Politico*, January 6, 2021 https://www.politico.com/2020-election/results/south-carolina/

Escalera, Arkee. "Harlem Renaissance at 100: Angelina Weld Grimké: Lesbian Poet Laureate." http://www.newnownext.com/harlem-renaissance-at-100-angelina-Grimké-lesbian-love-letters-poems/02/2020/

Everhart, Karen. "With 'Tales of the City,' public TV earns extremes of scorn and praise." *Current*, January 31, 1994 https://current.org/1994/01/with-tales-of-the-city-public-tv-earns-extremes-of-scorn-and-praise/

Gackler, Megan, "18th Century Pride: The Sexuality of John Laurens." https://www.18thcenturypride.com/the-sexuality-of-john-laurens/

Goldblatt, Gloria Rudman. *Ada Clare, Queen of Bohemia: Her Life and Times*. http://digital.lib.lehigh.edu/cdm4/nysp_viewer2.php?col=clare

Hambrick, Greg. "Blogger Lane Hudson exposes hypocrisy." *Charleston City Paper*, September 5, 2007 https://www.charlestoncitypaper.com/story/blogger-lane-hudson-exposes-hypocrisy?oid=1111322

— "North Charleston hosts the Lowcountry's first gay pride event." *Charleston City Paper*, May 12, 2010 https://www.charlestoncitypaper.com/story/north-charleston-hosts-the-lowcountrys-first-gay-pride-event?oid=1968201

Hogan, Maura. "How the Garden & Gun Club upended Charleston's starched social order in just a few years." *Charleston City Paper* https://www.charlestoncitypaper.com/story/how-the-garden-and-gun-club-upended-charlestons-starched-social-order-in-just-a-few-short-years?oid=25672282

Human Rights Campaign Fund. "The Human Rights Campaign Municipal Equality Index for 2020, Charleston, SC." https://hrc-prod-requests.s3-us-west-2.amazonaws.com/MEI-2020-Charleston-South-Carolina.pdf?mtime=20201202124450&focal=none

Jones, Mark. "Gordon Langley Hall." https://markjonesbooks.com/tag/gordon-hall/

Knox, Liam. "S. Carolina law banning LGBTQ sex ed is unconstitutional, judge rules." ABC News, March 12, 2020 https://www.nbcnews.com/feature/nbc-out/s-carolina-law-banning-lgbtq-sex-ed-unconstitutional-judge-rules-n1156501

Lincoln Conspirators.com. New Gallery: Joseph Adrian Booth | LincolnConspirators.com

Mallory, Christy and Brad Sears. *Research that Matters: Discrimination Against LGBT People in South Carolina*. (UCLA School of Law Williams Institute, July 2019) https://williamsinstitute.law.ucla.edu/publications/lgbt-discrimination-sc/

"Mapping the Gay Guides: Visualizing Queer Space and American Life." https://www.mappingthegayguides.org/

Millen, Lainey. "Gay bingo Moves to Convention Center." *Q Notes Carolina,* July 12, 2019 https://qnotescarolinas.com/gay-bingo-moves-to-convention-center/

Moredock, Will. "So Long, John Graham Altman." *Charleston City Paper*, November 13, 2013 https://charlestoncitypaper.com/so-long-john-graham-altman/

"MUSC Health Named A Leader in 'LGBT Health Care Equality.'" https://web.musc.edu/about/leadership/institutional-offices/communications/pamr/news-releases/2016/musc-health-named-a-leader ---

Out History."Adam Badeau (1831-1895)." https://outhistory.org/exhibits/show/badeau/badeau

Out History. "Alexander Hamilton and John Laurens: 1779-1782." https://www.outhistory.org/exhibits/show/rev/hamilton-laurens-letters.

Painter, George. "The Sensibilities of Our Forefathers: The History of Sodomy Laws in the United States: South Carolina." https://www.glapn.org/sodomylaws/sensibilities/south_carolina.htm

Ray, Timothy David. "Achievement vs. Service: Dr. Wilfred Delphin — Lifetime Achievement Reward Recipient." *The New Orleans Age*, January 27, 2016 https://myemail.constantcontact.com/Achievement-vs--Service--Dr--Wilfred-Delphin---Lifetime-Achievement-Award-Recipient.html?soid=1011087220895&aid=aFC0EaeqQ78

Revolutionary-Demosthenes. "As sincerely as a Republican can be to a Royalist." — Letter, Francis Kinloch to Johannes von Müller,... (tumblr.com)

Seaman, Marley. "A Funny Man of Good Report." *Northwestern: For Alumni and Friends of Northwestern University* (Winter 2005) https://www.northwestern.edu/magazine/winter2005/alumninews/close-ups/colbert.html;

South Carolina State House. "Report of the Joint Legislative Committee to Screen Candidates for College and University Boards of Trustees," March 13, 2004. https://www.scstatehouse.gov/CommitteeInfo/Universities&CollegesScreeningCommittee/ScreeningReports/Screenings%20Transcripts%20For%20March%2013%202014.pdf

The Center for HIV Law & Policy, "South Carolina." https://www.hivlawandpolicy.org/states/south-carolina

"Worst List: The Absolute Worst Campuses for LGBTQ Youth: Charleston Southern University." https://www.campuspride.org/worstlist/

List of Illustrations

Figure 1, page xii. Rainbow Row. Photograph by Michael Nolan.
Figure 2, page 2. "Hermaphrodites." Engraved image by Theodore de Bry, ca. 1590. Author's collection.
Figure 3, page 9. Sailors, USS *Charleston*. Photograph, ca. World War I. Author's collection.
Figure 4, page 18. John Laurens. Miniature portrait by Charles Wilson Peale, 1780. National Portrait Gallery, Smithsonian Institution; acquired with the generous support of an anonymous donor. Conserved with funds from the Smithsonian Women's Committee.
Figure 5, page 36. Charleston prostitutes repenting, 1886 earthquake. *National Police Gazette* (January 15, 1887). Author's collection.
Figure 6, page 40. Charlotte A. Myers. Daguerreotype, ca. 1850. Charlotte A. Myers Collection, College of Charleston Libraries, Charleston, SC, USA.
Figure 7, page 41. Rufus Griswold. Engraved portrait, ca. 1855. Author's collection.
Figure 8, page 53. Edwin Booth. *Harper's Weekly* (January 13, 1866). Author's collection.
Figure 9, page 55. Judah Benjamin. "Secesh Chain" Confederate portrait cover, ca.1860s. Author's collection.
Figure 10, page 62. Emancipation Day Celebration, Marion Square (detail). *Frank Leslie's Illustrated News* (February 10, 1877). Internet archives.
Figure 11, page 66. Ethel Waters as Hagar in *Mamba's Daughters*. Photograph by Vandamm Studio, 1939. Author's collection.
Figure 12, page 69. Oscar Wilde. Satirical cartoon by Thomas Nast. *Harper's Weekly* (September 9, 1882). Author's collection.
Figure 13, page 83. Laura M. Bragg. Photograph, ca. 1960s. John A. Zeigler, Jr. Papers, College of Charleston Libraries, Charleston, SC, USA.
Figure 14, page 87. Night Owl Bookplate of Laura M. Bragg. Author's collection.
Figure 15, page 92. Edmund Thornton Jenkins. Photograph ca. 1920s. Courtesy of Karen Chandler and the Charleston Jazz Initiative.
Figure 16, page 96. Edward I. R. (Ned) Jennings. Newspaper image, ca. 1927. Author's collection.
Figure 17, page 100. Harry Hervey. Photograph ca. 1922. Author's collection.
Figure 18, page 101. *The Gay Sarong* by Harry Hervey. Dust jacket, 1926. Author's collection.
Figure 19, page 105. DuBose Heyward, Gertrude Stein and Dorothy Heyward in front of the Villa Margherita. Photograph, 1935. DuBose Heyward Papers (#1172.00), South Carolina Historical Society.
Figure 20, page 108. Anne King Gregorie. Photograph, 1912. Visual Materials Collections (#VM 30-4 Gregorie) South Carolina Historical Society.
Figure 21, page 110. Flora Belle Surles. Business card. Anne King Gregorie Papers (#1254, container 28-4-1) South Carolina Historical Society.
Figure 22, page 114. Bus ticket to Charleston, SC Navy Yard, ca. 1940s. Author's collection.
Figure 23, page 118. Rathskeller matchbook, n.d.. Author's collection.
Figure 24, page 124. Harrison Randolph. Photograph, ca. 1930. College of Charleston photographic scrapbooks, College of Charleston Libraries, Charleston, SC, USA.
Figure 25, page 126. George Grice. Photograph, ca. 1940. College of Charleston photographic scrapbooks, College of Charleston Libraries, Charleston, SC, USA.
Figure 26, page 140. Edwin Peacock and John Zeigler in front of the Book Basement. Photograph, ca. 1950. John A. Zeigler, Jr. Papers, College of Charleston Libraries, Charleston, SC, USA.
Figure 27, page 142. Book Basement. Postcard by Prentiss Taylor. Author's collection.
Figure 28, page 142. *Charleston Battery*. Lithograph by Prentiss Taylor, 1934. Smithsonian American Art Museum.
Figure 29, page 148. *The Strange One*. Photographic lobby card, 1957. Author's collection.
Figure 30, page 150. Anchor Bar and Hibernian Hall. Photograph by Wes Laurence, 1960. Courtesy of Kevin Eberle.

Figure 31, page 151. James Blake. Photograph by Alex Gotfryd, 1971. Author's collection.

Figure 32, page 157. Club 49 matchbook, ca. 1950s. Author's collection.

Figure 33, page 180. Leonard Matlovich. *Time* Magazine, September 8, 1975. Author's collection.

Figure 34, page 185. Armistead Maupin and the cast of *Tales of the City*. Promotional photograph, 1993. Author's collection.

Figure 35, page 188. John Paul Simmons and Dawn Langley Simmons in front of Charleston City Hall. Photograph, 1969. Aubrey Hancock Papers, College of Charleston Libraries, Charleston, SC, USA.

Figure 36, page 196. Carriage House matchbook, ca. 1960s. Author's collection.

Figure 37, page 199. Mr. and Ms. King Street Garden & Gun Club pageant contestants. Photograph, early 1980s. George Thomas Lamme Papers, College of Charleston Libraries, Charleston, SC, USA.

Figure 38, page 200. Bar coupon. King Street Garden & Gun Club, ca. 1978. George Thomas Lamme Papers, College of Charleston Libraries, Charleston, SC, USA.

Figure 39, page 202. Two men in formal drag, Walterboro, SC. Photograph, ca. 1950s. Aubrey Hancock Papers, College of Charleston Libraries, Charleston, SC, USA.

Figure 40, page 202. Gay men in chorus line at a party. Photograph, ca. 1960. Aubrey Hancock Papers, College of Charleston Libraries, Charleston, SC, USA.

Figure 41, page 204. Bryan Seabrook as Africa in front of the Villa Margherita. Photograph, ca. 1988, used with permission and licensed by Greg Day. Greg Day Papers, College of Charleston Libraries, Charleston, SC, USA.

Figure 42 page 207. *Gay Charleston*, March 1981. Author's collection.

Figure 43, page 210. Delphin and Romain. Photograph by Christian Steiner of piano duo Wilfred Delphin and Edwin Romain, n. d. Author's collection.

Figure 44, page 211. Streetcar (bar) advertisement. *Gay Charleston*, February 1981. Author's collection.

Figure 45, page 216. *Charleston Alternative*, 1, 1 (November 1982). Author's collection.

Figure 46, page 217. Barry Kohn "The Bisexual Window." Column masthead, *The Charleston Alternative*, 1, 1 (November 1982). Author's collection.

Figure 47, page 225. William van Hettinga. Photograph, ca. 1985. Author's collection.

Figure 48, page 226. Cory Jerome Glover. Photograph ca. 1994. Courtesy of Jenny Turner.

Figure 49, page 232. AIDS Handbill protesting Governor Carroll Campbell, early 1990s. Joe Hall Papers, College of Charleston Libraries, Charleston, SC, USA.

Figure 50, page 237. Logo/Letterhead, Lowcountry Gay and Lesbian Alliance. Lowcountry Gay and Lesbian Alliance Papers, College of Charleston Libraries, Charleston, SC, USA.

Figure 51, page 239. *Rainbow Times*. Lowcountry Gay and Lesbian Alliance newsletter, November 2000. Lowcountry Gay and Lesbian Alliance Papers, College of Charleston Libraries, Charleston, SC, USA.

Figure 52, page 246. We are Family marchers, Myrtle Beach, SC Pride Parade, 1988. We Are Family Papers, College of Charleston Libraries, Charleston, SC, USA.

Figure 53, page 247. Linda Ketner at the Democratic National Committee's Gay and Lesbian Leadership Council, ca. 2008. Linda Ketner Papers, College of Charleston Libraries, Charleston, SC, USA.

Figure 54, page 257. GAYLA Announcement, Alliance for Full Acceptance, November 2014. Alliance for Full Acceptance Papers, College of Charleston Libraries, Charleston, SC, USA.

Figure 55, page 258. Melissa Moore. Photograph courtesy of Melissa Moore.

Figure 56, page 260. Wilhelmina Hein. Photograph courtesy of Wilhelmina Hein.

Figure 57, page 280. Program, Lezz Fest Guide, 2013. Lynn Dugan Papers, College of Charleston Libraries, Charleston, SC, USA.

Figure 58, page 281. Lynn Dugan. Photograph courtesy of Lynn Dugan.

Figure 59, page 282. Program, first Charleston Pride Parade, 2010. Lynn Dugan Papers, College of Charleston Libraries, Charleston, SC, USA.

Index

1812 Overture (Tchaikovsky), 194

A
Abbott, Abiel, 10
Academy of Music, 67, 68, 103
Ackerman, Conni, 172, 212-213
ACT UP, 232
Adams, Francis Colburn, 135
Adopt a Highway Program, 237
Adoption, 275
Adult cinema, 237
Adventures of Roderick Random, The (Smollett), 19-20
Advocate, The (magazine), 267
Africa (drag name), See Seabrook, Bryan Alston
Aiken's Row (Charleston), 42
Alabama College, 109
Albemarle (ship), 4
Alchiso, Sarah, 60
Alcoholics Anonymous, 241
Alexander, Isabel, 279
Algren, Nelson, 150
All for Love (Simmons), 189
Allen, Karen, 2790
Allen, Louise Anderson, 83, 86
Allen University, 90
Alliance for Full Acceptance, 243, 251-261, 263, 265, 279, 283, 285, 288
Allston, Benjamin, 28-29
Allston, Charles, 28-29
Allston, R. F. W., 28
Altman, John Graham, III, 264-265, 270
Amahl and the Night Visitors (Menotti and Frost), 107, 193
American Association for Personal Privacy, 218
American Civil Liberties Union (ACLU), 212
American Medical Student Association, 221
Anchor (bar), 149-150, 196
Anderson, Ed, 73
Anderson, Kristin, 289
Angkor Wat, 99
Anglican Church, 253
"Annabel Lee," (Poe), 114
Ansonborough, 187
Anti-Semitism 191

Arena Stage, 198
Arrington, Robert, Rev., 283
Arthur Ravenel Bridge, 277
Ashley, Alice, 37
Ashley Hall, 26, 128
Augusta, GA, 281
Autobiography of Alice. B. Toklas, The (Stein), 109-110
Avery Research Center for African American History and Culture, 87, 89

B
"Baby Love" (The Supremes), 169
Badeau, Adam, 51-53
Baker, Robert, Bishop, 269
Balboa, Vasco Núñez de, 3
Ball, Edward, 190-191
Ball, Robert, Dr., 219, 222-223, 224, 244
Bankhead, Tallulah, 111
Baptist College, 274
Barber, Samuel, 192
Barkley, Nella, 193
Barry and Alice: Portrait of a Bisexual Marriage (Kohn and Matusow), 216
bars, 113, 118, 134-136, 144, 149-150, 156-157, 163-164, 169, 171, 178, 195-203, 210, 211-212, 214, 217, 218, 228, 239, 263. *See also* names of individual bars
Basin Street South (bar), 197
Bat Room (bar), 197
Bates, Alan, 56
Bates, Miss (school), 33
bathhouse, 237
Battery, The 8, 68-69, 141, 142, 143, 164-165, 167, 184, 190, 201, 203, 210, 213, 224, 230, 278. *See also* White Point Garden
Baynard family, 146
beard (partner of closeted person), 127, 163
Beau (magazine), 286
Beauvoir, Simone de, 151
Bechdel, Alison, 191, 270-271
Bender, Ronald, 138
Bender, Trish, 236
Benemann, William, 9, 16, 20

Benjamin, Judah, 54-55
Bennett, John, 95, 99
Bennett, Kayla, 287
Bennett, Murray, 112-115, 116, 122, 136-137, 142
Bennett, Susan, 99
Berries, Denali, 286
bestiality, 4, 41, 81, 175
Betty Parsons Gallery, 112
Biden, Joseph R., President, 287
Big Brick (Bar), 135
Bisexuals and bisexuality, 34, 53, 103, 113, 129, 215, 216, 219, 239, 263, 2778
Bishop England High School, 161, 167, 176, 182
Black Enough, Man Enough (Smalls), 249
Black Lives Matter, 165
Black, Georgia, (aka George Cantey) 130-133, 145
Blackburn, Jean, 107
Blackburn, Paul, 107
Blacksburg, SC, 79
Blake, James, 150-152, 196
Bleckley, Nichols, 287
Blind Tigers, 80
Bloomsbury, 98, 107
Boatwright, David, 205
Boisseau, Wentworth, 11
Boissevain, Jan, 103
Bonnet, Stede, 7-8
Book Basement, 139-140, 142, 144, 147-148, 149, 162, 272, 273
Boone Hall Plantation, 185
Booth, Edwin, 51-53
Booth, John Wilkes, 54
Booth, Joseph, 54
Booth, Junius Brutus, 51
Bosch, Hieronymus, 178
Boston marriage, 83
Bowman, Oliver, 181-182, 273
Boyd, Blanche, 185, 190-191, 208
Boykin State Prison, 162
Boyle, Michael, 222
Brackett, Anna, 30, 49-50, 51, 53, 179, 271
Bragg, Laura Mary, 82-87, 91, 95, 97, 109, 138, 139, 169, 237
Brennan, Gerald, 98

Brick (Bar), 135
Bridge Over the River Kwai, The (motion picture), 147
Bridges, Melissa, 279
Brinson, Joe, 79
Brittlebank Park, 277
Broadway, 22, 65, 101, 102, 113, 146, 271
Brody, Misty, 279
Bronski, Michael, 55, 56
Brooke, Rupert, 113
Brooks, Africa (drag name). See Seabrook, Bryan Alston
Brooks Motel, 205
brothels, 35-38, 71-73, 76, 79, 134, 135, 187, 195. *See also* prostitutes and prostitution
Brown vs. Board of Education, 182
Brown, Conrad "Buster", Rev., 254
Brown, Henry, US Congressman, 265-266
Brown, J. Arthur, 176
Brown, Luther, 151-152
Brown, Millicent, 175-176
Brown, Rita Mae, 191, 256
Bry, Theodor de, 1
buggery, 4-6, 35, 41, 58, 73, 79, 81, 125, 138, 145, 162, 174, 212, 261, 273
Bundy, Eli, 286
Burke High School, 176
Burnham, Thuel, 154-155, 169
Burns, Harry, 233
Burton, E. Milby, 24, 26
Bush, George H.W., President, 222
Butler, Nic, 25-26, 45
Buzzard (pseudonym), 36-38, 59, 73

C

Cadmus, Paul, 143-144
Cainhoy Miracle Revival Center, 177
Calhoun, John C., 11, 23, 33, 78
Camden, Billy (pseudonym), 187
Camelot (bar), 197
Camelot (Lerner and Loewe), 200
Campbell, Carroll, Gov., 224, 232, 233
Campbell, Celia, 50
Campbell, Kevin J., 236, 238
Campbell, Richard, 243
Campsen, George, 159, 160, 243
Campsen, George E. "Chip", 243
Campus Pride, 274
Candlestick murder, xii, 156-162, 163, 171, 236

Cannon, Al, Sheriff, 287
Cannon Street Y.M.C.A., 222
Cannonsboro (Charleston), 24
Cantey, George, *See* Black, Georgia
Capote, Truman, 149
Carnegie Mellon University, 95
Carolina (ship), 4
Carolina Art Association, 155
Carolina Day, 178
Carriage House (bar), 196
Carrington, Dora, 98
Cat on a Hot Tin Roof (Williams), 112, 146
Catawba Indians, 3
Catholic Charities, 238
Catholic Diocese, 238
Center for Women (Charleston), 213
Charleston (dance), 96
Charleston (motion picture), 205
Charleston Alternative, The (newsletter), 166, 215-217, 219
Charleston Area Arts Council, 238
Charleston Area Transgender Support (CATS), 278, 283-284
Charleston Battery (Taylor), 141, 142
Charleston Black Pride, 283
Charleston Blockade Rugby Football Club, 286
Charleston City Council, 288
Charleston City Hall, 15, 78, 277
Charleston City Paper, 263, 277-278
Charleston Communications Center, 203
Charleston County Hospital, 221
Charleston County Jail, 174
Charleston County Planning Commission, 265
Charleston County Probate Court, 287
Charleston County Public Library, 45, 84, 87, 237
Charleston County Magnet School of the Arts, Gender & Sexual Identity Alliance, 286
Charleston Etchers Club, 95
Charleston Female Seminary, 50
Charleston Gay Task Force, 180-181, 205
Charleston Hotel, 67, 195
Charleston Interfaith Crisis Ministry, 238, 247
Charleston Jewish Federation, 284
Charleston Library Society, 19-20, 70

Charleston Light Infantry, 18
Charleston Maritime Center, 231
Charleston Mayor's Committee on Homelessness and Affordable Housing, 247
Charleston Museum, 23, 82, 95, 138
Charleston Navy Base, 112, 152, 171, 198
Charleston Place Hotel, 199
Charleston Port Society for the Promotion of the Gospel Among Seamen, 11, 12
Charleston Pride, 259, 280
Charleston Renaissance, 84-102, 134, 141
Charleston School Board, 264, 267
Charleston Social Club, 276
Charleston Southern University, 274
Cheeks (bar), 196
Chernow, Ron, 19, 20, 21-22
Cherokee Indians, 2
chickenship (of sailors), 10
Chicora Wood Plantation, 28
Childers, Jim, 79
Children's Hour, The (Hellman), 82, 90, 107, 149
Childress, Alice, 191
Chitlin' Strut Festival, 185
Chorlton, Tom, 267-268
Chris, George, 138
Christian Service Hospice, 238
Chronicle, The (newspaper), 205
Circular Congregational Church, 247, 284
Citadel, The, 62, 104, 138, 146-148, 155, 162, 167, 181, 240, 272-273, 275, 282. *See also* South Carolina Military Academy
Citadel Pride Society, 273
Ckhioati, Prince, 125
Clare, Ada, 33-34, 40, 52, 98
Clark, Mark, General, 162
Clements, Gabrielle de Veaux, 93-95
Clemens, Samuel L., 34
Clemson University, 14
Cleopatra (drag queen), 166, 167
Clifton, Ida, 37
Clinton, William Jefferson, President, 266
Closet, and closeted sexuality, 50, 57, 66, 83, 87, 103, 104, 111, 115, 116-132, 145, 152, 162, 164, 172, 192, 194, 216, 234, 235, 242, 247, 251, 262-263, 272, 273

C

Club 49 (bar), 144, 156, 157, 196
Club Bacchus (bar), 197
Club David (bar), 197
Coates, Mr. 29
Coffee Cup, (listed in gay guides), 197
Cofitachequi, Lady of, 31
Coleman, Richard, 135
College of Charleston, 33, 78, 82, 87, 111, 116-130, 145, 193, 206, 208, 209, 211, 240, 249, 254, 266, 267-268, 270-271, 284, 285; Communication Museum of, 240, 269; Gay and Lesbian Alliance of, 240, 2; Gay and Lesbian Film Festival, 240, 269
Collins, Moll, 37
Columbia University, 124; Law School, 78
Columbia, SC, 26, 175, 214, 221, 222, 223, 229, 232, 234, 238, 275, 276, 281, 286
Coming out, 174, 238, 240, 241, 245, 247, 267, 278, 285. *See also* Outfest
communism, 129, 147, 159
Condon, Colleen, 287
Confederate Defenders of Fort Sumter, statue, 141, 165
Congai (Hervey and Hildreth), 101
Conroy, Pat 147, 273
Conservatives, Inc. (newsletter), 174
Continental Congress, 19
Conversion therapy, 254, 285-286
Conway, SC, 267
Cooper, Dan, *See* Brown, Luther
Copland, Aaron, 141
Corndog Man, The (motion picture), 205
Courier, The (newspaper), 35
Cove (bar), 113, 114, 144, 157, 196
Coward, Noel, 111, 152
Cox, Martha, 37
Craft, Ellen, 59, 61
Craft, William, 59
Crawford, Beulah J., 88-90, 93
Creek Indians, 2
Cross-dressing, 18, 34, 46-47, 58-66, 73, 160
Crouse, Daryl, 263
Cruising, 8, 68, 100, 113, 114, 141-143, 164-166, 195-196, 213, 278
Crunelle, Tanner, 254
Cushman, Charlotte, 53
Cypress Gardens, 105

D

D'Anna, Dorothy, 153, 169
Dart Hall, 87
Dartmoor Prison, 13-14
Daughters of Bilitis, 148, 195
Dawn: A Charleston Legend (Simmons), 189
Dawson, Mrs., 70
Day, Greg, 176-177, 203-204, 205, 294
De Veaux, Gabrielle Esther, 93-95
Dean, Howard, 256
Declaration of Independence, 77
Delphin, Wilfred, 208-210
Delphin and Romain (piano duo), 208-210
Demarest, Emma, 37
Democrats and Democratic Party, 48, 265-267, 268, 270
Denishawn Dancers, 95
Derfner, Joel, 208, 229
Dhose, Chris, 214
Dialogue on Religion and Sexual Orientation, A, 256
Dickens, Charles, 33
Dietrich Marlene, 102
Dillon, George, 103
Dining with Friends, 231
Dobbins, Jack, 156-162, 169, 196, 243
Dock Street Theatre, 150, 152, 153, 155, 156
Dolphin Snack Bar (listed in gay guides), 197
Don Juan (Byron), 45
Don Juan (Strauss), 117
Don't Ask, Don't Tell, 183, 238, 260, 262, 272
Donehue, J. Douglas, 168-173
Doonan, Scott, 211
Douglas, Alfred, Lord, 69, 70
Downing, Martha, 37
Drag and drag queens, 65, 79, 99, 165, 166, 177, 188, 191, 196, 200, 202-205, 212, 280, 286-287
Drayton, Ed, 72, 73
Drayton, Frank, 76
Duberman, Martin, 28
Ducks Unlimited, 231
Dugan, Lynn, 275-282
Duggins, Regina, 283
Duncan, Isadora, 95
Duncan, Patrick, 24-26
Dunn, Lieutenant, 72
Dunn, Susan, 230
Dwork, Melvin, 137, 183, 184

E

E None of the Above (gay organization), 215
Eakins, Thomas, 94
East Cooper Baptist Church, 254
Ebony Magazine, 122, 130-132
Edens, Bill, 229, 230
Edwin Poems (Zeigler), 139
Ehrhardt, W. H., 159, 160
Eisenhower, Dwight, President, 167
Elbow Room Cocktail Lounge (bar), 144, 157, 196
Eliot, Ida, 49
Ellis, Havelock, 51
Ellsey, Samuel, 79
Emanuel AME Church, 238, 287
End as a Man (Willingham), 145-148, 273
Episcopal Church, 80, 284
Equal Time (radio show), 259-260
Equality Hub (Charleston), 259, 284
Esquire (magazine), 191
Estes, Patricia, Rev., 259
Evans, Cathy, 269
Exoo, George, Rev., 213-214, 215, 224

F

Faderman, Lillian, 83
Feminism and women's rights, 30, 49, 108-109, 110, 212, 213
Femme soles, 32
Ferro-Grumley Award, 191
Fineman, Irving, 106, 107
First Baptist School, 278
Fischinger, Peter J., Dr., 221-222
Fisher, Clara, 37
Fleet's In, The (Cadmus), 143
Florence, SC, 205
Focus on the Family, 265
Foley, Mark, US Congressman, 266
Folk Art Media Project, 203
Folly Beach, SC, 134, 135-136, 140, 194, 195, 273, 277
Footlight Players, 153
Ford, Robert, State Senator, 243
Ford's Theatre, 54
Fort Moultrie, 138
Fort Sumter, 48, 54, 141, 164
Fort Sumter Tours, 243
Fortune (magazine), 152
Foster, George, 44
Fox, Terry, 199

Frannie's (bar), 211
Fraser, Walter J., 7
Freedom parties, 262
Freud, Sigmund, 51
Friends Unlimited Bowling League, 240
Frost, Frances, 106-108
Fudenberg, H. Hugh, Dr., 221
Fun Home (Bechdel), 270-271, 272
Fun Home (Kron and Tesori), 271

G

Gage Hall, 214
Gaillard, Hester, 84, 85
Gallatin, Albert, 17
Game, McKrae, 285-286
Garden & Gun (magazine), 200
Garden & Gun Club, *See* King Street Garden & Gun Club
Gaud School, 244
Gay American History (Katz), 19
Gay Bingo, 287
Gay Charleston (newsletter), 206-207, 210-215, 251, 277,
Gay Daze (newsletter), 239
Gay Haiku (Derfner), 208
Gay Men's Health Crisis, 228, 234
Gay Sarong, The (Hervey), 99, 101
Gazzara, Ben, 146; photo, 148
Gergel, Richard, Judge, 287
Gershwin, George, 111, 194
Gibbes Museum of Art, 86
Gide, André, 151
Gilbreth, Edward, 201
Gilbreth, Frank, 105-106, 219, 223, 224, 230
Glenn, Chase, 257, 283
Glenn, Cheryl, 279
Glover, Cory Jerome, 225-228
Gone with the Wind (Mitchell), 56
Gone with the Wind (motion picture), 185
Goose Creek, SC, 244
Gospelfest, 233
Gottschalk, Louis Mourey, 34
Gould, Graydon, 57
Grace, John P., Mayor, 80
Grace, Norene Carr, 108
Graduate, The (motion picture), 148
Grant, Ulysses S., President, 52
Grass Roots League, 129, 159, 170, 174-175
Gray, Mark, 228
Graziano, Kristin, Sheriff, 287-288
Great Mischief (Pinckney), 141

Greeleyville, SC, 131
Green Book, 196
Green, Gus, 73, 74, 75, 76, 77
Green, Henry, 73
Green, Julien, 56-57
Greenberg, Reuben, Police Chief, 8, 213, 261
Greene, Harlan, 208
Gregorie, Anne King, 108-110, 169
Gress, Warren, see Redman-Gress, Warren
Grey, Zane, 128
Grice, George, 124-130, 145, 159, 169-170, 193, 268, 272
Grice, Marguerite, 127
Grice Marine Lab, 129
Griffen, Al, 166, 167
Grimes, Joseph, 18
Grimké, Angelina, 32
Grimké, Angelina Weld, 32
Grimké, Henry, 32
Grimké, Sarah, 32
Grimké, Thomas S., 78
Griswold, Charlotte Myers, 39-45
Griswold, Mary Caroline, 42, 44
Griswold, Rufus, 39-45, 74
Grocery Store Chorus Girls (store), 212
Groff, Sue, 275
Grossman, Paula, 268-269
Growing Up Gay (conference), 247
Gunter, Freeman, 166, 169, 193-195
Gwillim, Linda, 250, 254

H

Hale, Edward Everett, 94
Hale, Ellen Day, 93-95
Hall, Gordon Langley. *See* Simmons, Dawn Langley Hall
Hall, Joe, 229-234, 242
Halsey, Louise, 140
Halsey, William, 95, 140, 155
Hamilton (musical), 22
Hamilton, Alexander, 18-22, 23, 45
Hamlin (community), 177
Hammond, James Henry, 26-28, 48, 141
Hammond, L., 71
Hammond family, 27
Hampton, Wade, 28
Hamrick, Tom, 165-166
Hanover (Bar), 195
Harlem, NYC, 32, 64, 79
Harlem Renaissance, 32, 140

Harleston, Affra, 312
Harleston, Edwin Augustus, 91
Harleston, Eloise, 92
Harleston Village (Charleston), 31
Harmon Field, 88, 89
Harper's Bazaar (magazine), 152
Harriott Pinckney Home for Seamen, 11
Harris, Hugh P., General., 273
Harris, Stan, Rev., 213, 215, 260
Hart, Jeffrey, 219
Hartman, Kathy, 236, 241
Harvard Business School, 244
Harvard College, 49, 50
Hastie, Drayton F., 74, 75
Hate Crimes legislation, viii, 284
Hawkins, Suellen, 230
Hayne, Paul Hamilton, 33
Heart is a Lonely Hunter, The (McCullers), 139
Hein, Wilhelmina, Rev., 259-260
Hellman, Lillian, 82, 107
Helms, Jesse, 265
Helping Hands, 228-229
Hennessy, Ellen, 37
Henry's (restaurant), 196
Hermaphrodites and hermaphroditism, 1, 2-3, 41, 43, 44, 45, 272
Hervey, Harry, xi, 98-102, 154, 185
Hettinga, William van, 208, 225
Heyward, Dorothy 63, 64, 105, 155
Heyward, DuBose, 62-65, 75, 85, 91, 104-105, 144, 155
Heyward, Isabel, 85
Higdon, Lee, 270
High School of Charleston, 77
Hildreth, Carleton, 99-102, 154
Hilton Head Island, 146
Historic Charleston Foundation, 86, 153
Hitt, Jack, 163, 189, 190
HIV/AIDS, 183, 209, 222, 243, 249, 253, 276, 299; in Charleston and South Carolina, 218-235, 238, 240, 247, 253, 260, 274, 277, 278, 285
Hobbes, Nicholas, 104
Hoffman, Wilmer, 153
Hogan, Maura, 200
Hoisington, Ralph, 242, 261
Holocaust, 271; monument in Charleston, 272
Holt, George, 206-208, 212, 213, 215, 217, 218
Home of the Better Baby, 89

Homophobia, 35, 57, 79, 182, 191, 193, 205, 219, 220-225, 230, 238, 242, 249, 263, 265, 268, 271, 273, 274, 282, 288; internalized, 116, 167, 230, 248, 256
Hope for Wholeness (conversion therapy), 285-286
Horry County, SC, 266
Horticultural Society (Charleston), 25
Hosmer, Harriett, 53
Hospital Worker's Strike, 178-179
Hotline, 238
Howard Association, 46
Hudson, Lane, 266-267
Hughes, Langston, 140
Human Rights Campaign Fund, 266, 274, 275
Hume, Sophia, 30
Hungry Lion (restaurant), 224
Hunt, Eugene, 176
Hustlers and hustling, see also prostitutes and prostitution, 157, 166-167, 188. *See also* prostitutes and prostitution

I

In and Out (motion picture), 2401
Inglis, Bob, US Congressman, 222
Intersex, 44, 45
Invisible Pursuit (Bennett), 115
Iron Widow, The (Hervey), 101, 102
Isle of Palms, SC, 139, 228
It Happened One Night (motion picture), 125

J

JCPenney (department store), 198
Jackie's Café Espresso, 214
James Island County Park, 240
James, Henry, 83
Jasper, William, Sergeant, statue of, 141, 143, 165
Jay, William, 24
Jeb and Dash (Russell), 145
Jenkins, Daniel, Rev., 92
Jenkins, Edmund T., 92-93
Jenkins, Eloise Harleston, 92
Jenkins, Lena, 92
Jenkins, Olive Harleston, 92
Jenkins Orphanage, 12, 92
Jenkins Orphanage and bands, 12, 92
Jennings, Edward I. R. (Ned), 84, 95-98, 100-101, 119

Jervey, Huger Wilkinson, 77, 78-79, 191
Jervey, Theodore, 74, 77, 88
Jewel Lounge (bar), 196
Jim Crow laws, 73, 164
Jipsta (rapper), 282
Johns Hopkins University, 77, 188
Johns, Jasper, 112
Johnson, David K., 176
Johnson, Owen, 103
Johnson Hagood Stadium, 282
Johnston, Henrietta, 31
Joint, The (Blake), 152
Jones, Jehu, 59, 61
Jones, Randy, 282
Jorgens, Elise, 270
Journal of Homosexuality, The, 86
Judy's (bar), 211

K

Kahal Kadosh Beth Elohim, 54, 284
Kameny, Frank, 182
Kate Trimingham (Frost), 107
Katz, Jonathan Ned, 19, 22, 51
Keats, Cheryl, 215-216
Kelly, Dominic, 279
Kelly, Henrietta Aiken, 50
Kelly, William F., Police Chief, 170-171
Ketner, Linda, 208, 230-232, 247-249, 251-253, 254, 255-256, 261, 262, 265-266
King Street Garden & Gun Club (bar and disco), 198-201, 203, 205, 211-212
King, Martin Luther, holiday, 264
King, Susan Petigru, 32-33
Kinloch, Francis (the elder), 22
Kinloch, Francis (the younger) 22-23
Kinsey, Alfred, 147
Kinsey Report, 149
Kirstein, Lincoln, 144
Kline, Kevin, 241
Knight Times (newsletter), 240
Knobs (Cade), 273
Kohn, Barry, 215-219, 225
Koon, Harold, 253
Kron, Lisa, 271

L

Ladies Calhoun Memorial Association, 33
Lambda Literary Award, 191, 208

Lambda of Charleston, 214, 218; survey by, 263
Lambeth Conference, 253
Lamme, Tom, 163, 218, 228
Lane, Hugh, 193
Lanterns on the Levee (Percy), 78
Latham, Dick, 236
Laudonniére, René Goulaine de, 1
Laugh-In (television program), 189
Laurens, Henry, 19, 20
Laurens, John, 15, 18-22, 23, 45
Lavender Scare, 159
Lavender Scare, The: The Cold War Persecution of Gays and Lesbians in the Federal Government (Johnson), 176
Lavia, Mariano, Dr., 221, 224
Law and Order League, 80-81, 135, 175
Lawfully Wedded Husband: How My Gay Marriage Will Save the American Family (Derfner), 208
Lawrence, Gertrude, 111
League of Women Voters, 175
Leather organization, see Trident Knights
Lee, Peggy, 166
Legerton, C. L., 71
Leland, Jack, 188, 189
Leland, Lee Ann, 279, 283-284
Lepre, Steve, 259
Les Jardins (bar and disco), 211-212, 214, 215, 221
Lesbians and lesbianism, x, 30, 32, 33, 34, 53, 56, 61, 64, 65, 78, 81, 82, 84, 90, 95, 101, 103, 104, 107, 111, 112, 138, 139, 143-144, 147, 149, 170, 172, 174, 176, 178, 185-186, 191, 192, 198, 201, 208, 211, 212, 213, 214, 215, 217, 222, 225, 226, 234-236, 237, 238, 240, 242, 244, 254-255, 258, 261, 262, 265, 268, 269, 270, 271, 273, 275, 276, 277, 287
Lezz Fest, 276
Liberace, 150
Liberty Square, 277, 278
Lilly, Beatrice, 111
Lincoln, Abraham, President, 48, 54
Lion's Head (bar), 197
Little Atlantic (bar), 135-136, 195
Little Big Man (motion picture), 148
Little Theatre School, 153
Little, Richard, 212, 221
Livingston, Fanny, 37

Lockwood, Henry, Mayor, 135
Loop, The (newspaper), 242, 262-263; readership survey, 262-263, 278
Loos, Margaret, 236
Lords of Discipline, The (Conroy), 273
Lords Proprietors, 3-4
Lost Morning (Heyward), 63
Love Inn (listed in gay guides), 197
Love's Labour's Lost (Shakespeare), 128
Lowcountry AIDS Services, 234, 238, 240, 247
Lowcountry Gay & Lesbian Alliance, (LGLA) 236-241, 243, 247, 248, 249, 251, 252, 253, 255, 277, 288
Lowcountry Palmetto AIDS Life Support Services, (Lowcountry PALSS), 225, 229, 230-234. *See also* Palmetto AIDS Life Support Services, (PALSS)
Lowell, Amy, 103-104
Lynching, 79
Lyons, Carol "Kit", 153, 169

M

Mabe, Tera, 279
MacArthur Fellowship, 271
MacDowell Colony, 106
Madden, Timothy, 79
Magnolia Cemetery, 79
Magnolia Drive In, 148
Magnolia Plantation, 74
Magnolia Room, 149
Mahon, John, 157-162, 167
Mamba's Daughters (Heyward), novel, 63, 75, 91, 144
Mamba's Daughters (Heyward and Heyward), play, 63, 64-66
Man into Woman: A Transsexual Autobiography (Simmons), 189
Mandate (magazine), 194
Marine Bible Society, 11
Marine Hospital (Charleston), 11, 92
Marine Washingtonian Total Abstinence Society, 12
Mariner's Church (Charleston), 12
Marion, Francis, 18, 93
Marion Square 62, 113, 136, 224, 238, 272
Market (Charleston), 11, 31, 134-135, 166

marriage equality, 263, 287. *See also* S.C. Constitutional Amendment Marriage Act.
Martin, James, Rev., 224
Martin, Mary, 60
Masick, Joseph, see Mazyck, Joseph
Masturbation, 28-29, 117
matelotage, 7, 10
Matlovich, Leonard, 161-162, 167-168, 176, 180, 182-183, 184, 186
Mattachine Society, 149, 159-160, 174, 195
Mattern, Kymberly, 221
Matusow, Alice, 215
Maupin, Armistead, 172, 184-186, 190, 206
Maxwell, Elsa, 111
Maybank, Burnett, US Senator and Mayor, 135
Maybank Hall, 212
Mazyck, Joseph, 13, 14
McBee, Mary Vardrine, 26
McBride, Mark, Mayor, 253
McCallum, Corrie, 140, 155
McClellan, Alonzo, 91
McCloud, Margaret, 36
McCormack, Helen, 85-86, 87, 88
McCullers, Carson, 138-139, 149
McCullers, Reeves, 139
McElhenney, Ada Agnes, (aka Ada Claree), 33-34, 40, 52, 98
McKinney, Mark, 259
McLaughlin, Michael, 228
McMaster, Henry, Governor, 288
McNerny, Todd, 271
Medical College of South Carolina, 137, 156, 179
Medical University of South Carolina (MUSC), 181, 220-222, 273-274; Alliance for Equality of, 274; College of Heath Care Professionals of, 285; LGTBQ+ Health Services and Enterprise Services of, 283
Melville, Herman, 10
Melvin, Patrick, 4
Memminger, Christopher G., 49
Memminger Auditorium, 271
Memminger Normal School, 49, 80, 179
Menken, Adah Isaacs, 34
Menotti, Gian Carlo, 107, 192-193, 196

Merchant Seaman's Club (bar), 13, 196
Metropolitan Community Church (MCC), 213-215, 218, 238, 260, 278, 283
Miami Shores, FL, 264
Mickey, Edward, 90-91
Mickey, Ellen, 90
Mickey family, 90
Middleton, Arthur, 77
Middleton Inn, 251
Middleton Place Plantation and Gardens, 103, 186, 194, 252
Midnight Sun (bar), 197
Milecewz, Peter, 228
Miles, William Porcher, US Congressman, 112-113
military police, 137, 162. *See also* police
Millay, Edna St. Vincent, 103-104, 113
Miscegenation, 37, 72-77, 79, 188-189, 222, 263
Misogyny, 36, 129
Miss Gay Charleston, 204
Mitchell, Henry, 73
Mitchell, Sharen, 279
Moldenhauer, Lynn, 249, 256, 274
Molloy, Robert, 195
Monrovia Cemetery, 227
Montgomery, Brannon, 279
Moore, Melissa, 259
Mordecai, Hortensia, 53
Moredock, Will, 264
Morrison, Nan, 128-129
Morrow, Jeremy (pseudonym), 187
Mount Pleasant, SC, 244, 261, 275, 277
Mourning the Death of Magic (Boyd), 190-191
Mr. Roberts (Heggen and Logan), 147
Ms (magazine), 191
Muller, Johannes von, 22
Murder Cure, The (Ross), 191
Myers, Charlotte. *See* Griswold, Charlotte Myers
Myers, Hesse, 41-42, 44
Myers, Mike, 57
Myers, Sarah, 41-42, 44
Myers, Tom, 228
Myers, Tom, Jr., 244-246, 248-249
Myrtle Beach, SC 134, 253, 282
Myrtle Beach Bitch (newsletter), 134

The Real Rainbow Row

N

Nall, Tom, 163-164, 172
Names Project AIDS Quilt, 238
Nathaniel Russell House, 28
National Association for the Advancement of Colored People (NAACP), 32, 91, 140, 144, 176, 195, 245
National Association of Gay and Lesbian Democratic Clubs, 268
National Endowment for the Arts (NEA), 205
National Institute of Health (NIH), 221
National Organization of Women (NOW), 212-213
National Police Gazette (New York), 36-38, 43
National Rifle Association, 266
Nerves (Boyd), 185, 190
New York Metropolitan Opera, 139
New York Society for the Suppression of Vice, 146
New York Times, 183, 241, 248
Newkirk, Carolyn, 250, 254
News and Courier, 104, 115, 168-175, 185, 191, 212, 219
Newsweek (magazine), 219
Nicholson, James, 24-26
North Charleston, SC, 167, 174, 197, 237, 249, 276, 277, 284
North Palm Ministry Center, 259

O

O'Sullivan, Florence, 3-4, 7, 31
Obergefell vs. Hodges, 287
Obie award, 271
Ocean Bar and Grill (bar), 197
One (Magazine), 159-160
One Eyed Jacks (motion picture), 148
Open Door Congregation, 260
Ordinance of Secession, 48
Orlando (Woolf), 186
Orvin, George, M.D., 181-182
Osborn, C. Dixon, 262
Otey, Edward, 156, 157, 160, 162, 169
Outfest, 240, 277
outing (of gays and lesbians), 222, 241-243, 266

P

Palmetto AIDS Life Support Services (PALSS), 225, 229, 234, 255 Palmetto Community Care (PCC), 285, 287
Paramount Pictures, 273
Parents and Families of Lesbians and Gays (PFLAG), 240
Parham, J. Edward, 217, 218, 219
Paris Review, 151, 152
Park Circle (North Charleston), 279
Parker, Reba, 279
Parsons, Betty, 112
Parsons, Schuyler Livingston, 112-113, 116
Pat's Lounge (bar), 197
Patience (Gilbert and Sullivan), 67
Patriot's Point, 232
Pea Island, SC, 151
Peacock, Edwin, 138-140, 144-145, 155, 162, 272
Pearlstine, Susan, 228
Peirce, James Mills, 50-51, 53, 94, 116, 120, 179
PEN/Faulkner Award, 192
Peninsula of Lies (Ball), 189
People Against Rape (PAR), 180
Percy, Walker, 78
Percy, William Alexander, 78
Peterkin, Julia, 107
Petigru, James Louis, 32
Pfaff's Cellar, 34
Phelps, Fred, 281
Phil Donahue Show (television program), 216
Philadelphia School of Design, 94
Phillips (community), 177
Phillips Andover Academy, 244
Piccolo Spoleto, 238
Pierson, Betty. *See* Parsons, Betty
Pinckney, Josephine, 13, 102, 103-104, 106-107, 112, 140-141, 195
Pink (pseudonym), 37-38
Pink House, 141
Pippa Passes (Browning), 128
Pirate House, 99
Pirates, and homosexuality, 6-8, 10, 71
Planters Hotel, 52
Planters and Mechanics Bank, 24
Plymouth Church, 89
Poe, Edgar Allen, 39-40, 43, 113
Poetry Magazine, 103
Poetry Society of South Carolina, 78, 85, 103, 104, 106, 113, 155
police, Charleston, SC and area, x, 6, 8, 35, 37, 46, 60, 61-62, 72, 76, 79, 80, 81, 132, 135, 137, 159, 165, 170-171, 174, 177, 184, 189, 213, 224, 261, 263, 278, 284. *See also* military police; Mount Peasant, SC, 261
Political Action Committees, 263
Pollitzer sisters, 32
Pols, Birgit, 236
Poor William's Omnibus (newspaper), 208, 225
Porcher, Octavius, 28
Porgy (Heyward) novel, 63, 64
Porgy (Heyward and Heyward) play, 155
Porgy and Bess (Heyward and Gershwin), 57, 63, 155, 194
Port Royal (ship), 4
Porter, Cole, 111
Portrait Over My Shoulder: Personal Recollections of a piano virtuoso surreptitiously gleaned by the author (Wragg), 155
Post and Courier, 201, 238, 254, 261, 269, 285
PrEP program, 285
Preservation Society of Charleston, 85, 86
Price, Melvin, US Congressman, 268
Pride Parade, Charleston, difficulties, 277-278, 281; North Charleston, 278-282
Prier, Gilly, 37
Prime Timers, 286
Prioleau, Huldah Josephine, Dr., 88-90, 91, 93
Problem in Greek Ethics, A, (Symons), 50-51
Prostitutes and prostitution (see also brothels and hustlers), 35-38, 71, 72-76, 80, 134-137, 178. *See also* brothels, hustlers and hustling.
Pruitt, J. B., Judge, 160-161

Q

Queer History of the United States, A (Bronski), 55-56

R

Racism and discrimination, viii, 76, 87, 169, 176, 182, 184, 187, 191, 200-201, 205, 213, 222, 230, 249, 287, 288
Rainbow Lounge (bar), 196
Rainbow Row (houses), xi, xii, 156
Rainbow Times (newsletter), 239
Rainbow Times Newsource (newsletter), 239
Rakoczy, Paul, 280

Randolph, Harrison, 123-130, 145, 169, 272
Randolph, John, 23
Randolph, Louise Wagener, 123, 130
Randolph Hall, 129
Rankin, Jeannette, 109
Rapley, Richard A., 16-17
Rathskeller (bar), 117, 118, 195
Rauschenberg, Robert, 112
Ravenal, Julian (pseudonym), 150, 152
Reagan, Ronald, President, 183, 222
Reardon, Allen, 236
Rebel Without a Cause (motion picture), 149
Reconstruction, 58, 164, 206
Red Cross, Colored Branch, 88
Red Ending (Hervey), 100-102, 186
Red Scare, 160
Redman, Jim. *See* Redman-Gress, Jim and Warren
Redman-Gress, Jim and Warren, 248
Reid House of Christian Service, 238
Remley's Point, SC, 177
Republicans and Republican Party, 224, 241, 242, 243, 248, 265-267, 270, 284, 288
Rest stops, 224
Revolution of Little Girls, The (Boyd), 191, 208
Revolutionary War, 15, 18-20, 93, 141
RFD (Magazine), 203
Rhett, William, 7, 31
Richardson, Ida, 61-62, 63
Right to Life campaign, 266
Riley, Joseph P., Jr., Mayor, 193, 250, 256, 261
Riners, Lucy, 37
Ripley, Clements, 155
Ripley, Katharine Ball, 155
Riverfront Park (North Charleston), 279
Rivers, Maria, 286
Robertson, Pat, 238
Robinson, Emmett and Pat, 155
Robinson, George, 61
Robinson, Johnny, 171
Robinson, Leonard, 203
Robison, Richard N. "Dick", 198-201
Rock Hill, SC, 275
Rocky D (radio host), 256

Rodriguez-Mendez, Carlos Guillermo, 249
Romain, Edwin, 208-210
Roper St. Francis Hospital System, 285; Ryan White Wellness Center of, 285
Ross, Ann B., 191
Royal Academy of Music, 93
Rubyfruit Jungle (Brown), 191
Running a Thousand Miles for Freedom (Craft), 59
Russell, Ada Dwyer, 104
Rustin, Bayard, 222
Rutledge, Henry M., 23
Ryan White Act, 223
Ryan's Steak House, 236, 248

S

Sabb, Willie, 132-133
Sackville-West, Vita, 186
Safe Space, 245, 284
Sailors Home (Charleston), 11
Sailors, and homosexuality, 9-14, 71
St. Andrew's Society, 17
St. Cecilia Society, 112
St. Stephen's Episcopal Church, 238, 245
Salvador, Francis, 15-17, 21, 24, 26
Salvador, Joseph, 15, 26
Salvador family, 26
Samuel and Regina Greene Family Fund, 272
Sarah Jane (cross-dresser), 61
Sartre, Jean-Paul, 150
Sass, Joseph, 236
Savannah, GA, 47, 56, 102, 281
Sawyer, Frederick Adolphus, 49
Schroeder, Sybil, 233
Schwacke, David, 241-242, 248, 261, 262, 264, 270
Schwarzott, Mike, 236, 237-238, 241
Scott, Alonzo, 125
Seabrook, Bryan Alston (aka Africa, Miss Africa), 165, 203-206, 212
Sears, James, 187, 268
Secession Convention, 27
Secular Humanists of the Lowcountry, 284
Sellers, Robert, 96
Sendak, Maurice, 140
Seraphin, Joanne, 212-213
Servicemembers Legal Defense Network, 262

Severens, Martha, 94-95
Sewanee. *See* University of the South
Sex Education, 175, 286
Shake-A-Plenty (drag queen), 177, 203
Shako, The, 138
Shalosky, Nick, 267-268
Shanghai Express (film), 102
Shapland, Jenn, 84
Shari's Lounge (bar), 211
Sheehan, Annie, 279
Shiloh AME Church, 188
Shilts, Randy, 180
Short Walk, A (Childress), 191
Shuler, Gil, 205
Shuler, Robin, 205
Silver Dollar (bar), 197
Simmons, Dawn Langley Hall (aka Gordon Langley Hall, Dawn Pepita Simmons), xii, 186-190, 272, 278
Simmons, John Paul, 188-189
Simmons, Leon, 125
Simms, William Gilmore, 33
Singleton, William, Rev., 189
Sissinghurst, 187
Six Mile (community), 178
Sloane, Amy, 279
Smalls, Gee, 249
Smalls, Sammy, 62-63
Smith, Alice Ravenel Huger, 94
Smith, Charlie, 208, 246, 249-250, 252, 264-265, 270, 276
Smith, Helen, Apostle, 177-178, 219
Smith, Loula Carson. *See* McCullers, Carson
Smollett, Tobias, 19-20
Snug Harbor, 86
Society for the Preservation of Spirituals, 95, 112
sodomy, 3, 136, 138, 175, 218, 261, 288
Solomon, Fay, 181
Sons of Confederate Veterans, 165
South Carolina Aquarium, 278
South Carolina Christian Action Council, 224, 269
South Carolina College. *See also* University of South Carolina
South Carolina Comprehensive Health Education Act, 175, 244, 286
South Carolina Constitutional Amendment, Marriage Act, 243, 258

South Carolina Department of Criminal Justice Police Academy, 261
South Carolina Department of Education, 286
South Carolina Department of Health and Environmental Control (DHEC), 223
South Carolina Department of Social Services (DSS), 226, 227
South Carolina Equality, 256, 258
South Carolina Historical Records Survey, 109
South Carolina Historical Society, 86
South Carolina House of Representatives, 264
South Carolina Inter-State and West Indian Exposition, 71
South Carolina Medical Ethics and Diversity Act, 288
South Carolina Military Academy, 61. *See also* Citadel, The
South Carolina Pride, and Pride March, 238, 246, 248, 253, 259, 268, 275, 276, 277, 279, 280, 281, 284, 283, 284, 288
South Carolina Provincial Congress, 15
South Carolina Public Television, 186
South Carolina Retarded Children's Habilitation Center, 173
South Carolina Society Hall, 103
South Carolina State Law Enforcement Division, (SLED) 261
South Carolina State Legislature, 263, 270-271, 273, 278
South Carolina State Ports Authority, 238
Southern Exposure (magazine), 165, 202
Southern Illinois University, 208
Spartanburg, SC, 285
Spearman, Molly, 286
Spiegel, Sam, 148
Spirit Line Cruises, 243
Spoleto Festival USA, 192-195, 198-199, 238
Stardust Lounge (bar), 197
Steam (magazine), 166
Stein, Gertrude, 104-106, 109-110, 192, 219
Stern, Theodore "Ted", 193, 209, 240

Steuben, Friedrich Wilhelm von, General, 19
Steven, Paul, 279
Stoddard, Charles Warren, 34-35
Stoil, Rebecca, 15
Stonewall Democrats, 268
Stonewall Inn, and riot, 178, 179, 184, 195, 267, 275, 286
Stonewall Ladies, The (Verner), 179
Stoney, Samuel Gaillard, 106, 107, 108
Stoney, Theodore, 160, 161
Strachey, Lytton, 98
Strange One, The (motion picture), 148-149
Streetcar (bar), 196, 211, 212, 218
Suchy, Julianne, 2790
Sud (Green), 56-57
Sue Kuhlen's Camp for Kids, 240
suicide, 85, 97, 100, 133, 138, 163, 178, 245, 258, 285
Sullivan's Island, SC, 4, 31, 138, 215
Summerville, SC, 244
Summey, Keith, Mayor, 278-279
Supremes, The, 169
Surles, Flora Belle, 108-110, 122, 155, 169
Surpassing the Love of Men: Romantic Friendships and Love between Women (Faderman), 83
Sweet Gum Head (bar), 205
Swish: My Quest to Become the Gayest Person Ever (Derfner), 208
Symons, John Addington, 50

T

T Sisters, 240
Tales of the City (Maupin), 186-187, 191
Tango (bar), 215
Task Force, The (newsletter), 181, 206
Taylor, Prentiss, 107, 140-144, 165
Taylor, William, 66
Tecklenburg, John J., Mayor, 288
Temperance Boarding House, 11
Tension, Florence, 61, 63
Terkel, Studs, 152
Tesori, Jeanine, 271
Thackery, William Makepeace, 32
Thickets, The, 94
This is Charleston (Stoney), 86
Thompson, Santi, 160
Thompson Auditorium, 84
Those Other People (Childress), 191

Three o'Clock Dinner (Pinckney), 102, 195
Thurmond, Strom, US Senator, 222
Time (magazine), 180, 266
Timrod, Henry 113, 115
Tobias, Andy, 256
Tobias, Rowena Wilson, 142-143
Toklas, Alice B., 104-106, 109-110
Tomb of the Unknown Racist (Boyd), 191
Tony Award, 271
Trans issues and transsexuals, 130-133, 186-190, 215, 239, 240, 255, 261, 268-269, 277, 278, 283-284, 288; *See also* cross-dressing,
Transgender Day of Remembrance, 283-284
Transparent Life, The: Learning to Live without a Mask (Game), 286
Transvestite bar, 197
Treaty of Ghent, 14
Trenholm, George A., 26
Trident Health District, 238
Trident Knights, The, 239-240
Trinity Episcopal Church (Miami, FL), 249
Trump, Donald J., President, 287
Tsang, Kwon, Dr., 221
Tucker, Bobby, 187, 196
Tucker's Tavern (bar), 196, 197
Turkey, and homosexuality, 10, 53
Turner, Jenny, 225-228

U

Uncle Snowball (Frost), 108
Unicorn (bar), 214
Unitarian Church (Charleston), 50, 51, 94, 179, 213, 214, 284
US Air Force, 156, 157, 160, 161, 176, 180, 182, 183
US Chamber of Commerce, 265
US Custom House (Charleston), 238
US House of Representatives, 109, 266; Armed Services Committee, 268
US Military Academy, 29
US Naval Academy, 91
US Navy Hospital Corps, 137
US Navy, 9, 12, 113-114, 134-137, 139, 152, 160-161, 163, 171-172, 183-185, 198, 206, 262
USS *Charleston*, 9
USS *Yorktown*, 233
US Supreme Court, 182, 287, 288

US Veterans of Foreign Wars, 265
United Way, 231
Unity Fellowship Church, 283
University Club (gay organization), 215
University of Arkansas, 123
University of South Carolina, see also South Carolina College, 26, 109; Medical School, 221
University of Southern Mississippi, 209
University of the South, (Sewanee) 77, 78
University of Virginia, 123
Unruly Desires: American Sailors and Homosexualities in the Age of Sail (Benemann), 9
Untold Friendships (Parsons), 112, 115

V

Vaca, Alvar, Núñez Cabeza de, 1
Valentine Museum, 86
Valk, Marguerite Sinkler, 111
Vanessa (Menotti and Barber), 192
Vanity Fair (magazine), 191
Vanuga, Mary Ann, (aka Mary Ann Zanuga) 60
Venable, Stephen, 203
Venereal disease, 134, 174
Verner, Elizabeth O'Neill, 94, 179, 185, 225
Vesey, Denmark, 25
Vidal, Gore, 149
Villa Margherita, 105; photo of, 105
Village People (disco group), 282
Village Voice, 191
Virgo Social Club (bar), 198
Vogue (magazine), 152
Volunteer Center of the Lowcountry, 238

W

Wagon Wheel (bar), 196
Walk in the Parks, A: A Guide to Those in the City (Young), 141
Walters, Caroline, (aka Caroline Wilson, Charles Wilson), 46-47
War of 1812, 13-14
Ware, Hettie, 37
Waring, J. Waties, Judge, 244
Waring, Thomas, 107
Washington, DC City Council, 268
Washington, Florence, 37
Washington, George, 19
Washington Park, 238
Waters, Ethel, 65-66
Watson, Don, 228
We Are Family (WAF), 228, 243-247, 249, 255, 258-259, 260, 278, 288
We Are Your Neighbors (documentary), 259
We Too Are Drifting (Wilhelm), 143
Welch, Kate, 36
Welch, Silas B., Police Chief, 171
West Ashley Revitalization Commission, 265
West Point. *See* United States Military Academy
West, Joseph, 3
Westboro Baptist Church, 281
Weston, Nancy, 32
What the Dead Remember (Greene), 208
Whisonant, Frank, 79
White, Mr., 97
White Jacket (Melville), 10
White marriage (see also beard), 112
White Point Garden, 164-165, 195, 203, 224. *See also* Battery
Whitfield, Holly, 283
Whitlock, Edwina, 90, 91
Whitman, Walt, 33, 34-35, 40, 41, 44, 45, 50, 113
Whitney, Isabel, 186
Wilde, Oscar, 66, 67-71, 72, 73, 74, 103, 113
Wilhelm, Gale, 143
Will and Grace (television program), 262
Willard, Steven, 243
Williams Fred, Rev., 214-215
Williams, Edward, 79
Williams, Tennessee, 113, 149, 163, 194
Williams, Tony, 268, 280
Williams, Willie, 138
Willingham, Calder B., 145-148, 152
Willington Academy, 28
Willis, Kimberly Butler, 285
Wilson, Caroline, 46
Wilson, Charles, 46, 47
Wise, Benjamin E., 78
Withers, Thomas Jefferson, 27, 28, 48, 141
Witte, Charles Otto, 26
Wizard of Oz, The (motion picture), 204
Woman of this Earth, A (Frost), 107
Women's International League for Peace and Freedom, 108-109
Woolf, Virginia, 186
Woolsey, Elsa Gamel, 97-98
Works Progress Administration (WPA), 109
World AIDS Day, 238
World War II, in Charleston, 56, 134-138, 169, 183, 195
WQSN radio, 212
Wragg, Russel, 154-156, 169, 273
Wragg Mall, 42
Wright, Frances, 236
Wylie, Elinor, 113

X

Xavier University, 209

Y

Yale College, 54
Y.M.C.A., 195-196, 222
Young, John R., 141

Z

Zanuga, Mary Ann, 60
Zebra Supper Club (bar), 197
Zeigler, John, 138-140, 144-145, 155, 162, 169, 272

A native of Charleston, Harlan Greene is an award-winning novelist, archivist, and historian. He has served as Assistant Director of the South Carolina Historical Society, Director of the North Carolina Preservation Consortium, Archivist of the Avery Research Center for African American History and Culture at the College of Charleston, and is now Scholar in Residence at the College's Addlestone Library. His novels include *Why We Never Danced the Charleston*, the Lambda Literary Award winner *What the Dead Remember*, and the Lambda-nominated *The German Officer's Boy*. He lectures frequently, and has published books and essays on various aspects of Charleston history. A certified tourguide, he chairs the city's Historical Commission. He manages the South Carolina LGBTQ Oral History, Archives and Outreach Project at the College of Charleston, and is married to Jonathan Ray.

www.ingramcontent.com/pod-product-compliance
Lightning Source LLC
Chambersburg PA
CBHW070749230426
43665CB00017B/2306